Praise for *They Turned the World Upside Down*

"Jesus taught us to pray, 'your kingdom come, your will be done, on earth as it is in heaven,' but so many professing Christians haven't stopped and asked, 'What does that mean?' In *They Turned the World Upside Down* Charles Martin dives deep into the realities of Jesus' kingdom come by asking needed questions pointing us to the revelation of God through His word made flesh. This book is for the person who knows that there has to be more to this life and that there has to be something more real than all these temporary experiences. In his charming yet challenging way, Charles takes us beyond the temporary and into the eternal realities our souls are craving, and by doing so, he guides us to the throne room of God's grace, where we find truth, life, and the way of Jesus."

—RYAN BRITT, EXECUTIVE MINISTRIES PASTOR, CHURCH OF ELEVEN22

"Imagination is a gift from God and one of the most important tools for your faith journey. Have you ever imagined what it was like to walk with Jesus and witness the first sparks as the church began to spread? This book will help you do that. Watch Peter raise a dead woman to life, see Paul walk out of the prison gate, witness thousands come to Jesus. What would it have been like to be there? What if your life today could look a lot more like theirs than you ever imagined? Through brilliant storytelling and convicting questions, Charles Martin invites you to challenge your status quo and experience the power that raised Christ from the dead in your every day. The truth is, you and I aren't different from those ordinary men and women whose proximity to Jesus changed everything for them. And just like they did, we have the opportunity to join the movement that turned the world upside down. Want to come along?"

—JONATHAN VINKE, MINISTRIES PASTOR, CHURCH OF ELEVEN22

"When *What If It's True* was recommended to me by a close friend, I had no idea that 'it's heavy stuff' meant that I was about to have my whole world gracefully wrecked. The stories were conveyed so vividly that I often felt like I was in the pages with the characters. The insightful attention to the often-overlooked details of these familiar passages revealed new aspects of Jesus that I'd once considered, but never had the language to verbalize. Charles Martin, by the Holy Spirit, has an uber-unique gift. His ability to boldly dig into the secret crevices of the soul of a man, yet gracefully lead the reader into a prayer that hits the nail on the head is nothing shy of supernatural. I'm on the edge of my seat with every line of *They Turned the World Upside Down*. Oddly enough, both works have done just that— turned my world upside down, and I wouldn't have it any other way."

—MARC DICKERSON, LEAD PASTOR, AMAZING LIFE CHURCH

"Charles does a magnificent job of bringing us to the feet of Jesus and God the Father and leading us by the Holy Spirit into doing the ministry of Jesus, which He left for us, as believers, to do here on earth."

—HANK BRINK

"I'm forever grateful for the goodness on these pages and the incredible gift Father God gave to Charles and even more grateful that my brother has chosen to share that gift with us. Having walked much of the testimony of this book with Charles, I know no other human who embodies living by faith and turning the world upside down more than Charles Martin. I think the saying 'walk the walk' was penned for him. Father God is the change agent, but if you press in, this book can and will change you as you hear the testimony of the power of God's Word in the lives of real people and how it powerfully answers the questions: What if these words are true, and what if signs and wonders really are supposed to be following us?"

—RICK CROWLEY

"*They Turned the World Upside Down* is the perfect follow-up to *What If It's True?* The opening of the gospel of John says that Jesus is the Word that became flesh, and if He is the Word and the Word is always true, then Charles unveils a paradigm shift to what the entirety of the gospel actually is and does. Having done life with Charles for more than twelve years, I can attest to not only his understanding of the Word of God but also to the freedom that comes with it this side of the cross. Jesus' finished work at Calvary wasn't just for salvation; it gives every believer the right to His authority and power, as sons and daughters, through the indwelling of the Holy Spirit. And this book explains it perfectly."

—GREG FARAH

"*They Turned the World Upside Down* should inspire every believer to look outside the walls of conventional Christianity and what our intimacy with the Master should look like. Journeying with Him and doing the same things Jesus did should be an everyday part of life. This will motivate you to grow in harmony with the Holy Spirit, listen for His direction, and move with compassion to see the lives of people changed through simple obedience. If you know there is more to your walk with Him than you are experiencing now, this book will change you . . . period!"

—MIKE HOHMAN

"Charles leads his readers along a path of redemption. He reminds us how ordinary men walked alongside Jesus and were empowered by the Holy Spirit. I believe this book will shake many readers to their core and lead them closer to Christ. The quote that stands out for me is 'there is more grace in Jesus than sin in us.' I am again reminded that forgiveness is the path that leads to redemption."

—DEAN KRUGER

"Charles Martin's *They Turned the World Upside Down* is a master class in not just how to have a deeper intimacy with our King and Savior, but how to understand our unique calling, role, and purpose. While a lot of books convey knowledge, this centers around your heart. Charles encourages a deep dive into who we are as priests and what our Lord has in store for us. If I'm honest, it isn't easy. Action and repentance are required. But oh, the reward! As he so eloquently states, 'Freedom is worth the pain.' I am indebted to Charles for not only leading me to my Father but encouraging me to participate in this exciting journey."

—JON LIVINGSTON

"Our society teaches that when the rescue mission is accomplished, the story ends. But when it comes to Jesus' perfect, sacrificial, sanctifying rescue of us, the story has only just begun. With this freedom comes the blessing of a scriptural mandate to go—as warriors, disciples, priests—and to go boldly, in full belief in the power of the Holy Spirit, in complete willingness to receive Him, and in total faith to allow Him to do His will through us. Easy to say, but harder to put into practice every day. That's what our guys' group talks, studies, laughs, cries, worships, and prays about every week, and it's what Charles, with his typical brilliant way of asking simple questions that have life-changing, and sometimes life-saving, implications, lays out in this book."

—JOHNNY SARBER

"To the broken, lost, and fearful . . . this book is hope. It is a lamp to the feet of those who follow the Lord. Charles Martin has given us a detailed blueprint of what Jesus desires from our hearts and actions."

—JASON WATSON

"*They Turned the World Upside Down* is a Holy Spirit–inspired complement to *What If It's True?* When I finished *What If It's True?* my reaction was 'that's a great way to think about it, but what do I *do*?' *They Turned the World Upside Down* answers that question."

—DAVID WAINER

They
Turned
the
World
Upside
Down

They Turned the World Upside Down

*A Storyteller's Journey with Those
Who Dared to Follow Jesus*

CHARLES MARTIN

W PUBLISHING GROUP

An Imprint of Thomas Nelson

ISBN 978-0-7852-3148-6 (Audiobook)
ISBN 978-0-7852-3144-8 (e-Book)

Library of Congress Control Number: 2020943252

ISBN 978-0-7852-3142-4

Printed in the United States of America

21 22 23 24 25   LSC   10 9 8 7 6 5 4 3 2 1

For The King

Contents

Prologue xiii

Chapter 1: The Death of the Only Innocent Man 1

Chapter 2: It Is Perfectly Perfect 10

Chapter 3: A Dead Man Walks. 21

Chapter 4: Shame—the enemy's First Weapon 34

Chapter 5: Problem Number One 46

Chapter 6: Their Problem Is Our Problem 57

Chapter 7: Moving from Faith to Faithfulness 79

Chapter 8: The Holy Spirit 101

Chapter 9: Willing to Be Willing 138

Chapter 10: Show Us the Father. 156

Chapter 11: The Kingdom of Heaven 183

Chapter 12: I Raise My Hand 220

Chapter 13: You're in a War 252

Chapter 14: What or Who Are You at War Against? 285

Chapter 15: They Turned the World Upside Down 297

Epilogue 319

Appendix A 325

Appendix B. 331

Notes 339

About the Author. 345

The sun is setting. A crimson line trails across a blue canvas. The air is cool. A breeze filters through. Jesus and the disciples exit Jerusalem, cross the brook Kidron, walk through the Garden of Gethsemane, and begin the ascent up the Mount of Olives. This is the same path Jesus walked after His arrest en route to His mock trial, His merciless beating, and the criminals' cross. Now they're walking it in reverse.

And all of them recognize it.

The eleven are laughing and shaking their heads. They're having a difficult time reconciling what they're seeing. Weeks ago, they watched and listened as Jesus died a gruesome death. When they took His body down, some brave soul reached up and closed His eyes. Then they carried His tortured and graveyard-dead body to a cold tomb and watched helplessly as the soldiers rolled the heavy stone into place and sealed it with an iron spike. It was the end of all things good and beautiful.

But that was before.

Now, they're walking alongside Him. Huddling close. Touching Him. Making sure. Listening as the laughter enters and exits His lungs. During His earthly ministry, Jesus was a jungle gym for the young. They climbed all over Him. Rolled in the grass. Played tag. The disciples watch in wonder as Jesus carries one of their children on His shoulders.* Skips along the trail. Sings with another.

---

* I realize Scripture does not say this. And I'm not claiming it does. I'm taking license—given what we know of His nature. Having said that, Jesus loved children. More than that, I think He made time for them. If I were a child, and Jesus were walking up a mountain trail, I'd be climbing all over Him. I've tried to think and write like that.

They wind up the worn path to a hilltop where they overlook all of Jerusalem. Jesus has been here many times. He has prayed here, wept here, and it is here that His sweat turned to blood. It is here that His blood began crying a better word than that of Abel. And it is here that He told his disciples to wake up. There's a time for sleep but this was not it.

Over the last few weeks, Jesus has opened their minds to the Scriptures. Allowed them to see what has remained hidden for so long. Blown their minds with each new revelation. To the south sits the City of David. The City of the Great King. Up that winding path, King David returned the ark of the covenant to Jerusalem. The spoken words of God returning to the City of God.

But here and now, that very Word is flesh and walking among them.

Jesus Himself. Eating. Laughing. Talking. Praying. And not one of them can explain it. It's simply too good to be true. In their minds, anything is now possible. Jesus, the only begotten Son of God, lived, died, was buried, and was resurrected. He walked out of the grave. They don't understand everything that means, but at its minimum it means Jesus is more powerful than death. They are on the cusp of something great. Never seen before.

This is storied ground. Mount Moriah. The mountain of God. The word *Moriah* itself means "Foreseen by God." Over there, Abram met Melchizedek in the valley of the five kings; over there, he laid his son Isaac on the altar and raised the knife. This is the mountain of which Abram spoke when he told his son, "God will provide for himself the lamb for a burnt offering."[1] Down there is the threshing floor of Ornan the Jebusite where God withdrew the plague from the people. Up there, King David brought the ark of God into the City of David. Over there, Solomon built the temple. Along that trail, Jesus rode into the city triumphantly seated on a donkey, and down there, under cover of night, He was arrested. On that serpentine path that winds out of the city, the innocent King carried a criminal's cross. And up there, over by the skull, He poured out His soul unto death. Just over there, His body was laid and sealed behind heavy stone. Three days later, out of that same rock, He rose again—in accordance with everything written before.

More has happened on this mountain than any mountain in the world—and has yet to happen. It is here, on this mountain, that the very rocks cry out. It is here, on and in this ground, that God Most High, Possessor of heaven and earth, has placed His name. Forever. And it is here that He will, at a time in the future of His choosing, prepare a lavish banquet for all peoples. Refined and aged wine. Choice pieces of meat. On this mountain, He will swallow up the covering which is over all people. Even the veil which is woven into the nations. On this ground and in His time, He will swallow up death, wipe away every tear, and remove the reproach of His people from all the earth.[2]

But that time is not yet.

And while this is storied ground, these are not storied men. At least not yet. They will be, but here on this mountain they're second string. The did-not-measure-ups. The could-not-cut-its. While they're good Jews, they're not straight A's and valedictorians. That's why most are fishermen. This does not mean they weren't smart. Far from it. Most could probably recite entire portions, verbatim, of the Law, the Prophets, and the Psalms. But to be a Pharisee, you had to be something special. A-team. And these were not. In the world's eyes, these men were your average Joes. B-team.

Which was Jesus' intention all along.

As they climb the hill, their minds spin with possibilities. Most want to stick it to Rome. They are waiting for Jesus to bring down fire from heaven. Elijah and the prophets of Baal sort of stuff. Given what they have seen the last few weeks, each has a question on the tip of his tongue. They all want to know the same thing. One of them voices it: "Lord, will you at this time restore the kingdom to Israel?"[3]

Ever patient, Jesus smiles and continues climbing up the mountain. Halfway up, He turns: "It is not for you to know times or seasons that the Father has fixed by his own authority. But you will receive power when the Holy Spirit has come upon you, and you will be my witnesses"—Jesus points to the land laid out before them—"in Jerusalem and in all Judea and Samaria, and to the end of the earth."[4]

Up there, the disciples can see what He's pointing at, but they don't really understand what He's saying. The words rattle around their brains. Words like *Father, power, Holy Spirit,* and *witnesses.*

They want something more concrete. They want to know when He will send lightning bolts through the chests of Pilate and Herod. They've got it coming. Their days are numbered.

What the disciples cannot see are the myriad angels that have arrayed around them. Resplendent white. Gold. The army of God has come on assignment. To escort the Son home. Banners. Musicians. Dancers. Warriors. They line the mountain. They line the city. They line the earth for miles. Each has six wings. With two they cover their faces. With two they cover their feet. And with two they fly. A living picture of worship and service. At the top of the mountain, God's very own chariot awaits. Driven by white horses.

Jesus can see this. They cannot.

Nearing the top, Jesus walks alongside each of His followers. Holding their hands. An arm around their shoulders. They're all here: Peter, John, James, Andrew, Philip, Thomas, Bartholomew, Matthew, James the son of Alpheus, Simon the Zealot, and Judas the son of James. His natural brothers are here too. Including James. As is Mary Magdalene and His mother, along with many other families. Jesus is not distant. Not indifferent. Not aloof, standing over there. He's a hugger. He is in their midst. He kisses their necks. Tickles their children. They can feel His breath on their faces.

A breeze blows. It is time. The Father has waited long enough.

Jesus turns, looks longingly at His city, at those He loves, and then down through time at you and me. He smiles. He knows the end from the beginning. Then He steps into His chariot, a cloud envelops Him, and He is lifted out of their sight, taking the breeze and the host with Him.

Silence rains down on the mountain.

Minutes pass. Nobody says a word. Children run to and fro through the grass. He has come and gone so many times lately, walked through walls of stone, surely this is one of those times.

But standing on that mountaintop, the disciples begin to wonder. And so the longing begins. The longing for His return.

When the smoke clears, two angels stand in the place where Jesus had stood. Dressed in white robes. They are nearing eleven feet tall. Towering. Powerful. Magnificent. One of them speaks: "Men of Galilee, why do you stand looking into heaven? This Jesus, who was taken up from you into heaven, will come in the same way as you saw him go into heaven."[5]

The disciples stand speechless, one singular question on the tips of their tongues. No one is yet brave enough to voice it. But each is thinking it: *Just what on earth do we do now?*

To answer this question, they will spend, devote, and sacrifice the rest of their lives.

But standing on that storied mountain, in the bosom of the world, they find no answer. As the sun falls over Jerusalem, they return down the mountain, scouring their hearts in search of an answer. And it is about here that they start remembering the words He said while He was with them. They spent three and a half years with Jesus as He traveled and spoke, and given their primarily oral culture, Jesus often said the same thing in every location. Chances are quite good they heard the Sermon on the Mount dozens of times. You might even call it His stump speech. Given this, they could recite His words from memory. Finish His sentences. Which is good. They'll need them in the days to come.

In His absence, they return to Jerusalem—an indescribable combination of sadness and joy. They pray. Sing. Share meals. Encourage one another. And they remember His words: "but you will receive power."

So they wait.

Given the loss of Judas, they cast lots; Matthias, a longtime follower and believer, is now numbered with the eleven. The chosen apostles once again number twelve. In total, the disciples number about a hundred and twenty persons.

Those who stuck with Jesus. Those who saw Him perform miracles, heal the sick, cast out demons, raise the dead, and bounce children on His knee. Those who laughed with Him, cried with Him, and sat on the edge of their seats listening to His every word. These are those who saw Him dead and then saw Him alive. And while they wait, this unlikely and unremarkable group of people begin to reconstruct the words He spoke. Trying to both remember and share that remembrance. As they piece it together, they are amazed at how the Scriptures support and reveal what Jesus said and did. When they stand in the temple and the Scriptures are read, they are astounded. All of the Law, the Prophets, and the Psalms point to Jesus. A jigsaw puzzle of words that begins to take shape.

How could they not have seen it before?

Given a healthy fear of both the Romans and the religious elite, they remain in Jerusalem and keep to themselves. Despite their new revelation into His words, they have a problem. Jesus gave them His authority and commanded them to do as He did, but currently they are powerless to obey Him, and they know it. His words echo: "you will receive power when the Holy Spirit has come upon you."

A week passes.

In the throne room of heaven, the Father is beaming. His Son is home. Seated at His right hand. All of heaven rejoices. The halls echo with "Glory!" "Worthy is the Lamb!" And "Holy, holy, holy!" Over His shoulder, the Holy Spirit awaits the Father's command. The same Spirit that hovered over the waters in creation and just recently raised the Son does nothing of His own initiative. He is sent and He obeys. He is the agent of both action and change, and nothing that is done gets done without Him. He stands. Patiently. Waiting. The three are inseparable, unified, and share perfect and unhindered communion. They are One.

Finally, the time has come. The Father nods. The Son hugs the Spirit. The Spirit leaves the throne room, carves a vapor trail as He exits heaven, and descends into Jerusalem.

Where the roof starts to shake.

Power to Obey

When I wrote *What If It's True?*, I hoped to confront you and me with this question: *What if every word in the Bible is true and I can trust it? With my life?* What if the words of Scripture are truer than my circumstances? And if they are, would I, would you, be willing to allow the truth of God's Word to shine a light on our own sin? To unearth the depths of us and encourage us to acknowledge what lies there, confess what we'd rather keep hidden, and give Him room and access to cleanse us and begin making us more like Him? Why and how does the Bible do this? Because it, the Word, is living and active. It pierces us. Divides truth from falsehood. By its very nature, it flings open the closets in our spiritual basements we'd rather keep sealed. One of my spiritual heroes, Derek Prince, used to describe the living nature of the Word this way: When you're reading your Bible, it's reading you. Giving the Word access to our hearts means giving the blood of Jesus the room and authority to work in us and for us and through us. A process theologians call sanctification. Paul told the Corinthians, "the plowman should plow in hope" (1 Cor. 9:10).

So, once again, I'm writing and hoping.

By picking up this book, I assume you're somewhere in that process called sanctification. Like I am. And if so, then just like the disciples, you may well be asking yourself, What now?

If that's you, you're in good company.

As I have wrestled with this and scoured His Word for answers, I've landed on something really simple: nowhere in Scripture does Jesus tell us to sit back and wait until the process is complete before we do what He said. Nowhere—not one single place—does He tell us to become spectators watching only the holy, the perfect, and the superspiritual live out His commands. That's like saying you have to get cleaned up to take a bath or you have to arrive at the destination before you can embark on the journey. He didn't do that with the disciples. He doesn't do that with us. Inexplicably, He uses cracked cups to pour water.

What makes me say this? The arrival of His Spirit. When the Holy Spirit filled believers like you and me on Pentecost, the Father made good on His promise. From that moment in time, the kingdom of God was not about talk, but power.

What kind of power did He give them?

The answer is simple: power to do what He said. To obey Him.

By God's immeasurable grace, I am a blood-bought, blood-washed, and blood-redeemed child of God. Transferred out of the kingdom of darkness and into the kingdom of the Son of His love. God withheld from me what I deserved, His wrath, and has given me what I don't: His *chesed*, which is His loving-kindness, mercy, grace, forgiveness, and Him-for-me kind of love all wrapped into one. He gave me His Son to take my place.

Included in this undeserved and unmerited gift is the right to become His child. Which I have. And I am. I am a child of God. Heir to the throne. That said, He didn't just pluck me out of the fire only to drop me at His house. I'm no latchkey kid left to fend for myself. There's more. A lot more. God the Father adopted me as His Son and then, unbelievably and miraculously, sent His Spirit—the same Spirit that raised Christ Jesus from the dead—to live in me. He's here right now. Dwelling. Kind of strange when I think about it—that the third member of the Godhead is located in my chest right this second.

The cool thing is that the offer is available to as many as would receive Him. Who believe in His name. Meaning, I'm not the only one. He can dwell in you too. All of us.

He promised this more than two thousand years ago.

In my own experience and my life in ministry, I've discovered that most of us have heard the Bible stories and we've nodded our heads and muttered, "Yeah, yeah, yeah." But the truth is we have no real idea what His Spirit dwelling in us looks like. We think we do, but I disagree. I think we've missed Him by a mile.

Case in point: What if right this second I knocked on your door and told you that you just won the $250 Million Powerball lottery? And I had the check and the bank officials and the media trucks to prove it. All you had to do was agree and sign. How would you respond? How would your thinking change? How long would it take for you to quit screaming and dancing like a fool? How long would it take you to sign on the dotted line?

Now, let's say I knock on your door and tell you that Jesus, the Messiah, the King of all kings and the One who created you from the dust of the earth, wants to send His Spirit—the same Spirit that was responsible for all of creation and through which Jesus performed every miracle while here on earth—to dwell in you. Not the person next to you, not those people over there, not some names out of history. You.

How would you react? Linger here. Wrestle with this one.

Because this book is that knock.

And yet some of you are far more excited about the Powerball. Which is evidence that you have an enemy—and that he's winning.

Scripture records that from that very hour on the day we know as Pentecost, those believers were empowered to do what Jesus commanded. And they did. They walked into the streets of Jerusalem and the gospel of the kingdom was preached and signs and wonders followed them. The blind saw. Lame walked. Demons were cast out. Dead were raised to life.

And slaves and sinners like you and me became children of God, transferred out of the kingdom of darkness and into the kingdom of the Son of His love.

In the months and years ahead, that unlikely group of people preached a message so powerful and transformational that it put Rome on its heels—the greatest military power the world had ever known—and gave rise to a state-sponsored terrorist named Saul (later called Paul) who hunted them down, dragged them from their homes, and killed them one by one. But despite loss of home and threat of imminent death, the disciples continued to boldly proclaim Jesus' words and unashamedly do what He said.

Before their lives were over, these men and women would turn the world upside down.

I write fiction for a living, and that is either the most ridiculous word ever spoken or it should rock our foundation. Shake some things loose. Trigger a long and honest look in the mirror.

Why Write This Book?

Time is often the enemy of movements, reducing them to little more than whispers, roadside markers, and faded banners. But this movement charged on like a freight train. Many messages have crossed the globe, but in the entire history of the world, only one message has been accompanied with power to back it up. By signs and wonders.

Given that this message has not only survived the chipping away of time, but grown exponentially, it's worth asking: What did these believers do?

What was the message they believed and taught?

And what if it's still true today? What if everything He meant for them He still means for us? How should I react? How should I then live? I'm not entirely sure but I don't think it should be muted or reserved.

Two thousand years ago, Jesus preached the gospel of the kingdom to all who had ears to hear. It was true then. It's true now. And it will still be true tomorrow. But how much do we really believe it, and what would happen if we did? Would our lives look different? Would the world?

I tend to think so.

The death and resurrection of Jesus the Christ is the single most important event in the history of humankind, and one drop of His blood is the most powerful thing in this universe or any other. Dead and crucified Jesus came back to life by the power of the Holy Spirit and He is alive today. Right now. Ruling in the midst of His enemies. His Father gave Him all authority in heaven and earth, and yet, unbelievably, He shares it with all who would but ask. Freely.

In *What if It's True?* I asked what kind of King gives His life for self-centered slaves like you and me, allowing rebels like us to become sons and daughters. In these pages, I want to know what kind of King not only dies for His subjects and adopts them as heirs but gives them His authority—and His power.

What kind of King would do such a thing? There's only one answer.

But Jesus didn't stop there. He promised us that when we exercise that authority, we will do greater things than He did (John 14:12). And don't downplay "greater things." Don't just tell me we'll speak to larger numbers of people given technology and larger stadiums. It means "miraculous works." Signs and wonders kind of stuff. The blind see. Lame walk. Epileptics are healed. Dead are raised to life.

If this is true, then the book of Acts should be a description of your walk with Jesus. A roadmap. All that stuff the disciples did—all those sick people healed, all those demons cast out, all those dead raised to life, all those sinners and slaves brought into the kingdom of God—you and I should be doing that too.

And right about here is where the rubber meets the road and the disagreement begins.

If you're having trouble with these ideas, don't worry. You're in good company. Wars have been fought over this stuff. Our enemy, using every tactic and weapon at his disposal, has attacked you and your belief of this gospel since it was spoken. he desperately does *not* want you to think Jesus is actually talking to you.* Or that Jesus' Word means today what it meant to those who first heard it. Many of us, either consciously or not, have trouble believing that the words Jesus spoke two thousand years ago have any bearing on or relation to our present-day lives. As if two millennia and several thousand miles of geography have somehow changed His meaning or reduced and diluted His commands.

As a result, we live in a crossfire of unbelief and doubt. And we're not quite sure what to believe.

But what if? *What if it's still true?*

The appearance of the Holy Spirit at Pentecost is our first clue that Jesus wasn't kidding. That He meant what He said. That the kingdom of heaven has come to us. That the dwelling place of God is with man. Otherwise, what's His Spirit doing in my chest? And why give us His authority if He didn't intend for us to use it? His intention and promise is that the third member of the Godhead, His very Spirit, the Spirit of holiness, will live inside you and me when we invite Him.

---

* I did not capitalize "satan" in *What If It's True?* and I don't intend to start now.

I was wrestling with this one day and thought I heard the Lord ask me a tough question: *Where's the evidence?*

I scratched my head, "What do you mean?"

Well—He pointed at my Bible—*My Spirit does stuff. Scripture records it. Just look at all the miracles.* He tapped me on the chest. *If My Spirit is in you, then why aren't you doing the same stuff as those who received My Spirit? Has My Spirit changed?*

My response was quick: "You're the same yesterday, today, and tomorrow. You never change."

Then where does the problem lie?

I didn't have much of an answer.

If I'm honest, I'm looking at His Word in one hand and the fruit of my life in the other, and one of these things is not like the other. Discrepancies abound. Causing me to wonder if I received His Spirit only to tell Him to sit quietly in the corner and not do anything without my permission. Don't get too crazy. What would people think? Which prompts an honest question: Did I receive the Spirit only to muzzle Him?

How about you? Have you received the Spirit? If so, great—*but have you muzzled Him?*

Don't skip over this. The end of this book will still be there whether you read fast or slow. First things first: Have you received the Holy Spirit as described in Acts? And don't tell me what your church has told you. Don't tell me what your tradition has told you. I'm asking you: Have you received Him? If so, what's happened since and where's the evidence?

Matthew says, "From the days of John the Baptist until now the kingdom of heaven has suffered violence, and the violent take it by force" (Matt. 11:12). In Luke, Jesus said, "The Law and the Prophets were until John; since then the good news of the kingdom of God is preached, and everyone forces his way into it" (Luke 16:16). Interpretations vary on this idea of violence or forcing, but let's look at it in the context of which it is spoken—a conversation about John the Baptist. John was a self-denying man, and the message he preached was self-denying too. He was eager to give up worldly pleasure and press without compromise into the harder things of the kingdom.

Further, Jesus' words come within the context of John the Baptist's arrest by Herod Antipas, encouraging some to lean toward an interpretation of this scripture that suggests those within the kingdom suffer violence by those on the outside—and I can't say I disagree. Jesus Himself said, "You will be hated by all for my name's sake" (Matt. 10:22).

But I believe there's more. I believe the phrase "the violent take it by force" is talking about you and me. I believe it's suggesting a type of holy violence, or pious violence, we commit against ourselves where we apply the words of Jesus against our lives and ask some hard questions. Holy violence is a daily gut check. Asking ourselves: *Am I really walking in repentance? Every day? Have I forgiven everyone of everything? Have I confessed my sin to another? Am I focused on holiness? Am I walking in the fear of the Lord? Have I humbled myself? Do I really believe the words of Jesus, and am I doing them? Am I laying down my life? Could I wash Judas's feet? Have I received His Spirit and released Him fully to work in my life as He wills?*

Holy violence, or forcibly pressing our way into the kingdom, is not achieved with a sword or gun, but with vigorous self-denial. How vigorous? We gauge that by the strength of our self and what amount of violence is needed to overcome it. Take King David, for example. We know he was both a man after God's own heart (1 Sam. 13:14; Acts 13:22) and a man of war. But look how he attacked his own soul in Psalm 69: "I wept and humbled my soul with fasting" (v. 10). And again in Psalm 35: "When they were sick—I wore sackcloth; I afflicted myself with fasting" (v. 13). David knew that his spirit and the Spirit of God within him were at war, so how did he wage war? He humbled and afflicted his self by denying it through fasting. That's holy violence.

Does God agree with this? Look at what He said through the prophet Joel: "Return to me with all your heart, with fasting, with weeping, and with mourning; and rend your hearts and not your garments" (Joel 2:12–13). Finally, these are the words of Jesus—look at how He spoke about sin: "If your right hand causes you to sin, cut it off and cast it from you" (Matt. 5:30 NKJV). A man who met his sin in this way would, according to Jesus, be violently pressing in or violently taking the kingdom to heart.

In the first century, "believer" didn't just mean someone who heard and agreed with Jesus. It meant someone who acted on that belief. Believers obeyed and did. And when the outside world saw these believers, they declared, "These who have turned the world upside down have come here too" (Acts 17:6 NKJV).

The first believers saw something. Experienced something. And you and I are having this conversation because they "believed" what they saw and experienced—and then did stuff. Before I get too carried away, they also died. Every last one of them, save John, died as martyrs. Not to mention Stephen and Paul and a host of others. They were killed because of that belief. Something so great had happened in the depths of their soul, way down deep in their knowingness, that they sold out completely. For Him. They were what we might call "radicals"—a word which, by the way, comes from the Latin *radix*, which means "that which gets at the root. The base or the beginning." Jesus had gotten to their root.

How about you? Do you believe Jesus that deeply? Has He gotten to your root? Would anyone label you a *radical* for Jesus?

What Would It Take?

What would it take for you to die for someone? If that question scares you, good. It scares me too. Would I have the gumption to do what the disciples did? Until I'm brought to that moment, I have no idea, but I do know this: Jesus is the model, and they followed His example. To a tee. They laid down their lives and picked up their crosses. And because they did what He did, you and I can have this conversation. They believed something so deeply and with such fervor that their actions upended the world in which they found themselves.

These disciples turned the world upside down because they saw a dead man come back to life by the power of God. And whatever that "knowing" and "seeing" did in them, it did it at a deep level because they spent their lives talking about Him and doing what He did. Further, they weren't just fair-weather friends. They stuck it out. Even when it got tough.

- Peter was crucified upside down.
- Andrew—the brother of Peter—was scourged, and then tied rather than nailed to a cross, so that he would suffer longer. Andrew lived for two days, during which he preached to passersby.
- James (son of Zebedee, aka James the Greater) was arrested and led to a place of execution, whereby his unnamed accuser was moved by his courage. He not only repented and converted on the spot but asked to be executed alongside James. The Roman executioners obliged, and both men were beheaded simultaneously.
- John was boiled alive. When that didn't work, they exiled him to Patmos where some say he died.
- Philip was scourged in Heliopolis (Egypt), thrown into prison, and crucified.
- Bartholomew, by two accounts, was either beaten and then crucified or skinned alive and beheaded.
- Thomas was run through with a spear.
- Matthew was stabbed in the back in Ethiopia.
- James (son of Alphaeus, aka James the Less) was head of the church in Jerusalem and one of the longest-living apostles, perhaps exceeded only by John. At the age of ninety-four, he was beaten and stoned by persecutors, who then killed him by hitting him in the head with a club.
- Thaddaeus, aka Judas or Jude, was crucified at Edessa (the name of cities in both Turkey and Greece) in AD 72.
- Simon the Canaanite was crucified in England.

What would do this in these men? What would it take to do this in you? Don't just skip over that one. They believed something so deeply that they did not turn tail and run when the executioner appeared with blood dripping off his axe. Would you? Would I?

What would it take for us to love Jesus like that?

Yes, God is a good Father. Yes, He gives us good gifts. What have we received that wasn't given to us by Him? Yes, He has lavished us with His love, and He is for us and not against us. But coming to Jesus is not about what we get, what makes us happy, or what provides for our comfort. If it is, then explain to me why these men lost everything, including their heads, and gave up what they wanted for what He wanted?

There was a reason for this. The truth is, when we come to Jesus, we give up everything. What will it take for us to love Jesus as those first disciples did? The ones who turned the world upside down?

Absolutely everything.

Once Free, What Next?

If we really believe what we say we believe concerning Jesus, our lives with Jesus should look different from our lives prior to Jesus. Our lives should look as though He turned them upside down—and probably inside out. There should be evidence, as there was in the disciples' lives. If we believe as they did, we should be doing as they did—and signs and wonders should follow us.

Maybe some of you were raised in legalistic churches that beat you over the head with the idea that your eternal worth and ability to get into heaven was somehow tied to all your good religious deeds and works. If that's you, hold on. Just bear with me. I hope you don't feel as though I've given you a list of things to "do." Also, for those of you who grew up like me in more charismatic circles that started well-meaning but grew into a charismania movement filled with experience junkies who held out their arms and tapped a vein saying, "Don't bother me with the Word, I'm just here for the experience," you, too, can relax. In my life in ministry, and in writing this, I've attempted to look at the Word and ask myself the same question I asked in *What If It's True?* If this Word is true, what does that mean? Like, really? What should be different about me? Where am I off in my thinking and my doing? And what would my life look like if I actually did what He said?

These first-century Jews, these fishermen, these tax collectors, these women, these believers—they all walked with a Man. They saw Him do unbelievable and miraculous things. They also saw Him falsely accused, arrested, whipped, mocked, crucified, dead, and buried.

And they saw Him rise from that death. Walk through walls. Eat fish. Build a fire. Laugh. Walk. Ascend. They saw Him alive.

That changed them. In every way. Forever.

As much as I know my own heart, I love Jesus. I talk with Him, talk about Him, write about Him. But despite my pledged love for Him, I'm not sure I walk through my day with the same gut-level knowingness with which they walked around. That the King of the universe is alive. In me. And that His power is mine. To exercise at will. And that I want what He wants. I'd like to tell you I do, but I know me too well. Sometimes I do, sometimes I don't. Sometimes I just want to do my own thing, which is not necessarily His own thing, which tells you a lot about how little I really love Him.

But I want to.

I want my life to look like theirs. I'd like for my King to stare through the floor of heaven, motion the angels to the window, point at us with a smile on His face, and add us to the number of those who came before who *turned the world upside down*. For Him. I'd like to be counted in that group. To add my name, and your name, to the great faith Hall of Fame in Hebrews 11.

I have a feeling you would too. Jesus has that effect on us.

"Do You Love Me?"

Let me ask again: What would your life and my life look like if we read His Word, believed it with all that we are, and then did what He said to do? No questions asked. Easy peasy, 1–2–3. Even the parts we weren't too sure about. Like healing, casting out demons, raising the dead, giving prophetic utterances, and speaking in tongues.

Okay, hold it. Some of you just winced. Thought about closing this book. Rolled your eyes. Muttered under your breath, "Oh, not that again. Is he one of those?"

I've just landed on a few hot buttons, and most of us reading this are really divided when it comes to these. While our responses may vary, they are typical: "We don't do that in my church." Or, "I'm not comfortable with that." Or, "TV preachers have totally ruined that for me." Or, "I was wounded in a church like that." Or, "A man I really respect says all that stuff died with the apostles." Or, "I just don't believe that." Or, name your problem.

I know. Me too. It's a mess.

But three inches from my fingers right this moment is my Bible. (Or one of them. I'm a bit of a Bible geek and I own something like a dozen.) I'm staring at Matthew 10:7–8. It's the only thing highlighted on the entire two pages. I did that on purpose. So I wouldn't forget. This is Jesus speaking: "And as you go, preach, saying, 'the kingdom of heaven is at hand.' Heal the sick, cleanse the lepers, raise the dead, cast out demons. Freely you have received, freely give" (NKJV).

Just look at the verbs, *preach, heal, cleanse, raise, cast out, give.*

It could not be simpler. But does that describe you?

Because it did describe the disciples.

I admit, while it sometimes describes me, it does not always. *But I want it to.* Before we turn another page, the questions you and I have to wrestle with are these: Is Jesus just talking to them, or is He also talking to us? With equal sincerity? Right this second?

Does He mean His Words for you and me, today, the same way He meant them for the disciples two thousand years ago?

Write your answer over there in the margin. And then circle it. It matters.

A lot.

If the disciples showed us anything, they showed us that the preaching-healing-cleansing-raising-casting-out-giving-foot-washing-forgiving-loving-your-enemies kind of life will turn the world upside down. And let me add, their goal wasn't to turn the world upside down. It just happened to be the effect. Nor am I suggesting it should be our goal. It was the fruit of their life and proof that they believed. Evidence of the transformation. I'm holding it up as a pattern for us not so we seek the glory of the upturning but so we dig around inside ourselves enough to gauge both our transformation and our motivation. No to mention the fact that Matthew 10 is a command.

That's right. Command. How often do I, do you, obey it?

When I read Matthew 10, I ask myself, If I believed as they believed, what about my faith would be different? And what would I "do" as a result? I'm not suggesting that my faith is based on my works. Don't read that into this. But when I look at the lives of the men who had great faith, their faith worked. They believed, they prayed, they were baptized with water and with the Holy Spirit—as Jesus said, they were *clothed with power*—they gave unselfishly, they forgave, they loved, they shared, they preached, they cast out, they healed, they raised the dead, and they taught others how to do this. And somehow, despite being totally unqualified through sin, mistakes, unbelief, and lack of faith, they were really good at it.

How do I know this?

Because you and I are sitting here talking about them.

Jesus does not call the qualified. He qualifies the called. If not, explain Moses. And Peter. And Paul. And Charles Martin. Their primary problem, which is also my and your primary problem, was *belief.* Followed closely by *obedience.* The two were then and are now intertwined. Inseparable. To do one meant the other.

Jesus said, "If you love me, keep my commandments." After His resurrection, when He stood in their midst, the disciples were startled and frightened and thought they were seeing a spirit (Luke 24:36–37). He looked inside them and saw doubt and unbelief. So He held out his hands and pulled up His shirt. "See." And when they still couldn't believe, *for joy,* He asked for fish and then sat down, took a bite, chewed, swallowed, and smiled. And when their jaws hit the floor, He put down the plate, tilted His head slightly, and said, "These are my words that I spoke to you while I was still with you, that everything written about me in the Law of Moses and the Prophets and the Psalms must be fulfilled. Then he opened their minds to understand the Scriptures" (24:44–45).

My prayer for you and me as we start this is that He would "open our minds" and our hearts to understand the Scriptures. And that we would *believe*, *obey*, and *do*. Every word. Just like a child. Or a sheep. Without deliberation. Without qualification. In Acts 15 He made this possible with Lydia. He opened her heart to pay attention to what Paul said. So why not us?

The writer of Hebrews cautioned this: "For this reason we must pay much closer attention to what we have heard, so that we do not drift away from it. For if the word spoken through angels proved unalterable, and every transgression and disobedience received a just penalty, how will we escape if we neglect so great a salvation? After it was at the first spoken through the Lord, it was confirmed to us by those who heard" (2:1–3 NASB).

You see those two words *drift away*? To me it describes a rudderless boat absent its anchor. Is that you? Are you missing both your rudder and your anchor?

You see that word *disobedience*? It means "to mishear." Or, "be unwilling or neglect or refuse to hear." How often have I done this?

I cannot count. And if I'm being gut-level honest, partial obedience is complete disobedience. Period. Always has been.

If Jesus Were Standing Here . . .

After a couple of years of listening to Jesus speak about the kingdom of heaven, the disciples started looking toward its imminent arrival. And, being the guys they were, they started jockeying for position. It comforts me to know that I am not the only one who suffers the sin of comparison. One day, they were arguing over who was the greatest when Jesus pulled a child into His lap and said, "Truly, I say to you, unless you turn and become like children, you will never enter the kingdom of heaven. Whoever humbles himself like this child is the greatest in the kingdom of heaven" (Matt. 18:3–4). When I hear this, two words catch my attention: *humbles* and *turn*. *Humbles* means to make or bring one's self low. To abase by choice. It describes a childlike person who stands without arrogance or self-exaltation. In 1 Peter, the word describes a free man who willingly puts on the apron of a bond servant—a slave by choice (5:5). The second word is *turn*. It means to reverse. "To turn toward or adopt another course." Jesus' response focused not on rank, but the condition of the heart.

My encouragement to you as you read these pages is to do so through a childlike heart.

After His resurrection, Jesus spent forty days with the disciples and some five hundred other believers. Listen to what He said after He rose from the dead.

> Afterward he appeared to the eleven themselves as they were reclining at table, and he rebuked them for their unbelief and hardness of heart, because they had not believed those who saw him after he had risen. And he said to them, "Go into all the world and proclaim the gospel to the whole creation. Whoever believes and is baptized will be saved, but whoever does not believe will be condemned. And these signs will accompany those who believe: in my name they will cast out demons; they will speak in new tongues; they will pick up serpents with their hands; and if they drink any deadly poison, it will not hurt them; they will lay their hands on the sick, and they will recover." (Mark 16:14–18)

I think if Jesus were standing here or sitting alongside us (both of which He is), He would point at our unbelief and hard hearts and say, "Come on, guys. Really? What more is it going to take?" Then He'd sit alongside us and open the Scriptures for as long as we were willing to listen. And we, if we really believed Him, would lift those words off the page and *do stuff*—no matter what we thought about it or how we'd seen it abused by others or how crazy it sounded or how impossible we might think it. We would believe and do. Believe and do. Believe and do.

And signs and wonders would follow us.

When Paul addressed the Corinthians, he said this:

I, when I came to you, brothers, did not come proclaiming to you the testimony of God with lofty speech or wisdom. For I decided to know nothing among you except Jesus Christ and him crucified. And I was with you in weakness and in fear and much trembling, and my speech and my message were not in plausible words of wisdom, but in demonstration of the Spirit and of power, so that your faith might not rest in the wisdom of men but in the power of God. (1 Cor. 2:1–5)

He would later tell the Ephesians, "Be strong in the Lord and in the power of His might" (Eph. 6:10 NKJV).

We are commanded to stand and walk in power that does not originate with us, and yet we as people have an ugly history of abusing and/or refusing the power we've been given—or choosing powers other than God Most High. The fact that He has entrusted us with power at all is mind-boggling when we look at our own track record. People and power don't often mix well. And yet, He gives it freely. What kind of King does that?

My hope in writing this book is not to pen a theological treatise but more a pastoral plea—to sit shoulder to shoulder with you, take an honest look at our faith, and ask ourselves if we are standing and walking in that same power. And not for power's sake. But for obedience's sake. For love's sake. For His glory.

My prayer is that this book is *not* a list of stuff you must do to call yourself a good Christian. I have no interest in adding to your already overstuffed backpack or holding up a measuring stick to show you and me how massively and miserably we fail to measure up. As much as I know my own heart, I am simply falling more in love with my King. Jesus. And from that love, and out of that love, I find myself wanting to accept His invitation. Because that's what this is.

It's an invite. Expressed in two words: "Follow Me."

To follow where Jesus is leading will require that we look at the lives of those who believed and followed Him, and then commit holy violence against ourselves by examining and asking if we're doing what they did. To quote the writer of Hebrews, "everyone who lives on milk is unskilled in the word of righteousness, since he is a child. But solid food is for the mature, for those who have their powers of discernment trained by constant practice to distinguish good from evil" (Heb. 5:13–14). It's time to move from milk to solid food. In the Charles Martin translation, I call it a gut check.

So take a deep breath and walk with me back into the words and actions of Jesus, and the lives of those who loved and walked with Him. Let's look at the stuff they did that turned the world upside down. It's not overly complicated. In fact, it's rather simple: *They saw a dead man walk. And they believed. And they did.*

My Prayer for You

Father, I lift to You the hands and heart holding this book. If they are not currently Your child, I pray You call them to Yourself, that You would grant them the gift of repentance, and that they would come to know You as the Christ, risen from the dead, Savior of the world, the promised Messiah. If they are Your child, I pray You call them into deeper intimacy where they hear Your voice distinct and apart from the chaos, noise, traditions, and abuse of both the world and the enemy. I pray Your Holy Spirit would guide them through each word, each page. Have Your way. Do what only You can do. I entrust this one to You and ask even now, in this moment, that You fall in power. I pray that they would believe at a deeper level, that their faith would grow exponentially, that they would run headlong into Your kingdom with reckless abandon, that they would raise their hands and renew their covenant with You, that they would climb up into Your lap and know the scent of their Father—and that at the end of the day, they would walk in the authority that You alone have given them and do greater things than You did because You are seated at the right hand of the Father. Lastly, Lord, I pray that we—as both Your body and Your bride—will walk in belief and obedience and faith in such a way that the effect of our lives lived out pleases You and turns the world upside down. Not so we somehow get credit for the upturning, but so the world will know that there is only One God and Messiah and Your name is Jesus. Yeshua HaMashiach.

Lord Jesus, I'm reading Your Word, and my life doesn't look like the lives of the disciples who turned the world upside down. Signs and wonders aren't following me, and I want them to. Not for what that says about me, but Father, for what that says about You. For Your glory. So the world will know that You alone are God and that the kingdom of heaven is here. But I don't even know where to start, so please open my eyes to Your Word and reveal to me what has long been hidden. Two thousand years of history does not excuse me from living as You commanded. Nothing's changed. The tomb is still empty. You're still alive, and so is Your Word. It's not dead. Your Word means today what it meant when You first spoke it, and nothing changes that. I want to be obedient. I want to believe and do. Please grant me all I need as I walk through this, and reveal to me the truth of Your Word. In Jesus' name.

Before we move forward, I suggest you adopt the same process I recommended in *What If It's True?* Read the pages of this book and do the stuff we talk about. Make this a field manual and not just something that collects dust on the coffee table. Read with a Bible in one hand and pen in the other. Mark up these pages. Write in the margins. Make this a two-way conversation. But not with me. Carry on your own conversation with the Lord. He matters. Not me. Ask yourself the questions I'm asking you. Be honest. Dig around a little. Challenge your long-held assumptions.

Some of what we talk about here might push you out of your comfort zone. Don't worry—me too. Let it push you. Go and do the stuff. Give it a try. What have you got to lose?

Conversely, what have you got to gain? Answer those two questions. Over there in the margins. That's what all that space is for. Your answer might reveal a lot about you.

Look, I'm in this with you. I'm not on the outside pointing in, saying, "You need to do better." I'm on the inside looking out, wanting a life of faith and belief and obedience and work that pleases my King. And my Father. And He wants that too. Fact is, the Father wants to give you a gift. The most precious gift imaginable.

Walk this journey with me. Let's return to the cross and allow resurrected Jesus to walk us to the tomb, the Upper Room, the southern steps of the temple, and then stand in awe and wonder as His Spirit baptizes us and empowers us to go to the far parts of the world—and do what He said. My hope for both of us is that we would listen to Jesus with uncalloused and circumcised hearts, honest about our prejudices and traditions and anything that would hinder our obedience, or our disciple-like kind of faith.

None of us has this faith walk exactly right. No one has perfect theology. Certainly not me. James says, "the demons believe—and shudder!" (James 2:19). Truth is, the demons probably have better theology than most of us; they've just chosen the wrong kingdom and they don't have faith or belief.

Without which it is impossible to please God.

Those who turned the world upside down had something—they believed His Word was God's Word and that it was absolutely true. So true they staked their lives on it. Fifty days after Jesus' crucifixion, they received His Spirit without limitation, and then they did what He said do. So join me and let's walk with the resurrected Son of God, the only innocent man to ever live, and pray like crazy that He will do the same in us.

CHAPTER 1

The Death of the Only
Innocent Man

For the last three hours, an inexplicable darkness has covered the earth. Jesus pushes Himself up on His nail-pierced feet and tries to breathe, but He can't. His lungs are filling. He's been at it six hours and He's drowning in His own fluid. It is nearing three o'clock. In the temple, just a few hundred yards away, the High Priest is sharpening his knife with which he will slit the throat of the Passover lamb while another catches the blood in a basin. The lamb was chosen five days ago. Last Monday. About the time Jesus rode in on a donkey. The lamb has been waiting ever since.

From before the foundation of the world, Jesus and His Father have known unfettered, unbroken, and uninterrupted intimacy. Even here on earth. But at this very moment, suspended between heaven and earth, Jesus—Infinite God made Son of man—who is able to see both into this world and the world from which He came, watches as the Father does something He's never done. The inexplicable. And without warning. He forsakes His own Son. Rejects Him. And Jesus watches it in real time.

With the last loud voice He will possess this side of the grave, Jesus stands on the nails and screams, "My God, My God, why have you forsaken me?"[1] Jesus hangs knowing the complete and total rejection of the Father. Its effect is incomprehensible.

Below Him, the soldiers are not impressed.

The Roman army is the most powerful in the world. Also the largest. The logistics of supporting and maintaining an army that expansive require planning and forethought. An occupying force has to be fed. And a fed army has to go to the bathroom. Which leads to sanitation concerns. Disease and bacteria spread like wildfire if not contained. In order to help stem the flow of sickness and maintain a sanitary army, soldiers are issued two things: a jar of vinegar and a *tersorium*. Or, sponge on a stick. After using the bathroom, they would dip the sponge in the vinegar, clean their backside, and repeat as needed. You can see where this is going.

"Immediately, one of them ran and took a sponge, filled it with sour wine and put it on a reed and offered it to Him to drink."[2]

Some have suggested the sponge-in-the-mouth was an act of mercy, having been dipped in opium-laced vinegar. We don't know that. And given the soldiers' treatment of Jesus until now, I highly doubt it. What we do know is that Roman society used sponges on sticks as toilet paper, and there on the cross they shoved it in Jesus' mouth. "Eat this and die!" It tells us what they thought of Him. This continued mockery would be consistent with the soldiers' attitude toward Jesus throughout His crucifixion—save one.

The fluid in His lungs has reached the tipping point. Jesus has but one breath remaining. What does He do with it? He arches His back, tightens His lips, and speaks a singular word: "And Jesus cried out again with a loud voice, and yielded up His Spirit."[3]

What did He say? What did He cry out? Seems like His last word would be important. Maybe we should listen. John tells us: "So when Jesus had received the sour wine, He said, 'tetelestai!' And bowing His head, He gave up His Spirit."[4]

Tetelestai.

The final word spoken on earth by the King of all kings.

The Throne Room

Jesus exhales, His Spirit departs, and the Son of God—God made man, the only perfect, sinless human to ever walk the planet, *Yeshua HaMashiach*—hangs dead on a tree. Those who love Him can't believe it. They are incredulous. Dumbfounded. *How can this be?* Those who hate Him couldn't care less. *Good riddance.* The soldiers shoo the spectators, "Move along. Nothing to see here."

Jesus' last word echoes out across the ancient city and then wafts heavenward. Darkness consumes the day. Lightning flashes. Thunder cracks. An earthquake tears through the Rift Valley. Rocks split. The veil in the temple is torn in two. And people long dead rise from their graves.

Matthew records it this way: "Then, behold, the veil of the temple was torn in two from top to bottom; and the earth quaked, and the rocks were split, and the graves were opened; and many bodies of the saints who had fallen asleep were raised."[5]

Darkness? Lightning? Thunder? Earthquake? Rocks split? Veil torn? Dead people rise? That must have been some word.

We most commonly translate *tetelestai* to mean, "It is finished."

It's possible that when they heard Him speak that word (because it is in the perfect tense and continues on forever), they translated it to mean, "It is perfectly perfect." Or, "It is completely complete." They think He is talking about His life. About the rebellion. About the attempt to take on Rome. About all the stuff they had hoped Jesus would usher in.

But Jesus is not talking about all that.

In fact, while His body hangs here, I'm not convinced He's looking at this earth. Jesus, God become man, is able to see both this world and the heaven from which He descended. His vision is 0/0. He can see what we can't.

I tend to think He's looking at what we see in Revelation 4 and Isaiah 6. The throne room of God.

After a thirty-three-year absence, the Son has returned.* He's in bad shape. Every sin that has ever been committed by anyone at any time or ever will be after this moment, is draped around His shoulders. Shoved like a spear into His chest. Soaked through and through. Infused with His DNA. "He made Him who knew no sin to be sin for us."[6] Sinless God is now identified totally and completely with sin. Nothing could be more horrific.

And yet Jesus walks in. This is Mount Zion, the city of the living God. Heavenly Jerusalem.

The Holy City sits on a high mountain. It is radiant. Clear as crystal. It has a great high wall with twelve gates. Angels guard each gate. And on the gates are written the names of the twelve tribes. The walls have twelve foundations, and on the foundations are written the names of the twelve apostles. Its walls are jasper, pure gold, clear glass, covered with every jewel, and the city's streets are gold. Nothing unclean is here. In this city, there is nothing detestable, false, unfaithful, or untrue. There is also no sun or external light source. God the Father is the source. This means no shadows. No unlit space.

The door is open. A throne sits at the far end. Miles away. Covered in Jasper. Carnelian. An emerald rainbow surrounds the throne. Twenty-four elders, clothed in white, lie flat on their face. They, too, have thrones, but when Jesus walks in, they launch themselves off their seats and bury their noses in the ground at His feet. The golden crowns they once wore have been cast at His feet. As He approaches, lightning flashes, thunder sounds, and seven torches of fire stand before the throne, surrounded by a sea of glass and crystal. Four creatures sit on each side. The creatures possess eyes fore and aft. One is a lion, one an ox, one a man, and one an eagle in flight. Each has six wings. Twenty-four hours a day, seven days a week, they say, "Holy, holy, holy is the Lord God Almighty, who was

---

* Admittedly, I am outside of Scripture here. I can put pieces together from Scripture, but I am using license to paint this scene. Don't take this as absolutely true. It's coming from my imagination. I'm trying to help us see what we can't and could not, but I tend to think it happened. Did it happen exactly as I say it here? Probably not. But I'm finitely writing what might have happened to an infinite God. Please forgive my limitations.

and is and is to come!" The elders lie prostrate in agreement, "Worthy are you, our Lord and God, to receive glory and honor and power." They proffer space, time, and matter. "You created all things, and by your will they existed."[7]

Innumerable angels are arrayed in festal gathering. They are here for Him. His return. This is the assembly of the firstborn, which He is. They worship continually before God, the judge of all. High and lifted up, righteousness and judgment are the foundations of His throne. He is a consuming fire. Always has been.[8]

Walking in, carrying His own blood in a cup, Jesus has proven that He alone is the faithful witness. The firstborn of the dead. He is the second Adam, born on the cross when the soldier shoved the spear in His chest and blood and water flowed.

In this moment, He is the ruler of every king everywhere. In this moment, He is undefeated, and His victory is undisputed and irrevocable. The angels are about to lose their minds. The Father has inched forward to the edge of His throne. His right foot is tapping. His pulse has quickened. He's had about all He can take. The next person to lay a finger on Jesus will be incinerated—10,000 degrees Fahrenheit in less than a millisecond.

Through a rescue mission, a prisoner exchange, Him for us, Jesus has freed, ransomed, and redeemed people of every tribe, tongue, color, and nation—which includes you and me—from our sins with His very own blood. Having made the journey there and back, the King has returned. And He has brought mankind, all of captivity, with Him. In the distance, He sees the construction that has taken place in His absence. His Father's house. Rooms have been added. Lots of rooms. He smiles. He loves family. Can't wait to share it.

There are two sounds: Jesus' footsteps and the pounding of His Father's heart. Every muscle is tense. Coiled. This place is about to explode in an expression of joy unlike any ever.

Jesus is not just a King. He is *the* King. And He's not just the ruler of a kingdom. He is the ruler of *the* kingdom. To Him belongs all power and authority and dominion, and in the next few seconds He will do something no king anywhere has ever done. He will transform and transfer the nation of slaves He ransomed into a kingdom of priests—priests to His God and Father. And then in His first act as King, He will do the unthinkable. The unimaginable. He will give us the authority He is given. Making us sons. Coheirs. With all the rights and privileges thereof.

Were it not true, it would be inconceivable.

These are the last steps of a journey that started back in the garden of Eden. Before, even. Jesus has come to make a payment. Final payment. In blood. His own. This propitiation ushers in those who believe in His name to serve alongside Him as priests before His God and Father.

Every eye is fixed on Him. He alone has done this. This is Jesus. The Alpha, Omega, first, last, who is and was and is to come. A stark contrast to when He humbled Himself and became a man. When He last left, He was clothed with a long robe, a golden sash around His chest, hair white like wool, like snow, His eyes a flame of fire, His feet burnished bronze, His voice like many waters, like Niagara or the break at pipeline. He holds seven stars in His hand, and from His mouth comes a sword. His face is like the sun shining in its strength.[9]

But here and now, He is the Son of man. Returning to His Father. He is "marred more than any man. And His form more than the sons of men."[10] With every step, His visage becomes more disfigured. By the time He reaches the throne, He is unrecognizable as a man.

It's not far now. Just a few more steps. Before He left, He humbled Himself and did not think equality with God something to be grasped. And He does not now, which is why He alone has been lifted up and given the name above every name.[11] Before Him, there is a river flowing from the throne of God. Those who want to get to the Father must wade the river. No exceptions. Except Jesus. He walks on top. On either side is the Tree of Life, with twelve kinds of fruit, producing fruit each month, and the leaves are for the healing of the nations. As He walks, He speaks: "I am coming soon, bringing my recompense with me, to repay each one for what he has done. . . . Blessed are those who wash their robes, so that they may have the right to the tree of life and that they may enter the city."

He glances outside the city. Outside of heaven. To the darkness covering His execution below. "Outside are the dogs and sorcerers and the sexually immoral and murderers and idolaters, and everyone who loves and practices falsehood."[12]

Jesus is not just closing the distance to His Father. He is mediating a new covenant. A "better covenant . . . established on better promises."[13] The blood of the old covenant cries up from the ground, "Guilty!" Which is true. We are. Every last one of us. But in His hand He carries the blood of the new covenant, which He has cut with mankind. One that fulfills every requirement, thereby establishing as New. In it, He is both the Just and the Justifier. The blood of this new covenant whispers, "Innocent." Jesus' voice thunders and shakes the earth.

This new covenant is a gift unlike any this world has ever known. Before or since. Never before has one member of mankind offered to live up to the requirements of both sides. In its simplicity, Jesus is the greater member of the two parties, telling the minor party, "I will pay the debt you owe me. No matter the cost." He is both guarantor and guarantee.

So infinite in its reach that outside of the context of the *chesed* of God the Father—the inexplicable and abundant loving-kindness and mercy and favor of Creator God—this new covenant is illogical in its provision. What will be its result? Listen to Jeremiah six hundred years prior: "For this is the covenant that I will make. . . . I will put My law within them, and write it on their hearts; and I will be their God, and they shall be My people. No more shall every man teach his neighbor, and every man his brother, saying, 'Know the LORD,' for they all shall know Me, from the least of them to the greatest of them. . . . For I will forgive their iniquity, and their sin I will remember no more."[14]

Had it not happened, it would be too good to be true.

But that's just it. It did and it is.

In His hands, Jesus holds a cup. It is the cup His Father gave Him. The cup of wrath. Now filled with His very own blood. As He approaches the throne, He holds out the cup for all to see. One final act. He turns it up and paints the mercy seat. Seven times. The blood drips from the pores of His sweat, to His beard that was plucked out, to His face that was struck by fist and rod, to His brow stuck with thorns, to His back where the flesh was torn off in chunks, to His hands and feet pierced with nails, and finally to His side split open by a spear. Jesus puts Himself on display for the entire universe to see, the complete shedding of His blood.

Propitiation.

One Thing Remains

Why do I think Jesus literally walked into a heavenly temple? A heavenly holy of holies?

Because years prior, God had warned Moses, "See to it that you make [all things] according to the pattern which was shown you on the mountain."[15] This meant when the Levitical priests entered the earthly tabernacle, they served "a copy and shadow of heavenly things."[16]

Copy? Shadow? Pattern?

What Moses built was a mirrored reflection, as best he was able, of the heavenly tabernacle. The writer of Hebrews tells us that when Jesus, "Holy, innocent, undefiled, separated from sinners . . . [did this] once for all . . . He entered through the greater and more perfect tabernacle, not made with hands, that is to say, not of this creation; and not through the blood of goats and calves, but through His own blood, He entered the holy place once for all, having obtained eternal redemption."[17]

From the cross on the road below, driven into the ground on a road outside the city walls where they burn the trash, through the first and second heaven, and now into this, the third heaven—heavenly Jerusalem—Jesus has painted a crimson trail. Halley's Comet times ten trillion.

Jesus stops. The focus of every eye. He is simultaneously the wrath of God on display and the wrath of God satisfied. Once for all. Tears pour off the face of the Father. His muscles are taut. The pounding of His heart is heard and felt throughout the kingdom. He wants desperately to speak the word and soothe His Son's wounds. To make all things new. To wrap Him in His arms.

But one thing remains. One word, yet unspoken.

Jesus stands before His Father. Before the hundreds of millions in the host of heaven. Before the court of God and with His last breath and one final squeeze of His hand proving His body is completely empty of blood, Jesus opens His mouth and screams at the top of His lungs:

"Tetelestai!"

CHAPTER 2

It Is Perfectly Perfect

And on the cross on the earth beneath, the Son of man dies.

Innocent blood shed. Payment made. In full. Mankind redeemed. Forever.

The Father—watching His Son die a gruesome and painful death—opens His mouth and releases the pain and agony He has known while His Son was away. He entrusted His Son to us and yet we on the earth despised Him, shamed Him, and considered Him smitten and stricken by God. Nothing could be further from the truth. Lightning flashes from His throne, sending bolts to the earth below; the heavens thunder and the light that once shone on the earth falls dark. Stones split and an earthquake shakes Jerusalem. Having waited patiently since the garden of Eden, God the Father reaches down into the Holy of Holies and rips the veil in two with His very own hands.

That veil is His Son.[1] God once again dwells with man.*

Heaven erupts. The angels of God come unglued. The Son has returned. Victorious. He alone has done what no one else could. "Once for all, the just for the unjust, so that He might bring us to God, having been put to death in the flesh, but made alive in the spirit."

---

* No, I can't prove it, but when Jesus spoke His final word, I believe He was hanging here and standing there—in the heavenly Holy of Holies, carrying His own blood with which He painted the mercy seat. His own flesh, the veil that was torn, on display for all of heaven to see. Torn in two.

As Jesus' Word echoes off the walls of heaven, God the Father launches Himself off His throne. At the speed of light, He wraps His Son in His arms and covers His face in kisses. Not because He is the prodigal returned, but because He is the righteous Son who by His very own blood has healed God's hurting heart. The heart of the Father that was broken in the garden when Adam and Eve fell. God the Father has wanted for so long to walk once again with the man and woman He created; and now His Son, His only Son, has bought back mankind, ransomed and redeemed, and erased the barrier wall erected by the sin of mankind. The Son has justified man and brought mankind back into the presence of a Holy God and Father.

I wonder sometimes about the moment in which God the Father was healing Jesus' wounds. One by one. Tending tenderly to His Son. Maybe it happened in the tomb. Maybe it happened here in the heavenly Jerusalem. Maybe it happened in a blink of an eye someplace else. I don't know. But it did happen sometime before He rolled away the stone. And in my mind's eye, when God the Father gets to Jesus' hands and feet, and the hole in His side, He fully intends to close up the holes. Make all things new. But then I think the two of them looked through time at us, you and me, and Jesus looked up at His Father, and in my mind He's laughing. He says, "Abba, given their unbelief, maybe You should leave those open. Because if you close them, they'll never believe it's me."**

With His divinity now uncloaked, Jesus is visible as fully God and fully man. His eyes are flames, and diadems rest on His head. He has a name which God gave Him but only He knows. He wears a robe dipped in blood, the train of which fills the temple, and the name by which He is known to us is "the Word of God." The armies of heaven are seated on white horses and arrayed in fine linen, white and pure. Their attention is

---

** This scene is total speculation on my part, but please allow artistic license under the admission that there is no support for this conversation in Scripture. Other than Jesus' baptism, the Transfiguration, John 17, and Jesus crying out on the cross, I have little to no idea what the conversations between Jesus and His Father sounded like. Nor do I pretend to understand their motives other than that they are totally and completely rooted in love—the likes of which I cannot fathom. Having said that, somewhere and somehow the Father healed the Son, and I believe He did so with great tenderness—yet He left those wounds open to the visible eye. There was a reason for that. And I think that reason had something to do with our unbelief.

trained on Him and they await His singular order. A sword extends from His mouth with which He will strike down nations. From His throne and with His scepter, He will rule with a rod of iron. He treads the winepress of fury of the wrath of God almighty. On His robe and on His thigh is written a name, the King of kings and Lord of lords.[3]

God Most High places a handkerchief in His Son's chest pocket. With it, He will wipe away every tear. The end of mourning has come. No crying. No pain. Jesus looks down at us and smiles. "I am making all things new."[4]

Having made payment, Jesus turns and stares across the sulfur lake that burns with eternal fire and speaks to the souls held in prison. "I am the Alpha and the Omega, the beginning and the end."[5] He holds out His hands, and in them are springs of water; it's free. No one has to pay. Those who conquer, who endure, will drink from His hand. He will be their God and they will be His people. But to those who say no, the cowardly, faithless, detestable, murders, sexually immoral, sorcerers, idolaters, and all liars, they will join satan in the sulfur lake. Eternal fire.

A book is opened before Jesus. On the cover is written "The Lamb's Book of Life."[6] It's the only copy. With His mouth He writes the words.

While darkness covers the earth below, and His body is moved into a freshly cut grave owned by a rich man, Jesus' work is not yet done. Peter described it this way:

> Christ also suffered once for sins, the righteous for the unrighteous, that
> he might bring us to God, being put to death in the flesh but made alive
> in the spirit, in which he went and proclaimed to the spirits in prison,
> because they formerly did not obey, when God's patience waited in the
> days of Noah, while the ark was being prepared, in which a few, that is,
> eight persons, were brought safely through water.[7]

Before He leaves, God the Father—the Ancient of Days, clothing white as snow, hair pure wool, throne wreathed in fiery flames—speaks. And as

He does, fire comes from His mouth. A thousand thousands serve Him. Ten thousand times ten thousand stand before Him. The Son of man is presented before Him, and God Most High presents the Son before every tongue, tribe, nation, and person. Then He grants Him all authority and dominion and glory and a kingdom. The Father speaks so everyone can hear, "From now on, all peoples, nations, and languages will serve You. Your dominion is everlasting, and it will never end, and your kingdom can never be destroyed."[8]

A wrinkle forms between Jesus' eyes. He is staring into hell. He holds up a finger and says, "This won't take long. Be right back." From heaven, He descends into hell where He is met by foaming hordes. Unaware of what just happened in heaven, they think they're about to feast on the battered body of Jesus. Roast Him over the spit. Carve Him into steaks.

The party is short-lived.

satan is not so ignorant. he turns to run but Jesus slams him to the dirt and places his head beneath His heel. His enemy now a footstool. He removes the keys of death and hades off satan's belt and dangles them for all to see. Then He shouts so all of hell can hear, *"Tetelestai!"*

The demons closest go up in smoke. Ten thousand degrees Fahrenheit in less than a second. Nothing but dark spots where their souls once stood. Jesus' voice thunders again, "I have redeemed mankind with My very own blood!" At the sound of His voice, locks are shattered and prison doors swing wide. Demonic hordes scatter. Prisoners long held captive run to freedom. Jesus is laughing. Tears streaming down His face. He knows the prisoners by name. He has missed them. Every last one. He watches their twisted and bent bodies exit, straighten, stretch, and put one foot in front of the other. Walk. Jog. Run. Kicking up dust. A mass exodus. Dying of thirst, they drink from His hand. Clear living water. Those who don't drink, drown.*

---

* Again, I am writing about an event in a timeline which you and I can understand but which according to Scripture occurred before the foundations of the earth. This makes my fuzzy little head want to explode. But time is what we have, so in an effort to help us understand, I've once again written about something in a time sequence which occurred outside of time.

Having freed all who want freedom, Jesus stares topside.* At His tomb. At those weeping. He can see their broken hearts. His own heart yearns. He can't wait.

Now the fun begins.

The Son of God brushes the dust off His feet—and returns.

The Return

Shrouded in shadow, Peter is spinning his sword on its point by its handle. His sweat has dried. His tears have not. He hasn't eaten. Hasn't slept. The wine does little to medicate the pain. He sits alone on a hill. Before him lies the tomb that holds the body. Soldiers hover like hornets. They've driven an iron spike into the wall of the tomb behind the stone. Sealing it. Preventing the stone from being rolled back. They're passing the wine around, retelling the story. Laughing. Slapping backs. One in particular cleans the tip of his spear. An odd mixture of blood and water. Another sits quietly by himself, shaking his head. He keeps staring heavenward. Muttering something about the Son of God. But he is the minority. A third sits atop the round stone, dangling his feet.

The man inside the tomb lies wrapped in cloth. A hasty job. His lips are blue, hair matted, body cold.

Graveyard dead.

Peter is mumbling. Talking to himself. He glances over his shoulder where the cross stands empty. Awaiting the next victim. He curses. "Should have been Barabbas. That murderer." Peter cannot wrap his head

---

* For the record, I cannot prove that Jesus descended into hell and administered the tail-whooping as I've written it here. I am encouraged in my artistic license by 1 Peter 3:19, which says, He [Jesus] *went and proclaimed to the spirits in prison,* and Matt. 12:40 in which Jesus says, *For just as Jonah was three days and three nights in the belly of the great fish, so will the Son of Man be three days and three nights in the heart of the earth.* The reason I feel compelled to add it to my narrative is because Jesus defeated satan and all of hell, and—with His very own blood—purchased our freedom. That is a fact. We who were once in a prison of our own making have been set free. How that looked when He did it is tough for me to say, but the picture I've painted here reminds us that He did do it. Past tense. *Tetelestai.* And for that reason, I've included this scene.

around the last seventy-two hours. He is tormented by questions: *What happened? Why did He let it?* And, *What now?* But maybe the most painful question of all has to do with himself. *How could I?* As daylight approaches, a nearby rooster crows. Again. He covers his ears. *Somebody should kill that thing.* But what good would it do? He knows that every single day for the rest of his life, he will never escape the sound or the memory.

Peter spins the sword again. The thought of it takes him back to the garden. The night of the unlawful arrest. When he cut off the ear of the high priest's servant. His friend's words made no sense then. They make less sense now. "Put your sword into the sheath. Shall I not drink the cup which My Father has given Me?"[9] Peter shakes his head, *What cup?* He continues mumbling. "But what about the kingdom? What about us? What about me?"

Peter has never known shame like this. It's more than he can bear.

A few blocks away, the mother of the dead man stares down at her hands. The same hands that held Him when He nursed as an infant. That tucked Him in on cold nights when He was a boy. That dried His tears when He skinned His knees. That taught Him how to make bread. That held His face when she kissed Him. The same hands that pointed to the pots of water at the wedding in Cana only three and a half years ago. "Do what He says." Her sorrow is unmatched in human history.

She is close to losing her mind.

Across town, another Mary, Mary of Magdala, is crying. Brokenhearted. A bubbling mixture of pain and anger. Of unvented rage. They falsely accused him. Unjustly arrested Him. Played out a mock trial. Stripped Him. Shamed Him. Beat Him mercilessly. Tortured Him. Shoved the sponge in His mouth. Then they just stood there, laughing, gambling, while He screamed at the top of His lungs. *Why didn't He do something about it?* Nothing He said came true. His words seemed so full of life when He spoke them. Now they're just as dead as He is. He could heal the sick, raise the dead, cast out demons, but when the time came, He could not save Himself. What kind of God would do that to a man? Much less His own Son?

Mary keeps looking over her shoulder as she turns a singular question over in her mind. The further she gets from Jesus' last breath, the more the fear torments her. And in this moment, it is raging.

Scattered about town, the defeated band of rebels are hurting. Living in hiding and fear of Rome, they have no answers. Rent down the middle. Trying to pick up the pieces. The disillusionment is suffocating.

The chief priests and elders are feeling smug. Secure. They slap each other's backs. Nod knowingly. Feeling justified that they have honored God, for no one can call himself the Son of God. The law forbids it. There's a ruckus at the door. Without warning, a former follower, a mealy-mouthed weasel of a man named Judas who turned rat and betrayed the deceased, returns. Guilt-riddled. He holds out the blood money. "I have sinned by betraying innocent blood."[10]

They couldn't care less. He's a pawn. They're incredulous. "What is that to us? You see to it." Judas throws down thirty pieces of silver.[11] The payment for his services. The very same amount required in Leviticus to purchase a slave. Distraught, he runs to a known field, climbs a tree, ties a noose, and jumps. Death by suffocation. By hanging. His body swings alone. But the tree limb he chooses is weak, so as his decomposing body swells in the hot sun, it breaks the limb, sending the man's body to the earth where, upon impact, it splits open, spilling his intestines on the ground. Hearing of this, and not wanting to add blood money to the temple treasury, the religious rulers later buy the field and call it *Akeldama*. Or, Field of Blood.[12]

The psalmist spoke of this very field a thousand years prior, and to this day, it is desolate and no one lives in it.[13]

Jerusalem is quiet. Save the drunk soldiers in Pilate's garrison who are singing, still rolling their eyes at the pathetic *King of the Jews*. They pass the wine skin. "What a joke!"

In the temple, the priests eye the veil. Inexplicably torn in two by the earthquake.

Throughout the night, Peter sits on the edge of a vineyard and stares down at the tomb. Owned by a rich man. He is lost in a slideshow of memories. Of words spoken. He is trying to remember the sound of his friend's voice, but the sound is fading. All he can hear is the echo of His cries. Screaming in pain at the top of his lungs. Peter tries to quiet the voices of regret and shame, but he cannot. In his mind's eye, the blood continues to drip. Just outside the round door of the tomb is the knee-deep depression in the rock where the vineyard workers crush the grapes to make the wine. Peter closes his eyes and buries his face in his hands. Arrested in an olive garden. Buried in a vineyard.

Oil and wine.

Daylight is less than an hour away. Mary of Magdala can sit still no longer. She has to do something. What she wants is a few minutes alone. To talk to the body. Tell Him goodbye. Joined by Mary the mother of James and Joseph (who is also the sister to Mary the mother of Jesus),[14] Salome, and Joanna the wife of Chuza, Herod's steward,[15] she walks through the darkness, carrying embalming spices. Intent on properly preparing Him for burial. Knowing that the stone is some five feet tall, and that the tomb is sealed with an iron spike, they ask the obvious, "Who will roll away the stone?"

But there's a problem.

In the darkness, they can just make it out. The seal is broken. The iron spike has been snapped in two. Like a toothpick. The massive stone rolled away. Soldiers gone. An eerie quiet blankets the garden. Mist rises off the earth. Mary Magdalene steps inside. Trembling. Her worst fears realized. She cannot breathe in or out.

The body is gone.

Matthew's gospel states a "severe earthquake had occurred."[16] An interesting word choice, although as a writer I'm not sure what else he would call it. Then he says an angel of the Lord rolled away the stone and sat upon it. I love that. His appearance was like lightning and his clothing white as snow. I wonder if his feet dangled—or can an eleven-foot angel sit upon a five-foot rock and not dangle his feet? Upon seeing this, the guards shook in fear and became like dead men.[17]

Frightened out of their minds and defying their orders—an act which brought with it a death sentence—the guards must have turned tail and run, because when Mary arrives they are nowhere to be found. Just empty wine skins. The way I read the account, there were three angels at the tomb. Or, at least three they could see. One sitting on the stone. Two inside. The one sitting outside preempts Mary's question and says, "Do not be afraid, for I know that you seek Jesus who was crucified. He is not here; for He is risen, as He said. Come, see the place where the Lord lay."[18]

Notice those words, "as He said." They matter. A lot.

Mary rubs her eyes. Her heart breaking further. Her anger grows and she aims it at the soldiers who left their post. Mary is wrestling with reality. As in, what's real in this moment. It's not every day that she talks to stone-rolling-away-eleven-feet-tall-angels who are shining like the sun. Also, let's back into what might be Mary's deepest fear at this moment. To the singular question spinning in her mind. Jesus delivered her from seven demons. She heard Him tell them to "Go." And when He did, she felt them wrench her, heard them scream in a voice that was not hers though it used her mouth, and she knew when they physically departed her body. She felt them leave. Since then, she has known and walked in freedom. But then she saw Him die.

And if He's dead, are they coming back?

He could deliver her, but not Himself. So what about the seven? Are they coming back? And if so, are they bringing more with them like Jesus said they would? Is that what she has to look forward to? Was her deliverance only temporary? What torment awaits her?

Needing to see, she pokes her head inside the tomb. To her surprise, two more angels sit at either end of where the body had lain. She doesn't know whether to fall down or start swinging. She eyes the angels. Suspiciously. One of them speaks, reiterating what the angel outside had just told her: "Why do you seek the living among the dead? He is not here, but is risen."[19]

That's twice they've said that. The mental picture of dead Jesus returns to Mary's mind. *Unrecognizable as a man.* Mary sucks in a breath. She rolls up a sleeve and braces herself. This could get ugly. But the word *living* bounces around inside her head. If true, no . . . it's too good to be true. She can't let herself go there. But if it is . . . no, she can't let herself think that.

It could just be a sick trick. Everyone knows Herod is crazy. She wouldn't put it past him.

The glowing man in white continues. "Remember how He spoke to you when He was still in Galilee, saying, 'the Son of Man must be delivered into the hands of sinful men, and be crucified, and the third day rise again.'"[20] This is the second time now in just as many sentences where the angel reminds Mary of Jesus' words. Why is that?

Mark records the conversation this way: "Do not be alarmed. You seek Jesus of Nazareth, who was crucified. He is risen! He is not here. See the place where they laid Him. But go, tell his disciples—and Peter—that He is going before you into Galilee; there you will see Him."[21]

Somewhere in that fog, Mary remembered His words.[22]

Also, notice that Peter is singled out. Why? Because he's worse than the rest? No longer a disciple because he so greatly denied Jesus? I don't think so. Not by a long shot. Remember, angels are messengers. They only speak what they're told to speak. This is a message from the throne: "Peter, I am coming for you." And more than anything, Peter needs to hear this.

Mary is in a fog as the words "He is risen" ramble about her brain. She mouths the words. Trying to connect the meaning. Then she voices them out loud. Little more than a whisper. "He is risen."

About then it hits her. She is incredulous. And she is angry. Very angry.

Mary hikes up her dress and bolts back to town. Knees and elbows pumping like pistons. Caught between belief and unbelief, hope and despair, and unadulterated rage, she flings open the door and lays blame squarely at the soldiers' feet, "They have taken away the Lord out of the tomb and we do not know where they have laid Him!"*

The disciples are so weary. They can't take anymore. It's too much. Each is in more pain than they can fathom. Why would Rome do this? They've won. Haven't they done enough? What else do they have to gain? This is piling on. "Their words seemed to them like idle tales."[23] Another

---

* This is my best attempt at reassembling the chronology established in the four Gospels. I'm focusing here on Mary's singular experience with Jesus because of John 20:2, which suggests she had an experience at the tomb prior to her weeping in verse 11.

translation reads, "These words appeared to them as nonsense" (NASB). But watch what happens next: "and they did not believe them."

Remember this. Belief, or rather unbelief, was the root of the problem of the people of God. It was in the garden. It was in Egypt. It was in the desert. And it is now. Here at the tomb.

Peter and John race outside the city. John, evidently the faster runner—although we're only told that in his gospel—arrives first. He stoops down, sees the folded linen but, afraid to enter, stops short. Peter arrives next. Breathing heavily. Hand on the hilt of his sword, he barges in. Peter's eyes fall to the face cloth that had been around the dead man's head. Now it lies neatly folded in a place by itself. Why would the soldiers take the time to do that? But the women spoke of talking angels, and neither Peter nor John see anything other than an empty tomb. They conclude that the women are distraught. Delirious from their pain.

They return to their homes.

Save one. Mary.

And she is close to losing her mind.

CHAPTER 3

A Dead Man Walks

Mary stood weeping outside the tomb."[1] When she stoops to walk in, the angels have returned. She tries to flag down Peter and John but it's too late. They ask her, "Woman, why are you weeping?" The unspoken impression being, *We already told you He's not here.*

Unable to make sense of any of this, she cries, "They have taken away my Lord, and I do not know where they have laid him."[2] It's almost comical how Mary still blames the soldiers while speaking with beings who look like bolts of lightning dressed in snow. But notice her beautiful words: *my Lord.* She doesn't say rabbi, teacher, prophet, or friend. Even now, Mary's proclamation is that Jesus is Lord. An amazing declaration given that nothing in her circumstances agrees with her.

Mary turns and bumps into the gardener. Finally, someone normal she can speak to. His voice is calm. Soothing. Like water. "Woman, why are you weeping? Whom are you seeking?"

Controlling both her anger and her grief, she says, "Sir"—and points at the tomb. Her finger is shaking. Tears and snot are pouring off her face. "If you have carried him away, tell me where you have laid him, and I will take him away."

Then, in what is certainly the single greatest moment in Mary's life, the man cracks a smile. He speaks, and Jesus uncloaks His divinity. "Mary."[3] And in that single word, the voice and person of Jesus has returned.

He is alive!

Every time I read this, I am amazed that Jesus returned first not to his buddies, but to a brokenhearted woman whom He had delivered from demonic torment. Why? I think it's pretty simple. Because he knew her pain was killing her. That her broken heart mattered to Him a lot. And because He knew she was worried about the seven returning with their friends and what hell that spelled for the rest of her life. She questioned the permanence of her deliverance, she was probably worried sick about it, and He just couldn't stand that—not in her, and not in us.

Mary reaches out and touches His face. Her fingers read His smile.

Mary screams, "Rabboni!" and launches herself airborne, catching Jesus across the chest. Wrapping arms and legs around Him. Smothering his neck in kisses. Some have suggested a romantic connection between Jesus and Mary. I am not. That's total hogwash. Or in biblical terms, *scuba-lon.* Jesus was without sin. Period. I am simply suggesting, whether rightly or wrongly I do not know, that if I saw a man die the death Jesus had died, and then bumped into Him outside His grave three days later looking like the local gardener, my reaction would not be subdued. Or casual. I would not mind my manners. Wouldn't bow slightly or curtsy. Or even genuflect. I'd come unglued. Shot out of a canon. Zero to spider monkey in less than a second. I'd launch myself through the air, sink my face into his neck where I could smell Him and kiss Him a thousand times over.

I'd lose my ever-loving mind.

And so does Mary. Why? Well, lots of reasons but one of them has something to do with the fact that if He is alive, then that must mean that everything He ever said is true. Forever. And if His words are true, then she is delivered. Forever. She's really free.

Jesus catches her and laughs. Certainly the most beautiful laugh in the history of laughter. He, too, is excited to see her. He's missed her. He knows she's been hurting. They all have. He can't wait to see them. It's why He stopped off here en route to His Father. And He would have gotten here sooner but had to take care of a few things first. He sets her down. "Do not cling to me, for I have not yet ascended to my Father; but go to my brothers and say to them, 'I am ascending to my Father and your Father, to my God and your God.'"⁴

Hold it. Hold it. Hold it. Stop right here.

I don't want to skip over this too quickly. This is a dead man speaking. But, by definition, dead people don't speak. Because they're dead. Which must mean this particular dead man is no longer dead. And make no mistake about it: He was. She saw it. They all did. With their own eyes. Mary had watched Him pray the prayer of a dying man, Psalm 31:5: Father, "into your hand I commit my spirit." Then she watched Him push up on His nail-pierced hands and do just that. She witnessed the soldier's spear pierce His chest and heard the sound of blood and water flowing and splattering. She had helped take Him down off the cross. Had she been the one to close His eyes? Someone did. She had worked hastily to prepare Him, but they didn't have time. While the soldiers had yelled at her from the doorway and told her to hurry up, she had spilled tears on His cold, dead, rigor mortis–stiff, blue-lipped, blood-caked, ashen body.

Mary saw Jesus doornail dead.

But now He's not. Jesus is alive. Speaking. And Mary knows it. She just heard His voice. Saw the light in His eyes. Felt the warmth of His skin.

Pause. Like really. Close this book. Close your eyes. See this for what it is. Let the image settle. Mary Magdalene has just bumped into Jesus and the impossible has happened. He spoke to her. She felt His breath on her face.

This changes everything. About everything.

For everyone who would believe it. Forever.

There's that word again. *Believe.* It's growing in its importance. Put a bookmark here. We're coming back to it.

They Saw Him Dead

John rather mundanely recorded that Mary came announcing to the disciples, "'I have seen the Lord,' and that He had said these things to her"

(John 20:18 NASB). Let the reader infer. For me, that description leaves a bit to be desired. Leaves me wanting more. Which may well be the point.

Matthew at least added that "they departed quickly from the tomb with fear and great joy" (28:8). He then added that Jesus met them, greeted them, or as it says in the NASB margin, "said hello," which strikes me as hilarious. "Hi guys." Matthew concluded by saying they then took hold of His feet and worshipped Him.

You think?

I love how spontaneous worship always follows true belief.

In my mind, Mary runs into town having levitated four feet off the ground. Screaming out of her ever-loving mind. The neighbors shake their heads and comment, "Somebody should medicate that woman. She's had a rough go." And if she said it once, she said it a hundred times. She is now the self-appointed town crier. She is drenched with sweat. Hair matted to her face. Arms waving. Fist-pumping. In the process of losing her voice. She has either gone mad or she has seen something or someone no other human has ever seen. Nothing about her is muted. Look at her words. "I have seen the Lord! I have seen the Lord! I have seen the Lord!"

Don't let your eye skip over two words: *seen* and *Lord*.

After this, Mark recorded an amazing occurrence. "And when they heard that He was alive and had been seen by her, they refused to believe it" (16:11 NASB).

"Refused to believe."

There it is again. This word *believe*. Or rather, unbelief.

Why did they refuse? Too good to be true? Did they simply not believe her? Was she not known for telling the truth? I think it's because it would hurt too much if it were not true. After three years of daily intimacy, walking, talking, eating, drinking, laughing, sleeping, preaching, baptizing, healing, casting out, cleansing, and raising the dead, they saw Him whipped, mocked, beaten, struck, crushed, pierced, wrapped, and laid out.

They saw Him dead. What is more permanent than that? Who comes back from that? Death is death. We all know that.

Having seen, heard, and lived what they had all experienced the last three days, these disciples simply would not, and maybe could not, let themselves go there. Their souls couldn't take it. Their love was too deep. Their pain too intense. The possibility too impossible.

Inexplicably, Luke's narrative then jumps to two men traveling that same day to a village called Emmaus—seven miles from Jerusalem.*

Jesus draws near and begins walking with them. And just as with Mary in the garden, He has again cloaked His divinity "so that they did not know Him." Jesus asks them, "What kind of conversation is this that you have with one another as you walk and are sad?"[5] The NKJV margin translation reads, "And they stood still looking sad."

Cleopas is dumbfounded. He scratches his head and looks at Jesus as if He's not in touch with reality. "Are You the only stranger in Jerusalem, and have You not known the things which happened there in these days?"[6] His words suggest just how public was the crucifixion of Jesus. Everyone knew. The death of Jesus was no quiet execution on a hidden street corner. Just as Moses lifted up the serpent in the wilderness, so Jesus was lifted up. All Israel saw it. Rome too. Think back a week to the triumphal entry. When all the city was waving palm branches and laying down their clothes. When, even if Jesus had made all of them be quiet, *the rocks would have cried out.* So Cleopas looks at this man and shakes his head, thinking, *Where has this guy been?*

Jesus, not ready to reveal Himself but wanting to keep the conversation moving as they walk, says, "What things?"

---

* One of the men was Cleopas, whom tradition holds as the brother of Mary's husband, Joseph. We don't know the identity of the other man, and while I can't prove it, I think he might have been a she. Here's why: most agree that Clopas in John 19:25 and Cleopas in Luke 24:18 are the same man. The reason for this centers on the description of the women standing at a distance from the cross—Jesus' mother and her sister Mary, the wife of Clopas. In this instance, *sister* is thought to mean sister-in-law, which is where we get the idea that Clopas was Joseph's brother. Mark 15:40 names the woman at the cross as Mary the mother of James (the Less). Mark then goes on to say that Mary, the mother of James, brought spices to prepare the body of Jesus, and Luke tells us that same woman appeared at the tomb, found it empty, and told the disciples. So, it makes sense to me that Cleopas and his wife, following the Feast of Passover, walked out the western gate of Jerusalem toward home—which routed them either through or to Emmaus. If they were a husband-and-wife team, and relatives of Jesus, it might help explain some of the context of what happens next.

"And they said to him, 'Concerning Jesus of Nazareth, a man who was a prophet . . .'"

Prophet? Cleopas shows just how deeply his Messianic hopes were crushed when he chooses this word. Jesus isn't going to let him get away with that.

Cleopas continues, "mighty in deed and word before God and all the people, and how our chief priests and rulers delivered him up to be condemned to death, and crucified him. But we had hoped that he was the one to redeem Israel. Yes, and besides all this, it is now the third day since these things happened. Moreover, some women of our company amazed us. They were at the tomb early in the morning, and when they did not find his body, they came back saying that they had even seen a vision of angels, who said that he was alive. Some of those who were with us went to the tomb and found it just as the women had said, but him they did not see."

Jesus responds, "O foolish ones, and slow of heart to believe all that the prophets have spoken!"[7]

At this point you probably don't need me to point it out, but there's that word again. *Believe.*

Jesus continues, "Was it not necessary that the Christ—"

Pause. "Christ" and "prophet" are not the same. And the Christ is about to show these two why and how.

Jesus again: "'—should suffer these things and enter into his glory?' And beginning with Moses and all the Prophets, he interpreted to them in all the Scriptures the things concerning himself."

And notice here what Jesus used: the Old Testament. If you're new to Scripture and you find the Old Testament cumbersome and difficult to follow, and you really like just diving into the New Testament and reading it over and over—have at it. Eat it up. You will not go hungry. But I have found in my own walk that the words in the New have led me to the words in the Old. And the more I've landed there, the more I've come to realize that they are intimately intertwined and inseparable. The Old reveals the New. The New manifests the Old. Loving one has meant I equally love the other.

I read both testaments as one complete Word. I have come to love and cherish the Psalms, the Prophets, and the law of Moses because of how they so fully and completely reveal what I treasure so dearly. Upon His resurrection, Jesus used the Old Testament and those very words to confirm the revelation of Himself. Somehow, for Jesus, those words were still very much alive and relevant. Of all the words He could have said, or the signs and wonders He could have performed, Jesus Himself pointed them to Moses and the Prophets as the living manifestation of those words. This won't be the last time.

After He interpreted the Scriptures for them, "they drew near to the village to which they were going. He acted as if he were going farther, but they urged him strongly"—

Why "strongly"?

Because His words had rekindled their hope. And their faith.

They pleaded with him, "'Stay with us, for it is toward evening and the day is now far spent.' So he went in to stay with them. When he was at table with them, he took the bread and blessed and broke it and gave it to them. And their eyes were opened, and they recognized him."

Oh, how I love this. The bread of life. Handing out life. This is so like Jesus. It was the last thing He did before He walked to the cross and the first thing He does upon His return. He's sending us a message.

I'm wondering if we've gotten it yet.

Having once more uncloaked His divinity and revealed Himself, He "vanished from their sight. They said to each other, 'Did not our hearts burn within us while he talked to us on the road, while he opened to us the Scriptures?'" (Luke 24:28–32).

When did their hearts burn? When He opened the Scriptures.

Which Scriptures? Moses and the Prophets.

What was the effect of this interaction on Cleopas and his companion? "They rose that same hour and returned to Jerusalem. And they found the eleven and those who were with them gathered together, saying, 'The Lord has risen indeed, and has appeared to Simon.' Then they told what had happened on the road, and how he was known to them in the breaking of the bread" (vv. 33–35).

Good news wouldn't wait, so they walked back seven miles through the night to tell their friends. And it's a good thing too. Because Jesus shows up again.

A Long Day

John says:

> On the evening of that day, the first day of the week, the doors being locked where the disciples were for fear of the Jews, Jesus came and stood among them and said to them, "Peace be with you." When he had said this, he showed them his hands and his side. Then the disciples were glad when they saw the Lord. Jesus said to them again, "Peace be with you. As the Father has sent me, even so I am sending you." And when he had said this, he breathed on them and said to them, "Receive the Holy Spirit. If you forgive the sins of any, they are forgiven them; if you withhold forgiveness from any, it is withheld." (John 20:19–23)

There's a lot here. First, it was the same day of the week. And it had been a long day. The disciples were hiding inside a locked room, talking about what to do. Is He really alive? Did the soldiers take the body? Was it someone else? We know they were not convinced that He was alive because the doors were locked and they were in fear, not of the soldiers, but of the Jews. They think they're next on the Jews' hit list and they'd seen what they did to Jesus. While they were speaking in hushed tones, and because He was no longer bound by time and space and matter, Jesus walked through a wall. Those in the room must have shrieked or screamed or fainted because His first words were, "Peace be with you." Suggesting they needed it.

Next, in answer to the one question every one of them shared—which was, What do we do now?—He said, "As the Father has sent me, even so I am sending you." Think of the magnitude. The enormity. These were their marching orders. Their raison d'etre. Forever. Their heads were spinning with more questions but possibly none louder than, Okay . . . how? Knowing this, He gave the answer . . . and the remedy: "Receive the Holy Spirit." Or, "Receive Holy Breath." The word He spoke is *ruach*. It means both Spirit and breath. But watch what He was doing. These were not random words. The Creator was creating. Making all things new. Right before our very eyes. In Genesis, we see, "The LORD God formed the man of dust from the ground and breathed into his nostrils the breath of life, and the man became a living creature" (2:7). That was the old man. The one Jesus came to ransom. When Jesus walked into the room, He breathed new life into His own. Just as He breathed life into Adam in the old creation, He now breathes life into His own to mark the new creation.

In my mind, this marks the transition, the turning of the page, from the old covenant to the new. This is Jesus, the life-giver, giving life to our mortal bodies, breathing redeemed, justified, sanctified breath into the lungs of everyone who believes. We see this signified when, on the cross, the soldier pierced Jesus' side and blood and water flowed. In that moment, Jesus birthed the new man—or new Adam. Here in this room and in this moment, Jesus was giving life to the new creation with His very own breath. They were born again. And in my mind, He didn't just casually speak it from across the room. A blanket statement. He was speaking to a room full of individuals, each of whom He fashioned from the dust of the earth and each of whom He came to save. Jesus walked up to each one, pressed His nose to theirs, filled His chest to capacity and exhaled. We do this with our children when they're babies. Why wouldn't Jesus do it with us when we're born again?

I love this. The first breath of their new life started in His lungs. And this is not a singular event. If He did it for them, He does it for you and me too.

His next statement is earth shattering. Literally. "If you forgive the sins of any, they are forgiven them; if you withhold forgiveness from any, it is withheld." Meaning, in the same way Jesus—through His Spirit—forgave us, He is giving us the power and permission to forgive sins. Let me take it one step further. If you will receive His Spirit, you get to choose what His Spirit chose. Forgiveness. Said another way, an unforgiving disciple is a disciple; he or she is just not a disciple of Jesus.*

I don't want to brush by this—Jesus knew their thoughts. He knew why they were in that room and what they wanted. And most of the conversation revolved around revenge and hatred. It was why Peter kept spinning his sword by its handle on its point. And Jesus was not having any of it. Jesus was saying to them in that room and to us here today, if they—if we—are going to breathe in His breath and then walk out of that room, or away from this page, then we need to choose to walk out and read on in forgiveness. He did. The love of Jesus forgives—even His executioners.

Trust me, this is hard for me too. You should try writing it.

Somewhere in here, the disciples started remembering His words and thinking to themselves, *I think He was really serious when He commanded us to forgive.* Somewhere in here, these believers started to look back upon His words and remember them.

Paul would later write this to the Corinthians:

Therefore, if anyone is in Christ, he is a new creation. The old has passed away; behold, the new has come. All this is from God, who through Christ reconciled us to himself and gave us the ministry of reconciliation; that is, in Christ God was reconciling the world to himself, not counting their trespasses against them, and entrusting to us the message of reconciliation. Therefore, we are ambassadors for Christ, God making his appeal through us. We implore you on behalf of Christ, be reconciled to God. For our sake he made him to be sin who knew no sin, so that in him we might become the righteousness of God. (2 Cor. 5:17–21)

---

* This does not mean that once we follow Jesus, we no longer wrestle with unforgiveness. Of course we do. I'm living proof. Please see ch. 7 in *What If It's True?* A "disciple" willingly chooses to be like their teacher. The "doing" is evidence of the "following." So, someone who follows Jesus chooses to daily crucify their own unforgiveness and not live in it. To choose forgiveness. Hence, a disciple who continually chooses unforgiveness, would not be following Jesus.

In this breath, Jesus is passing the ministry of reconciliation to us.

Despite the fact that He was standing there, they couldn't believe their eyes. They were dumbstruck. So, to help them out, He showed His hands and side. Those first few eyewitnesses in that locked room wanted to make sure. To know for sure. And notice they never had to ask for the proof. Jesus offered it. Jesus anticipated their unbelief so He "showed them his hands and his side" (John 20:20).

They—like everyone else—needed to see and touch. We would too. What better way to confirm what you're seeing? John records they were, "glad when they saw the Lord" (v. 20). Glad? I don't think so. I think they were coming-out-of-their-skin elated. Screaming. Hugging. Fist-pumping. Dancing. Crying. Think of the range of emotions released in that moment. They'd never, not ever, known joy like they knew in that moment.

For some reason, the disciple Thomas was not in the room. John picks up his narrative eight days later, and Thomas wanted what they received. That finger-dipping moment.

Thomas has received a lot of grief through the ages for his statement regarding what he needed in his first face-to-face with the risen Jesus. Hence, the Sunday school nickname "Doubting Thomas." We'll tackle this more later, but it's unfortunate. I've never liked it. Thomas didn't doubt any more than anyone else in that room. They all doubted. He was simply the first to voice it.

Eight days later, they were all gathered inside again. Doors locked. Jesus walked through the wall and again said, "Peace to you" (20:26 NKJV). Then He walked up to Thomas, whose jaw had just hit the floor, and spoke. And He didn't say this in some condemning tone. (Remember Romans 8:1.) He said this in the intimate invitation from one friend to another. His tone was low, accepting, inviting. He extended His hands. "Thomas . . ." He turned them over for examination. Exposing the stretched nail holes. "Put your finger in here. Really. Go ahead. I know, weird isn't it?" He pulled aside His garment. The slice was deep and several inches wide. Large enough for a hand to enter. Several in the room gasped as they waited for His heart and lungs to spill out of His chest. Jesus moved His arm out of the way.

"Go ahead. You can't hurt me." The implication in this interaction is that Thomas's doubt didn't offend Jesus. He just wanted Thomas to bring it to Him. Which he did. Then in characteristic Jesus fashion, He leaned over while Thomas's fingertips were touching His heart, His face inches from Thomas's, His breath blanketing Thomas. He smiled and whispered, "Do not be unbelieving, but believing" (John 20:27 NKJV).

There's that word again.

Thomas nodded and smiled. He got it. Look at what Thomas said while his finger was still stuck in the hole. "My Lord and my God!" (v. 28). Out of the mouth of Thomas came the first recorded post-resurrection, face-to-face, verbal submission to the lordship of Jesus—the recognition of the God-ness of Jesus and the willful surrendering to His righteous reign. If anyone planted the address of their spirit squarely in the kingdom of heaven, it was this magnificent man, Thomas. To be fair, we should name him "Believing Thomas."

Jesus wrapped His arm around him. "Thomas because you have seen Me, you have believed. Blessed are those who have not seen and yet have believed" (v. 29 NKJV).

There's that word again. Twice. And in using it, He's talking about us. You and me.

I think Jesus was talking about how we are blessed because we believe without sight—that's true. But I also think Jesus was talking about the life Thomas was soon to have. Because of this finger-hand-chest moment, Thomas will lead others to belief. And who better to do it? Thomas will wiggle his fingers, wave his hand, and make a fist. "I know He's alive. I felt Him." Jesus' words to Thomas were a beautiful invitation—and as we will see, Thomas accepted.

Maybe you feel like a Thomas. You doubted. Didn't believe. Be encouraged—you'd make a great disciple. God can use you.

But not all are so happy about the empty tomb. Having been frightened out of their minds, the soldiers tuck tail and return to, oddly enough, the chief priests. Why the chief priests and not their own superiors? I think we learn why in Matthew. "And when they had assembled with the elders and consulted together, they gave a large sum of money to the soldiers" (Matt. 28:12 NASB).

Money. Rotten treachery for hire. The same thing they gave Judas.

The chief priests continued, "You are to say, 'His disciples came by night and stole Him away while we were asleep.' And if this should come to the governor's ears, we will win him over and keep you out of trouble" (vv. 13–14 NASB).

So the soldiers took the money and spread the lie. *As it is to this day.* Deception was there in the garden with the first Adam, and he was there at the resurrection in the garden with the second Adam. Spreading his lies. Continuing his all-out, never-ending assault on the truth. On our belief. Why? Because he is deathly afraid that you and I might actually *believe* this story. That it actually happened. As it happened. And he knows, better than you and I, that faith comes through hearing—and hearing through the word of God (Rom. 10:17).

And he hates that. Can't stand the thought of it. The idea that this retelling of an actual event might actually feed and grow your and my faith, which is more valuable than gold, is totally unacceptable to satan. Why? Because he loses. Again.

Thus begins the continued assault on the truth. The very same assault that happened with "Did God say?" in the garden. Jesus talked about this in the parable of the birds of the air (Matt. 13). That very same assault on the truth that is happening right this second.

These men and women did not have the luxury of the end of the story. They were present in it, living it minute by minute, while we see more of the whole. But make no mistake: you and I live in no less a crossfire. Truth versus falsehood. And the enemy's strategy then and now is simple: blitzkrieg. Shock and awe. Pour in copious amounts of doubt, hoping to reduce the truth to fragments, separate from the whole.

Are you aware of the assault on the truth you hold? Think of both you and me like a juggler with three bowling pins. Manageable. Now give him fifteen more. And seat him on a unicycle. It's a good picture of us.

CHAPTER 4

Shame—the enemy's First Weapon

Jesus tells the disciples to return to Galilee. So they do. Peter, Thomas, Nathaniel, James, and John, and two unnamed disciples. Unlike the rest, Peter has a problem. A self-inflicted wound. A telephone pole sticking out of his chest. And Jesus is about to expose and heal it.

Peter, opening his big mouth once again, announces to the group, "I'm going fishing." They all pile in the boat with him. Notice what he's doing. He's returning to his former life. Fishing for fish. Why? His shame has convinced him that he's disqualified himself for the life to which Jesus had called him. One and done and all that.

Jesus is having none of this. Just as Jesus crucified every assault the enemy could level at us, He is about to show Peter (and those around him . . . and us) that He wasn't kidding when He said, "It is finished." And that "finishing" includes shame, regret, and self-inflicted wounds.

So, they fish all night with no luck. Jesus, again having cloaked His divinity so they can't recognize Him, stands on the beach and yells, "Children, have you any food?"[1]

First, He calls them "children." Which they are. As expressed by the fact that they are standing in their former life, not living in the new life He has given them. The truth of the resurrection hasn't yet set in. But it will. Pentecost is coming. Later in his life, John will write, "See how great a love the Father has bestowed [other translations say "lavished." I like "lavished" better] on us, that we would be called children of God; and such we are. . . . Beloved, now we are children of God."[2] When he wrote that, I wonder if he was thinking of this interaction on the beach with the risen King?

Back on the beach, the question is a two-in-one. Yes, He's asking them if they've caught anything. But He's also asking them if they have any food for their souls. Bread of life kind of stuff. They corporately answer, "No."

He laughs. "Cast the net on the right side of the boat." The implication is, "Do what you're not doing."

Not knowing who He is, they look at Him with squinted eyes. These guys fish for a living. They're pros. They know what they're doing. They mumble among themselves. "Who's this guy think He is? Left or right side doesn't matter." Nevertheless, they cast the net, and wonder of wonders, they are unable to haul it in it's so full of fish. A foretelling of what's to come. Of what's about to happen.

Sensing that something is amiss, John scratches his head and says to Peter, "It is the Lord!"

You think?

Having stripped down for work, Peter is standing in his undergarments. Hair pulled back in a ponytail. Sweat dripping off him. Seeing the Lord, he puts on his outer garment—and takes a swan dive off the bow. Notice, while he is going forward, he is also covering up. Who does this remind you of? It reminds me of two people. The first is Adam in the garden. Ashamed, he and Eve sewed fig leaves to cover their nakedness. What drove them to do this? Shame. Contrast that with man number two, who was blind Bartimaeus at the gate in Jericho. When he came to Jesus, he threw aside his garment.[3] Why? He had nothing to hide. No shame. Peter has everything to hide and he is draped in shame. Don't think so? Okay, let me ask a pragmatic question—who covers up when he's about to jump in the water?

Notice also what Peter doesn't do. He doesn't ask the Lord to tell him to come to Him so that he might walk on water. He doesn't feel worthy. Shame is crushing his spirit. Peter is a mess. He swims to shore and walks up on the bank. In the meantime, his fishing buddies row to shore, dragging the filled-to-capacity net.

The Charcoal Fire

Onshore, they see Jesus cooking fish—over a charcoal fire. Uh-oh. Back up a week. This does not bode well for Peter:

> Simon Peter was following Jesus, and so was another disciple. Now that disciple was known to the high priest, and entered with Jesus into the court of the high priest, but Peter was standing at the door outside. So the other disciple, who was known to the high priest, went out and spoke to the doorkeeper, and brought Peter in. Then the slave-girl who kept the door said to Peter, "You are not also one of this man's disciples, are you?" He said, "I am not." Now the slaves and the officers were standing there, having made a charcoal fire, for it was cold and they were warming themselves; and Peter was also with them, standing and warming himself.[4]

Smoke rises from the beach. The smell of fish cooking. Peter sees the fire and freezes. Ice water trickles through his veins. That night returns. As does his denial. Peter's heart shatters on the beach. From the mountaintop victory at Caesarea Philippi and Peter's vocal proclamation to Jesus and the whole world, "You are the Christ," he has bottomed out here. Sea level. The single greatest failure and betrayal of his life and Jesus is bringing him back to that moment. With a charcoal fire. Peter shakes his head.

Jesus speaks over His shoulder, "Bring some of the fish which you have just caught."[5]

Peter grabs the net and singlehandedly hauls it to shore where somebody counts out 153 large fish. Testament that since the time of Jesus, fishermen have kept track of their catch. Jesus tells everyone, "Come. Let's have some breakfast."

Jesus takes bread and fish and gives it to them. This was the third time Jesus had revealed Himself to them. Amazingly, Jesus lets them eat. They're elated to see Him. All save one. They sit down alongside Jesus. Like old times. Only don't think for a second that they've grown accustomed to this whole risen-from-the-dead thing. They haven't. He appears. Walks through walls. Disguises Himself. Disappears. Speaks. Eats. They still don't know what to make of all this. Don't know what'll happen if they get too close. All they know is that He's alive; but as evidenced by the fact that they're in the water in a boat, led by Peter, they still don't know what to do with the rest of their individual and corporate lives. They are lacking direction—and none more so than the big, mouthy guy in the middle.

And in order to get some direction, their leader needs to get his head straight. So Jesus is about to straighten Peter's way of thinking. And heal his heart.

One of the beautiful moments in this event for me is the tenderness with which Jesus loves on Peter. He had every right to shame him. Deride him. Poke him in the chest. But He doesn't. Instead, I think He sits alongside and wraps an arm around his shoulder.

Peter is sitting by himself. His hair dangling down over his eyes so Jesus can't see the whites. Peter is afraid to look at Him. Despite his braggadocious claims to the contrary, he did the very thing Jesus said he would do after promising not to. Sitting on the beach, Peter is a liar and a backstabbing coward. Better than no one.

Which makes him a perfect disciple.

Jesus fills a plate and sits down. Shoulder to shoulder. He hands Peter the plate. Peter pushes the fish around. Afraid to look up. His heart is breaking. He wants to vomit. Jesus leans in. His face inches from Peter's. "Peter . . ." Jesus glances at the men spread across the beach. "Do you love me more than these?"

The implication is clear. Before Jesus' crucifixion, Peter said he did.

What happened next? Imagine a man on a rescue mission. Saving prisoners. All of them. Once they are free, our hero hears the helicopter coming. He makes it to the evac zone. Sees the helicopter. Waves at the pilot who gives him a thumbs up and tells him "good job." Then, just as the hero thinks he is about to climb aboard and be air-lifted to safety, the pilot pulls up on the stick and disappears while the enemy in the grass surrounds our hero and shoves their bayonets through his chest.

This is exactly what Peter did to Jesus.

He pulled up on the stick and watched as the enemy pierced His side. And before you or I get self-righteous, this is exactly what every one of us has done a thousand times over. To think otherwise is to hold a tainted view of your sin. Our sin is filthy rags. Used feminine products. None is righteous, no not one. So in this moment, when He's speaking to Peter, He's speaking to us.

Peter knows exactly what Jesus is referring to. It's all he's been thinking about. Can't get it off his mind. Peter won't look at him. He nods. "Yes, Lord." He exhales. His chest is tight. A shallow inhale. "You know that I love you."*

Peter sets down the plate and finally looks at Jesus. Tears pouring off his face. He is shattered at his own betrayal. His bottom lip is trembling. Tears trail his face and snot is pouring out of his nose. In his spirit, he is begging his friend, his Lord, his King, to take him back. Give him another

---

* Much has been made of Peter's response, and for good reason. Jesus asks Peter if he *agape* loves Him. *Agape* is sawcrificial love. It's Jesus on the cross, me-for-you kind of love. Peter responds with, *Yes Lord, you know that I love [phileo] you.* *Phileo* love means to have affection toward. Or, a personal attachment. Like a favorite pair of shoes. Or maybe the chair you like to sit in while you flip channels. One comes from the Father. The other comes out of our humanness. They're not even in the same stratosphere.

Jesus responds with, *Feed my lambs.* This response strikes Peter as a bit odd. He scratches his head. Who feeds sheep?

Jesus asks again. *Agape.* Peter responds again. With *phileo.* Jesus says a second time, *Tend my sheep.* Peter is starting to get irritated. Who tends sheep?

Jesus, knowing both what Peter needed and was capable of, asks a third time. Only this time, He uses the same word Peter has been using—*phileo.* It doesn't quite have the punch of *agape.* *Phileo* is friendship. Affection. To share the same interests. No strings. *Agape* is a choice at a deeper level. Few choose it. Peter had once said he could *agape,* but when push came to shove, he couldn't even *phileo.* Jesus has come down to his level. But truth is, Peter knows that when pressed at that charcoal fire more than a week ago, he didn't even *phileo* Jesus. He betrayed Him. Rejected Him.

shot. End this misery. For the first time, Peter knows how truly unworthy he really is, and yet he is sitting at the feet of his King, asking for a return to the team, to the lineup, when he knows he doesn't have a leg to stand on. "Please take me back. Please Lord, give me one more chance."

Jesus will do one better. It's why He's here. He loves this stuff. Almost as much as He loves Peter.

Jesus presses His forehead to Peter's. Friend to friend. Brother to brother. Jesus knows the ache of Peter's heart. It's why He built a charcoal fire. To take him back to the moment. But to heal the wound, He's got to pick the scab. Only then can He dig out the shrapnel. Jesus holds Peter's face in both His nail-pierced palms and speaks softly, "Feed my lambs."

Somewhere in here, it strikes Peter that Jesus is restoring him. Bringing him back in. He's no longer an outcast. He's forgiven. Further, he's been charged with tending and feeding sheep. That makes him a shepherd. Something he is now uniquely qualified to be since he understands lost sheep.

Jesus is not finished with him. Not by a long shot.

Peter's desire—the singular cry of Peter's heart—is to show Jesus that he loves Him. Jesus knows this. So, He looks into the future and gives Peter a glimpse. He wraps His arm around Peter and says, "Most assuredly, I say to you, when you were younger, you girded yourself and walked where you wished; but when you are old, you will stretch out your hands, and another will gird you and carry you where you do not wish."[6]

Jesus is speaking of Peter's death.

I've heard people interpret this as a seething indictment of Peter. As if Jesus is saying, "This is what you've got coming. And being the two-faced traitor that you are, it's all you deserve." I don't see it that way. Peter has been broken. Jesus knows this. He is telling Peter He can see the future, and in the future, Peter does not and will not deny Him as he did before the cross. He'll finish the race. Keep the faith. He'll die the same kind of death. And to Peter, this is the greatest news he could ever hear.

Peter weeps. That he is counted worthy to suffer for Christ and that Christ knows it. He wants nothing more.

Finally, Jesus, in perfect grace-filled, forgiving, pulling-for-us, lover-of-our-souls fashion, speaks to Peter the first words He ever spoke to him. And He does it after wrapping His arm around him and bringing him back into the fold. As if He's saying, "Enough of this foolishness. Let's get on with it. We have work to do. There's stuff to be done."

He leans in, and once again the *ruach* of God is breathing life into one of His own. Resurrecting another dead sinner. He could have said anything. The same voice that upholds all things by the word of His power and spoke ten trillion stars into the universe and calls each by name, is whispering the only two words Peter's heart needs to hear. He makes eye contact, smiles, and whispers, "Follow Me."

For the first time since that night, Peter drinks in a deep breath with no taint of smoke. He holds it. One second. Two. Then he lets it out slowly. Remember what he just did: chained as a slave in the prison of his making, having failed miserably he returned to his former life, but when he sees the Lord, he turns from his old life, dives in, and escapes from Egypt in the same way Israel did fifteen hundred years prior. One more deliverance through water.

For Peter, this is a do-over. The most beautiful do-over in the history of do-overs. In the ages to come, when pained parents and their broken children look up "do-over" in the dictionary, when shattered husbands and tortured wives stare across the pieces and look up "do-over" in the dictionary, when you or I rub our faces and stare back through the wreckage, they and we will see a picture of this moment. And Peter, to his great credit, takes it and never looks back. To me, this is what makes Peter great. He followed Him—again.

Remember, Jesus despises shame. And here He is driving a stake through its chest.

Peter is free. From himself. From his past. From his pain. And from his shame. Two simple words shattered its hold. Peter has been welcomed back in. He is now what he once tasted and has always wanted to be.

Peter is a child of God.

More Grace

While this moment is significant for Peter, it is even more so for you and me. God is the God of do-overs. Our enemy tries to tell us otherwise, and he does so with shame. But shame is a lie from the pit of hell.

Here's the truth of this God we worship: *There is more grace in Jesus than sin in us.*

You should let that sink in. Highlight it. Write it in the margin in your own hand. It might shake a few things loose. Yes, we are all depraved. More than we think. But our depravity is best understood under the banner of grace. Think of grace like an unpoppable balloon filled with air. The air is our sin. But no matter how much we inflate the balloon, it is always larger than the air that fills it and continues to cover all of it.

Take a deep breath. Close your eyes. Let this sink to your bedrock.

There is more grace in Jesus than sin in us.

Last time I was in Israel, I was standing waist-deep in the Jordan along with several of our pastors, and we were baptizing people. People were shouting. Screaming. Hands held high. New life all around. When finished, even though I'd been baptized there in that same river two years prior, my pastor—and friend—turned to me and proffered the water. A smile on his face. "You want some of this?"

"Yes." I nodded, wading through the water lapping against my waist. "Yes, I do."

He asked me, "Charles, who is Jesus to you?"

"My Lord, my Savior, and my King."

And down I went. Again.

Why? Because of my magnificent friend Peter. And when my pastor pressed my face, head, and chest down into that cold water, the picture in my mind's eye was this one: Peter diving in, swimming to Jesus.

Now before you get too axle-wrapped on the theology of being baptized more than once, and the possible heresy or blasphemy of such an unholy act, here's my thought: I was washed clean and made new the first time. Buried with Him. Resurrected with Him. A new man took the dead man's place. I've been crucified with Christ. It stuck then. It's sticking now. Stake driven in the ground. Proclamation made. As for the second? Well, for starters I was standing in the Jordan River. Jesus was baptized there. What else was I going to do? "No"? Get serious.

I'm trying to make the argument that I'm a big believer in getting baptized. It matters. Jesus did it and He commanded it. You should do it. I'm also a big believer that if you're standing in the Jordan and you have the opportunity to do it again, then dive in. It's for freedom that He came to set us free, and for me, some of that freedom has been freedom from the religious traditions of men of which Jesus didn't think too highly nor have much use for (Mark 7). I'm not making a statement about what my first baptism wasn't or lessening its significance. The do-over was just a really cool reminder. My liquid Ebenezer. And truth be told, if someone asks me to do it again, I'm going swimming.

Back to Peter. A lot has been made about Peter the Rock. Peter the apostle. I get it. And I'm a fan. But the reason I'm a fan is not so much what he did as recorded in the book of Acts, but what he did that day in the boat. He despised his own shame and dove in the water toward his Savior. He couldn't take it any longer. He had to be with Jesus. Hear His voice. Even if it meant a scolding—which it didn't.

I said this earlier, and it's the reason I wrote this chapter: your enemy wants to take your shame and drape it about your shoulders as if it identifies you. As if that's what you are. The sum of your screwups. Your King wants you to know that's a lie from hell. Yes, we are all guilty and none of us is worthy, but that's the mystery and majesty of the cross. "While we were still sinners, Christ died for us" (Rom. 5:8 NKJV). I can't say that enough. It means at our worst and most despicable, Jesus loved us enough to climb up on the cross. Why? "For the joy set before Him" (Heb. 12:2 NASB). And even after we've denied Him and thumbed our nose at Him, He beckons, sits alongside us, lifts our chin, and says, "Follow Me."

There is more grace in Jesus than sin in us.

Let's Pray

Lord Jesus, due to my own sin, shame is wearing me out. I can see nothing else. It's all I think about, and until we deal with it, I'm not much good for anything else. Jesus, shame is a liar. he keeps reminding me of who I was. What I did. Father, I know what I did. I can remember. My sin is always before me. And I alone am guilty for my sin. Jesus, like King David, I pray—create in me a clean heart, renew a steadfast spirit within me, cast me not from your presence and take not your Holy Spirit from me (Ps. 51).

Jesus, please take my shame. I don't want it any longer. Shame is a liar and it's time we tell him to go. I repent wholeheartedly for the sin that allowed it and brought it on. Jesus, I know conviction comes from You. And I welcome the conviction from Your Spirit because through that You confront me with the reality of me. And I desperately desire to see the truth of me. Through Your eyes. But I have an enemy who sees my sin, my broken heart, and attacks it and me with shame. To constantly remind me of who I was. Father, my enemy takes Your conviction and twists it into condemnation. And through that, he tries to tell me that's who I am. That my sin identifies me. But in You, there's no condemnation (Rom. 8:1).

Jesus, You're the only One who gets to tell me who I am. You're the only One who gets to declare my identity. Yes, I'm a sinner. Yes, I betrayed You and those I love. Yes, I did what I said I wouldn't do. Yes, I was selfish, self-centered, and I repent for all of that. Please forgive me. Forgive the act of my sin and all the thinking and all the actions that led me to that place. Please wash me and cleanse me. I'm so sorry. Jesus, I agape You. I love You. I desperately desire to return to a place of intimacy and closeness with You. My problem is that shame keeps whispering in my ear telling me I'm not worthy. And the truth is, absent You, I'm not. But Your death—Your blood—declares me, while still a sinner, worthy. I can't earn it and don't deserve it, but I come before Your throne of grace and I am asking to receive Your grace and mercy because I believe there is more grace in You than sin in me (Heb. 4:16). Would You please take my shame and nail it to Your cross with all the rest of shame, where You made a public spectacle of it (Col. 2)?

In the name of Jesus, by and because and through the blood of Jesus, I tell shame to leave me now. Get out of me. Get off my heart. Get out of my mind and take all of your images and reminders with you. You can't live rent free any longer. You're a liar.

Jesus, Your Father made You who knew no sin to be sin for me, that I might become the righteousness of God (2 Cor. 5:21). And if I confess my sin, You are faithful and just to forgive me and cleanse me from all unrighteousness (1 John 1:9). For by a single offering, You have perfected for all time those of us who are being sanctified. And within the covenant You make with us, You remember our sins no more (Heb. 10:14–17). You do not deal with me according to my sins but remove them from me as far as the east is from the west. (Ps. 103:10–14). I know You bore my sin, my shame, on Your body on the tree so I might die to sin and live to right-eousness; for by Your stripes I am healed—and delivered. I strayed like a sheep but have now returned to the Shepherd and Overseer of my soul (1 Peter 2:24–25).

I thank You, Jesus, that You love me. That You have cleansed me. That You have given me the right to be Your child and that You are not ashamed of me. I worship You and You alone. In Jesus' name.

If this chapter described you and if you prayed this prayer in ear-nest, let me do for and to you what Jesus declares we who believe in Him and have received His Spirt are authorized and empowered to do. When Jesus was resurrected, He appeared to the disciples and said, "'Peace be with you. As the Father has sent me, even so I am send-ing you.' And when he had said this he breathed on them and said to them, 'Receive the Holy Spirit. If you forgive the sins of any, they are forgiven them; if you withhold forgiveness from any, it is withheld'" (John 20:21–23).

So let me speak this over you:

- Your sins are forgiven you.
- Washed away.
- White as snow.
- Forgotten by the Father.
- Removed as far as the east is from the west.
- They don't define you any longer.
- You are free.

CHAPTER 5

Problem Number One

Matthew concluded his gospel with these amazing words: "And when they saw him they worshiped him, but some doubted" (Matt. 28:17). Some doubted.

Are you kidding me?* He was standing in front of them.

Stop. Look at the influence of doubt in your life. Has anything good ever come from it? Has doubt ever done anything? Freed anyone? Laid down its life for anyone? Doubt, like fear, is a thief and liar. A destroyer of all things good. And if it was at work then, do you honestly think it's any less at work now?

Mark ended with this scathing account: "He appeared to the eleven themselves as they were reclining at table, and he rebuked them for their unbelief and hardness of heart, because they had not believed those who saw him after he had risen" (Mark 16:14).

Rebuked them? Unbelief? Hardness of heart? Because they had not believed? Sounds like me. Sounds like us. Which means we could make really good disciples. It also means we have some work to do. If doubt and belief was their first problem, then it's also ours.

---

* But before I get all self-righteous, let's be honest. I'm no better. How many times have I looked at something that can only have been accomplished through the singular and sovereign and merciful hand of God, and come up with some rational explanation that reduces Him? A lot. And Lord, I'm really sorry for every single time.

Luke offered this detail: "And while they still disbelieved for joy and were marveling, he said to them, 'Have you anything here to eat?' They gave him a piece of broiled fish, and he took it and ate it before them" (Luke 24:41–43).

Jesus was standing in front of them, and yet they were marveling and they "still disbelieve." It's almost comical. Jesus scratched His head and asked Himself, *What more is it going to take? I know, I'll eat something in their presence. That'll convince them.* So He chewed, swallowed, and the fish disappeared. I wonder if any of them sort of crept around behind Him and checked to see where it went. Like a circus act. *Where's He hiding it?*

> Then he said to them, "These are my words that I spoke to you while I was still with you, that everything written about me in the Law of Moses and the Prophets and the Psalms must be fulfilled." Then he opened their minds to understand the Scriptures, and said to them, "Thus it is written, that the Christ should suffer and on the third day rise from the dead, and that repentance for the forgiveness of sins should be proclaimed in his name to all nations, beginning from Jerusalem. You are witnesses of these things. And behold, I am sending the promise of my Father upon you. But stay in the city until you are clothed with power from on high." (Luke 24:44–49)

There's a lot here but let's start with this: "He opened their minds to understand the Scriptures."

Before we tackle what they did, we have to wrestle with the same thing they wrestled with upon His return. The Word. In order to understand Jesus, they had to change the way they viewed the Word. From beginning to end. They needed a paradigm shift. Scales off.

Which brings me back to us. *What's your relationship to the Word?*

This was one of the first questions I asked in *What If It's True?* Hence, the title. So maybe we should start where we left off. If when Jesus returned and met with His disciples, He used the Law of Moses, the Prophets, and the Psalms—what we would call the Old Testament—to identify and point to Himself, then shouldn't we? Jesus literally stood in a room, flipped to the pages (or scroll), pointed, and said, "See that? That's Me. I am the singular manifestation of that revelation." And this blew their minds.

Does He not still do that with us? The Old Testament is the revelation of Jesus. In the New Testament, Jesus manifests Himself as that revelation. They're flip sides of the same coin. Every writer in the New Testament used the Old to preach the gospel we claim to preach. Jesus Himself said He didn't come to abolish the Old, He came to fulfill it. To make it perfectly perfect and completely complete.

Let me jump forward slightly in the story. And there's a reason for this. Paul has appealed to Caesar and is under house arrest in Rome:

> When they had appointed a day for him, they came to him at his lodging in greater numbers. From morning till evening he expounded to them, testifying to the kingdom of God and trying to convince them about Jesus both from the Law of Moses and from the Prophets. And some were convinced by what he said, but others disbelieved. And disagreeing among themselves, they departed after Paul had made one statement: "The Holy Spirit was right in saying to your fathers through Isaiah the prophet: 'Go to this people, and say, "You will indeed hear but never understand, and you will indeed see but never perceive." For this people's heart has grown dull, and with their ears they can barely hear, and their eyes they have closed; lest they should see with their eyes and hear with their ears and understand with their heart and turn, and I would heal them.' Therefore let it be known to you that this salvation of God has been sent to the Gentiles; they will listen."
>
> He lived there two whole years at his own expense, and welcomed all who came to him, proclaiming the kingdom of God and teaching about the Lord Jesus Christ with all boldness and without hindrance. (Acts 28:23–31)

Couple of things. First: "Some were convinced but others disbelieved."

There it is again. Same old problem. We will unpack this more in the next chapter.

Second, you see that word *understanding*. It means "to put together, to comprehend, to send or bring together as soldiers for a battle." We see the same word used above in Luke 24:45 describing Jesus after His resurrection: "He opened their minds to understand the Scriptures." To prove that all Scripture points to Him. How'd He do this? The Law of Moses, the Prophets, and the Psalms. If you include both direct quotations and allusions, both from the *Tanakh* (Hebrew Scriptures) and the Septuagint (Greek translation of the Hebrew), New Testament writers quote what we call the Old Testament Scriptures more than seven hundred times. When you include possible allusions, the number exceeds nine hundred. Both Jesus and those who followed after Him did this to prove that Jesus is the living revelation, manifestation, and fulfillment of everything spoken of the Messiah in the Old Testament Scriptures.

When Jesus met His followers on the outskirts of Jerusalem, He started talking Isaiah 53 and Psalm 22. If He did that with you, could you make the connection? Could you hear the quotation and think to yourself, *He's talking about Himself; I've never seen that before?* And once that lightbulb flickered, how many more would light up the inside of your mind? The epicenter and foundation of our faith is the resurrection. Period. And if we are to walk in the power of that resurrection, power that He both promised and gave us, we're going to need to grow in our belief and our faith. When Jesus bumped into this very issue with His friends, He took them to those words. In a gross oversimplification, Jesus led them to the words of Moses, the Psalms, and the Prophets as if to say, "See, it's always been about Me. I'm Him."

And according to those who followed Him, the result of that reminding was belief and faith within men and women who turned the world upside down.

If I were our enemy, I'd work really hard to chip away at this "understanding." My battle tactic would be to convince the opposing army that the most powerful weapon in the history of weapons—the one right there in their hand—isn't a weapon or isn't as sharp as it used to be or that there are better ones out there. This is like some foreign ambassador convincing our president that the nuclear football is useless. And so convincing is he that the president pitches the briefcase in the trash heap. The ability to annihilate the world and everyone in it lies at the bottom of a maggot-infested dumpster covered in spaghetti and half-eaten chicken bones. Would that make sense to anyone?

And yet we view the Word of God with less belief.

Lastly, while under house arrest in Rome, Paul quoted Isaiah. A prophet who served 600 years prior to Jesus and some 2,600 years prior to us. Incidentally, Jesus quoted this very verse when scolding His disciples in Matthew 13 about why He spoke in parables. Notice in three verses, Jesus quoted Deuteronomy, Ezekiel, and here—along with Paul—the prophet Isaiah: "For this people's heart has grown dull, and with their ears they can barely hear, and their eyes they have closed; lest they should see with their eyes and hear with their ears and understand with their heart and turn, and I would heal them" (Matt. 13:15; Acts 28:27; Isa. 6:9–10).

They are us. And like them, our hearts have grown dull.

John ended his gospel a bit differently. He said: "This is the disciple who is bearing witness about these things, and who has written these things, and we know that his testimony is true. Now there are also many other things that Jesus did. Were every one of them to be written, I suppose that the world itself could not contain the books that would be written" (John 21:24–25).

As a writer, I love this. John, probably some sixty years after the death and resurrection of Jesus, addressed both the unspoken and spoken unbelief of the critics and nonbelievers as an eyewitness who didn't have time for all the disbelief and doubt. His account is true. Period. Take it or leave it. Not only has he, John, testified to it, but he's raising the bar on what it means to believe, admitting that he hasn't scratched the surface at telling all of what Jesus did. There's more. Lots more. His unspoken implication to the reader is, *You think this much is tough to digest? This is a fraction. Wait until heaven and you'll hear the whole story.*

Remember when John met glorified Jesus on the island of Patmos? He didn't recline on His bosom. He fell down as though dead. John had witnessed the difference between Jesus eating fish and Jesus having been seated at the right hand of God Most High. Then he was tasked with writing about it in his Revelation. How'd you like that job? As a writer, I wonder if John ever looked at the enormity of the revelation laid out before him and then tapped the paper with his pencil. *Just how in this world do you want me to explain that?*

Here's my point: if satan can cause you to believe, even for a moment, that the tomb is not empty, that Jesus is still in there, your faith is useless. If satan can fill your heart with enough doubt, you have nothing to stand on and you're going to get your lunch handed to you as soon as you step foot on the battlefield. Why? Because you don't actually believe what you say you do, which means you don't actually believe in the weapons you've been given. Which means your battle is lost until you decide differently.

Matthew recorded Jesus' last words this way: "All authority in heaven and on earth has been given to me. Go therefore and make disciples of all nations, baptizing them in the name of the Father and of the Son and of the Holy Spirit, teaching them to observe all that I have commanded you. And behold, I am with you always, to the end of the age" (Matt. 28:18–20).

Mark recorded this:

"Go into all the world and proclaim the gospel to the whole creation. Whoever believes and is baptized will be saved, but whoever does not believe will be condemned. And these signs will accompany those who believe: in my name, they will cast out demons; they will speak with new tongues; they will pick up serpents with their hands; and if they drink any deadly poison, it will not hurt them; they will lay their hands on the sick, and they will recover." So then the Lord Jesus, after he had spoken to them, was taken up into heaven and sat down at the right hand of God. And they went out and preached everywhere, while the Lord worked with them and confirmed the message by accompanying signs. (Mark 16:15–20)

Luke recorded these words. This is Jesus speaking:

"Thus it is written, that the Christ should suffer and on the third day rise from the dead, and that repentance for the forgiveness of sins should be proclaimed in his name to all nations, beginning from Jerusalem. You are witnesses of these things. And behold, I am sending the promise of my Father upon you. But stay in the city until you are clothed with power from on high." And he led them out as far as Bethany, and lifting up his hands he blessed them. (Luke 24:46–53)

Despite these farewells, the disciples are confused. They still don't get it. So, one of them asks:

"Lord, will You at this time restore the kingdom to Israel?" He said to them, "It is not for you to know times or seasons that the Father has fixed by His own authority. But you will receive power when the Holy Spirit has come upon you, and you will be my witnesses in Jerusalem and in all Judea and Samaria, and to the end of the earth." And when he had said these things, as they were looking on, he was lifted up, and a cloud took him out of their sight. And while they were gazing into heaven as he went, behold, two men stood by them in white robes, and said, "Men of Galilee, why do you stand looking into heaven? This Jesus, who was taken up from you into heaven, will come in the same way as you saw him go into heaven." (Acts 1:6–11)

From there we know the disciples "worshiped him and returned to Jerusalem with great joy, and were continually in the temple blessing God" (Luke 24:50–53).

Look what happens next. Look at the viral effect of the word they spoke.

The group in Jerusalem numbers about 120 people and included Peter, John, James, Andrew, Philip, Thomas, Bartholomew, Matthew, James the son of Alpheus, Simon the Zealot, and Judas the son of James. There are also many women including Mary His mother, and His brothers. This small ragtag group of people return to Jerusalem, to an upper room, and begin waiting. They're not sure what they're waiting for, but it has something to do with "power" and some sort of baptism.

While they wait, Peter looks around, notices their numbers are down one man, and suggests they nominate someone to take Judas Iscariot's place. In doing so, and in speaking of Judas, he quotes Psalm 69 and 109. "May his camp become desolate, and let there be no one to dwell in it." And, "Let another take his office."[3]

These are no small words Peter has spoken. Yes, they are soon to choose Judas's replacement, but in quoting these two psalms, Peter shows us that he's starting to get it. His paradigm is shifting before their very eyes.

By casting lots for Judas's replacement, the disciples are showing us that the veil and scales have been taken off their eyes and they are beginning to see Jesus through the beauty of the Law of Moses, the Prophets, and the Psalms. It's starting to sink in.

They cast lots, and the lot falls to Matthias. The Eleven are now once again Twelve.

Pause—look at their faces. What do you see? I see a group of people who, despite their faults and problems, now live in a world where Jesus lives. Where He's not dead, but alive. And not only does Jesus live, but His Word lives. The Word of God has come alive like never before.

As I have read back through the accounts of the eyewitness events of the resurrection of Jesus, I had to ask myself, *Do I live in a world where Jesus lives, and does His Word live in me?*

Like, really. I know I talk about it. I write about it. I tell others about it. I'm doing that right now with you. But in my heart of hearts, down where my love and faith and hope live, do I live in a world where I believe that I believe that I believe that Jesus lives and His Word means today what He meant it to mean today? I say I do, but in reality, I'm rather spiritually lazy. And I'm comfortable. And I wrestle with a fear of man and acceptance. And I have wounds from my past. And . . .

The truth is, I don't live every day with the *He's alive* thought running through my mind. Nor do I take seriously all those things He said.

Doubt, unbelief, hardness of heart, fear. This was the reaction of those who knew Him and loved Him after they encountered Him. They were just a bunch of ordinary folks like us. But let's be honest. Before I, and possibly we, get overly self-righteous, while doubt and unbelief was their problem, it is also mine. And yours.

But then something happened. And after that something happened, they *turned the world upside down*. God used them to change eternity for all of us. And He did it with His resurrected life and with His Word.

From those moments when they touched His side, watched Him eat some fish, felt His breath on their faces, and walked alongside Him, those first disciples functioned in a world where a dead Man lives. Rose up out of the grave. Walked out shining like the sun. They saw dead Jesus live. Walk. Talk. Eat. Drink. Swallow. Laugh. Love. Hug. Dance. Sing. Clap. Make a fire.

Despite their unbelief, they lived in a world where Jesus is alive—and something in their heart and their gut came into agreement with that. And despite the soup of their own unbelief, Jesus led them back to His Word. It mattered then. It matters now. Everything they needed to feed their belief then, and everything they would ever need, had already been written. Same is true for us. Everything we need now, and everything we will ever need to grow our belief, is in His Word. But something has to change in how we view it. We need Jesus to help us "understand."

We need to become like the psalmist: "I have stored up your word in my heart, that I might not sin against you" (Ps. 119:11). We need to become like Jeremiah: "Your words were found, and I ate them, and your words became to me a joy and the delight of my heart" (Jer. 15:16). We need to believe like Isaiah: "The grass withers, the flower fades, but the word of our God will stand forever" (Isa. 40:8). And we need to stand with Moses, and more importantly, Jesus, when He said, "Man shall not live by bread alone, but by every word that comes from the mouth of God" (Matt. 4:4).[4]

Why should we live like this? So what is written about the last days can be said of us: "And they have conquered him by the blood of the Lamb and by the word of their testimony, for they loved not their lives even unto death" (Rev. 12:11).

You know what's coming. If I'm asking me, then I'm about to ask you. Do you love the Word like this? Are you betting your life on the Word as they did? How true is it to you?

Ask yourself. Be honest. Spend a day or a week right here.

If Jesus is alive—as in, He's alive right this second, sitting next to you, resurrected, tomb empty—how deeply do you believe His Words? I'm reading the Word, and the accounts of the disciples' lives following the resurrection, and the more I read, the more I scratch my head. You don't need a graduate degree to understand. They believed. They obeyed. They devoured His Word. They did what He did. "And they did not love their lives to the death" (Rev. 12:11 NKJV).

Can that be said of me? Of you? Why not?

If we are going to walk with belief where the rest of this book will take us, we need to wrestle this one.

So, let's pray about that.

Let's Pray

Jesus, I confess my belief is lacking. In fact, it's pathetic. I have not taken every thought captive to the obedience of Christ and I have allowed the enemy to tell me what's true about You rather than Your Word as revealed by Your Spirit. I have listened to the whispers of the deceiver rather than You. I'm so sorry. Admittedly, it's easier to listen to the lies because believing a lie doesn't require faith. It only requires doubt. And doubt is easy. It costs me nothing. Faith? Faith costs me everything, starting with my life.

I can see now how I am exactly like these same men and women who walked with You. I am filled with unbelief and doubt, and my heart is hardened. Please forgive me. I want to believe Your Word. I want to hide it in my heart. I want Your Word to be truer to me than my circumstances or what I can see or hear. I want Your Word to be the foundation upon which I think and make every decision. I want my plumb line to be Your Word. Period.

Jesus, I choose belief. Today. Right now. This second. I choose to say to my enemy, "Be quiet! Be muzzled in the name of Jesus. You don't get to speak to me anymore about my King. You don't get to tell me what's true." Jesus, Your Word tells me what's true and in it You tell me what to believe. Today, I choose You and Your Word as the sole source of what I hold true and my understanding about You. The only thing that colors or influences my perspective of You is Your Word as revealed to me by Your Holy Spirit.

So come Holy Spirit. Open the Scriptures and reveal my King to me. And Jesus, as You do this, please protect that Word in me and let it take deep root. Don't let the enemy steal it away like the birds steal the seed. Guard it in me. Command Your angels concerning me and please wage war against any enemy who would seek to lessen, steal, or chip away at the truth of You. In Jesus' name.

CHAPTER 6

Their Problem Is Our Problem

Standing in the streets of Capernaum, the woman with the issue of blood no longer has the issue. She's healed. Twelve years of shame and rejection are washing themselves out of her heart as she dances her way down the street. Jesus laughs as she twirls. She is a mixture of tears and sobs as she screams at the top of her lungs, "He called me 'daughter'!"

The town is amazed.

The only one not impressed is Jairus, the leader of the synagogue, whose daughter lies at the point of death. He's sweating, hasn't eaten in days, and he's worried. She was hours from death when he left the house and even now it may be too late because Jesus has been messing around with this smelly woman in the street. He got to Him first and yet, for some reason, Jesus held back. Jairus is exasperated. While he's waiting on Jesus to finish with this woman, someone runs from his house. Their face tells the picture. Bad news. His daughter is dead. Don't trouble the teacher any further.[1]

Jesus picks up on their quiet conversation. And Jairus's body language. The shoulder-shaking sob. He knows what they said. He also knows there's no pain like kid pain.

He touches Jairus on the shoulder. "Do not fear, only *believe*."

Don't fear? Are you kidding me? Get serious. Jairus is riddled with fear. He's afraid of what he will find when he walks in the door. Afraid of not being able to comfort his wife. Afraid of holding his dead daughter's body. And as for believe? Believe what? Believe that she's dead? Believe that he never should have left her side? Jairus spits and cusses beneath his breath. He knew he never should have left the house. At least he could have been with her when she passed out of this life.

Dreading what awaits him, Jairus leads the way. Followed by Jesus, Peter, James, and John. The next couple of days for the disciples will be rather action-packed, and Jesus is using this as their training ground.

When they arrive, the house is in turmoil. People are wailing. Loudly. Tearing their clothes. Piling dirt on their heads. Jesus raises a hand, grabs their attention, "The child is not dead, but sleeping."

How insensitive. They laugh Him off. He's lost his mind.

Jesus is tired of both their laughter and what lies beneath it. He puts everyone outside save the father and mother and His three disciples and goes in with the child.

He pokes His head around the corner and smiles. He knows her. He made her. She's twelve, which means she's lived as long as the woman back in the street had the issue of blood. After this they can share their story. Compare notes. It's obvious to everyone in the room that she is dead. She looks it. Plus, they heard her breathe her last and she hasn't breathed since. No one can hold their breath that long. Everyone in the house can confirm beyond a shadow of a doubt that Jesus is too late and that the girl is, in fact, dead. It's why they're wailing. And they'd better get busy if they're going to get her buried before sundown.

Jesus kneels next to the bed, pushes the girl's sweaty hair out of her cold, blue, dead face, and then slips His hand inside hers. The mother is clinging to Jairus who is clinging to his wife. Both are shattered. They thought the Teacher could help her. He was their last hope. For who can raise the dead?

Jesus leans forward and speaks softly. As if to wake the girl gently, "*Talitha cumi*." Which means, "Little girl, I say to you, arise."[2]

At this moment, Scripture records an amazing thing: "Immediately the girl got up and began walking."

A dead girl sat up, stepped out of bed, and began walking.

Now look at her parents. What do you imagine they are doing?

Jesus and His disciples leave the house where a party—shouting, singing, dancing, drinking—has taken the place of a funeral wake. Everyone wants to see the little girl. To touch her. Word spreads like wildfire. *She's alive!*

From there, Jesus comes to His hometown. He is recognized as the carpenter, the son of Mary and Joseph. Most know Him as the kid who used to help His father, who played in the barn with His brothers, helped His mother with dinner, who had an innate ability to remember large amounts of Torah by heart. Now He's all grown up and He's returned with a bit of a following. A posse. Some who heard Him were astonished at His wisdom. Others were offended. *Who does He think He is?*

Regardless, Scripture records, "He could do no mighty work there, except that He laid His hands on a few sick people and healed them. And He marveled because of their unbelief."[3]

Jesus just raised a dead girl to life and yet, in His hometown, He bumps into unbelief and "can do no mighty work there."

Is there a correlation?

In the days that follow, Jesus feeds five thousand men, walks on water, and then interestingly, when He gets out of the boat at Gennesaret, everybody wants to touch the hem of His garment. Thanks to the woman who no longer has the issue of blood, word has spread. In the region of Tyre and Sidon, He marvels at the faith of the Syrophenician woman and drives out the demon in her daughter without ever laying hands on the child. He then heals a deaf and mute man in the region of the Decapolis on the shores of the sea of Galilee—probably near Magdala. He does so with one word: *Ephphatha.* Or, "be opened."[4]

All these things brought more attention and more crowds, so Jesus again feeds them. This time, four thousand. He then heals a blind man at Bethsaida, and He and the disciples start their walk north to Caesarea Philippi, where Peter confesses, "You are the Christ."[5] By this time, the disciples' heads are on swivels. The miraculous is coming at them faster than they can comprehend.

What can this Man *not* do?

Then six days pass and Peter, James, and John find themselves alone with Jesus on the side of a tall mountain. Then some stuff happens to blow their minds.

Now Peter, James, and John are walking down the snow-covered slopes of Mount Hermon.* Following Jesus. Their eyes are big as Oreos. They keep poking each other in the shoulder. Shaking their heads. "Did you see that?"

Jesus laughs.

Before their very eyes, Jesus appears in a conversation with Moses and Elijah. That's right. Moses. And Elijah. All three are shining like the sun. Not to be outdone, God Himself speaks to them from the cloud. "This is my beloved Son, with whom I am well pleased; listen to him."[6]

Even though they've seen it with their own eyes, the three of them are still having trouble believing it. They're rehearsing what they will tell the other nine, but they have no words to describe what just happened. It doesn't matter. No one will believe them anyway.

Meanwhile, the unsuspecting nine are waiting at the bottom of the mountain where things are not going well.

Jesus approaches a crowd in the midst of a heated argument that revolves around a kneeling father and a tormented boy who is seizing and foaming at the mouth. The father holds his son's head to keep it from slamming against the gravel road and pleads with Jesus, "Lord, have mercy on my son, for he has seizures and he suffers terribly. For often he falls into the fire, and often into water. And I brought him to your disciples, and they could not heal him."[7]

Mark, probably recording Peter's eyewitness account, records the interaction this way: "Teacher, I brought my son to you, for he has a spirit that makes him mute. And whenever it seizes him, it throws him down, and he foams and grinds his teeth and becomes rigid. So I asked your disciples to cast it out, and they were not able."[8]

---

* Scripture does not say the Transfiguration occurred on Mount Hermon. This is my opinion. But, given the location of Caesarea Philippi, it is highly possible.

Jesus eyes the crowd, then His disciples, and shakes His head. "O faith-less and twisted generation."[9]

Faithless is "disbelieving." Unbelieving. Incredulous. Without trust in God. "Twisted" is also translated "perverse," which means to turn one's self around. Adopt another course. Turn aside from the right path. To plot against the saving purposes and plans of God.

So to be faithless and twisted, or unbelieving and perverted, is to plot against the saving purposes and plans of God. Jesus said, "Whoever is not with me is against me, and whoever does not gather with me scatters."[10]

Before we can start doing what those first disciples did, before we can do the stuff, we have to first address the very thing Jesus first addressed in them when He rose from the dead and walked through the wall.

Unbelief.

For some of us, what we say we believe and what we do with that belief, or how that belief works itself out our fingers, doesn't really line up.

In other words, there's a disconnect between what we say we believe and what we do. For some reason, we give ourselves a pass when it comes to doing what Jesus did and told us to do.

If your answers to my questions are not too impressive, and you're part of this disconnect, be encouraged. You're in good company and you'll make a great disciple. But in order to make a great disciple, we have to be gut-level honest about where we currently stand.

Back to the story. Jesus says, "Bring him to me." The boy is brought forward, at which point the demon in the boy sees Jesus and, because he knows his time in the boy has come to an end, he throws the boy on the ground whereby the boy flops about and foams at the mouth. Jesus asks the father how long this has been happening. And He doesn't do this for His own benefit. He knows the answer. He does it for the benefit of the crowd. The father explains, "From childhood. And it has often cast him into fire and into water, to destroy him. But if you can do anything, have compassion on us and help us."[11] Another translation says the spirit "mauls" or "shatters" him.

Remember the context into which this man is speaking. Jesus had already sent out the seventy-two. They had experienced casting out demons. They'd seen Jesus do it and they'd done it. When they returned, they said with joy, "Lord, even the demons are subject to us in your name!" And Jesus said to them, "I saw Satan fall like lightning from heaven. Behold, I have given you authority to tread on serpents and scorpions, and over all the power of the enemy, and nothing shall hurt you."[12]

Don't let your eye skip over that too quickly: "I saw Satan fall like lightning from heaven." Jesus is telling His followers that He was in heaven when God the Father cast satan out of heaven. Jesus' suggestion is essentially, "Keep watching. You haven't seen anything yet."

Jesus responds, almost as if to Himself, "If you can." Then He follows it with this: "All things are possible for one who believes."[13] When Jesus responds to the man, He is speaking to the crowd. Which, incidentally, includes you and me.

I want to focus on two words: *all things*. How much of *all things* do you believe? Does that still apply today? As you walk through your daily life, do you hear the promise of *all things*, or do you hear the whisper of impossibility shouted by your enemy?

Immediately, the father of the child cries out and says, "I believe; help my unbelief!"[14]

The crowd presses in. Everybody wants to see. Jesus focuses on the boy yet speaks to the demon in the boy, "You mute and deaf spirit, I command you, come out of him and never enter him again."[15]

The spirit cries out, convulses the boy terribly, and comes out, leaving the boy looking like a corpse. Those in the crowd say, "He is dead."

Jesus slips His hand inside the boy's, lifts him, and "the boy was healed instantly."[16] And Jesus dusted him off and "gave him back to his father."[17]

Now, let's return to where we started this book—the resurrection. Remember, the disciples are staring at Jesus. In the flesh. Risen.

Matthew concludes his gospel with this: "And when they saw him they worshiped him, but some doubted."[18]

Mark ends this way: "Afterward he appeared to the eleven themselves as they were reclining at table, and he rebuked them for their unbelief and hardness of heart, because they had not believed those who saw him after he had risen."[19]

Luke concludes this way: "As they were talking about these things, Jesus himself stood among them and said to them, 'Peace to you!' But they were startled and frightened and thought they saw a spirit. And he said to them, 'Why are you troubled, and why do doubts arise in your hearts?'" Then He shows them His hands and feet and some still "disbelieved."[20]

In that moment, the disciples are characterized by doubt. Unbelief. Disbelief. And hardness of heart. And yet, He's standing in front of them. Complete with holes and no blood. And probably a smile.

John finishes with this: Jesus said, "Do not disbelieve, but believe. . . . Blessed are those who have not seen and yet have believed."[21]

Right there, Jesus is talking about us.

What Exactly Do You Believe?

Throughout the earthly ministry of Jesus, and leading up to and through the resurrection, the apostles' problem was our problem. Belief. This has always been *the* problem.

So let me dig at you a bit: What *exactly* do you believe? Let me put some teeth into this question.

- If God asked you to build an ark, would you?
- If He asked you to sacrifice your son, would you?

Okay, let me bring it closer to home.

- If He asked you to pray for the sick—someone who was in a coma on life support attached to a ventilator, moments from being "unplugged"—would you?
- If He asked you to cast out a demon, would you?

- If He asked you to pray for a dead person, to bring them back to life, would you?

Still too tough? Okay, what if He asked you to:

- Forgive someone who didn't deserve it—at all. Would you?
- Tell the Muslim with the prayer rug in the cubicle next to you about Him. Would you?
- Risk a relationship with someone you love in order to tell them that their sin is not righteousness—even though they adamantly and defiantly claim that it is. Would you?
- Go to a friend's house to pray for their child who is a cutter. Would you?
- Tithe before you pay taxes and your bills, when money is already tight. Do you?

According to Jesus, the kingdom of heaven has come to us (Rev. 12:10). If you are in Him, then you are in the kingdom. He also tells us that unless we become like a child, we cannot enter the kingdom of heaven (Matt. 18:3). Why is that?

I think it's because children trust their fathers without needing to know why they should trust them. They just do. Peter hopped out of the boat as a child. Then began walking like an adult.

How would a child respond to the questions above? How would you?

A few weeks ago, on a Sunday afternoon, I found myself in a pool in my neighborhood with a bunch of our friends. Lots of people, kids, much chaos. One of my friends was playing with his son who's two. Mind you, he—the two-year-old—can't swim. At all. And yet that boy jumped a hundred times off of the edge of the pool and into his dad's arms. And most of the time, it was when his father wasn't looking. Why is that? Because he believes in, has faith in, his father. Period. He has yet to let the water speak into his mind what it can do to him.

And it can kill him.

The word for "belief" is *pisteuo*. It means to "have faith in." Or, "put trust in." Like that little boy jumping off the edge into the arms of his father. *Pisteuo* isn't simply a decision of your head. It's an action of your heart. And legs.

Take bungee jumping. Let's say you and I are standing on a bridge where people are bungee jumping. It's one thing to stand there, point at the rope and the little apparatus they lock around their ankles, and then watch as the folks take a swan dive off the bridge as we comment casually from the comfort of the sideline, "I believe that rope will hold me and so will that thing around my ankles." It's another thing entirely to walk onto the bridge, strap the rope around your ankles, and take a Peter Pan off the bridge.

Positionally, standing there and watching others jump is *believing that*. Strapping it around your ankles and jumping into nothingness is *believing in*.

Big difference. The latter is *pisteuo*.

At the ends of the Gospels, Jesus was rebuking His friends for failing to *believe in*. For failing to *pisteuo*.

People who believe that, watch.

People who believe in, jump.

What gets people from the edge of the bridge to sailing through the air? I'm not sure I can answer that except to say that they do something: they respond to the invitation. "Come." "Follow me." And all the others. I can articulate the difference between the watcher and the jumper in one word.

Faith.

Faith acts. And it acts on what Jesus did and said.

Your and my first problem is that we don't really believe what He said. If you really press us, we think that two thousand years has somehow changed His meaning. That time and science and medicine and the further development of humankind has somehow changed all that. That we know better today. That His command in Matthew 10:8 two thousand years ago doesn't mean what Matthew 10:8 means today.

Amazingly, immediately after Jesus rebuked the disciples for their unbelief and hardness of heart, He told them:

"Go into all the world and proclaim the gospel to the whole creation. Whoever believes and is baptized will be saved, but whoever does not believe will be condemned. And these signs will accompany those who believe: in my name they will cast out demons; they will speak in new tongues; they will pick up serpents with their hands; and if they drink any deadly poison, it will not hurt them; they will lay their hands on the sick, and they will recover." (Mark 16:15–18)

These are the words of Jesus. To you and me. If we don't believe in Him in the first place, how will we ever do what He said?

Secondly, we're afraid of what people think. It's called "fear of man," and I'm as guilty as anyone. The fear usually comes in the form of an unspoken question. A whisper that we hear. It sounds like this: *What if I do or say this and they reject me? What if I'm shamed? What if they make fun of me?*

The third problem we have is, *I did that before and it didn't work.* (Admittedly, a big one for me. I hear this whisper often.) Or, *I didn't see the result I wanted or hoped for.* I get it. Trust me. I've prayed for a lot of people who, when I or we finished praying, saw no visible sign of any change. Even after weeks. Some stayed sick. Some kept their disease. Some even died shortly after I prayed. Right this second I can see a man's face on the back of my eyelids—someone for whom I prayed and yet he died days later. I, and a whole lot of people, loved that man.

But I've also seen people healed. Like, completely. (As I'm typing this, I get a text from a buddy in my Bible study. He just got a phone call from a guy several of us had prayed for a couple of months ago. I'll call him Steve. Steve was traveling back and forth to Mayo for months with an incurable disease. They told him he might very well die. Steve was afraid. Several of us prayed. No big deal. No fireworks. I can't tell you that I saw anything happen in that moment. And yet, Steve just called to say Mayo says he's totally healed. Completely. Like, "You don't need to come back." And they didn't even do anything. No surgery. No medicine. Just scratching their heads. Can I explain that? No. But I do know we prayed.)

In truth, I've seen more not healed than healed. But I don't pray because everybody is healed. I pray out of obedience. Because He said to. If I stop praying, the problem is me. Not Him. So, regardless of outcome, I keep praying. I am *believing in*.

I think our final problem is that we just don't care. Or at least not enough to uproot us from our lazy, self-satisfied, smug, electronics-filled, screen-staring worlds. And if you are thinking that for one second I'm excluding myself from this last problem, don't. I'm writing from experience.

It might help you understand what I'm saying if you read *What If It's True?* In that book, we came to Jesus with hurts. With broken places. With need. And we opened up our chests and invited Him to heal those broken places in us. To redeem us. And He did. In this book, we have come to Jesus with eyes open wide and hearts eager to follow Him. In answer, He directs our gaze at those around us who are broken and in need of healing. And as we stare, He speaks to us, He commands us to use the authority and power He's given us to do in others what He did in us. To be His hands and play a role in that process for another.

Said another way, in *What If It's True?*, the blood of Jesus worked *in* us and *for* us. In this book, the blood of Jesus is working *through* us.

First *in* and *for*, and only then *through*. And in order for the blood of Jesus to work *through* us, we must circle back and confront our problem.

We must *believe in*.

What Does Faith Do?

Faith steps out of the boat. Faith builds an ark. Faith prays.

Think about it. We have reduced Noah to a Sunday school crayon sketch, but he was a man with a family. God told him to do something that both then and now sounded crazy—and yet he did it. He was mocked. Laughed at. People said he had lost his mind. Turns out, he hadn't.

Could you do the same? Would you? Where does your faith begin and end?

Faith conquers a land populated by giants. Faith walks down into the Valley of Elah and picks up five smooth stones. Faith prays for the sick. Faith casts out demons. Faith raises the dead.

Simply, faith does what Jesus said to do. Faith obeys.

Again, I don't have a monopoly on this. But if we are going to follow Jesus and do what He did, we have to move from *believing that* to *believing in*. To faith. Belief is a head action. Faith is a heart action. So how do we move our heads and hearts into a parallel path with Jesus? I'm not sure, but I think it has something to do with being like that two-year-old in my neighborhood pool. We have to jump into the arms of our Father—even if we know in our head that we could drown.

The opposite of belief is not unbelief, it's faithlessness. More often than not, we are a faithless people when Jesus is calling us to faith. Paul put it bluntly: "Whatever does not proceed from faith is sin" (Rom. 14:23). It's an astounding statement. *Whatever.* How much of your and my Christian walk is hedged? How much is controlled? How much is not faith? For me, it's more than I care to admit. And I'm sorry for that. I don't want to be that way. How about this one? "Without faith it is impossible to please him" (Heb. 11:6). How much of your walk with Him is pleasing to Him? And how much is not?

Here's the good news: if you don't have faith, you can get it. It's a gift. "Faith comes from hearing, and hearing through the word of Christ (Rom. 10:17). I think the bigger questions are, Do you want it? What are you willing to do to get it? And what will you do with it once you have it?

Are you content *believing that* (which by the way requires very little), or do you want to move to *believing in* (which will require most everything you have)? If so, have you asked for it? And if He gave it to you, would you act on it? That last question is a biggie. Don't skip over it. If God gave you faith like Abraham, would you act on it?

"Abraham believed God, and it was credited to him as righteousness" (Rom. 4:3 [Gen. 15:6; Gal. 3:6; James 2:23] NASB). What did he believe? He believed that his post-menopausal, ninety-plus-year-old wife could and would have a child. By any medical standard, an impossibility. Why did Abraham believe? Because God said so. Period.

To quote Jesus: "All things are possible to him who believes" (Mark 9:23 [Matt. 19:26; Mark 10:27] NASB).

Be honest. Would you have believed God if you were Abraham? Would you have laughed? To me, that promise sounds about as crazy as an angel telling a virgin she's going to give birth to the Christ without ever having sex. If you had been that virgin, would you have responded with, "Let it be to me according to your word" (Luke 1:38)?

Paul described Abraham this way: "In the presence of the God in whom he believed, who gives life to the dead and calls into existence the things that do not exist. In hope he believed against hope, that he should become the father of many nations, as he had been told" (Rom. 4:17–18).

"In hope . . . against hope." I've wrestled with the meaning of this. As best I can understand, it means letting your heart hope for what your mind tells you is just plain crazy.

Hope against hope. Does that describe you? Your prayers? Your encouragement to others? Paul went on to say, "He did not weaken in faith when he considered his own body, which was as good as dead (since he was about a hundred years old), or when he considered the barrenness of Sarah's womb. No unbelief made him waver concerning the promise of God, but he grew strong in his faith as he gave glory to God, fully convinced that God was able to do what he had promised. That is why his faith was 'counted to him as righteousness'" (Rom. 4:19–22).

You see that line "fully convinced that God was able to do what he had promised"? We need to put that on a bracelet. Paint it above the doors of our homes. Print T-shirts. The question remains: Are you fully convinced?

The Abuse of This

I know what some of you are thinking. Trust me, I've thought it too. I've been doing this Jesus thing long enough to have seen this teaching on faith and belief abused. I've seen it twisted. Seen practitioners claim stuff that makes me just want to vomit. The abuses of this faith thing both within and without the church are many. We have lots of reasons to acquiesce. To not try. To take a pass and let ourselves off the hook. To point at those who have in selfishness made a mockery of the name of Jesus and think to ourselves, *They're a bunch of idiots and I don't want to be looped in with them. I'll pass.*

But despite all the excuses we have and the abuses we've seen, here is what is at stake: you or I may have a friend call us one night and say, "Jane was in an accident. She's on life support. Doctors are telling us we need to disconnect her. Will you come pray that she is healed?"

So how will you answer? In my experience, it's better to wrestle with what you believe before the phone call comes.

If we are in Jesus, then He, the unvanquished and undefeated King of all kings, has given us power and authority to do what He did. Not only that, He has commanded us to walk in that power and authority. After two millennia, something has happened to us and we don't believe this any longer. Not really. But why? Why don't we believe? Said another way, why haven't the very words of Jesus taken root in us and now stand as towering oaks alongside the bank of the waters that flow from His throne?

Jesus answered this in Mark 4 when He described the sower actively sowing seed. Which He is doing in us. When He does sow, like right now, one of four things happens.

First, the birds come and eat the seed. That means the enemy—satan—comes and steals His Word out of your heart. This is offensive, active, guerilla warfare and it is consistent with the enemy who has come to steal, kill, and destroy. In this moment, he is stealing the Word, killing your belief, and destroying your faith. This is just what he does; he did it in the garden; he's been doing it ever since. Nothing new here. I think this is why God commanded us through His son Solomon to, "Watch over your heart with all diligence" (Prov. 4:23 NASB). I actually like the NIV translation here better: "Above all else, guard your heart." But I think my favorite is the Darby Bible Translation: "Keep thy heart more than anything that is guarded." Why did God instruct Solomon this way? Jesus answered that right before He told the parable of the sower: "The mouth speaks out of that which fills the heart" (Matt. 12:34 NASB).

Second in Jesus' parable, seed is sown on stony ground. Meaning there's little to no soil. Which suggests hard, impenetrable hearts. At the first sight of heat or friction or suffering—what Jesus called persecution or tribulation—it withers. Shrinks back. Dies.

Third, there are thorns. These are the cares of the world. The deceitfulness of riches. The desire for things other than His Word. These choke His Word and it proves unfruitful.

Fourth, there is good soil where the seed takes root and bears a crop. Even to a hundredfold.

Why did Jesus speak this way? According to Him,

"I speak to them in parables; because while seeing they do not see, and while hearing they do not hear, nor do they understand. In their case the prophecy of Isaiah is being fulfilled, which says, 'You will keep on hearing, but will not understand; you will keep on seeing, but will not perceive; for the heart of this people has become dull, with their ears they scarcely hear, and they have closed their eyes, otherwise they would see with their eyes, hear with their ears, and understand with their heart and return, and I would heal them.'" (Matt. 13:13–15 NASB)

All of us fall somewhere in this story. We are all attacked and we are all guilty of all the above. It's the reason for the parable. But Jesus did not teach us all this to grant us a pass allowing us to compromise and acquiesce—but rather to confront us with the truth so we might be set free.

If you woke up this morning to find someone had emptied your bank account while you slept, what would you do? Let me ask another way, what would you not do?

Okay, would you, do you, spend the same energy on His Word

deposited in your heart? And yet God tells us it's more valuable than silver and gold.

Over the years, as I've both lived and taught this, I find most of us on a spectrum—a pendulum swinging between two options.

On one side is "good man" Jesus. A good moral teacher. An honest walkabout prophet who loved animals, told people how to live good lives, and just hoped to make the world a better place. But in reality, He had no lasting power. When push comes to shove, Jesus left you here to deal with life because He is powerless against your enemy, who is—as you've always known—stronger than your King, and between here and death it's just a suck-fest and you're pretty much on your own. So suck it up. Life is no better this side of the grave, and between here and there you're simply concerned with limiting your losses and mitigating the suffering. The best you can hope for is to not hack off your enemy and make it to the pearly gates with a white-knuckled death grip on your salvation.

On the other side is Jesus, the Son of God, who died, was buried, rose again the third day, and who is right this second seated at the right hand of God. Whose name is above every other name and at whose name every knee will bow and who is returning to judge all of us and who gave us all authority to do what He did. He is a rewarder of those who seek Him and gives us the petitions for which we ask (Heb. 11:6). He defeated the enemy and has given us the tools and authority to maintain that defeat. To fight *from* victory rather than *for* it. That greater is He who is in you than he who is in the world, and the commands in Matthew 10 and Mark 16 are spoken to us: to preach, cast out, heal, raise, cleanse, and speak in new tongues.

Stand shoulder to shoulder with me and let's take an honest look at us. Let the mirror reflect our response to the birds and depict the nature of our soil. Now let the image settle. Where are you on the pendulum swing? What do you really believe? What I'm trying to get at here is that, in my experience, most of us are holding on to a shadow view of what it means to follow Jesus, and many of us have accepted a powerless gospel. For a host of reasons, we have acquiesced to the point of continual compromise, and the power we claim is about equal to a gnat in a hurricane. We were given 747s and fighter jets, yet we act like kids on tricycles. This was never Jesus' intention.

I am trying to add strength to your spine and echo the words of Paul that ours is a gospel of power and the Spirit we have received is a Spirit of power: "My speech and my message were not in plausible words of wisdom, but in demonstration of the Spirit and of power, so that your faith might not rest on the wisdom of men, but in the power of God. . . . For the kingdom of God does not consist in talk but in power" (1 Cor. 2:4–5; 4:20).

At the core of our problem is what we believe about Jesus, which was one of the reasons I wrote *What If It's True?* A man who said and did what Jesus said and did is not a walkabout prophet with a posse. He's either a nutcase or the Son of God. There's no middle ground. It's either-or. Think about it: Jesus commanded us to eat His flesh and drink His blood. Again, you're either a lunatic on the level of a poached egg, or you're really the Son of God. There's no gray here. And if this sounds a lot like C. S. Lewis, you're right. I probably first confronted this truth in *Mere Christianity*.[22]

So, who is Jesus to you? And just as importantly, what is your relationship to the words, the commands, of Jesus? Because, that's what they are. They're commands.

How Do You Answer?

Spend a minute here. Fill the margin. Ask yourself a hard question. Write the answer. Who is Jesus, and do you believe His Word? Every word? How much? Is He talking directly to you, or is it just a record of words He spoke two thousand years ago to a bunch of folks now dead? Little more than helpful history? Is Jesus speaking directly to you or not? And if He is, in what power are you walking?

For the record: I believe Jesus is God's only begotten Son. He is the perfectly perfect manifestation of every Old Testament prophecy that told us He was coming. He is Alpha and Omega. He created us by His very own words and with those very words He upholds everything—and I do mean everything. He is the sovereign ruler of the kingdom of heaven and there is nothing we encounter that hasn't first been sifted by His sovereign hand. He is undefeated, and His death and resurrection rendered an irrevocable and irreversible defeat to satan. Jesus is God. He is Lord. And He's coming back. And I believe every word He said while here.

I believe the Word, our Bible, was and is inspired by the Holy Spirit and there's not a single word in there that He doesn't want in there. It's perfect. Further, the Old Testament beautifully reveals Jesus, and incarnate Jesus is the singular manifestation of that revelation because He fulfilled every Old Testament prophecy. The Old and New Testaments are inseparable. Flip sides of the same coin.

I believe the new covenant is a better covenant than the old, based on better promises, and that, when you look closely, it requires something of us. In many ways more. The New Testament raised the bar. It didn't lower it. It requires us to love like Jesus. The Old Testament didn't include the me-for-you sacrifice we see in Jesus. The New Testament does. It commands a lay-down-my-life sacrifice.*

I believe the gospel of the kingdom of heaven as preached by Jesus. Every word. From "In the beginning" to "Amen." And I believe He's serious about us doing what He did. All of it. I believe He's the King of a kingdom, and we are created rebels, aiding and abetting the enemy. Yet in His mercy, He offers us adoption. Deliverance from the kingdom of darkness to the kingdom of the Son of God's love. There's just one condition: in order for us to set foot inside that kingdom, we are required to repent, believe, and confess. We have cheapened grace to suggest anything less.

God required repentance then and He requires it now. No exceptions. Without complete and total repentance, there is no entrance into the kingdom. And when we step across the threshold, and our picture of King Jesus clears a little, we can't help ourselves but fall at His feet, worship Him, declare Him King, and surrender fully. No longer full of ourselves, we empty ourselves and come bringing nothing. Just us. We

---

* I explain this more fully in "The Peg on Which Everything Hangs" in *What If It's True?*

yield completely. We give up our rights and give Him the right to either give them back or keep them. That giving and the keeping is His alone. What's ours is surrendering all, demanding nothing. There is no salvation without lordship. Accept the invitation to become His child, declaring His will be done, not ours.

I believe He chose us, and yet if we don't choose Him, we end up in hell, which is a real place and it's really bad and there will be people who really go there because they rejected Jesus.

And I believe He's coming back. Soon.

When the disciples believed, they obeyed. And when they obeyed, stuff happened. Did their obedience transform them all of a sudden into perfect, non-sinning human beings? I don't think so. It's easy to romanticize and overspiritualize the apostles because of what they did, but I think they were a lot like us. The difference was that they saw a dead man walk. And they believed.

All of us find ourselves on the spectrum waffling somewhere between belief and unbelief. But are you willing to let the Holy Spirit challenge your unbelief and move you further toward faith? Are you willing to be willing? The answer will matter as we move through this book.

If you knew me, you'd know I'm not all that qualified to write this book. If I was stretching my limits in *What If It's True?*, then I'm way outside my box with this one. Not because I don't know what the Word says, but because I pick and choose when I do what He says to do rather than just being on call 24–7 and doing it. By definition, that makes me a hypocrite. I don't like saying that, and I don't like being that, but I'm being honest.

I've asked the Holy Spirit to help me with this. My sanctification is ongoing. I'm more like Him today than I was yesterday. Or, I am most days. I'm not writing this book from a place of having-gotten-here. I'm writing from a place of want-to. Of looking at the Word, then myself, and shaking my head at the gap between. The same is true of every one of the men and women who followed Jesus. They were all misfits. All B-team. None were qualified. None had their stuff together.

Jesus doesn't call the qualified or the equipped. He qualifies and equips the called.

Big difference.

Which is why you can make a great disciple. But—belief alone won't get you there. Remember: the demons believe, and they probably have better theology than us, but they're in the wrong kingdom. We have to move from finger-pointing and passive *belief that* to the middle of the bridge with that thing tied around our ankles, leg muscles taut—*belief in*. In my own life and experience, when I've struggled to have faith, or I'm banging my head against a wall of unbelief, I've found that repentance, or lack thereof, was really my problem. And when I repented, faith followed.

Are you convicted by your own unbelief? Can you see its effect in your own life? Do you see how it spreads and infects other areas? Do you see how really evil unbelief is? When the disciples asked Jesus, "What shall we do, that we may work the works of God?" Jesus answered, "This is the work of God, that you believe in Him whom He sent" (John 6:28–29 NKJV).

It's really that simple.

Believe *in*.

Let's Pray—in Faith

- I thank You, Father, that You made no distinction between us and them, having cleansed our hearts by faith (Acts 15:9).
- I thank You, Jesus, that faith is the assurance of things hoped for, the conviction of things not seen (Heb. 11:1).
- I thank You, Lord, that without faith it is impossible to please You, for whoever would draw near to You must believe that You exist and that You reward those who seek You (Heb. 11:6).
- I thank You, Lord, that we do trust in You with all our heart, and do not lean on our own understanding but in all our ways we acknowledge You, and You will make straight our paths (Prov. 3:5–6).

- I thank You, Lord, that no unbelief made us waver concerning the promise of God, but that we grow strong in our faith as we give glory to God, fully convinced that You are able to do what You have promised (Rom. 4:20–21).
- I thank You, Father, that we always give thanks to You, because our faith is growing abundantly, and the love of every one of us for one another is increasing (2 Thess. 1:3).
- I thank You, Jesus, that on the day I called, You answered me, and my strength of soul You increased (Ps. 138:3).
- I thank You, Lord Jesus, that we walk by faith, not by sight (2 Cor. 5:7).
- I thank You, Father, that we draw near to You with a true heart in full assurance of faith, with our hearts sprinkled clean from an evil conscience and our bodies washed with pure water (Heb. 10:22).
- I thank You, Lord, that You equipped me with strength and made my way blameless. That You train my hands for war, so that my arms can bend a bow of bronze. That You have given me the shield of Your salvation, and Your right hand supports me, and Your gentleness makes me great. That You gave a wide place for my steps under me, and my feet did not slip. For You equipped me with strength for the battle; You made those who rise against me sink under me (Ps. 18:32–39).

Jesus, I confess I'm just like the men and women with whom You walked. I'm sorry. I repent. I lack belief. I lack faith. I am covered up in unbelief, disbelief, and if I'm honest, I've given more credence to the enemy whispering what You can't do than Your voice confirming what You can. I realize my unbelief costs me nothing, belief that costs me very little, and belief in costs me a lot. Actually, everything. My problem is I'm still acting as the lord of me. I've put me and what I think on the pedestal where only You can stand. I've enthroned me and what I think above You. I'm sorry. I don't want to do that anymore.

So, here and now, I tear down my throne and lift You alone high on Yours. Here and now I am choosing to believe in and not just that. And Jesus, I choose faith over fear. Perfect love casts out fear, so please fill me up with Your love. Please help me, by the power of Your Holy Spirit, to walk out the faith I've chosen. I choose to bring every thought captive to You, and if that thought doesn't agree with You, I'm throwing it out. Unbelief and hardness of heart can no longer live rent free in the middle of my chest. Only You can.

So, come Lord Jesus. Please forgive me and grant me belief and faith so great and so deep that the unbelievers around me are shaking their heads telling me I'm crazy. In Jesus' name.

CHAPTER 7

Moving from Faith
to Faithfulness

I've taught this message enough to know that some of you aren't quite with me. You're reading me through squinted eyes and praying these prayers with half-breaths because you know if you actually believe all this stuff that Jesus said, you might actually have to do it. And that makes you uncomfortable. You're okay with maybe 50 to 75 percent of what Jesus said to do, which in your way of thinking is good enough. Most of what Jesus said was optional anyway. Extra credit. The realm of the superspiritual.

At the close of the last chapter, some of you took a deep breath, "Good, glad we're through that. Now on with the rest of the book." But therein lies the problem. There is no "rest of the book" if you miss this. The problem I often encounter from this point is that it requires more to move people to the edge of the bridge. Throughout the life and ministry of Jesus, He continually and intentionally moved His disciples, His followers, the true believers, from faith—to faithfulness.

In the lives of those who loved and followed Him, belief led to action. Faith became faithfulness. And the stuff of faithfulness is what we would call *works*. Listen to the brother of Jesus: "What good is it, my brothers, if someone says he has faith but does not have works? . . . Faith by itself, if it does not have works, is dead" (James 2:14, 17).

You say you have faith? Faith in whom? Jesus? Okay, let's do this: in the margin on the left side of this page, list the commands of Jesus. The stuff He said to do. You might start in Matthew 10:8 (He said the same thing in Mark 3:13–15 and Mark 16) but there are lots of places. Next, list the stuff He did. Look at His actions. And only use verbs. (Hint: these two lists will be identical, because Jesus did what He said.)

Okay, using the margin on the right, drag and drop every command and action of Jesus that you're actively doing.

Now compare the lists.

Not fair? These are the words of Jesus: "Truly, truly, I say to you, whoever believes in me will also do the works that I do; and greater works than these will he do, because I am going to the Father" (John 14:12).

Belief in Jesus becomes faith, which when repeatedly put into action becomes faithfulness, which produces fruit called works.*

The Antidote

Look at Jesus' response to faith. Look at what He said about it when He bumped into it.

When the centurion asked Jesus to heal his servant, telling Jesus He didn't need to come to his house, he said, "Only say the word." Jesus marveled and said, "with no one in Israel have I found such faith" (Matt. 8:8–10). This was a Roman centurion. A Gentile. And his faith is registering off the charts. This means there's hope for us.

When the men lowered their paralyzed friend down through the roof, Jesus saw the faith of the men holding the ropes and responded to the paralyzed man, "Take heart, my son; your sins are forgiven" (Matt. 9:2). The

---

* For the record, I am not saying your salvation is a function of works. I think you know me better. Works are the organic outgrowth of true faith. Faith first, then works. It's like a rose. Seed. Root. Stem. Finally, fruit. The rose petal is proof of the root established in fertile soil. Logically then, if you have faith, you should have fruit. You can't have one without the other. Faithfulness by its very nature produces something. It's that something I'm asking you to look at.

paralyzed man was healed not by his own faith, but his friends' faith. This means there's hope for us.

When Jesus turned and saw the woman with the issue of blood after she had held the wing of his shirt, He said, "Your faith has made you well" (Matt. 9:22). Her faith healed her. This means there's hope for us.

When Jesus encountered blind Bartimaeus at the gate in Jericho, Bartimaeus was crying aloud, "Jesus, Son of David, have mercy on me." Jesus touched his eyes, healed him, and said, "your faith has made you well" (Mark 10:52; Luke 18:42). His faith healed him. This means there's hope for us.

When one of the ten lepers returned after having been cleansed by Jesus, and thanked and worshipped Jesus, the Lord said, "Rise and go your way; your faith has made you well" (Luke 17:19). Faith healed the leper. This means there's hope for us.

When Peter walked on water, he saw the wind and became afraid and began to sink. Jesus said, "O you of little faith, why did you doubt?" (Matt. 14:31). Peter's mind (his eyes) took over, convinced him walking on water wasn't possible. So he sank. His unbelief crushed his faith. This means there's hope for us.

When Jesus encountered the Canaanite woman who begged him to deliver her daughter from an evil spirit, telling Him that even the dogs eat the crumbs that fall from the master's table, Jesus responded, "O woman, great is your faith! Be it done for you as you desire" (Matt. 15:28). And her daughter was healed instantly. Her great faith healed her daughter who wasn't even in the same room. This means there's hope for us.

When the disciples came to Jesus and asked Him why they could not cast out the demon from the boy suffering seizures, Jesus said, "Because of your little faith" (Matt. 17:20). This, too, means there's hope for us.

And when the disciples saw that the fig tree had withered, Jesus told them, "Whatever you ask in prayer, you will receive, if you have faith" (Matt. 21:22). This means there's hope for us.

When the disciples began to understand they needed faith, they asked Jesus, "Increase our faith!" (Luke 17:5). How did Jesus respond? He walked into Jericho and set His face for Jerusalem. Why? So they could experience the soul-crushing experience of watching Him die a gruesome death? Powerless against His accusers?

No. So, they could see Him walk out of a tomb. Stick their fingers in the holes. Watch Him eat fish. Ascend on high.

The antidote for unbelief is not *belief that*, but *belief in*. And *belief in* is faith. If we are going to become like the disciples, we need to inject faith into the wound that is harboring unbelief.

The Elephant in the Room

Now hold it. Let me address the elephant in the room before I lose some of you. I know where this can go, and I know some of you are sitting in hospitals right this second with chemo dripping into your veins or staring up from a wheelchair or staring down on your child's tombstone, and you're scratching your head. Or you're starting to get angry. "But Charles, I have faith."

I believe you. I do. Again, I've prayed for and with a good many sick people. Some have been healed. Some have not. Some have had great faith. Some have prayed that the Lord would help their unbelief. And some who had great faith were not healed and died. Whatever the case, I am not placing blame—and I don't believe Jesus is either. And if you knew me, you'd know that my heart hurts for you. A lot. I know the enemy likes to use a message like this one to whisper into your wound and tell you, "If you had enough faith, you'd be healed." (Or they would have been.) Please don't hear that from me.

I am trying to herald the truth that our circumstances don't dictate God's reality. His Word does. And in His Word, He tells us, *Whatever you ask . . .* And, *All things are possible to those who believe . . .*

I am trying to encourage you that if we lack faith, we can get it. Faith is like a muscle. You flex it and it grows. Don't, and it atrophies. My point is this: I don't want to be one more preacher or writer browbeating those of you who have been praying for healing and haven't seen it. In some ways, I'm in that camp. I have prayed and am praying for healing for several people, and we have yet to see it. There are three guys in my Bible study right this second, diagnosed with disease. And yet I believe and I have faith that God can and will heal them. Will He? I have no idea, but I don't want anything to stop my praying. I love Him and them too much. I don't want to let the fact that you or they are not yet healed allow us to acquiesce, expect less, pray less, or throw up our hands, saying: "Well, I guess this is just my lot in life." I don't believe that. I also don't understand the ways of God—His ways are higher than mine.

I realize I'm running a fine line here, but I want to add steel to your spine. If you need healing and you've been praying and have seen no results, hang in there. Keep praying. Ask others to join you. Fast. A lot. I realize this is easier said than done. But the testing of your faith is producing something in you more valuable than gold. I believe Jesus wants to give you more faith and that no one wants your healing more than Jesus. Don't believe me? Let me walk you back to the cross. "He Himself took our infirmities" (Matt. 8:17 NKJV). That's past tense.

When God used Peter and John to heal the man born lame—who had been that way for forty years—Peter responded to the religious rulers, "His name—by faith in his name—has made this man strong whom you see and know, and the faith that is through Jesus has given the man this perfect health in the presence of you all" (Acts 3:16).

When Paul encountered the man at Lystra who could not use his feet, he looked "intently at him and seeing that he had faith to be made well, said in a loud voice, 'Stand upright on your feet.' And he sprang up and began walking. And when the crowds saw what Paul had done, they lifted up their voices, saying in Lycaonian, 'The gods have come down to us in the likeness of men!'" (Acts 14:9–11).

Notice those two phrases: *by faith in His name* and *he had faith to be made well*. Do either of these miracles happen without faith? Not according to Scripture.

From Faith to Faithfulness

Belief is the soil. Faith is the root. The Holy Spirit is the water. The Father is the Gardener.

As we move from *believing that* to *believing in*, we grow in faith.*

Absolutely nothing happens in the Christian life without faith. Period. Faith is synonymous with obedience. With doing. Let me encourage you with this: "Faith comes from hearing, and hearing through the word of Christ" (Rom. 10:17). Which means if we don't have it, we can get it.

I want to shift or change the way we think about this. When we say "faith," we should really think "faithfulness." It's an attitude. A heart thing. It's a choice and it grows out of belief. It's a loyalty toward. And it's not one single act. It's a bunch of acts.

Faith is expressed in faithfulness.

Without faith, there is no faithfulness. But you cannot walk in faithfulness unless you are acting on what you believe. Faith without expression, without acting, is not faith. It's simply belief, and even the demons believe.

Let me end with this: Moses and the nation of Israel have entered Shechem. They are standing between Mount Ebal and Mount Gerazim. The tribes of Simeon, Levi, Judah, Issachar, Joseph, and Benjamin stood on Mount Gerazim to bless. And Reuben, Gad, Asher, Zebulon, Dan, and Naphtali stood on Mount Ebal to curse. When positioned, Moses said, "Keep silence and hear, O Israel: this day you have become the people of the LORD your God. You shall therefore obey the voice of the LORD your God, keeping his commandments and his statutes, which I command you today" (Deut. 27:9–10).

The word we translate above as "obey" is a very special word. One of the most special in the Hebrew language. The word is *shama,* and it

---

* And notice, too, what is up to us and what is up to Him. We are the soil in which faith, the Holy Spirit, and the Father work. What does the soil do? Very little. It's just soil. The Gardener does the work. Tilling. Watering. Pruning. That should take some pressure off us. It reminds me of Ephesians, "stand firm," and Philippians, "it is God who works in you both to will and to work for His good pleasure." Don't wig out if you lack faith. You can get it, and it is His great pleasure to give it to you.

actually means "to hear." I've also heard it defined as "listen listening" or "listen with both your ears and your heart"; it's the same word we find eighteen words prior when Moses said, "Hear, O Israel." It's also the same word used twenty-one chapters prior in the greatest commandment: "Hear, O Israel: the LORD our God, the LORD is one. You shall love the LORD your God with all your heart and with all your soul and with all your might. And these words that I command you today shall be on your heart" (Deut. 6:4–6). We see it again in Deuteronomy 28: "If you faithfully obey the voice of the LORD your God, being careful to do all his commandments that I command you today, the LORD your God will set you high above the nations of the earth" (v. 1). Here we find the word *shama* translated as "faithfully obey."

In every use, the word is imbedded with both the idea of hearing and obedience. With doing. They are synonymous. *Shama* means to hear with attention to obedience, to give your undivided attention to, or to hear with an intent to do. It means to *obey . . . and keep.*

It was that simple then. It's that simple now. The difficulty is in the doing.

Belief without works is faithlessness.

Belief with works leads to faithfulness.

The command then was "hear and do." The command today is "hear and do." Incidentally, the voice speaking to Moses then was the same voice speaking to the disciples—which is the same voice speaking to us.

Help My Unbelief!

Back to the father with the little boy—the man who prayed the magnificent prayer, "Help my unbelief!" (Mark 9:24). He's no different from us. He is us. He's come to Jesus with a need. Something he can't fix. His heart is breaking; he's helpless and he knows it. And he comes to Jesus knowing Jesus alone can do what he's asking, but he doesn't know how or when He will or even if He will.

But the father comes anyway.

That's us. We don't know how Jesus will answer our prayer or when He will or even if He will in the way we want it answered, but we come anyway. And when we do, He asks us, "Do you believe I can do this?" He's not asking for His benefit. He's asking for ours.

I am trying to encourage you to respond from your gut with this: "Yes, Lord, help my unbelief!" I am trying to get you and me to the place Job found himself after his trial and after having lost everything, including his ten children, and after his final conversation with God, when he responded with, "I know that You can do everything, and that no purpose of Yours can be withheld from You" (Job 42:2 NKJV). Job also said, "Though he slay me, yet will I hope in him" (13:15 NIV). That word *hope* can also be translated "serve" and "trust."

I am trying to herald the faith of Shadrach, Meshach, and Abednego when they responded to Nebuchadnezzar after he said:

> "But if you do not worship, you shall immediately be cast into a burning fiery furnace. And who is the god who will deliver you out of my hands?"
>
> Shadrach, Meshach, and Abednego answered and said to the king, "O Nebuchadnezzar, we have no need to answer you in this matter. If this be so, our God whom we serve is able to deliver us from the burning fiery furnace, and he will deliver us out of your hand, O king. But if not, be it known to you, O king, that we will not serve your gods or worship the golden image that you have set up." (Dan. 3:15–18)

I want a faith like that. A faith that says our God is able to deliver us from the furnace and He will deliver us from the enemy's hand, *but* even if He does not, we're not bowing down to him and any other god. Ever.

I know some of you well enough to know that even after this encouragement, you shake your head. "I did that, and He didn't answer. They died." I know. Trust me, I feel your pain. But Jesus is looking for a people who return to Him in faithfulness even when they don't understand, who don't allow their circumstances to dictate who they believe He is. The rubber meets the road of faith right here. There is a war in our mind between our circumstances or what we've experienced and the pain attached to it—and His Word. The same war that existed in Peter's mind when he walked on water. His mind told him, *This is not possible.* And yet Jesus said, "Come."

Jesus is saying to us, *Come. Follow me. Do what I do. Believe what I'm telling you. Act on what I'm telling you. Walk in faithfulness.* Specifically, He's sending us and saying as we go, "Go . . . proclaim . . . 'The kingdom of heaven is at hand.' Heal the sick, raise the dead, cleanse lepers, cast out demons" (Matt. 10:6–8).

We as people have excuses and we have experiences in which we tried and it didn't work and we have hesitancies like fear of man and we have unbelief and lack of faith—and *none of that* excuses us from any of this.

Something happened in the minds and hearts of the disciples and those who followed Jesus to take what they knew of Him in their minds and migrate it south into their hearts where they put that knowingness, that belief, into action. Where they did what their belief was spurring them to do. Only then did they upend the world. We will get to what happened in the next chapter, but my point is this: belief alone will do nothing. The demons show us this. But belief acted upon, well . . .

Nothing in this book is possible if we're functioning with hard hearts and in unbelief. That stuff has got to die if we are to live in Him. So let's drive a stake through it. You don't have to have disciple-level faith right this second. I'm just asking you: *Do you agree that Jesus is asking us to believe Him, and are you willing to ask Him for that kind of faith and then walk it out as faithfulness?*

Before faith is Faith and before Faith is Faithfulness, it is obedience. "Stretch out your hand." "Pick up your mat." "Rise and walk." These are commands to be obeyed. Think about it. They did not receive their healing until they did. I'm not suggesting your and my healing is somehow up to us. Some sort of bootstraps thing. That we do and we are healed. Not at all. But Jesus does command us. Will you obey? The first command is simple.

Believe.

The Enemy of Faith

Why have I spent two chapters talking about this? Why devote this much space to a single topic? Because if you "get" this, then God the Father, through you, will turn the world upside down. *And* because you have an enemy who fears this—who does not want you to have faith. At all. he's afraid of your faith because he knows what it can do. he's seen it. The enemy of belief is not unbelief but faithlessness, and the enemy of faith is not doubt, but *fear*. Jesus is looking for people of faith in a culture overridden with fear. I believe fear is both an emotion—one that God created and gave us and can be helpful, like "Run, that bear wants to eat you"—but it can also be a demon who attacks us. (i.e., "a spirit of fear" [2 Tim. 1:7]). In order to wrestle with your own fear, you've got to come to grips with the fact that you're in a war.

Stop there. You're in a war, and you're in one whether you like it or not and whether you agree or not. You have an enemy and he's real and he hates you and he wants to post your head on a stake outside the city walls. You have been in a war from the moment you opened your eyes on planet earth. Most of us medicate or numb our fear with some form of medication— drug, drink, sex, power, money, pick your poison—rather than the Word, but all we've done is closed the closet door on fear. he's still in there. Down in the basement. Why? Because to fight him, we have to stand on something. To muster some gumption. To be more like Caleb and less like the ten spies who said the land was populated by giants. John tells us "perfect love casts out fear," which means fear has to be cast out, or removed forcibly (1 John 4:18). And when he said this, he was speaking from experience.

How can faith and fear reside in the same house when they are not compatible? If you're nodding your head and this is you—hang in there. The remedy is coming. We live in an epidemic of fear, and most of us have no real idea that it is controlling us. That it is the master of our house. The strong man. Fear is rampant because our faith is weak. God knew this, which is why Scripture says, "Do not fear" 365 times. One for every day.

It's easier to be fearful than faithful because fear is a liar and requires nothing—save agreement with its lies—while faith will require something, which is often everything. Faith the size of a mustard seed will upend the world. Fear is passive agreement with a defeated foe, while faith is a gift from an undefeated King, which you can refuse. Faith is a choice to believe when belief is not reasonable, and faithfulness is an active choosing, no matter the lie. And while the differences are striking, we choose one or the other. Daily.

All of us vacillate somewhere between believing the whispers and lies of fear versus God's Word. And often, fear is not necessarily a conscious choice. It can be a subconscious reaction where we fail to bring every thought to the captivity of Christ. Whether conscious or not, this place of decision is where the rubber meets the road. Lies or Word. It's "The land is populated with giants" or "We are well able."[1]

Again, the opposite of faith is not doubt but fear—and if you are not walking in faith then you are by definition walking in fear. What about your life right this second requires a God kind of faith? What about your life is requiring any kind of faith at all? Where are you needing Him to show up? Like, if He doesn't show up it will fail. If the answer is not quick in coming then chances are good you've agreed with the liar and sacrificed your faith at the altar of your comfort, convenience, and self. Jesus is returning to a people of faith. How will He find you when He does? Will He find you seated on the sideline, cozied up with fear, indifference, and resignation? Or standing on a tabletop screaming, "They are our bread"?[2]

Will you step across the threshold?

What Hinders You?

One last question: How much of your belief is informed by your tradition, and how much is informed by the Word? Don't skip over this. Think about your faith and the expression of it. Where'd it come from? Where'd you learn it? You and I are guilty of having allowed others—and many times they are well-meaning—to tell us what to think and both what the walk of our faith and the expression of our faith should look like. Jesus bumped into this same problem with the Pharisees in Mark 7. They were complaining that His disciples were not following the traditions of the elders in how they washed their hands prior to eating. The tradition had to do with holding the cup correctly, pouring a certain number of times with each hand, etc. None of which came out of the Word of God. The intricate rehearsal was a man-made tradition that they had taken as greater than the Law of Moses.

Jesus was annoyed by their petty insistence and shook His head: "And he said to them, 'Well did Isaiah prophesy of you hypocrites, as it is written, "This people honors me with their lips, but their heart is far from me; in vain do they worship me, teaching as doctrines the commandments of men" (Mark 7:6–7 [Isa. 29:13]). Don't let your eyes skip over the lips-and-heart part. This is where we get the phrase "lip service." The Pharisees' worship was in vain, and not only had they taught the commands of men as doctrine but they'd accepted it as doctrine. But Jesus wasn't finished. He then said this about them: "thus making void the word of God by your tradition that you have handed down. And many such things you do" (Mark 7:13).

Another translation says, "invalidating the word of God" (NASB).

Making void and *invalidating.* I know of nothing else on planet earth that can make void or invalidate the Word of God. The enemy is powerless to do this, and yet we do it daily. By our traditions. So back to my question: Where are you allowing your tradition to inform what your faith looks like more than the Word? In some ways this is a difficult question. It's like asking a fish to describe water. It's all he's ever known. It's been working pretty well up to now. And he's comfortable with it and sees no reason to change. But therein lies the tension.

Comfort. If we are anything, we are comfortable. Comfort is an idol, a god, even, and our lives are totally geared toward achieving it or acquiring what comforts us.

The kind of faith Jesus' disciples had doesn't just happen to us. We don't just wake up one day and *whammo*, we're titans of faithfulness. Steps are taken, and one of the first is taking an honest look at what limits and hinders us; most often those limitations are man-made constructs.

And don't accuse me of being antitraditional. I'm not. There's much I love about the history and practices and expressions of our faith. *But* tradition has a way of replacing faith and becoming an idol. Why? I'm not sure I can answer this except to say I think it has something to do with the comfort and faithlessness required in continuing to do what we once did and not stopping long enough to ask the Holy Spirit if He is still doing that, or wants to. If I am to follow Jesus, if you are, we would do well to put everything on the table, and if something we are doing or accepting is limiting or hindering our growth in faithfulness or our experience in the kingdom of heaven here on earth, then I want to know it—so that I can stop doing that.

I realize wars have been fought over this question, but does your tradition look like the ministry of Jesus? Does it hinder you?

Here's the writer of Hebrews. He's cautioning his readers:

Take care, brothers, lest there be in any of you an evil, unbelieving heart, leading you to fall away from the living God. But exhort one another every day, as long as it is called "today," that none of you may be hardened by the deceitfulness of sin. For we have come to share in Christ, if indeed we hold our original confidence firm to the end. As it is said, "Today, if you hear his voice, do not harden your hearts as in the rebellion." For who were those who heard and yet rebelled? Was it not all those who left Egypt led by Moses? And with whom was he provoked for forty years? Was it not with those who sinned, whose bodies fell in the wilderness? And to whom did he swear that they would not enter his rest, but to those who were disobedient? So we see that they were unable to enter because of unbelief. (Heb. 3:12–19)

Unbelief Is a Killer

You don't have to kill a warhorse to take it out of the battle. Just hobble it. You can render wholly ineffective the most powerful, awesome weapon in the army by tying up one leg. A two-pound piece of rope can render mute fifteen hundred pounds of fury and destruction. Where is unbelief hobbling you? Where have you sacrificed your faith at the altar of a two-pound piece of rope called "unbelief"?

An unbelieving heart is evil. And it will cause you to fall away from God. Our hearts are hardened by the deceitfulness of sin—and everything not of faith is sin. Meaning, unbelief is a killer.*

Use the margin. Write over there, Where has unbelief hobbled you? Maybe your answers look something like, "my marriage," "my work," "my life in ministry," "my relationship with my kids," "my relationship with my ex-wife," "my broken heart," "in my inability to step out and walk in to the calling to which He has called me," or "in the amount of fear I live with on a daily basis."

Or maybe it's just one answer, "in my unwillingness to lock that thing around my ankles and take a Peter Pan off the bridge."

If we are going to walk with Jesus and do what He did and said, with hopes of having a faith that upends the world, we need to admit unbelief.

---

* Moses was leading the people of God into the promised land. And unbelief kept them out. Think about it. Unbelief kept them out of the very land God had promised and set aside for them. Not a foreign enemy or foreign power or weapon of destruction. But, unbelief. From this perspective, not only is unbelief a killer, but look at what God says about lack of faith. Just before Moses died, God was giving a final command to Moses and He told him to go up on Mount Nebo, view the land of Canaan, and then die. Think about the amount of time, the percentage of his life, spent trying to get into the promised land and yet God kept him out. He allowed him to see it from a mountaintop and yet not enter it (until the transfiguration). Why did God do this? *Because you broke faith with me in the midst of the people of Israel at the waters of Meribah-kadesh, in the wilderness of Zin, and because you did not treat me as holy in the midst of the people of Israel* (Deut. 32:51).

Confess it. To crucify our own unbelief and our stubborn, evil, faithless hearts. And we need to do it quickly. Every day. Maybe we should add one picture to the list you just created over there in the margin. Draw a cross above all of it. Then write these words above it: *This he set aside, nailing it to the cross. He disarmed the rulers and authorities and put them to open shame, by triumphing over them in him* (Col. 2:14–15).

I love that. *Triumphing.* It's one of those tenses which means not only has He done it, but He is continuing to do it and will continue to do it. It never stops.

And if you're enjoying the process, why don't you write this one too. Paul wrote in his second letter to Timothy, *Remember Jesus Christ, risen from the dead* (2 Tim. 2:8).

Pray with Me

As we pray, let's start with what Scripture says about faith. Let's speak these proclamations over ourselves in prayer. I think we need reminding, so let's remind our hearts what Scripture says about faith. Saying it out loud is better. And saying it out loud with another person is even better.

- The righteous live by faith (Rom. 1:17; Gal. 3:11).
- The faithless are haters of God, inventors of evil, and heartless (Rom. 1:30–31).
- We have been justified by faith (Rom. 5:1).
- When we confess with our mouths that Jesus is Lord and believe in our hearts that God raised Him from the dead—we proclaim the word of faith (Rom. 10:8–9).
- Our faith does not rest in the wisdom of men, but in the power of God (1 Cor. 2:5).
- If Christ has not been raised from the dead, our faith is futile, and we are still in our sins (1 Cor. 15:17).
- We walk by faith, not by sight (2 Cor. 5:7).

- We are not justified by works of the law but through faith in Jesus Christ (Gal. 2:16).
- We have been crucified with Christ, and it is no longer we who live, but Christ who lives in us. And the life we now live in the flesh we live by faith in the Son of God, who loved us and gave himself for us (Gal. 2:20).
- We received the Spirit by hearing with faith (Gal. 3:5).
- Through the Spirit, by faith, we wait for the hope of righteousness (Gal. 5:5).
- Faithfulness is part of the fruit of the Spirit (Gal. 5:22).
- By grace we have been saved through faith, which is the gift of God (Eph. 2:8).
- Christ dwells in our hearts through faith (Eph. 3:17).
- Our righteousness comes through faith in Christ and depends on faith (Phil. 3:9).
- By holding faith and a good conscience, we wage the good warfare (1 Tim. 1:18–19).
- We are to pursue righteousness, godliness, faith, love, steadfastness, gentleness, and fight the good fight of faith (1 Tim. 6:11–12).
- We are to flee youthful passions and pursue righteousness, faith, love, and peace (2 Tim. 2:22).
- When we fight the good fight, finish the race, keep the faith, there is laid up for us a crown of righteousness, which the Lord, the righteous judge, will award to us on that day (2 Tim. 4:7–8).
- If the message (of the good news) is not united by faith through listening, it will not benefit those who hear it (Heb. 4:2).
- The foundation of the elementary doctrine of Christ is repentance from dead works and faith toward God (Heb. 6:1).
- If we shrink back in our faith, God's soul has no pleasure in us. But we are not of those who shrink back and are destroyed, but those who have faith and preserve our souls (Heb. 10:38–39).
- Faith is the assurance of things hoped for, the conviction of things not seen (Heb. 11:1).

- Jesus is the founder and perfecter of our faith (Heb. 12:2).
- The testing of our faith produces steadfastness (endurance) (James 1:3).
- We show our faith by our works (James 2:18).
- Belief alone is not enough. Even the demons believe and shudder. Faith apart from works is useless (James 2:20). So we are justified by works and not by faith alone (v. 24).
- Our faith is more precious than gold when tested by fire, and the outcome of our faith is the salvation of our souls (1 Peter 1:7, 9).
- The victory that has overcome the world is our faith (1 John 5:4).

Having said all this, now let's remind ourselves what faith does. (Just look at the number of times you see the phrase "by faith" in the words below, and note what verbs follow.)

- By faith we understand that the universe was created by the word of God, so that what is seen was not made out of things that are visible (Heb. 11:3).
- By faith Abel offered to God a more acceptable sacrifice (Heb. 11:4).
- By faith Enoch was taken up so that he should not see death (Heb. 11:5).
- Without faith it is impossible to please him, for whoever would draw near to God must believe that he exists and that he rewards those who seek him (Heb. 11:6).
- By faith Noah, being warned by God concerning events as yet unseen, in reverent fear constructed an ark for the saving of his household (Heb. 11:7).
- By faith Abraham obeyed when he was called to go out to a place that he was to receive as an inheritance. And he went out, not knowing where he was going (Heb. 11:8).
- By faith Sarah herself received power to conceive, even when she was past the age, since she considered him faithful who had promised (Heb. 11:11).

- By faith Abraham, when he was tested, offered up Isaac, and he who had received the promises was in the act of offering up his only son (Heb. 11:17).
- By faith Isaac invoked future blessings on Jacob and Esau (Heb. 11:20).
- By faith Jacob, when dying, blessed each of the sons of Joseph (Heb. 11:21).
- By faith Joseph, at the end of his life, made mention of the exodus of the Israelites and gave directions concerning his bones (Heb. 11:22).
- By faith Moses, when he was born, was hidden for three months by his parents, because they saw that the child was beautiful, and they were not afraid of the king's edict (Heb. 11:23).
- By faith Moses, when he was grown up, refused to be called the son of Pharaoh's daughter, choosing rather to be mistreated with the people of God than to enjoy the fleeting pleasures of sin. He considered the reproach of Christ greater wealth than the treasures of Egypt, for he was looking to the reward (Heb. 11:24–26).
- By faith he left Egypt, not being afraid of the anger of the king, for he endured as seeing him who is invisible (Heb. 11:27).
- By faith he kept the Passover and sprinkled the blood, so that the destroyer of the firstborn might not touch them (Heb. 11:28).
- By faith the people crossed the Red Sea as on dry land, but the Egyptians, when they attempted to do the same, were drowned (Heb. 11:29).
- By faith the walls of Jericho fell down after they had been encircled for seven days (Heb. 11:30).
- By faith Rahab the prostitute did not perish with those who were disobedient, because she had given a friendly welcome to the spies (Heb. 11:31).
- For time would fail me to tell of Gideon, Barak, Samson, Jephthah, of David and Samuel and the prophets—who *through faith* conquered kingdoms, enforced justice, obtained promises, stopped the mouths of lions, quenched the power of fire, escaped the edge of the

sword, were made strong out of weakness, became mighty in war, put foreign armies to flight. Women received back their dead by resurrection. Some were tortured, refusing to accept release, so that they might rise again to a better life (Heb. 11:32–35).

Now let's pray:

Lord Jesus, I repent for my unbelief, my hard-heartedness, my stubbornness, my chronic failure to obey. For having allowed myself to be deceived by sin. I'm so sorry. Please forgive me. Forgive any remnant of unbelief. Help me move from belief that to belief in. Please give me the gift of faith. Give me a double portion of faith. I want an Abraham kind of faith that hopes against hope. That believes in Your ability and desire to speak that which is not as though it is.

Father, You have rescued me from the kingdom of darkness and transferred me into the kingdom of the Son of Your love, and yet I don't live that way. I'm sorry for trusting more in the power of the enemy than in Your power and authority. I'm sorry I haven't done what You said to do. But I want to. With all that I am, I want to. I want a Hebrews 11 kind of faith. The kind that pleases You and that You write about.

Holy Spirit, come fill me now with faith. Father, in my weakness I have chosen unbelief because it's easier. Because it requires nothing. Forgive me. Help my unbelief. Lord, my enemy is fear. So, in agreement with Your Word, I rebuke, bind, cast down, reject, and repel the spirit of fear in my life now and forever. Get out! Go! I'm calling you out. You must flee now in the name of Jesus.

And where there is a generational curse of fear passed to me by my ancestors, I break that curse in the name and by the blood of Jesus. I proclaim that Jesus has given me—past tense—a spirit of power, love, and a sound mind. I receive the Holy Spirit now and release Him to abound and grow in my life. Father, please show me as we walk out of here any place where I am encouraging my own faithlessness. Please show me any door of unbelief. Please show me any wound of my past or experience that is limiting or hindering my deeper faith in You.

Father, please reveal what is hidden in me that limits me or causes me to be fearful or unbelieving. Lastly, I thank You for the gift of faith, and I receive it. I open my eyes, my ears, my head, and especially my heart to faith. Father, I believe. I believe in You, in all You did, and all You said to do. And from this day forward, I have a God kind of faith that obeys— that preaches the kingdom, heals the sick, casts out demons, cleanses the lepers, and raises the dead. In Jesus' name.

For some of you that might be the first time you prayed something like that. No worries. You're in good company. In order for it to sink in, you might pray it a few times. It's like anything in life; practice brings about muscle memory. To help your muscle remember, write it out in your own hand. Take my prayer above, and write it out on the page next to this one, and then add to it. Make it your own. Change where needed. If you need more space, use a legal pad. Martin Luther isn't the only one who gets to have fun. Write your own prayer of faith, your proclamation of what you believe, and then nail it to the door of your house. Trust me, if you're wanting an occasion to talk about your faith, this prayer nailed to your door will do just that.

CHAPTER 8

The Holy Spirit

Jesus has brought them to the Mount of Olives. He is leaving, but they don't know it. He does. Just before His feet lift up from earth, He tells them: "Thus it is written, that the Christ should suffer and on the third day rise from the dead, and that repentance for the forgiveness of sins should be proclaimed in his name to all nations, beginning from Jerusalem. You are witnesses of these things. And behold, I am sending *the promise of my Father* upon you. But stay in the city until you are *clothed with power* from on high."[1]

The disciples return. Worship daily in the temple. The wait drags on. A week passes. They begin trying to remember what He said while He was still with them. Then the memories return: after He washed their feet the night before He was crucified. The last words He spoke to them as a group. The last words of a man who knows He's going to die: "And I will ask the Father, and he will give you another *Helper*, to be with you forever, even the *Spirit of truth*, whom the world cannot receive, because it neither sees him nor knows him. You know him, for he dwells with you and will be in you. I will not leave you as orphans; I will come to you. Yet a little while and the world will see me no more, but you will see me."[2]

Upon hearing this, Judas (not Iscariot) speaks for the group. "Lord, how is it that you will manifest yourself to us, and not to the world?"[3]

It's an honest question, and everyone is thinking it.

Jesus answers him, "If anyone loves me, he will keep my word, and my Father will love him, and we will come to him and make our home with him. Whoever does not love me does not keep my words. And the word that you hear is not mine but the Father's who sent me. These things I have spoken to you while I am still with you. But the *Helper*, the *Holy Spirit*, whom the Father will send in my name, he will teach you all things and bring to your remembrance all that I have said to you."[4]

Then just to make sure they are listening, Jesus says it again: "But when the *Helper* comes, whom I will send to you from the Father, the *Spirit of truth*, who proceeds from the Father, he will bear witness about me. And you also will bear witness, because you have been with me from the beginning."[5]

Then, just before He is arrested, hoping it sinks in, He says it a third time: "It is to your advantage that I go away, for if I do not go away, the *Helper* will not come to you. But if I go, I will send him to you. And when he comes, he will convict the world concerning sin and righteousness and judgment: concerning sin, because they do not believe in me; concerning righteousness, because I go to the Father, and you will see me no longer."[6]

I'm not sure the disciples have any real context for this. I think most are standing there scratching their heads. This is speculation on my part, but I think every time they hear Jesus say the word "Helper" or "Spirit," they immediately think of the words of King David: *"O Lord, be my helper!"* (Ps. 30:10); *"God is my helper"* (Ps. 54:4); *"The Lord is on my side as my helper"* (Ps. 118:7). And, *"Cast me not away from Your presence, and take not your Holy Spirit from me"* (Ps. 51:11).

Or, maybe they remember these words of Jesus: *"What father among you, if his son asks for a fish, will instead of a fish give him a serpent; or if he asks for an egg, will give him a scorpion? If you then, who are evil, know how to give good gifts to your children, how much more will the heavenly Father give the Holy Spirit to those who ask him!"* (Luke 11:11–13).

Waiting in the Upper Room, the disciples know they are waiting on someone, but they don't have much to go on. They do know He will come from the Father, He will teach them, bear witness about Jesus, and help them remember what Jesus told them while He was with them. They also know

He will be a Spirit, He will help them and empower them (but in what way they're not sure), and He will convict the world, but that's about all they know.

And given their experience with Jesus, they have no idea what's about to happen.

So they wait. In the same way that the crucifixion and resurrection are historical facts, so is Pentecost. It happened. God did, in fact, pour out His Spirit on all flesh. This immediately gives rise to a question: Did Jesus intend that release of His Spirit in and through them as a one-time event, or is the power at work at Pentecost available to work within us? Equally?

We can argue semantics over whether the Spirit falls on us or baptizes us from without or wells up from within us. And I realize the phrase "baptism in the Holy Spirit" is difficult for some. Lord knows it's been abused. But my point is that we have become comfortable with a powerless gospel. I'm not okay with that. Neither is Jesus. According to Scripture, to walk in the power we are commanded to walk in we must first receive His Spirit and give Him permission to be released in and through us. We are conduits, not cul-de-sacs. Streams, not puddles.

Can I argue that everyone at Pentecost functioned in all the gifts? No. But I do know that "the . . . Spirit . . . apportions to each one individually as he wills" (1 Cor. 12:11). And Paul does tell us to "earnestly desire the higher gifts" (1 Cor 12:31). More than once (see 1 Cor. 14:1). If you say that you have received the Spirit of Christ Jesus, have you released Him to do as He wills? Have you put a collar on Him or cut Him loose? I'm not advocating chaos. I'm championing surrender. Absolute yielding.

If You Were Your Enemy

Let me ask you this: If you were your enemy, and you knew Jesus had promised to not only send His Spirit but fill you with Him and then dwell in you so that you'd be empowered to be His witness and actually do the stuff He commanded us to do, how hard would you work to prevent that? What exactly would you do to stop it?

Let me ask it this way: What if you knew that Jesus' followers needed power to defeat you, and you knew that the source of that power was the Holy Spirit. How hard would you work to subvert everything about that source of power? Is there anything you would *not* do, and is there any extent to which you would *not* go to attack that idea and that power?

If I were your enemy, I'd wage a frontal assault on the idea that Pentecost actually happened in the first place. Then I'd simultaneously argue that if it did happen, it happened only for a select few and no one else and whatever they received died with them. Then I'd chip away at what the Spirit did when those who had received Him released Him to do as He willed. Then I'd attack the credibility of anyone who actually believed this archaic "nonsense" and claimed to walk in that power, and I'd work overtime to discredit any signs and wonders that followed.

In short, there's nothing I wouldn't do to keep believers from actually believing what Jesus claimed about His Spirit and *the* promise of the Father. Prophecy is real. Tongue-speaking is real. Interpretation is real. Miracles are real. Healings are real. Discerning of spirits is real. Casting out the demonic is real. It would be easy here to get axle-wrapped around one thing, but God is the giver of the gifts, and some of us wouldn't know the Holy Spirit if He kissed us on the cheek. And because of this, we are missing the power and the joy and the fight.

According to Jesus, it was His desire while He was here, and it was His desire when He left, and it is still His desire, that *every* believer be filled with—baptized with—His Spirit.

When John introduced Jesus, he said, "I myself did not know him, but he who sent me to baptize with water said to me, 'He on whom you see the Spirit descend and remain, this is he who baptizes with the Holy Spirit'" (John 1:33). Two things: from the beginning, John identifies Jesus as not only the Lamb of God who takes away the sin of the world, *but also* as the One who will baptize with the Holy Spirit. And the image is clear: "I'm dunking you in water. Soaking you from head to toe. He's going to do the same with His Spirit." Secondly, God told him Jesus would do this. It has always been God's design that His children are baptized in His Spirit.

Other than the crucifixion and resurrection, there are only two events shared by all Gospels: the feeding of the five thousand and John's statement about Jesus: "I baptize you with water for repentance, but he who is coming after me is mightier than I, whose sandals I am not worthy to carry. He will baptize you with the Holy Spirit and fire. His winnowing fork is in his hand, and he will clear his threshing floor and gather his wheat into the barn, but the chaff he will burn with unquenchable fire" (Matt. 3:11–12 [Mark 1:8; Luke 3:16; John 1:33]). Every writer, speaking through the inspiration of the Holy Spirit, thought it significant to include this description of Jesus. They wanted to make it clear that this is what He—Jesus—will do for us and to us.

Jesus reminded us of John's introduction just before His ascension: "Wait for the promise of the Father, which, he said, 'you heard from me, for John baptized with water, but you will be baptized with the Holy Spirit not many days from now'" (Acts 1:4–5).

You and I have a problem, and it's twofold: first, our enemy has worked tirelessly to pervert, corrupt, weaken, even eradicate our perception of and our desire for the Holy Spirit since Pentecost. To poke fun at Him. To mock Him. To belittle and make Him seem less than. To enthrone our minds so that we look down on the work of the Holy Spirit and what we might not understand. Secondly, our enemy has used broken, selfish, and evil people who have misused the power of the Holy Spirit to cause us to want nothing to do with Him or them. We have channels of TV preachers who give us ample excuse to run the other direction. Preachers who claim, "the Holy Spirit said," when I really doubt the Holy Spirit said anything of the sort. If there is one area of the church where we have seen the greatest abuse, it may well be right here.

Life Is Warfare

Let me pause and reiterate something I said in *What If It's True?* Life is warfare. You are in a fight whether you like it or not, whether you invited it or not, whether you agree or not, and you've been in that fight since before you opened your eyes on planet earth. And to make things interesting, you didn't start it, your enemy doesn't care that you didn't start it, you cannot see him with your physical eyes, and it is a fight to the death. Right this second, you have an enemy who wants to enslave you, dominate you, and kill you.

Period.

And one of his most powerful weapons is to make you think he's not real and/or that he's more powerful than your God.

Paul knew the church needed to understand this, which is why he wrote this to the church in Ephesus: "Be strong in the Lord and in the strength of his might. . . . For we do not wrestle against flesh and blood, but against the rulers, against the authorities, against the cosmic powers over this present darkness, against the spiritual forces of evil in the heavenly places" (Eph. 6:10, 12). Paul's assumption is that we do wrestle. It's close. Hand to hand. But it's not with physical bodies.

To the church in Corinth, he said: "For though we walk in the flesh, we are not waging war according to the flesh. For the weapons of our warfare are not of the flesh but have divine power to destroy strongholds. We destroy arguments and every lofty opinion raised against the knowledge of God" (2 Cor. 10:3–5). Another translation reads, "pulling down strongholds [and] casting down arguments" (NKJV). The assumption is we do wage war. We destroy and pull down. And we do so with weapons that have divine power and that are not of the flesh.

John, in his Revelation, when looking at the last days and the battle with satan, said, "they have conquered him by the blood of the Lamb and by the word of their testimony, for they loved not their lives even unto death" (Rev. 12:11). The assumption is that in order for there to be a conquering, there is first a battle and one side "conquers" the other. And we're not playing for pizza. It's a life-and-death struggle.

The Father has known this since before the foundation of the world. Before there was war here, there was war in heaven. He knew that if He sent us out in the same way He sent His Son, we would need empowering. Why? Because we're in a power struggle.

These are the words of John: "Little children, you are from God and have overcome them, for he who is in you is greater than he who is in the world" (1 John 4:4).

This is Paul: "The god of this world has blinded the minds of the unbelievers, to keep them from seeing the light of the gospel of the glory of Christ, who is the image of God" (2 Cor. 4:4).

And this is Peter: "Be sober-minded, be watchful. Your adversary the devil prowls around like a roaring lion, seeking someone to devour" (1 Peter 5:8).

Jesus Himself said, "And if Satan is divided against himself, how will his kingdom stand?" (Luke 11:18). Don't miss the fact that satan does have a kingdom. And according to Paul, that kingdom is organized and has various levels of rulerships or principalities.

John again in his revelation: "Then the dragon became furious with the woman and went off to make war on the rest of her offspring, on those who keep the commandments of God and hold to the testimony of Jesus" (Rev. 12:17). Do you keep Jesus' commands? Do you hold to His testimony? Then, by default, you have an enemy who is making war on you whether you like it or not.

One more: Daniel was fasting and praying for the people of Israel. In his own words, he was "mourning" (Dan. 10:2). Three weeks passed and nothing happened. Crickets. Finally, he met a messenger of the Lord. The messenger said, "From the first day that you set your heart to understand and humbled yourself before your God, your words have been heard, and I have come because of your words. The prince of the kingdom of Persia withstood me twenty-one days, but Michael, one of the chief princes, came to help me" (vv. 12–13).

Daniel's prayers set all of heaven in motion. He was heard, and a response sent as soon as he prayed. The first day. But the angel had to fight his way through the kingdom of darkness to get to Daniel. And he needed help to break through. There was real struggle. And real war. This is not specific to just Daniel. It includes all of us who keep Jesus' commands and hold to His testimony.

Paul said to the church in Corinth, "I know a man in Christ who fourteen years ago was caught up to the third heaven" (2 Cor. 12:2). If there is a third, there must logically be a first and second. I believe the first is the heaven we can see, the second is inhabited by the enemy because he was "cast down," and the third is the seat of the throne of God. Can I prove this delineation? No. But it does help paint a picture to explain the nature of the warfare that we face.

My point is this: if we do not acknowledge the enemy's presence and his hatred of us and warfare against us, and if we don't obey and receive both God's Word and His Spirit, then we have folded our hands in defeat and we are powerless against the enemy. Further, if we put limitations on the extent to which we do receive His Spirit, and/or the extent to which we release Him to empower and work through us, then we put limitations on the extent to which we can defeat the enemy.

All of hell is hell-bent on stealing glory from God. Everything he does is geared toward the thievery of glory. You and I wake up daily in a world where the enemy is waging war to prevent you from receiving the Spirit, and being willing to let Him work through us as He desires.

I am trying to make the argument that you cannot do this on your own. You need help. God knew this. He provided a way. Hence, Pentecost and the command to "receive the Holy Spirit." Right this second, God is standing in front of us, holding out His hand, offering His Spirit.

He's offering. Making good on His promise.

I will you ask one more time: Have you received the Holy Spirit *and* if so, have you released Him, have you given Him permission to work through you in whatever way He desires, no matter what that looks like?

Back to the Upper Room

Following Jesus' ascension, this ragtag group of believers has spent their time in the city of Jerusalem, worshipping Him and blessing God in the temple. Scripture also says they were filled with great joy.[7]

Who's in the room? Luke recorded that Peter, John, James, Andrew, Philip, Thomas, Bartholomew, Matthew, James the son of Alphaeus, Simon the Zealot, Judas the son of James, several women, Mary the mother of Jesus, and His brothers were there. Luke also records they were all in unity and devoting themselves to prayer.[8]

How long have they been waiting? Jesus was raised from the dead on the third day, and we know He presented Himself to them on the evening of that day. He then spent forty days with them, so it's possible He ascended to the Father on the forty-third day after His crucifixion. Why does this matter? Because it suggests the disciples have been waiting in the Jerusalem room for about a week with the door shut due to a healthy fear of Roman soldiers doing to them what they did to Jesus.

Finally, the day of Pentecost arrives. "Pentecost" is actually the Greek name for the Jewish feast called Feast of Harvest or Feast of Weeks, which occurred fifty days after Passover.[9] The Jews celebrated two harvests each year. The early harvest of May and June and the latter harvest of the fall. Leviticus 23:16 says to count seven weeks or "fifty days" from the end of Passover to the beginning of the next holiday which was called the Festival of Weeks, or Weeks in the vernacular. From this stretch of time, the Greek-speaking Jews coined the phrase Pentecost, or "fifty days." The reason for observing or celebrating the feast was rather simple. God told the people through Moses: "You shall remember that you were a slave in Egypt."[10]

So this group of people is gathered in Jerusalem, whether in an upper room or in the temple, I do not know, but they are gathered and they are remembering that they were once slaves. Which can be said of all of us.

It also means there are a lot of Jews in Jerusalem. Certainly, the most since Passover. The Feast of Weeks is one of three times during the year when all the Jewish males were commanded to appear in Jerusalem.[11] The streets are swimming with heads of households and their households. Which will be significant when Peter stands on the southern steps of the temple to speak his first sermon.

Now let's turn our attention to the kingdom of heaven. Specifically, the throne room. The seat of God Most High, Possessor of heaven and earth. The Ancient of Days. After a thirty-three year absence, Jesus, the only begotten Son of God, has returned. The sinless Son has come home. All of heaven, hundreds of millions in attendance, wait at the door with bated breath. They are giddy with expectation. God the Father sits on His throne tapping His fingers. The angels drive the chariot homeward, through the first heaven, through the second, and into the third—the throne room of God. The epicenter of this universe and every other.

The chariot stops at the doors to heaven, and Jesus exits wearing what He wore when He left—a loincloth. Like David before the ark, the King is returning to the Holy Jerusalem. Doorkeepers whisper, *"Welcome home King of all kings . . . King of Glory,"* and then swing wide the doors where all of heaven hits their faces. Prostrate. Laid out. Every lip pressed to the crystal-clear floor of heaven. Hands raised. Infinite worship. Every voice singing "Holy is the Lord" at the top of their lungs. Jesus returns. He's home.

No sooner has His foot cleared the threshold than God the Father launches Himself off His throne. He will wait no longer. He crosses the expanse of heaven in a thunderbolt, wraps His arms around His Son and covers His face in kisses. Smearing the tears He has held for thirty-three years across a face that had been marred more than any of the sons of men. (I know Scripture says there are no tears in heaven. I think that Scripture is talking about ours. We will have no tears in heaven. And He will dry our eyes. I don't think that Scripture is suggesting that God doesn't know sorrow. I think He does. If we have seen Jesus, we've seen the Father. And Jesus wept over Jerusalem. Over you and me.)

Before all of heaven, God the Father welcomes home the obedient, righteous, spotless, victorious, conquering Son. Heaven erupts. The roar is deafening. The elation inescapable. Jesus lifts chins, hugs friends, kisses children, laughs, sings. Then like David before the ark, Jesus dances to the throne. Where the elders have yet to come off their faces. Where their crowns have been cast at His feet. Jesus dances through heaven. Flinging sweat from His fingertips. Joy untold. Children join him, twirling in circles, climb on Him like a jungle gym. Mothers and fathers laugh, sing, cry. The Son is home! He did it. Jesus won. He defeated . . . everything. He ransomed and redeemed all of mankind with His very own blood. Forever. Rendering an irrefutable and irrevocable defeat to the enemy.

Reaching God's throne, the Father clothes His Son. A banquet awaits. He is given a new robe. His train fills the temple. Sword. Ring. Crown. Diadem. Jesus' hair is white. Eyes flames of fire. Feet burnished bronze. During the clothing, God the Father glances at the wounds in His hands, feet, and side. It's obvious He doesn't like them. They have no place in heaven. The Father touches each tenderly, ending at the hole in His side, then He speaks a word, and the wounds disappear. No scar. No residue. Jesus is perfect. All of heaven rejoices. Angels swing from the rafters. Millions upon millions upon millions dance, sing, laugh. Unhindered freedom and inexpressible joy. Jesus joins in and works His way through the crowd. The rumble of the Father's laughter is heard and felt one heaven down.

One thing remains. The Father grants His kingdom to His Son and gives Him the seat to His right. And then He gives Him the name at which every knee will bow and every tongue confess. Jesus is not just the ruler of a kingdom. He is the ruler of *the* kingdom. He is all-powerful, all-knowing, and everywhere—both inside of time and outside of it. There is no power that can contend with His. And on His throne, His enemies have been made His footstool. He is the only King and there is no other.

A week passes and as the celebration continues, the Father turns to the third member of the Godhead. His Spirit. Holiness is his name. The Father intends to make good on His promise. The Spirit hugs the Father and the Son. They have been together since the beginning. The Spirit hovered over the waters at creation, and nothing that has ever been created was created without the Spirit. He has been intimately involved in every creative act performed at the will of the Father. And on the earth below, His next creation awaits. Possibly His most beautiful. His most magnificent.

The Father turns to the Spirit. "You ready?" The Spirit looks to and fro across the earth beneath. Scanning all of mankind. Throughout the ages. There is much work yet to be done. He nods. "Been ready." The Father laughs, opens His lungs, fills them to capacity, and exhales. The roar of heaven. Niagara. The break at pipeline. A hurricane absent the carnage. The sound shakes the foundations of the mountains and the oceans on earth beneath.

The Spirit smiles. He's been waiting eagerly for this moment. He loves to create, and because of the shed blood of Jesus, a new creation awaits. He is giddy with the thought that He gets to press His lips to those of us who will receive Him and fill us with His breath. To take residence in us. To dwell in us. To share with us the love of and intimacy with the Father. He exits the throne room with a swan dive, careening to earth like a lightning bolt bathed in the shouts, cheers, and cries of victory. At the speed of both light and sound, He roars His way earthward. To His new home. The new temple that is man.

You and me.

And there in Jerusalem, oblivious as to what, or rather who, is coming, the roof starts to shake. And it sounds like a freight train is about to split the room down the middle.

"They were all together in one place. And suddenly there came from heaven a sound like a mighty rushing wind, and it filled the entire house [some suggest the word *house* could better be interpreted "temple"] where they were sitting. And divided tongues as of fire appeared to them and rested on each one of them. And they were all filled with the Holy Spirit and began to speak in other tongues as the Spirit gave them utterance."[12]

Now look at the reaction of those who saw this:

There were dwelling in Jerusalem Jews, devout men from every nation under heaven. And at this sound the multitude came together, and they were bewildered, because each one was hearing them speak in his own language. And they were amazed and astonished, saying, "Are not all these who are speaking Galileans? And how is it that we hear, each of us in his own native language? Parthians and Medes and Elamites and residents of Mesopotamia, Judea and Cappadocia, Pontus and Asia, Phrygia and Pamphylia, Egypt and the parts of Libya belonging to

Cyrene, and visitors from Rome, both Jews and proselytes, Cretans and Arabians—we hear them telling in our own tongues the mighty works of God." And all were amazed and perplexed, saying to one another, "What does this mean?" But others mocking said, "They are filled with new wine."[13]

Some are bewildered, amazed, and astonished. Others mock. "They're drunk." It's always been this way.

An amazing thing happens next. Peter, whose last public act was to deny Jesus, stands on the southern steps of the temple, opens his mouth, and throws down the gauntlet. Peter in the garden of Gethsemane had a sword in his hand. Now he's got one in his mouth, and it may well be the best sermon ever given by a follower of Jesus.

But Peter, standing with the eleven, lifted up his voice and addressed them: "Men of Judea and all who dwell in Jerusalem, let this be known to you, and give ear to my words. For these people are not drunk, as you suppose, since it is only the third hour of the day. But this is what was uttered through the prophet Joel: 'And in the last days it shall be, God declares, that I will pour out my Spirit on all flesh, and your sons and your daughters shall prophesy, and your young men shall see visions, and your old men shall dream dreams; even on my male servants and female servants in those days I will pour out my Spirit, and they shall prophesy. And I will show wonders in the heavens above and signs on the earth below, blood, and fire, and vapor of smoke; the sun shall be turned to darkness and the moon to blood, before the day of the Lord comes, the great and magnificent day. And it shall come to pass that everyone who calls upon the name of the Lord shall be saved.'

"Men of Israel, hear these words: Jesus of Nazareth, a man attested to you by God with mighty works and wonders and signs that God did through him in your midst, as you yourselves know—this Jesus, delivered up according to the definite plan and foreknowledge of God, you crucified and killed by the hands of lawless men. God raised him up, loosing the pangs of death, because it was not possible for him to be held by it. For David says concerning him, 'I saw the Lord always before me, for he is at my right hand that I may not be shaken; therefore my heart was glad, and my tongue rejoiced; my flesh also will dwell in hope. For you will not abandon my soul to Hades, or let your Holy One see corruption. You have made known to me the paths of life; you will make me full of gladness with your presence.'

"Brothers, I may say to you with confidence about the patriarch David that he both died and was buried, and his tomb is with us to this day. Being therefore a prophet, and knowing that God had sworn with an oath to him that he would set one of his descendants on his throne, he foresaw and spoke about the resurrection of the Christ, that he was not abandoned to Hades, nor did his flesh see corruption. This Jesus God raised up, and of that we all are witnesses. Being therefore exalted at the right hand of God, and having received from the Father the promise of the Holy Spirit, he has poured out this that you yourselves are seeing and hearing. For David did not ascend into the heavens, but he himself says, 'the Lord said to my Lord, "sit at my right hand, until I make your enemies your footstool."' Let all the house of Israel therefore know for certain that God has made him both Lord and Christ, this Jesus whom you crucified."

Now when they heard this they were cut to the heart, and said to Peter and the rest of the apostles, "Brothers, what shall we do?"

And Peter said to them, "Repent and be baptized every one of you in the name of Jesus Christ for the forgiveness of your sins, and you will receive the gift of the Holy Spirit. For the promise is for you and for your children and for all who are far off, everyone whom the Lord our God calls to himself." And with many other words he bore witness and continued to exhort them, saying, "Save yourselves from this crooked generation." So those who received his word were baptized, and there were added that day about three thousand souls.[14]

There's a lot here so keep a finger on this page; we're coming back to it. First, in a beautiful act of mercy, Peter gets a do-over, and with the whole world as his stage, he is now counted as a believer. A follower. One of Jesus' own. No denial this time. Peter is doing now what Jesus asked him to do on the beach. He is shepherding the flock and feeding His sheep with spiritual food. And Jesus' prayer is coming true—Peter's faith is not failing him.

Secondly, the proof of Jesus' divinity is Scripture. Look with what ease Peter quotes Joel and David. How seamlessly a prophet and the psalmist fill his language. Peter demonstrates how he can and does now view Scripture through the lens of how it reveals Jesus. That Scripture is *the* revelation of Jesus.

Thirdly, he's clear in his diagnosis: "You killed the Christ. You are a long way from God and you will die in your sin. But that's not His desire."

Lastly, he ends with a simple command. Peter's first public command is also the first public command of John the Baptist, Jesus, Stephen, Paul, and it is commanded in five of seven of the letters to the churches in Revelation: *repent*. The only way to a right relationship with Jesus and the Father begins with repentance. Period. Total surrender. No exceptions.

Then he finishes with one final word: "Receive the gift of the Holy Spirit."

In my way of understanding there are several spiritually significant moments in history: creation, the death and resurrection of Jesus, the pouring out of His Spirit, and His return. In my read of the Gospels, everything was looking forward to and building up to Pentecost. Jesus Himself pointed us to it. And on that day, something was birthed. In our traditions of faith, we primarily look to the cross and the resurrection—and don't think for a second that I am reducing their significance. But once resurrected, Jesus Himself looked to Pentecost.

As well we should.

Does He Still Do Today What He Did Then?

Some argue that the Holy Spirit is no longer functioning the way He did in the book of Acts. I say that's a lie from the pit of hell, and the only one who has anything to gain by it is the enemy. "Well," you say, "my church doesn't do any of that." I understand. And you're not alone. There are a lot of churches who have no expression of the gifts of the Holy Spirit. But who are you listening to, your church or the Word? Again, I go back to Mark 7. It is the traditions of men that make void or nullify the Word of God. So, have you in your traditions made void the work of the Holy Spirit in your life? In your church? If so, do you really want to live that way?

The disciples did nothing in the kingdom until they had received the promise of the Father—and that promise was and is His Spirit poured out and into them, flowing through them. Only then did they turn the world upside down. And only then were their own lives turned upside down. Jesus is King of a kingdom, and in His kingdom His subjects receive His Spirit. "For all who are led by the Spirit of God are sons of God" (Rom. 8:14). Peter didn't know how to preach on the southern steps of the temple in Acts 2:14 until he'd received the Holy Spirit. For the early believers, Matthew 10 and Mark 16 only became possible once the Spirit of God had filled them, clothed them, and endued them with power.

I've been doing this long enough to know there is vigorous discussion over this whole "baptism of the Holy Spirit" thing and whether or not it's a "second baptism" or it occurred immediately when you believed. Several modern-day traditions hold that you and I received the Holy Spirit when we obeyed Romans 10:9—when we confessed, believed, and were born again. Opposite that are several modern-day faiths who argue for a second event.

Let's look at Scripture—there are multiple examples from Scripture to support the "second baptism" theory. Obviously, the disciples at Pentecost are Exhibit A before the jury. So are several others. But before we declare that the only way, there's also Paul's question in Acts 19 to the new believers at the church in Ephesus: "Did you receive the Holy Spirit when you believed?" (Acts 19:2). Implied within his question is the possibility that they could have. Meaning, according to Paul, it was possible.

Personally, I don't care whether you received the Spirit when you first believed or whether it occurred later. The timetable matters not. What does matter to me is Paul's question: "Did you receive Him?" And you'd know if you did. He's a He. A person. You know when you meet someone. Some of what we argue about is semantics, so let's keep the main thing the main thing: Did you receive Him? And if so, my next question would again be, Where is the evidence? Because for those who did receive Him, there was evidence.

Regardless of how you and I answer these questions, for most of us, there is one question that has been left out of our tradition and our experience, and our enemy loves its exclusion: "Did you receive the Holy Spirit when you believed?" (Acts 19:2).

Well?

Think before you answer. Really. Wrestle with this. Don't take someone else's word for it. Don't tell me what your church would tell me. Don't tell me what your tradition would tell me. If the answer is yes, then where is the evidence? And don't compare yourself to the culture you live in. Compare yourself to the book of Acts. Do signs and wonders follow? I'm not asking this question with my finger in your face. I'm asking with my arm around your shoulder. Walking side by side. I want this for you and I want this for me, and if we're going to walk where He's leading, we'll need His Spirit. Plus, it's a lot more fun.

I'm also not asking this question to make you into something you're not or get you to join some group or compare you to another group. What's more, your answer doesn't have to satisfy me. You don't even have to answer me. I'm asking you in writing in this book so you can take it to the Lord. You'll never meet me in the street or church or wherever with my finger poking you in the chest, "Hey—where's the evidence?" Lord forbid. I'm just asking you to hold up your life to the lives of those in Acts and compare. Was their experience yours? You be the judge.

According to Paul, the Spirit at work produces fruit. This is Paul detailing that fruit for the church in Corinth:

Now there are varieties of gifts, but the same Spirit; and there are varieties of service, but the same Lord; and there are varieties of activities,
but it is the same God who empowers them all in everyone. To each is
given the manifestation of the Spirit for the common good. For to one
is given through the Spirit the utterance of wisdom, and to another the
utterance of knowledge according to the same Spirit, to another faith by
the same Spirit, to another gifts of healing by the one Spirit, to another
the working of miracles, to another prophecy, to another the ability
to distinguish between spirits, to another various kinds of tongues, to
another the interpretation of tongues. All these are empowered by one
and the same Spirit, who apportions to each one individually as he wills.
(1 Cor. 12:4–11)

Does any of this describe you?

I'm trying to challenge each of us to step outside the confines of our
upbringing or our biases or prejudices and just look at the Word and at the
lives of those who loved Him and followed Him, and to say, "They did it; I
want it." In the book of Acts, in the lives of the apostles, there was evidence
of the baptism of the Holy Spirit. Why should our lives look any different?
I know that we, individually and collectively, have all kinds of baggage
from labels like Pentecostal, to charismatic—which is probably just a
kinder label of a Pentecostal—to the host of late-night television propaga-
tors with big hair and expensive jets and girlfriends their wives don't know
about, to snake handlers and strychnine drinkers, to name-it-and-claim-it
screamers, and more. I get it. I do. I've seen them. Heard them.

*But none of that and none of them excuses you and me from looking at the
Word and saying, "That's what it says. I want to be obedient. Come, Holy Spirit."*

The Holy Spirit was promised by God thorough the prophets long
before Jesus. When here, Jesus said He would go to the Father and send
His Spirit. He did that. Pentecost proved it. Since that moment, there's
been a war, an all-out war, to cause us to look down our noses and
reject Him.

I don't want to do that anymore. I don't want to ever look into the face of my King and tell Him that I rejected the most precious thing He could send me, His Spirit. Even if that means that I look foolish to all of mankind.

If you think otherwise, whose fool are you?

Through Jesus, the Father has offered us a gift. I want to receive that gift. No matter what the gift looks or sounds like. Because He gives good gifts. Every time.

Trust me, I get your apprehension. Me too. As a child, I saw the beauty and power and wonder of the charismatic movement morph into charismania as believers moved away from the Word and gravitated toward experience. And while this is dangerous, so is the flip side—where we want nothing to do with the baptism. Where we lock the Spirit in a box and throw away the key. Jesus wants us to have both His Word and His Spirit. It's not either-or. It's both-and. In fact, they're inseparable.

Those who witnessed the outpouring of the Holy Spirit on Pentecost accused those who had been filled as being drunk with wine. Peter's response was that it's only the third hour of the day (9:00 a.m.). Would anyone ever look at your walk with Jesus and accuse you of being drunk? Sure, you can take my question too far, but is it valid? Is there anything about your having been filled with the Holy Spirit that takes you out of your comfort zone?

For many of us, our churches are comfortable and our expression of worship is comfortable—and yet when I compare us to the book of Acts, I see some glaring differences. I'm not down on our churches. We should all be in one. I thank God for His bride and I love my church. But the believers in Acts were willing to look foolish, to risk their precious dignity, for whatever the Spirit wanted. Are you? When David danced before the ark, he described himself as "undignified."[15] Is there room in your life, and in your church, for unhindered expression? To dance in the presence of God?

While I'm praising expressive worship, I've also seen practitioners of the baptism descend into chaos and claim it is fruit. God is the God of freedom, not chaos. There's a difference.

We Have Enthroned Our Mind

We, as a culture, put such priority on our ability to rationally understand something, that we can't quite make sense of what isn't sensical. Maybe this is one of the true ripple effects of Descartes: "I think therefore I am." We have enthroned our idolatrous appetite for control through reason over childlike obedience to the Father. Our problem is that we've enthroned our mind above our spirit. But we bump into trouble because we are spiritual beings housed in a soul, living in a physical body. By enthroning our mind and our ability to reason above our spirit, we've subjugated the Spirit to the soul, requiring it to exit and enter our body through the skeptical and doubting filter of our mind. King David knew this. It's why he often commanded his soul in the Psalms (Pss. 42–43). Even humbled it with fasting (Ps. 69:10).

I know this is a huge rabbit trail and we could get lost in here, but if what I'm saying is true, we have a problem. And the problem is rather simple: we think we know better. Which is ugly arrogance. And your enemy is happy you think you know better. God gave us each a mind, for which I'm grateful, but it is the spirit of man which possesses wisdom and understands (Eph. 1:17; Dan. 5:14; Acts 6:3; Isa. 11:2). Paul said it this way: "Now we have received not the spirit of the world, but the Spirit who is from God, that we might understand the things freely given us by God. And we impart this in words not taught by human wisdom but taught by the Spirit, interpreting spiritual truths to those who are spiritual" (1 Cor. 2:12–13).

If the Holy Spirit sat down next to you right now and held out His hand, and in His hand was a gift, would you refuse it? We would fight over miracles and healing, but what if it was the gift of tongues? Think about the absolute absurdity of refusing anything He would offer.

Most of us are afraid of looking foolish. But therein lies the tension. We're more concerned with how we look to others rather than being a vessel of the Holy Spirit—which is both fear and pride. Both of which need to be crucified.

What if the Holy Spirit wants to pour out every good gift in you? Healings, miracles, prophecy, knowledge, tongues, interpretation. Would you accept them? And how? With or without limitations? What if accepting them meant He would push you out of your comfort zone? Do you think Jesus is looking to pour out His Spirit on a people who cherry-pick what gifts they want—"I'll take that one but You can keep that one"—or a people who open up and say, "Here I am. I'm available. Have Your way, Lord."

The Pendulum Swing

There is another swing to this pendulum that is equally dangerous. It's to so remove our minds that we open ourselves up to any spirit that would have us. We "empty" ourselves and welcome all comers. The result is chaos and ownership by a spirit that is not the Holy Spirit. Or we claim a move of the Holy Spirit when it's nothing of the sort. This is not wise, and we will get to the remedy shortly. Scripture says in the last days, "False christs and false prophets will arise and perform great signs and wonders, so as to lead astray, if possible, even the elect" (Matt. 24:24).

Signs and wonders don't necessarily verify or guarantee the presence of the Holy Spirit. When Moses went to Pharaoh, Jannes and Jambres opposed him and performed miraculous signs and wonders. When Peter and John went to Samaria in Acts 8, they bumped into a man named Simon. Simon was a magician who claimed to be someone great, and as a result, the people of Samaria said of him, "'This man is the power of God that is called Great.' And they paid attention to him because for a long time he had amazed them with his magic" (Acts 8:10–11). When Peter and John laid their hands on the people of Samaria, and the people of Samaria received the Holy Spirit, Simon saw the power they now exercised and said to Peter and John, "Give me this power also, so that anyone on whom I lay my hands may receive the Holy Spirit" (v. 19).

Notice Simon's words though. He didn't ask for Jesus. He wanted nothing to do with relationship. He wanted power. Period. Peter picked up on this quickly and rebuked him, "May your silver perish with you, because you thought you could obtain the gift of God with money! You have neither part nor lot in this matter, for your heart is not right before God. Repent, therefore, of this wickedness of yours, and pray to the Lord that, if possible, the intent of your heart may be forgiven you. For I see that you are in the gall of bitterness and in the bond of iniquity" (Acts 8:20–23). Simon's response to Peter was telling. He said, "Pray for me to the Lord, that nothing of what you have said may come upon me" (v. 24).

Here's my point: the pendulum can swing both ways. Just as there is danger in rejecting the baptism of the Holy Spirit outright, there is also danger that we receive Him only for the power He brings.

Years ago, I was in Nicaragua with a group of guys. Ministry stuff. We were walking the streets of León, one of my favorite towns. A man stopped us and asked us about our group. Evidently, we stuck out. Gringos do that. (I think he had seen us pray for someone in a coffee shop.) Interestingly, as soon as he stopped us, my radar started dinging; and the more questions he asked us, the more I began thinking about Simon the sorcerer and Acts 8. Standing in the street, one of my buddies began telling him about Jesus. About how Jesus has healed him (my buddy) from disease. Our friend in the street nodded receptively. He, too, wanted healing and he wanted to pray for people. But he also had an answer for everything, and it sounded like he'd taken about eight different world religions and rolled them into one. Somewhere in the conversation, my friend asked him if he knew Jesus. The man responded yes, but then he said something interesting. He said, "You pray for me." And the way in which he said it just smacked of Simon. As the conversation played out, the man in the street didn't want Jesus. "Wanting Jesus" requires surrendering and yielding to Him and His lordship, and the man in the street wanted nothing to do with that. He didn't want the Holy Spirit. And he didn't want to repent. He wanted power. The same spirit in Simon in Samaria that wanted power is still walking around today, and he is working to deceive even the elect.*

---

* I am not for one second claiming to discern every spirit. I, too, have been deceived. But I am saying I picked up on this one. We all did.

My point is this: I know this is a slippery slope, and sometimes it can be difficult to know what's really a move of the Holy Spirit and what isn't. But the fact that it's slippery and difficult is not a justifiable excuse to refuse the Holy Spirit. If there is one area in the church we as church people have abused, it is this whole thing surrounding the Holy Spirit. I know that. And the mess is a lot bigger than my characterization here. But when I look at the Word and what the believers did who loved Jesus, I am left with this singular overriding understanding: if we want to move from unbelief to belief, if we want faith, if we want to see the sick healed when we pray for them, if we want to see miracles, utter prophecy, give words of knowledge, speak in and/or interpret tongues, if we want to see cancer eradicated from a diseased body, or want to see epilepsy cured, or—how about this one—if we want to see the dead raised to life, then you and I are going to need the Holy Spirit, and we are going to need to cut Him loose to do what He wants without our interference.

That means receiving Him how He desires to be received. Without prejudice and without limitation.

Let me circle back around to the timing issue. On resurrection Sunday, Jesus walked through a wall, breathed on the disciples, and said, "As the Father has sent me, even so I am sending you. . . . Receive the Holy Spirit" (John 20:21–22). Then, moments before His ascension, He said, "You will receive power when the Holy Spirit has come upon you, and you will be my witnesses in Jerusalem and in all Judea and Samaria, and to the end of the earth" (Acts 1:8). My question is this: If they already had everything they needed that they received from Him on resurrection Sunday, why did He tell them to wait for more? I don't know. I only know that He did. And I find it wise that we do the same. From Acts 2 onward, the baptism, or receiving the Holy Spirit, always refers to the Pentecost Sunday experience.

The purpose was and is to receive power to be witnesses, and this promise was fulfilled on Pentecost when the believers received boldness to witness, insight into Scripture, and were released to the apostolic mission. As a result, all Jerusalem felt the impact. To quote the city authorities in Acts 17, "they turned the world upside down" (v. 6).

The resurrection Sunday experience resulted in life. The Pentecost Sunday experience resulted in power. We need both.

According to Paul these can happen simultaneously, while, for most, these were two separate events.

A lot of us meet Jesus and receive life but we never wait or ask for the Pentecost Sunday experience to receive power.

And if I was your enemy, I'd be glad you didn't.

We are powerless to do anything in the kingdom without the Spirit. And yet, Jesus told us He would not leave us orphans and He would come to us.

And He has. In the Holy Spirit.

Three Examples

In Acts 8:12, when the people of Samaria believed Philip, they were immediately baptized with water. Hence, they were saved. To quote Paul, "If you confess with your mouth that Jesus is Lord and believe in your heart that God raised him from the dead, you will be saved. For with the heart one believes and is justified, and with the mouth one confesses and is saved" (Rom. 10:9–10). In short, they had checked this box. At this point in their lives, they had received new life, but they had yet to receive power.

The disciples picked up on this, but look at their response: "Now when the apostles at Jerusalem heard that Samaria had received the word of God, they sent to them Peter and John, who came down and prayed for them that they might receive the Holy Spirit, for he had not yet fallen on any of them, but they had only been baptized in the name of the Lord Jesus. Then they laid their hands on them and they received the Holy Spirit" (Acts 8:14–18).

If they already had been baptized when they believed, if they'd already been empowered, then why send the apostles?

Example number two. Peter was summoned to the house of "Cornelius, a centurion of . . . the Italian Cohort, a devout man who feared

God with all his household, gave alms generously . . . , and prayed continually to God" (Acts 10:1–2). Peter appeared, spoke an abbreviated version of the sermon he gave in Acts 2, and then: "While Peter was still saying these things, the Holy Spirit fell on all who heard the word. And the believers from among the circumcised who had come with Peter were amazed, because the gift of the Holy Spirit was poured out even on the Gentiles. For they were hearing them speaking in tongues and extolling God. Then Peter declared, 'Can anyone withhold water for baptizing these people, who have received the Holy Spirit just as we have?' And he commanded them to be baptized in the name of Jesus Christ" (Acts 10:44–48).

For starters, if you're a Gentile like me, this is really good news. Also, notice that they were already saved when the Spirit fell. And look at what evidence surfaces to verify they were filled.

Number three. Acts 19. Paul came to Ephesus. There he met some new disciples. He asked them, "'Did you receive the Holy Spirit when you believed?' And they said, 'No, we have not even heard that there is a Holy Spirit.' And he said, 'Into what then were you baptized?' They said, 'Into John's baptism.' And Paul said, 'John baptized with the baptism of repentance, telling the people to believe in the one who was to come after him, that is, Jesus.' On hearing this, they were baptized in the name of the Lord Jesus. And when Paul had laid his hands on them, the Holy Spirit came on them, and they began speaking in tongues and prophesying. There were about twelve men in all" (Acts 19:1–7).

They were disciples. They believed. They had received new life. They had yet to receive the Spirit. Paul's response? He laid his hands on them, prayed that they would receive, and they did. And again, there was evidence: they spoke in tongues and prophesied.

The Seal of God

According to Scripture, God's Spirit in us is His guarantee. His guarantee of what? That we are His. These are the words of Paul to the Corinthians:

"And it is God who establishes us with you in Christ, and has anointed us, and who has also put his seal on us and given us his Spirit in our hearts as a guarantee" (2 Cor. 1:21–22).

The word for seal is *sphragizo.* It means to stamp, like a signet ring or private mark for security or preservation. It comes from another word that means to fence or enclose. I love this. And I want it. Because when my enemy comes hunting me, I want him to find me sealed, fenced, and enclosed with the Spirit of God.

Here Paul was speaking to the church in Ephesus: "In him you also, when you heard the word of truth, the gospel of your salvation, and believed in him, were sealed with the promised Holy Spirit" (Eph. 1:13).

And here: "And do not grieve the Holy Spirit of God, by whom you were sealed for the day of redemption" (Eph. 4:30).

Finally, this was John writing his revelation:

And the fifth angel blew his trumpet, and I saw a star fallen from heaven to earth, and he was given the key to the shaft of the bottomless pit. He opened the shaft of the bottomless pit, and from the shaft rose smoke like the smoke of a great furnace, and the sun and the air were darkened with the smoke from the shaft. Then from the smoke came locusts on the earth, and they were given power like the power of scorpions of the earth. They were told not to harm the grass of the earth or any green plant or any tree, but only those people who do not have the seal of God on their foreheads. They were allowed to torment them for five months, but not to kill them, and their torment was like the torment of a scorpion when it stings someone. And in those days people will seek death and will not find it. They will long to die, but death will flee from them. (Rev. 9:1–6)

I cannot pretend to understand all of this, and I am no expert on Revelation, but I can logically deduce that things do not turn out well for those without the seal of God on their forehead. And according to Scripture, the seal is the Holy Spirit.

Just to show you the perfect totality of God's Word, He sets this up for us in Exodus. And if you're a Gentile like me, this is also really good news. After the exodus from Egypt, the nation of Israel included a mixed multitude of people who were not the children of God but foreigners. Slaves. They were people who, enduring the plagues, looked at Pharaoh and compared him to this God that Moses represented and said to themselves, "Forget Pharaoh. I'm with Moses and his God." Then they walked out of Egypt. That's me. Maybe that's you. But look at what God says next: "If a stranger shall sojourn with you and would keep the Passover to the LORD, let all his males be circumcised. Then he may come near and keep it; he shall be as a native of the land. But no uncircumcised person shall eat of it. There shall be one law for the native and for the stranger who sojourns among you" (Ex. 12:48–49).

See those words "he shall be as a native of the land"? This is why Paul said, "But a Jew is one inwardly, and circumcision is a matter of the heart, by the Spirit" (Rom. 2:29). And the seal of all of this is the Holy Spirit.

Where Did He Come From?

The Holy Spirit has been at work in the universe from creation onward. We see Him in the first few lines of Scripture: "And the Spirit of God was hovering over the face of the waters" (Gen. 1:2). He was there at the beginning. And He's described as "hovering," which can also be said of a bird, which is how He's described in John when He falls on Jesus.[16] And not only was He hovering, but He was instrumental in creation: "By the word of the LORD the heavens were made, and by the breath of his mouth [spirit] all their host" (Ps. 33:6).

When I read Psalm 139, David is describing the Lord who is one with the Holy Spirit. Look at the verbs and what he attributes to the Lord and apply them to the nature of the Holy Spirit:

O LORD, you have *searched* me and *known* me! You *know* when I sit down and when I rise up; you *discern my thoughts* from afar. You *search out my path* and my lying down and are *acquainted with all my ways.* Even before a word is on my tongue, behold, O Lord, you know it altogether. You *hem me in,* behind and before, and *lay your hand upon me.* Such knowledge is too wonderful for me; it is high; I cannot attain it.

Where shall I go from your Spirit? Or where shall I flee from your presence? If I ascend to heaven, you are there! If I make my bed in Sheol, you are there! If I take the wings of the morning and dwell in the uttermost parts of the sea, even there your hand shall lead me, and your right hand shall hold me. If I say, "Surely the darkness shall cover me, and the light about me be night," even the darkness is not dark to you; the night is bright as the day, for darkness is as light with you.

For you *formed* my inward parts; you *knitted* me together in my mother's womb. I praise you, for I am fearfully and wonderfully made. Wonderful are your works; my soul knows it very well. My frame was not hidden from you, when I was being made in secret, intricately woven in the depths of the earth. *Your eyes saw* my unformed substance; in your book were written, every one of them, the days that were formed for me, when as yet there was none of them. (Ps. 139:1–16, emphasis added)

I love all of that, but maybe none more than "lay your hand upon me." The Holy Spirit has been inspiring and empowering people for a long time. In the Old Testament, when God commanded the construction of the ark, the tabernacle, and the mercy seat, He said, "See, I have called by name Bezalel the son of Uri, son of Hur, of the tribe of Judah, and I have filled him with the Spirit of God, with ability and intelligence, with knowledge and all craftsmanship" (Ex. 31:2–3). Of Joshua God said, "And Joshua the son of Nun was full of the spirit of wisdom, for Moses had laid his hands on him" (Deut. 34:9). Then in Judges: "The Spirit of the Lord clothed Gideon" (6:34). And finally, in the last words of King David, "The Spirit of the Lord speaks by me; his word is on my tongue" (2 Sam. 23:2).

Nowhere does Scripture say that what happened in Acts is dead. I realize there are schools of theology dedicated to the contrary. Obviously, I disagree. He—the Holy Spirit—is alive today. Moving as He moved then.

Still is. Still wants to. In fact, we have it better than when Jesus was here: "It is to your advantage that I go away, for if I do not go away, the Helper will not come to you. But if I go, I will send him to you" (John 16:7).

We either fail to realize or we take for granted that One member of the Godhead is here now, dwelling in us. Ruling. Reigning. Empowering us. We are handcrafted and hand-carved tabernacles, custom fitted for His Spirit. "Do you not know that you are God's temple and God's Spirit dwells in you?" (1 Cor. 3:16). "Or do you not know that your body is a temple of the Holy Spirit within you, whom you have from God?" (6:19).

The gifts of the Holy Spirit could not be given until Jesus sat at the right hand of God, and then He was poured out on us. How sure are we that if we ask, He will give Him to us? "If you then, who are evil, know how to give good gifts to your children, how much more will the heavenly Father give the Holy Spirit to those who ask him!" (Luke 11:13). "But the Helper, the Holy Spirit, whom the Father will send in my name, he will teach you all things and bring to your remembrance all that I have said to you" (John 14:26).

When Jesus breathed on the disciples, He said, "Receive the Holy Spirit" (John 20:22). Possibly a better translation might read, "receive Holy Breath." Interestingly, the same word used to describe breath in secular Greek is used to describe a flute player. It means to play the flute. And when someone does that, they place their lips on the instrument. I think this means Jesus breathed into each one, intimately, through their lips and nostrils. That may make you uncomfortable, but He did the same in Genesis, so there is a pattern in His creation for it. "Then the LORD God formed the man of dust from the ground and breathed into his nostrils the breath of life, and the man became a living creature" (Gen. 2:7). In the Upper Room, resurrected Jesus was the new Adam breathing resurrected life into His new creation.

Forty days later, just before He ascended, He told them there was more to come: "I am sending the promise of my Father upon you. But stay in the city until you are clothed with power from on high" (Luke 24:49).

Whatever He did to them on resurrection Sunday wasn't completed until Pentecost. So they waited for it.

Let me ask this: If you refuse God's gift, do you really love Him? How do you talk about the gifts of the Holy Spirit? Do you talk down or poorly about Him? Do you do so with irreverence? Are you mocking the Holy Spirit by making fun of Him? *"Every good and every perfect gift is from above coming down from the Father of lights, with whom there is no variation or shadow due to change"* (James 1:17). He—the Holy Spirit—is God, and He's a person, and He comes with a personality no different from Jesus or the Father. He comes from above because the Father sends Him. The Holy Spirit is a good gift, and to refuse the gift is to not love God.

We Think We Have Him

Let's return to Pentecost. Acts 2. The southern steps of the temple. Peter has just finished preaching. People are prophesying and speaking in tongues. Devout Jews from every nation under heaven are bewildered, amazed, and astonished. Peter quotes Joel: "I will pour out my Spirit on all flesh."[17] Then speaking to the crowd, Peter beckons to those prophesying and speaking in tongues: "Having received from the Father the promise of the Holy Spirit, he has poured out this that you yourselves are seeing and hearing." Peter continues, "Repent and be baptized every one of you in the name of Jesus Christ for the forgiveness of your sins, and you will receive the gift of the Holy Spirit. For the promise is for you and for your children and for all who are far off, everyone whom the Lord our God calls to himself."[18]

That last sentence is for us. We are "you." And "all who are far off . . . whom the Lord our God calls to himself." That's us.

Notice what happened next. Three thousand people were added to their number. The Spirit fell, and people repented. A move of the Holy Spirit leads to corporate and individual repentance and worship. If what you are experiencing, whether in church, small group, or individually, does not somehow include a spirit of repentance and worship of Jesus, I question whether it is in fact a move of the Holy Spirit.

I wonder sometimes if we're fooling ourselves into thinking we have all the Holy Spirit has to offer. Look closely at Paul's admonition to Timothy:

> But understand this, that in the last days there will come times of difficulty. For people will be lovers of self, lovers of money, proud, arrogant, abusive, disobedient to their parents, ungrateful, unholy, heartless, unappeasable, slanderous, without self-control, brutal, not loving good, treacherous, reckless, swollen with conceit, lovers of pleasure rather than lovers of God, having the appearance of godliness, but denying its power. Avoid such people. For among them are those who creep into households and capture weak women, burdened with sins and led astray by various passions, always learning and never able to arrive at a knowledge of the truth. (2 Tim. 3:1–7)

Don't skip this—he's talking to us. *Do you have a form of godliness but deny its power? Are we always learning yet not arriving at a knowledge of the truth?*

A few verses later Paul tells Timothy, "All who desire to live a godly life in Christ Jesus will be persecuted, while evil people and impostors will go on from bad to worse, deceiving and being deceived" (vv. 12–13). Have you been deceived or even robbed of the truth of the Holy Spirit? Let me ask it this way: Has your tradition robbed you of experiencing the Holy Spirit as He desires to be experienced by you?

What if, somewhere in our history, we—as a body of believers—departed from a right and sincere faith because we were duped by someone or someones who deceived us through teaching the doctrines of demons? Is it possible? Look at Paul's warning to Timothy: "Now the Spirit expressly says that in later times some will depart from the faith by devoting themselves to deceitful spirits and teachings of demons through the insincerity of liars whose consciences are seared" (1 Tim. 4:1–2).

If you were your enemy would you work really hard to make that happen? For me, it's rather simple—I'm looking at my faith and comparing it to Acts, and I see some differences; and the most glaring is my and others' experience with the baptism of the Holy Spirit and the lack of signs and wonders following. I think we've been robbed of something special. And magnificent. And powerful.

And what's worse, I think most of us are okay with that.

This is the writer of Hebrews describing the early church: "How shall we escape if we neglect such a great salvation? It was declared at first by the Lord, and it was attested to us by those who heard, while God also bore witness by signs and wonders and various miracles and by gifts of the Holy Spirit distributed according to his will" (Heb. 2:3–4). Does it describe you?

Let me ask it this way: If Jesus were to walk into your Bible study, your church, your daily walk as a believer, would He find His Spirit free to do as He wished? Would He find signs following? If not—and if you believe the Word of God is true—you have to wrestle with this: there's a problem with your walk with Him, and either you are the source, or He is. And according to Scripture, He is not. I realize it can come across as supremely arrogant of me to suggest "we think we have Him," implying that we don't. Maybe you do. Again, I'm reading His Word and comparing it with my faith in Him, and one of these things is not like the other.

Both then and now, real obedience of the heart does not occur until we understand we are dealing with a real, living, and powerful God. If Scripture is true, it is God's intention and design to confirm His message with signs and wonders, and He does that through people like the Twelve and Paul and Timothy and you and me who've been baptized with His Spirit. But therein lies the one thing that set them apart—they had been baptized with His Spirit.

Are You Thirsty?

Paul, when speaking of his own ministry, said, "I will not venture to speak of anything except what Christ has accomplished through me to bring the Gentiles to obedience—by word and deed, by the power of signs and wonders, by the power of the Spirit of God—so that from Jerusalem and all the way around to Illyricum I have fulfilled the ministry of the gospel of Christ" (Rom. 15:18–19). As I read back over this I am impressed with the idea that nothing was accomplished in Paul's ministry absent the Spirit of God. Nothing.

This is the last sentence of Mark's gospel: "And they went out and preached everywhere, while the Lord worked with them and confirmed the message by accompanying signs" (Mark 16:20). If Mark were here writing today, would he write this about you? About me?

So how does the Spirit manifest in our lives? In other words, what does He do? Remember Paul's encouragement to the church in Corinth: "To each is given the manifestation of the Spirit for the common good" (1 Cor. 12:7). Which begs the question: If we're not experiencing the manifestation, what are we doing to prevent Him?

Just before Jesus was taken up from the Mount of Olives, He said, "You will receive power when the Holy Spirit has come upon you" (Acts 1:8). The word for power is *dunamis*. It means miraculous power—or the power to perform miracles. It's the same word used to describe what had gone out of Jesus when the woman with the issue of blood touched the hem, or wing, of his garment. One with *dunamis* exercises dominion authority. Which Jesus had and has. The question you and I need to wrestle is, did He really give that to us?

When God spoke through the prophet Isaiah some six hundred years before Christ, He said: "I will pour water on the thirsty land, and streams on the dry ground; I will pour my Spirit upon your offspring, and my blessing on your descendants. They shall spring up among the grass like willows by flowing streams" (Isa. 44:3–4).

What happened in Acts 2 was the fulfillment of Isaiah 44 and Joel 2. Keeping His promise, God poured out His Spirit. On all flesh. Are you "all flesh"? If you read more closely, there's a condition. The reason the willows spring up is because the thirsty land and dry ground is drinking from the flow of the stream. Which prompts the obvious question:

Are you thirsty?

Every time I read this, I am reminded of my West Texas father who is known for what I call his Texas-isms.* One of which is, you can lead a horse to water, but you can't make him drink. Like all of his phrases, it paints a picture. I wonder sometimes if he didn't get it from King David: "He leads me beside still waters. . . . my cup overflows" (Ps. 23). It was true with David and it is true with us; the Lord will lead us to His water, but He will never make us drink. That's our job. We open up and receive. In my own life, if I'm not thirsty for His Spirit, I'm either complacent, indifferent, or battling resignation—none of which comes from the Spirit of God. The disciples upended the world, yes, but before they did, their own lives were upended. They gave up their comfort for whatever the Holy Spirit wanted. We say we want to turn the world upside down, but I wonder how many of us would sacrifice our comfort to do so.

I can ask the question because I'm guilty. But I don't want to be.

This is what I know: we wait, we receive, and we accept. Most of us acknowledge the Holy Spirit, even allow Him in the room as long as He stays where we tell Him and doesn't do anything without our permission. This is especially true in church. But that is not the biblical model. And we are not inferior to the disciples. We receive the same Spirit. Or we can. We have unfettered access. Just as fully. Just as completely. We are not second-class believers. Remember, too, confession and belief precede the Spirit. I think they clear the way and tell Him that He's welcome.

Are You Willing to Be Willing?

If you are currently reading me through one slanted eye, and you're looking at your tradition or your pastor or your group of friends and you're still not convinced and you're comfortable where you are, and you're thinking,

---

* If you read *Chasing Fireflies*, my fifth novel, you got a pretty good dose of this.

Nope, this jump is just too big. Too many crazies. Don't trust them, I can't really disagree with you. You probably have good reason for saying that, but I would just ask you to read Acts and compare your life to theirs. How about these two verses: "God was doing extraordinary miracles by the hands of Paul, so that even handkerchiefs or aprons that had touched his skin were carried away to the sick, and their diseases left them and the evil spirits came out of them" (Acts 19:11–12).

Just being honest: that does not describe me. But I want it to. And Paul and I—and you—have access to the same Spirit. That same power is available today. I find no place in Scripture where it says that well has dried up. In fact, I've found a bunch of places telling us He's still pouring. "Whoever believes in me will also do the works that I do; and greater works than these will he do, because I am going to the Father" (John 14:12). Jesus wants to pour His Spirit on us and in us. But I don't see that power exercised very much in our churches, and not seeing is no excuse whatsoever to stop asking for it. And the fact that I don't see it or that it's not the norm is not justification that He, the Holy Spirit, isn't moving today like He moved then.

The argument that says, "I don't believe the Holy Spirit is here today or available or intends to fill us today the way He did in the book of Acts because I don't see Him working here today the way He did in Acts" is like saying, "I don't believe in nuclear weapons because I don't see them in use today." I'd be willing to bet that 99.999 percent of us have never seen a nuclear weapon explode. And yet I'd also be willing to bet that same 99.999 percent believe nuclear weapons exist, and not only that they exist but that they can explode—with the push of a button. Compared to the Spirit of God, the sum total of our nuclear arsenal isn't equal to a gnat in a hurricane—and yet most of us give more credence to the gnat.

If we, as the people of God today, are going to be used by Him to turn the world upside down, we will not do it with our own strength. Not possible. We will do it only as we open ourselves to receive the Holy Spirit and His power. Do I know what that looks like today? Not really. But neither does that excuse me or you from asking. If I'm being honest, when I wrote *What If It's True?*, I was rather hesitant to put chapter 8 in the book. Not because I didn't believe it, but because chapter 8 deals with generational curses and blessings, and whenever I've taught that I've suffered the worst warfare of all my other teachings combined. The enemy hates that teaching, and yet I've seen great freedom come as a result of it. Case in point—Christy and I (along with the guys in my Bible study) have prayed with a few couples who were having trouble getting pregnant. All kinds of trouble. Legitimate, physical inabilities and limitations. They tried every form of medical help. (And I'm not knocking medical help. I'm for it. I'm thankful for doctors, hospitals, and medicine. I'm just describing their process.) They came to us frustrated. A last resort of sorts. Then I walked them through the teaching of generational curses and blessings, and we prayed through the prayer at the end of chapter 8. As I write this, there are children walking around this planet who were born to those couples after we prayed and broke those curses. I've held them. Got their pictures on my phone. I'm not writing theory—I've seen this work. Like Peter and John, I respond, "How can I but speak of what I've seen and heard?" And for the record, it's not me breaking the curse. It's the Holy Spirit. He's the hurricane.

My response to this chapter on the Holy Spirit is similar. I can hear the labels now, and I realize I'm swimming upstream. There is a part of me that is reluctant to add this one to the table of contents. Many of you don't want to speak in tongues because as soon as you do, you're worried what others will think or how they will loop you in with all the other crazies. But God's Word is His Word, and in His Word He tells us He wants to pour out His Spirit on all of us—and when He does, and only when He does, are people healed, freed, delivered, and raised up. That's the bride to whom He is returning. A Spirit-filled bride. One who does not shun or reject any aspect of His Spirit.

What would it look like for us to repent of that and for Jesus to pour out His Spirit on us and in us, to clothe us, to baptize us, completely in Him? I don't know, but I welcome both the process and the experience. "It's a fearful thing to fall into the hands of the living God" (Heb. 10:31).

What would it look like for you to be willing to be willing to receive the Holy Spirit? And if you say you've already received Him, then great. What would it look like for you to be willing to be willing to release Him to pour Himself out fully into your life? To bring all the gifts God has planned for you?

Are you willing to be willing?

Pray with Me:

Lord Jesus, before we step into the baptism, I think maybe I need to correct the record. For lots of reasons, I have not been willing. I've kept Your Spirit at arm's length because, honestly, I can't control what He might do when I give Him control—and that scares me. And I don't want to look foolish. I'm sorry for that. I don't want to be that way anymore. I'm sorry for letting both pride and fear keep me from Your promise. For the record, I'm willing. And where there is still a remnant of unwilling-ness in me, I'm both asking You and giving You permission to make me willing. Do the work in me to make me good soil so you can sink a deep root. This is my heart's sincere desire. Come, Lord Jesus.

CHAPTER 9

Willing to Be Willing

I love that phrase: *willing to be willing.* It takes the pressure off of us to have it all figured out and just puts us in the posture of looking inside ourselves and commanding our will to receive what He promised. Much in the same way King David often said, "Why are you cast down, O my soul, and why are you in turmoil within me? Hope in God; for I shall again praise him, my salvation" (Ps. 42:5, 11; 43:5).

Because the disciples were willing, you and I are having this conversation. I know there are places in my own life where I walk in the full expression of the Holy Spirit, but there are certainly more. I have no monopoly here. There's more for me. There's more for you.

In Acts 3, Peter and John are going to the temple for prayer at the ninth hour—about three in the afternoon. A man lame from birth is being carried to the gate of the temple called the Beautiful Gate where he was brought daily to beg alms. The man is over forty years old, so he's been doing this whole begging thing a long time. This is the sum of his life. His metal cup is worn, and his eyes glazed over with boredom and indifference. He rattles his cup at Peter, who looks down at him and says, "Look at us."[1] The man looks up, expecting money and nothing more. But Peter has something else in mind.

He says to the man, "I have no silver and gold, but what I do have I give to you. In the name of Jesus Christ of Nazareth, rise up and walk!" Then

Peter grabs the lame man by the right hand, lifts him up, and Scripture records an amazing thing: "immediately his feet and ankles were made strong."[2]

Is there any logical explanations for what just happened? Of course not. But can you hear this guy screaming? Can you see him dancing? Twirling. Hugging Peter and John. I think the man is near to out of his mind. But, watch what he does: "And leaping up, he stood and began to walk, and entered the temple with them, walking and leaping and praising God."[3] I think he was doing more than leaping. I think he was probably doing backflips.

Then he walks into the temple. Why? Because he's been lame since birth, and according to Leviticus, "no one who has a blemish shall draw near, a man blind or lame."[4] Which means he was excluded from temple worship. For his entire life. No fellowship with God. He was born and has always been a complete and total outcast. But not any longer. Now he's included. A child of God. And he's jumping around in amazement, screaming and laughing at the top of his lungs. "And all the people . . . were filled with wonder and amazement at what had happened to him."[5]

The people are dumbfounded. Peter, not one to avoid a chance to preach, opens his mouth and gives a shortened version of the same sermon he gave on the southern steps. "You killed Jesus. You denied the Holy Spirit. And faith in the name of Jesus has given this man perfect health. Therefore repent and turn back, that your sins may be blotted out."[6]

But anytime the Holy Spirit shows up, so does the enemy. So the priests, the captain of the temple, and the Sadducees burst onto the scene because Peter is teaching that in Jesus is the resurrection from the dead.[7] They arrest them, and as they are carted off to the prison someone takes a head count and another amazing thing has happened. "Many of those who heard the word believed, and the number of the men came to about five thousand."[8] The church is growing.

The next day, the rulers, elders, and scribes gather along with Annas the high priest and Caiaphas. These names should be familiar. These are the men who killed Jesus. They bring in Peter and John, and notice what single question they ask: "By what power or by what name did you do this?"[9] So Peter, again not wanting to miss a chance to preach, lays down the gauntlet: "This Jesus is the stone that was rejected by you, the builders, which has become the cornerstone. And there is salvation in no one else, for there is no other name under heaven given among men by which we must be saved."[10]

The elders are skeptical, but they have one insurmountable problem: the healed man. He's standing there nodding. And no one can deny his healing because they've been stumbling over him for more than forty years. Unable to argue with the truth of what they're seeing, they command Peter and John to "speak no more to anyone in this name." Peter and John shrug, saying, "Whether it is right in the sight of God to listen to you rather than to God, you must judge, for we cannot but speak of what we have seen and heard."[11]

You should underline that. "For we cannot but speak of what we've seen and heard." Better yet, write it in the margin in your own hand.

They release Peter and John, and all the believers lift their voices together and offer this prayer: "Now, Lord, look upon their threats and grant to your servants to continue to speak your word with all boldness, while you stretch out your hand to heal, and signs and wonders are performed through the name of your holy servant Jesus."[12] But notice what happens next. "And when they had prayed, the place in which they were gathered together was shaken, and they were all filled with the Holy Spirit and continued to speak the word of God with boldness."[13]

Cheating Ourselves

We are cheating ourselves, those we love, and those in our churches if we suggest that the Holy Spirit was given once and only at Pentecost. Acts 2 was not an isolated event. Nor was it intended to be. God is a good Father and He loves to give good gifts. Especially those which He promised. If we're evil and we know how to give good gifts, what makes us think for one second that God wouldn't continually pour out His Holy Spirit on those of us who are thirsty and ask Him? You may disagree with my theology and you may argue to the contrary, but let me ask this: Do you honestly believe that if you ask for the Holy Spirit and then expect to receive Him as the believers did in Acts, God is going to look down on you and shake His head? Waggle His finger? Why? Because you believed His Word? I don't think so. I think He's going to pull you up into His lap and lavish you with His Spirit and knock your socks off and destroy your puny expectations and weak limitations.

Let me give you one final caution. Two chapters later in Acts, Stephen, "full of grace and power, was doing great wonders and signs among the people," and is arrested.[14] He's dragged before the high priest, accused by false witnesses, and told to give an account of why he's doing what he's doing and with what power. Stephen, who had evidently been listening to and taking lessons from Peter, holds forth and commences giving the leaders of the law an education in the law—which only increases their hatred of him. And as he's finishing, he says: "Yet the Most High does not dwell in houses made by hands, as the prophet says, 'Heaven is my throne, and the earth is my footstool. What kind of house will you build for me, says the Lord, or what is the place of my rest? Did not my hand make all these things?'"[15] Stephen is telling these temple-goers that God inhabits His people. That we are His temple. That He has poured His Spirit into us. Then He gazes even more intently saying, "You stiff-necked people, uncircumcised in heart and ears, you always resist the Holy Spirit. As your fathers did, so do you."[16]

So enraged, they kill him.

But let's turn the mirror. Let's assume for a second that Stephen was speaking to us. That we are them. That he's trying to wake us from our tradition and blindness. Our hard, calloused hearts. If that sounds like the last chapter, it should.

What if we're the ones who are "always resisting the Holy Spirit." What if that's us?

Do you really want that to be said of you?

Sometimes in my experience, I have seen people come to the Holy Spirit, excited through what they've heard, open themselves up, raise their hands, and welcome all that He has. And I'm for that—we should dance, sing, laugh, worship, and pour ourselves out in repentance. There should be joy and tears and intimacy with the Father. According to Scripture, the unbelievers should accuse us of being drunk. But there is danger in the pendulum swinging too far where we chase experience at the expense of the Word, becoming experience junkies. We show up to church, hold out our arm, tap a vein, and say, "Don't bother me with the Word, I'm just here for the experience." This is really dangerous. We need both Word and baptism. In equal amounts. And in truth, I'd argue for a greater dose of the Word because the Word is our protector and our guarantee against false experience, in that the Word reveals the Spirit.

Notice what Scripture says about the disciples. They were daily in the temple and they gave themselves to the ministry of the word and prayer.[17] Think about it—all they had was the Old Testament, and it perfectly revealed Jesus. They lacked nothing. Think how much better we've got it.

I've also seen folks adopt this posture with spirits other than the Holy Spirit, so when they show up in church, they're carrying more than one spirit. This, too, is dangerous. How do we guard against this? The Word and mature leadership—but if I go much further down this rabbit trail I'll write another book, so let me just close with this: I'd encourage you to proceed to the feet of Jesus, and only Jesus, with an open heart and receive the Spirit He would give you and only His Spirit. Then test the spirits.

I don't want us to get too sidelined with what might go wrong. More on that later. What I do know is this—Jesus said, "I will pray the Father, and he shall give you another Comforter" (John 14:16 KJV). The word for "comforter" is *parakletos*. It means advocate. Helper. Intercessor. Consoler. And my favorite, encourager. Also, the word for "another" is *allos*. It means "one of different quality but equal to Himself." That means the Holy Spirit is equal in every way to Jesus.

When His Spirit filled His followers in Acts, stuff happened, causing bystanders to accuse them of being drunk at 9:00 a.m. What's one thing most really drunk people do? They fall down. Pass out. Laugh. Cry. Late-night TV is full of wild-haired preachers smacking people in the head. One or two have smacked me, and it was all I could do not to punch them in the teeth. I get it. Really. I too am suspicious when I see that. I was like, "Dude . . . get your hand off me. Go smack somebody else. Can't you see I'm trying to meet Jesus here?" But their abuse doesn't change the fact that when the Holy Spirit touches people, they really do fall down. Including me—and I had no intention of going down. In fact, I was bracing against it. Maybe this is because the word *glory* means "weight" and when the "weight" of the presence of God falls on us, there's not a human alive who can stand up under Him.

John showed us this on the Island of Patmos when he fell down flat as though dead when he met Jesus.[18] There have been times when I've prayed for people and they've fallen flat out. One minute they're standing there, the next minute they're flat on their back. I can't explain that. Nor can I control or create it. At other times, I've prayed for people who all of a sudden start speaking or praying in tongues. And this has happened when we had never discussed it. I can't explain that either.

I prayed for a guy in prison once, and as soon as I laid my hand on his shoulder, he started praying in tongues. Or stammering in tongues. However you want to describe it. It surprised me, so I stopped him. I was curious and I wanted to know if he had come from a Pentecostal background or if he was yanking my chain. "You do that often?" He shook his head. His eyes were the size of Oreos. "Never done that before." It's even happened in foreign countries with people who did not speak English. And no, they weren't speaking their language either. I checked. The translator had no idea what they were saying.

Look—I'm not naïve. I get all the baggage and abuse that comes with this. But if you argue that baggage and abuse nullifies or negates the reality of the manifestation of the Holy Spirit, then don't you have to simultaneously argue that counterfeit money negates the value of real? Sure, there are counterfeit bills in circulation, millions of them, but their existence does not mean that we immediately run into the streets waving it like a flag, screaming, "We found counterfeit bills! Therefore, all money is counterfeit. Everybody burn their money." If we did, how many fires do you think we'd see?

The pendulum swings here between two extremes: the Word of Faith movement (out of which the prosperity gospel grows) and what I call the "doctrine of suffering." I defined this in *What If It's True?* "Prosperity" does not mean health, wealth, happiness, toys, cash, and prizes. It means accomplishing the orders of your superior officer. The prosperity gospel is an abomination to the gospel of the kingdom. As is the doctrine of suffering.

Do we suffer? Yes. Did Jesus? He learned obedience through what He suffered, and it was His Father's good pleasure to crush Him. Did Paul suffer? Just a little. Did God swallow Jonah into the putrid belly of a whale? For three days and nights. In Hebrews 11, the great faith hall of fame, do we learn that some were sawn in two and some run through with the sword? And in Revelation do we learn that some were beheaded for the gospel? Yes, and yes. Did all the disciples suffer and die save one for the cause of the gospel of the kingdom? Yes. Does God use suffering to accomplish His purposes?

Scripture records that God brought Job to satan's attention. He put Joseph in iron fetters. He enslaved His own people. There is no doubt that He uses suffering to forge in us something more valuable than gold. But I cringe when people use their suffering as a crutch to excuse them from praying in faith for what God commands us to pray for—healing. Deliverance. Again, I herald two responses in Scripture, from Daniel and his companions: "Though He slay me, yet will I serve Him." And, "He can save us, He will save us, but even if He doesn't, we will worship Him alone."

Listen to Paul echo Daniel as he encourages the church in Corinth: "We do not want you to be unaware, brothers, of the affliction we experienced in Asia. For we were so utterly burdened beyond our strength that we despaired of life itself. Indeed, we felt that we had received the sentence of death. But that was to make us rely not on ourselves but on God who raises the dead. He delivered us from such a deadly peril, and he will deliver us. On him we have set our hope that he will deliver us again" (2 Cor. 1:8–10). Can you find any evidence in Scripture that Paul stopped walking in the power of the gospel because of his suffering? Paul accepted his suffering as God's sovereignty and then, like Shadrach, Meshach, and Abednego, he declared that God delivered us, and He will deliver us again. That posture is one of faithful obedience regardless of present circumstances, outcome, or cost.

So, What Now?

When Peter preached at the house of Cornelius, "the Holy Spirit fell on all who heard the word" (Acts 10:44). If the same Spirit hasn't fallen on us, I wonder if we're listening. The word for "fall" is *epipipto*. It means to embrace with affection or seize with violence, and it comes from a root that means to alight like a bird. To descend upon.

If God the Father sent His very Spirit and He embraced me with affection, I'd cry my eyes out. Maybe even laugh some. And if He seized me with violence, I'd fall out. Flat. Maybe some would accuse me of being drunk.

Whatever it looks like, provided it's from the Lord, I want everything He has for me, and I have a feeling He intends more and has more. And if I'm being honest, the reason I have yet to receive it and Him is my fault. I've kept Him at bay. At a distance.

I tend to think we've taken other people's word for whether or not we have all that the Holy Spirit intends for us. Most of us operate in an unhealthy fear of man, which is just fear disguised as false piety. It's ugly. It's evil. And I, too, am guilty. But if I take the book of Acts and lay it like a grid across my life, I see some glaring differences. I'm the problem, not Him, and I think we're missing out. A lot. I don't think we have it all. Not by a long shot. That should bother us. What if we swept away every bias, everything we thought we knew about what the filling of the Holy Spirit ought to look or sound like, and everything everybody else told us about Him, and we just asked Him to fill us. To "fall" on us. To overflow us. And what if we did that without limitation or reservation and no matter what it looked or sounded like?

What would happen if we just set everything aside save the Word and then lie prostrate before His throne with one unified request: "Holy Spirit, have Your way. You're welcome here. Do as You like. We put no limitation on You. We want everything You want for us." And what if this took weeks? Months even. Would you hang in there? Would you wait? Could you?

In my experience of walking with the Lord for something like forty-five years, our traditions often put the Holy Spirit in a box because we're not comfortable with what He might do if we let Him out. We have a "form of godliness" but we deny its power (2 Tim. 3:5 NIV). We can't control the Holy Spirit, and because we're fearful He might push us out of our comfort zone, we "shush" Him into something we can manipulate. *Sit there and be quiet. You're scaring people. And we worked too hard to get people in here for You to run them off.* And because one nature of the Holy Spirit is that of a dove, He doesn't protest. He waits patiently. Cooing.

For the record, getting us out of the way so that the Holy Spirit can have His, requires wise and mature leadership—people with real discernment—because the enemy loves to take that well-intended opportunity and turn it into unorganized chaos and convince the naïve people of God that what they are experiencing is a move of the Holy Spirit. Not necessarily. Signs and wonders and warm fuzzy feelings don't guarantee a move of God. Maybe, maybe not. You are better off to test the spirits. It could be a head-fake by the enemy. A wolf disguised as a sheep. It could also look like a false teacher telling you something you want to hear. Deceiving even the elect. The same can be said of me, so test what I'm telling you. I'm not suggesting we become legalistic, dictating how, when, and where the Spirit manifests. I'm simply saying we test the spirits, and there's wisdom in the council of many.

There is no simple recipe for how to do this, but you can help guard against chaos by starting with repentance and true worship. The enemy hates both.

The Supernatural

The gifts of the Holy Spirit are the entrance into the supernatural, and you can't have a discussion of the first-century church, the church in Acts, without the supernatural. Without signs and wonders. I'm sorry if that freaks you out, but if you say you are a believer, then that's what you're in for. For those of you who say salvation is a supernatural sign and wonder, yes. I totally agree. It is and I thank God for it. But it's the doorway. The entrance. Not the culmination. There's more. Salvation is also inward, while the gifts are external manifestations.

If your discomfort causes you to want to remove the supernatural from Acts, cutting each chapter that involves the supernatural, you have to cut out every chapter. All twenty-eight. Might as well rip the whole thing out of your Bible. There is no book of Acts without the supernatural from beginning to end. And the first evidence of signs and wonders in the church in Acts was people giving prophetic utterance, words of knowledge, and speaking in tongues.

Jesus said, "Out of the abundance of the heart the mouth speaks" (Matt. 12:34). When the Spirit fills us up, the first overflow is with the mouth. From the Jews at Pentecost to the Gentiles in the household of Cornelius, the first evidence of the supernatural gifts of the Holy Spirit was speaking in tongues. If your theology does not make room for this, then is your theology based on Scripture? And if your first reaction is to want to argue this point, let me ask you this: Do you really want to open the Word, read and accept it at its face value, and do what it says, including receiving everything the Holy Spirit has to offer—or do you want Him on your terms, dictating how He manifests, if at all?

This was not the response of the first-century believers.

I'm trying to make the argument that "receiving" the Holy Spirit is an event. I don't care when you received Him, but can you say that doing so was an event? Yes, receiving is an experience, but more than that it is an event. You are meeting a Person. Intimately. And you'd know if you met Him. Can you be a believer without the event? Sure, but what fun is that? That's like getting married but never going on a honeymoon. Why would you?

When the believers in Acts received the Spirit, the place shook and bystanders accused them of being drunk. They gave words of knowledge, made prophetic utterance, and spoke in tongues. Then, signs and wonders, the supernatural, followed them. I also don't think this is a one-time event any more than intimacy in marriage is a one-time event. We as people leak, so we need refilling. Sometimes often. And the Holy Spirit loves to do just that. He's not one and done.

In my life, and in the lives of those I walk with closely, this filling and refilling is often governed and limited by our pride. Our arrogance. If you're questioning whether you've experienced the event, or you've been praying and haven't, press into your pride and ask the Lord to show you if it's a hindrance. Are you limiting you? For me this has been true—for others not so much.

Remember how I told you to keep a finger on Peter's sermon? Flip back with me one last time. He declares the people aren't drunk, but affirms Joel's prophecy: that God has poured out His Spirit on all flesh—as He promised. Signs and wonders are accompanying these who believe. Meaning, belief is step one. And all who call upon the name of the Lord are being saved. The NASB says "delivered." I love this because you and I are included in both "all" and "everyone." The condition is that we call upon Him.

Will you call upon Him? What if He doesn't answer the first time? Will you keep calling?

If I receive these words, maybe as a child would receive words from his or her Father, then salvation includes the event of the pouring out of the Holy Spirit in such a way that external manifestations are witnessed by others. Let me suggest this: just pray. "Father, if there's truth in these words, please show me and give me a heart that is willing to receive both the answer and the gift. And if my pride is in the way, please forgive me. I don't want to let me get in the way of You."

For those of you who have been praying and seeking and asking, and haven't received the answer or experienced the baptism or witnessed the healing you'd hoped for, let me speak the words of Jesus over you: "These signs will accompany those who believe: in my name they will cast out demons; they will speak in new tongues; they will pick up serpents with their hands; and if they drink any deadly poison, it will not hurt them; they will lay their hands on the sick, and they will recover" (Mark 16:17–18).

This is His promise. And if His Word is true, and it is, then His promises are true.

One final word from Jesus. And here He's not speaking about conversion or salvation, He's speaking about the Spirit: "If anyone thirsts, let him come to me and drink. Whoever believes in me, as the Scripture has said, 'Out of his heart will flow rivers of living water.' Now this he said about the Spirit, whom those who believed in him were to receive, for as yet the Spirit had not been given, because Jesus was not yet glorified" (John 7:37–39).

Jesus pours out His Spirit on the thirsty. Are you thirsty?

If so, are you willing to drink?

Drink (Pray) with Me

Acts 2:38–39: "Peter said to them, 'Repent and be baptized every one of you in the name of Jesus Christ for the forgiveness of your sins, and you will receive the gift of the Holy Spirit. For the promise is for you and for your children and for all who are far off, everyone whom the Lord our God calls to himself.'"

Lord, I accept that promise as for me and spoken to me, and I repent. Holy Spirit, I receive You. I repent for keeping You at a distance. For shunning You. For telling You to sit quietly in the corner and do nothing without permission. I'm so sorry for not revering You. For treating You as anything less than who You are. You are a member of the Godhead sent to empower and fill me and dwell in me, and I've held out my hand like a stop sign and said, "No." Forgive me, please. I ask Your forgiveness for ever muting You. For making decisions that silence You. For shutting the door on You. For not letting You in. I know that I have grieved Your heart and I am so sorry. I would never do that to Jesus or God the Father, and yet for some reason I've been comfortable shrugging my shoulders at You. Which is ridiculous when even before creation You hovered over the waters. In every creative action in Scripture, You created.

Please remove any barrier or hindrance that I have either knowingly or unknowingly put between You and me that would hinder the release of Your Spirit in and through me. Please, come now. Fill me. Overflow. Baptize me. I want everything You intend for me. I put no restriction or limitation on You. I want every gift You desire to give me, and yes, that means the gift of tongues—which I don't really understand and think sounds kind of funny, but I'll get over that. For so long, I've enthroned my mind and my ability to understand or control above You. I've said, "If I can't understand then I don't accept." I don't want to do that anymore. I trust You. I'm pretty sure the disciples and every person in that Upper Room did not understood any of what You did that night or any of what You did on the day of Pentecost but they accepted You and what You were doing. I want to be like them.

I choose right now to trust You with me and the decisions You make. I'm taking my mind off the throne of me. This doesn't mean I'm dumbing me down. It is simply acknowledging that I'm a spirit housed in a soul living in a physical body. My mind exists in my soul and was created to serve my spirit. Not the other way around. I thank You for my mind and the awesome creation it is, but somehow I've allowed my mind to limit You. To not grant You access to me. To close You off from me. I don't want to do that anymore. I know that You give good gifts and every good and perfect gift comes down from the Father of lights in whom is no variableness neither shadow of turning, so I want everything You've got for me:

wisdom, words of knowledge, faith, healing, working of miracles, discerning of spirits, tongues, interpretation of tongues. I want everything that You want for me, and I receive You now. All of You.

Come, Holy Spirit. Shake my house. Blow the roof off. Let tongues of fire rest on me. Let Your kingdom come and Your will be done. Also, I know according to Scripture that while we are possessed by the Holy Spirit we as believers can be both affected and effected by more than one Spirit. In simpler terms, it's called "being demonized." Whether by sin, generational curse, wounding, whatever, I know that we can operate or function with two spirits. One of those Spirits is You. And the other is not. If that describes me, I don't want to house two spirits anymore. I want to give You sole ownership of me. Sole possession. So, right now, in the name of Jesus, and by the precious and magnificent and undefeated blood of Jesus, I rebuke, bind, cast down, and spew out of my body any spirit that is not You and doesn't bow to the King of all kings, Jesus. Get out. No vacancy. Your lease is revoked in the name of Jesus.

I know that You, Holy Spirit, are the promise of the Father. So today I receive the promise. This day and every day. I receive You in every corner of my person, even those subconscious areas that I'm not aware of. Your Word says You are both the lamp of God and the finger of God so I give You permission to shine a light in all the closed and dark closets in me. Fling the doors off the hinges. And if You find anything in those closets that shouldn't be there, then throw that out too. I'm done with it. Don't want it anymore. In agreement with Your Word, I am Your temple. I am Your dwelling place. I was made to house You. So, I do and I am.

According to Your Word, Your Spirit gives wisdom, understanding, knowledge, creativity, and might. For so long I've tried to muster those up without Your help. Pretty dumb, I know. I'm done with that. Your servant, King David, when he was dying, said, "the Spirit of the LORD speaks by me; his word is on my tongue" (2 Sam. 23:2). I want that. Please let that be said of me. I know that when You asked Moses to build the tent of meeting, the ark of the testimony, and the mercy seat that You filled Bezalel with Your Spirit and gave him ability, intelligence, *knowledge, and all craftsmanship. Please pour that into me. I know that before Moses died, he laid hands on Joshua, and You filled Joshua with a spirit of wisdom. Please pour that into me. I know that in the valley of Jezreel, when Gideon blew the trumpet, Your Word says You "clothed" him. Please clothe me in the same way. I know that when Your servant Peter stood on the southern steps of the temple and gave his great sermon in Acts 2, that he quoted Your prophet Joel through whom You said, "I will pour out my Spirit on all flesh," and You did (Acts 2:17). And You are still pouring out Your Spirit today. Pour into me. Fill me up. Overflow my banks.*

Lastly, I know I have an enemy who from the day of Pentecost has worked tirelessly to cause me and all of us to doubt You. To make fun of You. For some reason, You and Your work have been hijacked, more often than not by the fringes, and because of that I've wanted nothing to do with You. I've seen the abuses, and because of that I've thrown out the baby with the bath water. Please help me discern what is You, and what is broken and selfish and evil people abusing Your power—and please don't allow me to be one of them. Please, when You empower me, show me what is the right use of the power You entrust to me. Your Word describes You like a dove. That Your nature is to wait patiently until called or invited. I'm inviting You to be more like an F-16 in me and my life.

Holy Spirit, breath of God, please baptize me. Clothe me. Imbue me. Soak me entirely in You, now. Let rivers of living water flow up and out of the overflow in me.

Lastly, Lord, if an evil spirit is blocking or hindering me from receiving You or believing any of this, I rebuke that spirit. I bind you, evil spirit. I cast you down. And I spit you out of me now in the name and by the blood of Jesus. Get out! You will rob me no longer of what My God promises me. In Jesus' name.

Because His Word is true, and we know that it is His delight to give us His Spirit, we should thank Him. The Scriptures below help me do that.

- I thank You, Lord, that we as men speak from God as we are carried along by the Holy Spirit (2 Pet. 1:21).
- I thank You that we are all filled with the Holy Spirit and begin to speak in other tongues as the Spirit gives us utterance (Acts 2:4).
- I thank You that we do repent and are baptized in the name of Jesus Christ for the forgiveness of our sins, and we do receive the gift of the Holy Spirit. For this promise is for us, for our children, and for all who are far off, everyone whom the Lord our God calls to Himself (Acts 2:38–39).
- I thank You that the Spirit of Him who raised Jesus from the dead dwells in us, He who raised Christ Jesus from the dead also gives life to our mortal bodies through His Spirit who dwells in us. So then, we are debtors, not to the flesh, to live according to the flesh. For if we live according to the flesh we will die, but if by the Spirit we put to death the deeds of the body, we will live. For all of us who are led by the Spirit of God are sons of God. For we did not receive the spirit of slavery to fall back into fear, but we have received the Spirit of adoption as sons, by whom we cry, "Abba! Father!" The Spirit Himself bears witness with our spirit that we are children of God, and if children, then heirs—heirs of God and fellow heirs with Christ, provided we suffer with Him in order that we may also be glorified with Him (Rom. 8:11–17).
- I thank You that He abides in us, by the Spirit whom He has given us (1 John 3:24).
- I thank You, Lord, that You baptize us with the Holy Spirit and fire (Luke 3:16).
- I thank You, Lord, that we are God's temple and that God's Spirit dwells in us (1 Cor. 3:16).
- I thank You that we have asked You and that You have given us living water to drink (John 4:10).
- I thank You, Lord, that You pour out Your Spirit on us and will make Your words known to us (Prov. 1:23).

- I thank You, Father, that You pour water on the thirsty land, and streams on the dry ground—and that You pour Your Spirit upon Your offspring, and Your blessing on Your descendants, and that we shall spring up among the grass like willows by flowing streams (Isa. 44:3–4).

- I thank You, Jesus, that it has come to pass that everyone who calls on the name of the LORD shall be saved. And I thank You that we can call on You—and we do. We call on You and You alone (Joel 2:32).

- I thank You, Lord, that we are strengthened with power through Your Spirit in our inner being, and that You, Jesus Christ, dwell in our hearts through faith. And that we, rooted and grounded in love, have strength to comprehend with all the saints what is the breadth and length and height and depth, and to know the love of Christ that surpasses knowledge, and that we are now filled with all the fullness of God (Eph. 3:16–19).

- I thank You, Father, that hope does not put us to shame, because Your love has been poured into our hearts through the Holy Spirit who has been given to us (Rom. 5:5).

- I thank You, Lord, that You gave and we have received the Holy Spirit just as Your first disciples did (Acts 10:47; 15:8).

- I thank You, Lord, that Your Spirit will rush upon us, and we will prophesy with them and be turned into another man (1 Sam. 10:6).

- I thank You, Lord, that whoever believes in You, as the Scripture has said, "Out of his heart will flow rivers of living water." And so we thank You that even now, rivers of living water are flowing out of us (John 7:38–39).

- I thank and praise You, Lord, that we have received not the spirit of the world, but the Spirit who is from God, that we might understand the things freely given us by God. And that You have imparted this in words not taught by human wisdom but taught by the Spirit, and that You interpret spiritual truths to those who are spiritual (1 Cor. 2:12–13).

- I thank You, Lord, that You were anointed with the Holy Spirit and with power and that You went about doing good and healing all who were oppressed by the devil, because God was with You—and that You have given us that same power and anointing over all the power of the enemy (Acts 10:38; Luke 10:19).

- I thank You, Lord, that You have given us one heart, and that You have put a new Spirit within us. That You and You alone have removed our heart of stone and given us a heart of flesh (Ezek. 11:19).

- I thank and praise You, Lord, that there is therefore now no condemnation for those of us who are in You—Christ Jesus. And that the law of the Spirit of life has set us free in Christ Jesus from the law of sin and death (Rom. 8:1–2).

- I thank You, Father, that the Spirit of the LORD rests upon us, the Spirit of wisdom and understanding, the Spirit of counsel and might, the Spirit of knowledge and the fear of the LORD. And that our delight is in the fear of the LORD. And that we do not judge by what we see with our eyes or decide disputes by what our ears hear (Isa. 11:2–3).

- I thank You, Lord, that You have anointed me (Isa. 61:1).

Last thing, I promise. You should know that I and several others have prayed much over this book. And we've prayed a lot over this very chapter and this specific moment. For you. Right here. Right now. He's here. So, don't leave this place.

Breathe In. Breathe out. And drink Him in.

CHAPTER 10

Show Us the Father

Scripture is silent on Jesus' appearance. We have no idea what he looked like. In fact, Isaiah declared He had no form or majesty that we should look at Him, and no beauty that we should desire Him (Isa. 53:2). The Charles Martin translation says, "He was nothing special to look at and nothing about Him would grab your attention."

I've published fourteen novels, and leaving out a character's physical description would never occur to me, nor would my editor let me get away with it. This absence of Jesus' description is purposeful on the part of the Holy Spirit. If we knew something of His appearance, we'd all be tripping over ourselves to look like Him.

While we know nothing of His appearance, we know a good bit about His first recorded public words. And first words, like last words, matter.

We pick up the narrative in Luke 2: "Now his parents went to Jerusalem every year at the Feast of the Passover. And when he was twelve years old, they went up according to custom."[1]

Remember this word, "up." Jerusalem sits at about 2,500 feet in elevation. Most everywhere in Israel is lower, so whenever someone came into the city, they walked uphill. This will matter shortly.

"And when the feast was ended, as they were returning, the boy Jesus stayed behind in Jerusalem. His parents did not know it, but supposing

156

him to be in the group they went a day's journey, but then they began to search for him among their relatives and acquaintances."[2]

If you're a parent, this should encourage you. Even Mary and Joseph didn't get it right all the time. In fact, they missed it by a mile.

"And when they did not find him, they returned to Jerusalem, searching for him."[3]

This means that after a day's journey, maybe twenty miles downhill, they turn around and walk back uphill into Jerusalem. I don't think they were too happy when they found Him.

"After three days . . ."

Three days. Think about it. Mary is pulling her hair out. She's beside herself. She can't find Jesus. Twelve years old. She's worried sick. And don't miss the obvious: the three days is significant. Foreshadowing.

"They found him in the temple, sitting among the teachers, listening to them and asking them questions. And all who heard him were amazed at his understanding and his answers. And when his parents saw him, they were astonished."[4]

I've always laughed at that translation. "Astonished." I'm the father of three boys, and if I had been unable to find them for three days, I don't think "astonished" would quite get at my condition. Maybe "my head was about to spin off" or, "out of my mind," but not astonished.

"And His mother said to Him, 'Son, why have you treated us so? Behold, your father and I have been searching for you in great distress.'"

I put that phrase "great distress" in the same category as "astonished."

Jesus is surprised. Taken aback. "And he said to them, "Why were you looking for me? Did you not know that I must be in my Father's house?"[5]

These are no small words He is speaking.

"My Father's house."

You could have heard a pin drop.

Mary and Joseph are stunned. Lost for words. As is depicted in the next verse in Scripture: "And they did not understand the saying that he spoke to them."[6] This idea of God as "Father" is world-rocking and paradigm-shattering. They have no context for this.

Is this as big a deal as I'm making it? Am I just overdramatizing Scripture?

So extreme is this statement that twenty-one years from that moment, these same people will gather on this same mountain, and they'll brutally and savagely murder the man this boy becomes. Why? For speaking two words: "My Father." The Jewish rulers explain this when they stand before Pilate, "We have a law, and according to that law he ought to die because he has made himself the Son of God."[7]

Why Does This Matter?

Prior to Jesus, God Most High was known to the nation of Israel by many names: Elohim, El Elyon, Yahweh, Adonai. His covenantal name in Exodus 34. All of these names describe parts of His character. Healer. Provider. Creator. Merciful. Loving. But prior to Jesus, this idea of God as "Father" was not real common.

God speaks prophetically through Isaiah,[8] Jeremiah,[9] and Malachi,[10] who all use the word *Father*. As do Moses[11] and David.[12] Throughout their writings, the word is most often used in a corporate sense and not necessarily to describe what He is on an individual level. He's the Father of a nation. Not yours and mine.

Maybe the most beautiful usage comes in Psalm 89, when, speaking through the inspiration of the Holy Spirit, the psalmist foretells of the Messiah and His relationship with God:

> I will crush his foes before him and strike down those who hate him. My faithfulness and my steadfast love shall be with him, and in my name shall his horn be exalted. I will set his hand on the sea and his right hand on the rivers. He shall cry to me, "You are my Father, my God, and the Rock of my salvation." And I will make him the firstborn, the highest of the kings of the earth. My steadfast love I will keep for him forever, and my covenant will stand firm for him. (Ps. 89:23–28)

This prophetic, Messianic psalm was fulfilled some thousand years later when twelve-year-old Jesus spoke of His Father—in His Father's house.

While prophesied and used corporately to describe God as Father of a people, the idea of God as an individual, intimate, personal Father was nonexistent in Jesus' day. And there was good reason for this: the Law of Moses forbade it (Lev. 24:16). Jesus was doing something at the age of twelve that no rabbi had ever before dared. He was calling God "My Father"—with emphasis on "My."

Those around Him were stunned.

As a twelve-year-old and throughout His earthly ministry, the word Jesus used to address God Most High is *Abba*. It's a transliteration. Meaning, translators wrote the sound of the word which the Hebrews spelled *Av*. Greek translators took the Aramaic or Hebrew *Av*, and they wrote the closest word they had in their lexicon, *Pater*. In Greek it means "Father," but Father in Greek and Father in Hebrew are not necessarily the same thing.

This problem of translation is similar to Jesus' name when He walked the earth. The disciples didn't call Him "Jesus," they called him *Yeshua*, which is actually closer to *Joshua* and means "The Lord is my Salvation" or "I am the One who avenges you."

In the Greek mind, the word *Pater* described what God is. It's along the same lines as describing God as Creator, Protector, Healer, Provider, etc. All are true and glorious, magnificent descriptions of God's character and person, but the Hebrew word *Abba* is inclusive. It combines the description of *what* God is but also includes *who* God is. It's both. It's *Pater* plus some intimate knowledge of. In English, we don't really have a word that does the same. *Daddy* gets close, but there's argument around this and I don't really like the comparison. When someone says *Pater* they can be simply describing a what—as distant as the name on a family tree—but when someone says *Abba* they're not only describing a what but they're speaking intimately to a who. Big difference.

In other words, someone who says *Abba* knows who he or she is speaking to. Intimately. Someone who says *Pater* or *Father*, might or might not.

In Jesus' day, slaves were forbidden to address the head of the family by this title. It was too intimate. In Jesus' darkest moments, when He was sweating blood in the garden, it's the word He used: "Abba Father, if it's Your will, remove this cup from me."[13] Also, the reason I think we read "Abba Father" is because the translator, by putting the two words side by side, is telling us, "We don't really have a word that means the same thing so we're putting our word next to this one so you (the reader) will have some idea what it means. Otherwise, you'll have no idea."

Abba carries innately inside the combination of its own letters a deep expression of intimacy and knowingness. It's *Father* in 4K Ultra HD. Etched into the word is identity, security, purpose, and ownership. Jesus' use of *Abba* caused the religious rulers of the day to hate Him. Despise Him.

Don't believe me? "For this reason therefore the Jews were seeking all the more to kill Him, because He not only was breaking the Sabbath, but also was calling God His own Father ["Abba"], making Himself equal with God" (John 5:18 NASB). Why? The Law of Moses declared it so: "Whoever blasphemes the name of the LORD shall surely be put to death. All the congregation shall stone him. The sojourner as well as the native, when he blasphemes the Name, shall be put to death" (Lev. 24:16). Every time He said it, Jesus was making Himself equal with God. A Son with all the authority, rights, and privileges thereof (Matt. 28:18; John 17:2). And every time He said it, the Pharisees were looking at Jesus and asking themselves, "Who does this guy think He is?"

Let's look at a few instances:

- "When you pray say: 'Father, hallowed be Your name'" (Luke 11:2 [Matt. 6:9]).
- "Fear not, little flock, for it is your Father's good pleasure to give you the kingdom" (Luke 12:32).
- "And he told those who sold the pigeons, 'Take these things away; do not make my Father's house a house of trade'" (John 2:16).
- "I and the Father are one" (John 10:30).

- "Father, glorify your name." Then a voice came from heaven: "I have glorified it, and I will glorify it again" (John 12:28).
- "All that the Father has is mine; therefore I said that he will take what is mine and declare it to you" (John 16:15).
- Jesus on the cross: "Father, forgive them . . ." (Luke 23:34).
- "Father, into your hands I commit my spirit!" (Luke 23:46).
- After the resurrection: "Jesus said to her, 'Do not cling to me, for I have not yet ascended to the Father; but go to my brothers and say to them, "I am ascending to my Father and your Father, to my God and your God"'(John 20:17).

Jesus used *Abba* more than any other word to refer to God. If He taught us anything about the One who sent Him here, who begot Him, He taught us that He was His Father. He uses the word more than 165 times in the Gospels. In John 5, when He healed the man at the pool of Bethesda, Jesus used the word fifteen times in two paragraphs. "I have come in my Father's name and you do not receive me. . . ." (v. 43). To the religious rulers, this was beating them over the head. Fingernails on the chalkboard. And they hated Him for it. In the Sermon on the Mount, He said it seventeen times. The high-water mark begins in the book of John chapter 14 and ends in what we call the High Priestly Prayer. In four chapters, Jesus said *Abba* or *Father* fifty-one times. Think about it: the last thing Jesus did before He went to Calvary was have a conversation with his closest friends about His Father—His Abba—and then a conversation with Abba in which we get to hear what He is saying.

When Moses walked up on the mountain alone with God, He asked God the single most burning question on the tip of his tongue: "Who are you? Who is this God who speaks from the cloud?" Jesus anticipated this from all of us and answered it 165 times. Paul then picked up on this and uses the word forty times in his own writings, bringing our total to more than two hundred times in the New Testament.

Why did Jesus do this?

In John, Jesus said, "In my Father's house are many rooms . . . I go to prepare a place for you" (John 14:2). Then there's this one: "I am the way, and the truth, and the life. No one comes to the Father except through me" (John 14:6). Why did Jesus risk His life to speak a singular word? Because He's taking us somewhere. The question is where. Which Jesus answers some 165 times.

He's taking us to the Father.

It could not be simpler. Paul would later explain: "Through Him we both have access in one Spirit to the Father" (Eph. 2:18). The Father's presence is the destination of the rescue mission.

If this revelation is not important, then why spend such time on it? Why take us there?

Before His crucifixion, Jesus said:

"If you had known me, you would have known my Father also. From now on you do know him and have seen him."

Philip said to him, "Lord, show us the Father, and it is enough for us."

Jesus said to him, "Have I been with you so long, and you still do not know me, Philip? Whoever has seen me has seen the Father. How can you say, 'Show us the Father'? Do you not believe that I am in the Father and the Father is in me? The words that I say to you I do not speak on my own authority, but the Father who dwells in me does his works. Believe me that I am in the Father and the Father is in me, or else believe on account of the works themselves." (John 14:7–11)

I want to offer you an invitation. The Lord wants to put a word in your mouth. It's a special word. Maybe *the* single most important and meaningful word we will ever speak. We used to know it. For most of us, it was the first word off our lips when we were born. It was resting there. Our lips make the sound naturally. It's the DNA-cry of our heart.

Abba.

Say it out loud with me: "Abba."

Your Abba wants to get at your image of Him. He wants unfettered access to the place in your heart where you hold Him. He is jealous to correct how you think about and know Him. He wants to reveal Himself to you as He is. And He wants to shatter the image the enemy has painted or tainted.

When our kids were born, we—like every parent including Mary and Joseph—had trouble getting them to sleep through the night. Sometimes they'd wake crying. For no apparent reason. Christy, because she had what they needed, would try and quiet them. Sometimes it worked. Sometimes not. When it didn't, she'd hand me this screaming, peeing, pooping, vomiting thing and say with this weary look in her eye, "Here . . . you do something." I'd take them in the den, strip them down to their diaper, and then I'd lie on the sofa with my shirt off. Their skin pressed to mine. Invariably, they'd curl their knees up under their stomach, turn their face into mine, and then nuzzle their snotty nose up against the base of my neck—where they could smell me. Eventually, they'd sleep. Christy would look at me in desperation, "I have the stuff but how do you do that?!" Many nights my boys slept on my chest where I could hear them breathing, smell them, and nuzzle their noses.*

As I was researching Hebrew meanings of *Abba*, I discovered that of the six, one of them means, "I long for your scent."

In Isaiah, God was speaking through the prophet. He said, "Hear, O heavens, and give ear, O earth, for the LORD has spoken: 'Children have I reared and brought up, but they have rebelled against me'" (Isa. 1:2). Seven hundred years before Jesus, and God Most High were calling us sons—and yet we don't know our Father.

So let me ask you: Do you know the scent of your Father?

I know some of you have had horrific experiences with your earthly father, and you hear me say stuff like this about our heavenly Father and His desire to be known by us, and you shake your head. You have no context for this. And you don't have the mental capacity to hope for this because your wound is too deep. I get it. I do. In *What If It's True?*, I

---

* For the record, Christy calmed our boys far more than I. This was just the one place where I could help. And I remember it because, to this day, I think they fell asleep when they smelled me.

said, "Rejection is the deepest wound of the human soul." I believe that more today than when I wrote it. And, if it is possible to separate rejection wounds into horrible and more horrible, the worst of the bunch are those caused by an earthly father.

My Friend Hank

I met Hank in Tallahassee my sophomore year of college. I'd cracked a vertebra in my back playing football at Georgia Tech and transferred to Florida State to try to become a student. My doctor believed the muscles in my back needed strengthening so he told me to get on a bike and pedal until I didn't feel like pedaling anymore. Given that I was a bit competitive, I started racing bikes. During a training ride early in my sophomore year, a guy pulled up alongside me and we struck up a conversation.

Throughout my time at FSU, Hank was a constant pal. We traveled, raced, trained. When I last counted, he and I have ridden over 25,000 miles together on bicycles. During this time, I learned a good bit about him. He had been adopted. Knew nothing of his biological parents. His adoptive parents divorced when he was five, meaning he was shuffled around a lot, and spent a lot of time with his grandmother—who I later met and who loved the Lord. Hank had no real relationship with his adoptive dad. He'd suffered abuse, abandonment, rejection, and his mother died the night of his senior prom. Rather than dance, he sat next to her bed and held her hand.

During our junior year, we raced in Gainesville at a rather large race. Sprinting toward the line, I heard a crash behind me. Sounded pretty bad. A few minutes later, one of my teammates carried Hank's bike to my car and pointed at the ambulance, "Hank's in there." That's all he said. Then he handed me his helmet—which was broken. I threw everything in my car and followed the ambulance.

The trauma center at the hospital was chaos. A multi-car pileup had filled most of the rooms, and people were screaming and crying down every hallway. I checked in at the desk, and the lady told me to wait. Which I did for an hour. With no update. Finally, when she vacated her seat for a few minutes, I reached around her desk and punched the security button opening both sliding doors. Down the first hallway, I saw medical personnel pull a sheet over a large woman and then work feverishly over the body of a boy in the next bed. Things were bad all around. But Hank was nowhere to be found.

Finally, I turned a corner and saw a supply closet with a cracked door and the light on. I pushed it open and found Hank lying in a fetal ball, shaking uncontrollably on a gurney. In the supply closet. His clothes were badly torn, his face was bloody, and he had road rash over his legs, arms, and hands. I reached through the bars of the gurney, "Can I pray for you?"

He nodded.

That was when we really started talking about the Lord. The scans were negative, so they sent us on our way, but standing in that supply closet it struck me, maybe for the first time, that Hank had nobody that cared whether he was in that closet or not. Nobody knew. Except me. Had I been in a wreck like that, the waiting room would have been full of family and my mom and dad would have been standing bedside. But that was not Hank's world.

Winter rolled around and to alter our training regime we would run the stadium steps in Doak Campbell Stadium. On Thursday nights, the football team would practice on the field, and we did this so much that I remember Bobby Bowden watching Hank and me run. The stadium had something like thirteen rows with eighty-seven steps in each row, and we'd run the whole thing for time. One night, after a hard workout, we were sitting on the top row and for some reason, at that moment, the Holy Spirit moved and Hank laid down his life and followed Jesus. Hank says it's probably the best thing to ever happen in Doak Campbell Stadium.

In the years that followed, Hank became my brother. He would later stand alongside my dad as the best man in my wedding, and today I've known him thirty years. As we've walked together with Jesus, one of the things I have routinely bumped into is a wound in the depths of his heart. It's his father-wound.

A wound I don't have and couldn't really understand until Hank lived it out before me. My dad loved me. Fought for me. Hung out with me. I don't have some giant gaping hole in my chest caused by my dad. My dad has hugged me and kissed me most every time I've seen him. Meaning, my earthly dad has hugged and kissed me ten thousand times. I know the love of a father. No, he's not perfect, but it's safe to say that I'm writing this book because he led me to love my heavenly Father.

Hank had no such model. Matter of fact, that place in Hank that his dad was supposed to fill was covered over in scars and pus. And every time he'd suffer a trial or some hardship and I'd press him to trust the Lord, he had trouble. Trusting was difficult. His father-wound was Everest. At the root. The thing I bumped into time and time again was this unspoken objection: "How can you expect me to believe in and much less receive the love of a heavenly Father, when I've never known it or seen it modeled on earth?"

Herein lies the insidious voice of the enemy. Itself rooted in fear. One more variation on the Did-God-say? lie. For Hank, it was an ever-constant whisper that said, *You and I both know that you can only trust your circumstances. Your experience is the only thing that's real. Not the words out of some old book.*

Over the years, as I prayed about this, I felt like my heavenly Father, Abba, said, "Bring him to Me." As best I've know how, I've done this.

Today, Hank is married to beautiful Laura, works with our church, and we are still the best of friends. I saw him last night—he's been in my Bible study since its inception—and his heart is one of the most tender and honest I've ever known. While I would have liked to see an overnight miracle where God healed the hole in his chest, the process has been slow and taken years. Evidence of the depth of the wound. The good news is that Hank knows the Father. Intimately. He spends time with Him. Loves Him. Trusts Him. And he leads other people into this place as well. I have often encouraged folks in our church, "If you're suffering a father-wound, you should ask Hank to pray for you. He has an anointing in this area and he is uniquely qualified to bring people into the presence of Abba. He knows the road."

One funny story—Hank's wedding day. We're standing in the basement of the church. Tuxedos. Music is playing upstairs. We are ninety seconds from walking down the aisle where Hank will say "I do" with Laura. Given that he's a bit nervous, he's drinking coffee. And he's shaking. Badly. I'm watching this Styrofoam Big Gulp of coffee with one slanted eye. Thirty seconds later, that entire cup drains down Hank's chest. Upstairs they are calling for us. We are inside of a minute. The clock is ticking. We walk into the bathroom and start stripping. "Gimme your shirt." Today, when you leaf through their wedding album, the pictures are magnificent. There's Laura, a vision in white. Hank, a GQ model. The church is historic and beautiful. Things could not be more perfect—and then there's me, standing there with a giant brown stain across my chest. (I'm sorry, Laura. We almost made it.)

To Know the Father

In my life in ministry, Hank is not alone. Maybe the deepest wound of everyone I've ever ministered to—from priest, to playboy, to prisoner, and this includes women—is a father-wound. And to each of them, that indescribable pain in their ribcage is a sucking chest wound. Everest. Unclimbable. And for most, their response when you try to touch it is this: "Don't touch it. Just let me lie here alone."

Let me ask you a question: If your Father's desire is for you to know Him as Father, and that desire was and is strong enough to cause Him to send His Son to die for you, do you think the enemy is okay with this? Think like your enemy for a second. If you were your enemy, would you jack with your image of the Father? Let me ask it this way: What would you not do to mess with your image of the Father? Is there any extent to which you would not go?

Your enemy—satan—is going to turn hell inside out to taint, ruin, sour, mess with, and poison your image of your heavenly Father. he will stop at nothing to do this.

When you think "Father," what comes to mind? How has the enemy tainted your image? What's your relationship like with your dad? And what kind of dad did you have? Abusive? Performance based? Passive? Absent? Angry? Life sucking? Or, maybe he was awesome and he loved you really well. Everyone has some version. But good or bad, your earthly dad is not necessarily the reflection of your heavenly Father. And herein lies the tension—your enemy wants your heart to think God is a mirror reflection of your past experiences.

I'm not glossing over your experience. But while your pain with your dad is real, he's not God. For many of us, this is tough to wrap our heads around. We can't hear the truth about our heavenly Father because our wound is too deep, it's Velcroed to our soul, and our knee-jerk defense is too quick and limits our ability to hear. If that's you and I'm picking at the scab of your wound and your pain, you should know that in my experience, God the Father may well access your image of Him through that wound. Through the very thing that hurts.

This means that in order for the wound to heal, you might have to forgive someone. Like your earthly dad. Even when he hasn't asked for it and doesn't deserve it and you've still got the scars—both inside and out—to prove what a sucky dad he really was. I'm sorry to break it to you, but forgiveness is not optional for the children of God. Jesus commands it. I know it's not fair, but the kingdom of heaven isn't built on fairness; it's built on righteousness. If it was built on fair, we would be hanging on the cross and not the only begotten Son of God.

The thief came to kill, steal, and destroy, and that destruction in your life may well have started with your earthly father. Why does God work this way? Can't He just zap the wound, heal it, and move on? Sure, but those I've watched forgive their dads have learned the inexplicable value and freedom of forgiveness at a level deeper than their wounds. And inevitably, in what is simply a miracle by the Holy Spirit, they then translate the depth of that knowingness to Abba. I don't understand the intricacies of this, but the act of forgiving their earthly dads unlocked an intimacy with their heavenly Father they didn't see coming. And that intimacy is stronger than any scar I've ever known.

Don't think that just because I'm writing this I've got it all figured out. Forgiveness is tough stuff. Maybe the toughest. Especially toward people who don't deserve it.

The enemy's plan in your and my life is to shatter our image of what and who our heavenly Father is and/or does. Always has been. The enemy wants you to question everything about your Father. Even whether He loves you. No, especially whether He loves you.

While this is your enemy's tactic, your heavenly Father—Abba— wants you to fall asleep on His chest. Tuck your nose into His neck. To know His scent.

I can hear the objections. I have. Often. "There is nothing in me that even remotely wants to engage with what you're telling me." Or, "Dude, do you see where I am? Look around you. You think I put me here?" Or, "You don't know my story. You have no idea how that man hurt me." You're right, I don't. But your Abba does. So let me press you—would you grant Him access to the wound? Would you give Him permission to change your perspective? Right this very second, you have an enemy who desperately does not want you to have a right "knowing" of Your Father— your Abba. Maybe more than anything.

Don't shortcut this and don't minimize it. And don't skip over it because it hurts. This is *the* battle for your heart—and whose thumbprint owns it. The rest of this book matters little at all if you don't dig into this one.

Here's why this is such a big deal. Jesus was praying in John 17. The High Priestly Prayer. It's the last thing He said before walking to the cross. It's His prayer for you and me: "Holy Father [Abba], keep them in Your name. . . . While I was with them, I was keeping them in Your name. . . . Righteous Father [Abba], although the world has not known You, yet I have known You; and these have known that You sent Me, and I have made Your name known to them, and will make it known, *so that* the love with which You loved Me may be in them, and I in them" (John 17:11–26 NASB, emphasis added).

What name has Jesus made known? Father. And don't miss the obvious: Jesus stands from His throne, takes off His ring, undresses His priestly and kingly garb, lays down His crown, leans His royal diadem in the corner, and takes a swan dive out of the throne room of heaven—why? To grab our hands and lead us to His Abba. *So that* we might know that kind of love.

The revelation of God as your and my Father was Jesus' first recorded words, and they were the last words before He went to the cross. When He rose from the dead, He said, "I haven't yet been to your and my Father."[14] In between He said it more than 165 times. So much so that the rulers wanted to kill him. This was *the revelation* He spoke more than any other.

If we knew God as Abba, what would we worry about? What would we fear? What would bother us? Name one thing.

You can't.

A year or so ago, I asked my Father to reveal Himself to me as Abba. If He wants me to know Him as my Father, then He ought to be able to speak that revelation to me in a way my heart can receive and understand. So, He played a slideshow of my boys as they'd grown up. In many of the slides, they'd come running to me in pain. Crying. Knees bloody. They'd reach up. I'd reach down. How long would I hold them? As long as they'd let me. Then He asked me, *Charles, where do you think those emotions come from? If you feel that for them, and you feel it that strongly, and you're evil and I'm good, how do you think I feel about you?*

And yet, for some reason most of us don't translate that response or initiative to our heavenly Father. To Abba.

Oftentimes, when I've found myself at this place of wrestling to trust my heavenly Father, I've felt a tap on my shoulder. When I look up, He points to the cross. And His Son. His question is simple and honest. *Charles, what more will it take to convince you? I gave you Him.*

Father, I'm so sorry. I have gospel amnesia.

The fact that I don't register God as the source of those emotions *and* give Him credit for both giving them to me and feeling them infinitely more strongly about me, shows the enemy's war against my relationship with My Father. My Abba. This disconnect, this fact that I don't give Him credit for allowing me some insight to how He feels about me through my own emotions, is the enemy's thumbprint. And it's evidence that the enemy has more influence on my heart than I'd like to admit.

Over the years, I've seen this same thumbprint in Hank. While his prayer atop the stadium steps in Doak Campbell is for me the date that Hank believed and confessed, and therefore God transferred Him out of the kingdom of darkness and into the kingdom of the Son of His love, this has been difficult for Hank to grab hold of. His wound has been so deep that even salvation itself is tough to own. Hence, early in his faith, I saw Hank walk down for umpteen altar calls in a dozen different churches or services. Not because it didn't take the first time but because there is a war raging in his heart. "Could God the Father really love me?" His heart simply had no box for this. Often, before he has stepped out in the aisle, he would look at me, wanting to go but wanting to know if I'd be angry with him—as if his unbelief and doubt is somehow a disappointment to me. In every case, I heard the Father say, "Bring him to Me." So I smiled, patted him on the back, and pointed, and Hank walked up front or prayed with someone else.

Over the years, I came to look at Hank's aisle-walking much like I do my own baptism experience. The Father is waiting for His son, and I don't think for one second that He's going to meet Hank at the altar with His hand toward his chest and say, "Um, excuse me, Hank, haven't we already done this a few times?!" Are you kidding me? The Father is waiting on Hank and you and me with arms outstretched. Every time. And when we appear in the aisle or the altar or coming back over the crest of the hill, the Father launches Himself off the porch and covers our face in kisses. And in those moments following, maybe when we're driving home or eating dinner, where Hank has wrestled with his recurring need to walk back up there or pray again, and the enemy is trying to condemn him for unbelief, I've just laughed with him: "Dude, think of it this way, you're the most saved man I've ever met."

So, What Now?

At its root, the problem is a galactic battle between our circumstances, or what we've lived, and what the Word of God says. On one side of our heart, our circumstances would scream that God can't be trusted because if He could, the things that have happened to us would never have happened and the things that are currently happening wouldn't be happening. What kind of good Father would allow that?

On the other side, His Word speaks: "All who are led by the Spirit of God are sons of God. For you did not receive the spirit of slavery to fall back into fear, but you have received the Spirit of adoption as sons, by whom we cry, 'Abba! Father!' The Spirit himself bears witness with our spirit that we are children of God, and if children, then heirs—heirs of God and fellow heirs with Christ" (Rom. 8:14–17). And it says, "And because you are sons, God has sent the Spirit of his Son into our hearts, crying, 'Abba! Father!' So you are no longer a slave, but a son, and if a son, then an heir through God" (Gal. 4:6–7). And in the Psalms, He says, "For as high as the heavens are above the earth, so great is his steadfast love toward those who fear him" (Ps. 103:11).

I want to add some context to this. "As many of [us who] were baptized into Christ have put on Christ" (Gal. 3:27). These verses mean that right this second, God's Spirit in us is crying out, "Abba! Father!"

And then there's this one, probably my favorite. And remember when you read this that Jesus told Philip, "If you've seen me, you've seen the Father." It might help you to interchange the words:

Who shall separate us from the love of Christ [the Father]? Shall tribulation, or distress, or persecution, or famine, or nakedness, or danger, or sword? As it is written, 'For your sake we are being killed all the day long; we are regarded as sheep to be slaughtered.' No, in all these things we are more than conquerors through him who loved us. For I am sure that neither death nor life, nor angels nor rulers, nor things present nor things to come, nor powers, nor height nor depth, nor anything else in all creation, will be able to separate us from the love of God in Christ Jesus our Lord. (Rom. 8:35–39)

If I read Paul correctly, then nothing I can conceive, and even what I can't conceive, can separate me from the love of the Father. Yet for many like Hank, these words stand in stark disagreement with past experiences and current circumstances. They are opposite ends of the spectrum. It can seem, and is, rather insensitive to tell someone with a sucking chest wound left by their abusive or absent dad, "Hey, chin up, pal. Your Father loves you." Those words will run off their heart like water off a duck's back. They stare in disbelief, shake their head, and point to their scars. "How is that true?"

If you know the Father and you're walking with someone who does not, I have found that no amount of convincing persuades them. The problem rests not in their mind but in their broken heart. Hence, "Bring them to Me." If you don't know the love of the Father and you're reading this nodding your head, saying, "Tell me about it," let me encourage you to take Paul's words and tape them to your bathroom mirror. Or your cell wall. Or the ceiling in your dorm. Make them the home screen on your phone. Drive them like a stake in the ground and strap yourself to them. Why? Because they are the very words of God. Your Father. Spoken from His lips to your heart. Nothing could be truer.

About here the enemy likes to whisper all kinds of stuff like, "It sounds like you're telling me to meet God halfway when He's the one who abandoned me." You can be ten million miles from the Father and yet when you turn your heart toward His, taking one single step, you will find no matter where you are that He's there waiting on you—and has been. He was there all along. But you have to discover that yourself.*

---

* I have wrestled with this theme for some two decades, resulting, at least on my part, in three novels. *Chasing Fireflies* (my fifth), *Thunder and Rain* (my eighth), and *Long Way Gone* (my twelfth). If you have some time and want to dive deeper, I'd encourage you to look them up. At the end of the day, for me, those novels stand as love letters from the Father to us. And when it comes to the love of the Father for His children, *nothing compares.*

How would it change your life, your prayers, your expectations to speak, "Abba, Father . . ."?

John wrote in Revelation that we overcome him (satan) by the blood and the word (Rev. 12:11). The word *confession* means to say the same as He (Jesus) has already said. What if our confession mirrored His? What if we cried out, "Abba"?

I've been in church a long time. Heard a lot of great teaching. That said, I know of no more important teaching than this one. This idea, this truth that God is our Father and, if we are in Him, we are His children is the most significant and life-altering truth we will ever hear. And if we take Jesus at His word, He would agree.

Some of you—given your wounds—need to know how much Abba loves you. Here, hold my hand. He answered that two thousand years ago. Walk with me back to the cross. Look closely. Whose place did Jesus take? Barabbas's. Now look closely at his name. Bar–Abba. It means "son of the Father." Jesus took the place of the son of the Father.

He took our place. Yours and mine.

You are worth Jesus.

When Jesus hung on the cross, the world turned dark. The light of the sun faded. For three hours. The natural order of the universe was upended. Yes, Jesus was crushed for our sin, but what do you think that did to the Father?

You are worth Jesus.

The father of lies would tell you that you're plastic pieces on a chess-board. Single-use disposable razors. Compost. That God is disconnected. Indifferent. Maybe He's amused by you. God Most High—who would like to be known by us as "Abba"—is not our coach. He's not our boss. He's not up there. He's not disconnected. Indifferent. Or sort of amused by you.

Hank is not an isolated event in human history. He's more the norm than not. And over the years, as I have ministered and walked with peo-ple—as I've been on my face for my friends as they've suffered and hurt, I've heard the Father say, "Bring them to Me."

I have attempted this here.

Abba wants us to reach up, crawl into His lap, to bring all our pee, poop, and vomit with us and curl into a fetal ball on His chest. And when we do, He whispers into our ear, "Son. Daughter. I am so happy you're here. I'm crazy about you."

I am writing this because I think it's the single most important word some of us will ever hear—and one most all of us need to hear. If I could, I'd stand on your roof and shout this at the top of my lungs.

I am trying to tell you, in whatever way I can, that Jesus redeemed us, sanctified us, and snatched us back out of the hand of the devil *so that* He could bring you and me to the Father. It's always been about a return trip for mankind. The love of the Father for His creation who were not yet His children—that's the reason. Period. Your Father sings over you, weeps over you, rejoices over you. He is jealous for you. Wants you to know Him without enemy interference. For mankind to walk once again in the cool of the mornings. He wants your image of Him to rightly reflect Him.

But There's a Catch

There is a popular teaching today that says we are all God's children. Some even include the idea that everyone is already saved, we just don't know it yet. Both are a lie. We are not all His children. At least not yet. This is Jesus speaking to folks like us, and this was no more popular then than now: "You are of your father the devil, and you want to do the desires of your father. He was a murderer from the beginning, and does not stand in the truth because there is no truth in him. Whenever he speaks a lie, he speaks from his own nature, for he is a liar and the father of lies" (John 8:44 NASB).

"Our father the devil."

Some of you see those words and you ask, "How is this so? I didn't choose him." Adam and Eve had no children inside the garden of Eden. Only out. Hence, every son of Adam is a rebel from birth. It's woven into our DNA. The lens through which we see. As a result of the fall, we are born into the kingdom of darkness, and by default our father is the father of lies. Yet, despite our complete and total depravity and the fact that we—as humankind—chose the father of lies who rules over the kingdom of darkness, our Father in heaven has given us all the right to become His children. To choose His kingdom over this present darkness. But herein lies both the truth and the tension: "But to all who did receive him, who believed in his name, he gave the right to become children of God, who were born, not of blood nor of the will of the flesh nor of the will of man, but of God" (John 1:12–13). What's more, the father of lies can do nothing about this. he can't hold you against your will.

The bottom line is that we must choose to become God's child, and until we choose the right Father, we're all just created rebels, born into the kingdom of darkness. Aiding and abetting the enemy. Serving a double-tongued liar. This may offend you, but this is the gospel and this is the truth of us. You and I are great sinners in need of a great Savior. And we desperately need to be transferred or delivered out of this dark kingdom. Until we come to grips with both our depravity and His unmerited grace, we're all headed for hell.

Some refute this, saying, "Well, why is a good God sending me to hell?" He's not. You are. His Word is the mirror that reflects the intersection of our sinful nature with His goodness. When we read it, when we *abide* in it, the truth causes the dross to rise to the surface. And the dross is the stuff in us that's not like Him. It's the truth that shines a light on the lies.

This is why He said, "If you continue in My word, then you are truly disciples of Mine; and you will know the truth, and the truth will make you free" (John 8:31 NASB). Further, it's His will that none "should perish, but that all should reach repentance" (2 Pet. 3:9). When Paul is speaking to us in Galatians telling us that God has sent His Spirit into us and by that Spirit we cry out, "Abba, Father," notice, he's talking to God's children. Rebels who chose adoption into the kingdom of God and out of the kingdom of darkness. Once in, having received the Spirit, it is that same Spirit who cries out, "Abba." You and I are born with the craving for intimacy with our Father, but it is His Spirit that puts the word on our lips. And until we receive His Spirit, we're babbling incoherently.

With His Spirit, we cry out, "Abba."

Without His Spirit, we cry out lies.

This means sonship is conditional. That's right. Conditional. To be received as a son, we have to submit to His discipline. If you don't, you're still a rebel who wants the benefits of sonship without the responsibility and accountability. Listen to the writer of Hebrews:

> Have you forgotten the exhortation that addresses you as sons? "My son, do not regard lightly the discipline of the Lord, nor be weary when reproved by him. For the Lord disciplines the one he loves, and chastises every son whom he receives." It is for discipline that you have to endure. God is treating you as sons. For what son is there whom his father does not discipline? If you are left without discipline, in which all have participated, then you are illegitimate children and not sons. Besides this, we have had earthly fathers who disciplined us and we respected them. Shall we not much more be subject to the Father of spirits and live? For they disciplined us for a short time as it seemed best to them, but he disciplines us for our good, that we may share his holiness. For the moment all discipline seems painful rather than pleasant, but later it yields the peaceful fruit of righteousness to those who have been trained by it. (Heb. 12:5–11)

Notice that phrase in the middle, "If you are left without discipline, . . . then you are illegitimate and not sons."

Why does God do this? For our good. So that we share in His holiness, which allows us to be brought into His presence. And in the end, to those of us who submit to it, His discipline yields the peaceful fruit of righteousness—without which no one will see God.

You want to see God one day as His child? Submit to His discipline.

The Choice

When I talk about "choosing to become," I'm starting to dance around this issue of God's sovereignty. People spend a lot of time here. Argue ad nauseum. If you're wanting me to satisfy your need to understand His sovereignty, I can't. His ways are higher than mine. He's the Creator, I'm the created. He spoke me into existence. Calls a hundred trillion stars by name. What I do know is this: He is sovereign. He does what He wants, when He wants, however He wants, and He asks no one's permission. And because we filter this through our sinful, carnal nature and the wounds therein, we are skeptical that much good can come from this. Not to mention the fact that we have an enemy whispering in our ears that our Abba is cold and calculating. Nothing could be further from the truth.

In God's sovereignty He chose me, and predestined me, and drew me to Himself; and yet if I don't choose Him, I'm going to hell. Jesus placed several decisions in our lap: repent, receive, forgive, and a host of others. Point is, we choose these.

For me, whenever I hear folks arguing or discussing this, I am reminded of Joshua, speaking to the people of Israel: "Choose this day whom you will serve, whether the gods your fathers served in the region beyond the River, or the gods of the Amorites in whose land you dwell. But as for me and my house, we will serve the LORD" (Josh. 24:15). Then and now, I am commanded to choose. So I do. I choose Him. And I choose to receive His Spirit.

Again, let me point you to Matthew 18. Jesus tells us to turn and become like a child or we won't enter the kingdom of heaven, but notice what He says following: "Whoever humbles himself like this child is the greatest in the kingdom of heaven" (Matt. 18:4). I can't begin to unravel all of the discussion surrounding God, His sovereignty, and what that means for you and me. In my relationship with Him—when it comes down to me and Him—I want to be like this child. I want to turn, humble myself, and climb into His lap—and trust Him. He's my Father.

I'm good with that.

Let's Pray

Let me close with this. This is Jesus speaking to people like you and me:

> If God were your Father, you would love me, for I came from God and I
> am here. I came not of my own accord, but he sent me. Why do you not
> understand what I say? It is because you cannot bear to hear my word.
> You are of your father the devil, and your will is to do your father's
> desires. He was a murderer from the beginning, and does not stand in
> the truth, because there is no truth in him. When he lies, he speaks out
> of his own character, for he is a liar and the father of lies. But because I
> tell the truth, you do not believe me. Which one of you convicts me of
> sin? If I tell the truth, why do you not believe me? Whoever is of God
> hears the words of God. The reason why you do not hear them is that
> you are not of God. (John 8:42–47)

We all choose a father. We either choose the father of lies, or the Father
who loves us. And if we don't actively choose our Father in heaven, then,
by default, we have chosen the father of lies. In one kingdom, the father
of lies tells us that we are little more than plastic pieces on a chessboard.
Single-use disposable razors. In the kingdom of God, our Father in heaven
pulls us into His arms and reclines on the couch where we crawl into a
fetal ball on His chest and turn our nose into His neck. And as we do, He
whispers the one word our hearts were created to hear . . . "Child."

The choice is yours—choose a father. Choose a kingdom. And do so
now, while the choice is still yours.

Again, this truth is not a head thing. It's a heart thing. Maybe even a
gut thing. The only One who can make this true in you, and cause you to
receive it down in that place where your love lives, is the Holy Spirit. He
has to do what only the Holy Spirit can. Make it true. This territory is His
alone. That's why I think He says, "Bring them to Me."

So, I'll leave you with Him. Let me recommend that you stay here.
Wrestle this out with your Father. No matter how long it takes, and it may

take a while. The wound took a while to form; it may take a while to peel back the layers and expose the shrapnel. Can He heal it in one fell swoop? Of course, but in my experience, He takes His time. No, I don't really understand that, other than He's not in a hurry and He loves the time with you and because He knows what He's doing and sometimes we don't always understand all that. Again, I'm okay with that.

The following prayer is a little different. It's my prayer to the Father— it's between me and Him, and I'm letting you read it so you'll know you're not alone, and maybe to offer you a model. I'd like to suggest that you do the same. Write Him your own letter. It's the reason for the space below. Write Him several. Write Him a dozen or a hundred. Fill a journal. If your wounds are raw and you're leaking and you need to vent your anger, cuss, and cry out, don't be afraid. Vomit all that stuff on the page. He's big enough to handle whatever comes out your mouth. You can't say anything He doesn't already know. Let me just encourage you to get it out your mouth and bring it to Him. Jacob wrestled God and God blessed him. So, wrestle your Father. I think when you do you'll find Him with arms outstretched, and when He covers your face in kisses, you'll come to know His scent.

Father, Abba, because Your Word promises me, I know that:

> *To all who receive You, who believe in Your name, You have given the right to become children of God, who were born, not of blood nor of the will of the flesh nor of the will of man, but of God. (John 1:12–13)*

> *In love You predestined us for adoption to Yourself as sons through Jesus Christ, according to the purpose of Your will. (Eph. 1:5)*

> *You are My Father who created me, who made me and established me. (Deut. 32:6)*

> *You know what I need before I ask. Because of that, I pray like this, "My Father in heaven, hallowed be your name . . ." (Matt. 6:8–9)*

> *You show compassion to Your children, and to those who fear You. (Ps. 103:13)*

> *All who are led by the Spirit of God are sons of God. For I did not*

receive the spirit of slavery to fall back into fear, but I have received the Spirit of adoption as a son, by whom I cry, "Abba! Father!" The Spirit Himself bears witness with my spirit that I am a child of God, and if a child, then an heir—heir of God and a fellow heir with Christ, provided I suffer with Him in order that I may also be glorified with Him. (Rom. 8:14–17)

You have said to me, that if I will go out from idol worship, be separate from those who do, and touch no unclean thing, then You will be a Father to me, and I will be Your son or daughter. (2 Cor. 6:17–18)

I have seen what great love You, My Father, have lavished on me, that I should be called a child of God, and so I am . . . I am Your child now. (1 John 3:1–2)

Father, I need You. And I need You to be more real than I've even known You to be. I need You to pierce me and my wounded and sometimes cold heart with the revelation that You are who Jesus reveals You to be. You're my Father. My Abba. And in faith, I believe in and agree with Your Word and speak this truth over me. I receive You, I believe in Your name, and I am Your child. You know what I need even before I open my heart. I give you permission right now to upend my image and notion of You. I want a right understanding and knowingness of You.

So please . . . do that in me now. Open my heart and my mind to receive You as You are and not as my history and my circumstances would suggest. You have lavished me with love, and while that's sometimes difficult for me to wrap my head around, I receive Your love of me. And because You have adopted me, and I am Your child, Your Spirit in me cries out, "Abba."

Father, my Father, my Abba, I long for Your scent. Can You and I just hang out for a while? Will You please walk with me? Just wherever You want to go. I know that I need You more than I need air. More than I need my next breath, I need You—My Father—to wrap Your hand around my shoulder and pull me to You. Let me smell You. Remind my heart who You are and who You intended me to be. If You would just speak to my soul and write Your great name on my heart—I'd like that.

For a long time, I've listened to and agreed with the whisper that You don't care and never did, and I'd like to send those lies packing. So, come like fire. Come like rain. Come like a hurricane. Come like the God who fashioned me and spoke me into existence. Who pressed His lips to mine and breathed into me the breath of life. My Father, breathe into me. Revive me according to Your Word. Revive my soul. Father, I know You in my head. I need to know You in my heart. So, please . . . fill me, Father. In Jesus' name.

CHAPTER 11

The Kingdom of Heaven

Seven hundred years before the birth of Jesus, the prophet Isaiah said this: "For to us a child is born, to us a son is given; and the government shall be upon his shoulder, and his name shall be called Wonderful Counselor, Mighty God, Everlasting Father, Prince of Peace. Of the increase of his government and of peace there will be no end, on the throne of David and over his kingdom, to establish it and to uphold it with justice and with righteousness from this time forth and forevermore. The zeal of the LORD of hosts will do this."[1]

Notice the words *government, throne,* and *kingdom.*

Now jump forward to the angel of the Lord who has just appeared to a virgin girl named Mary. Mary is listening with eyes wide. Nothing like this has ever been said to anyone. Anywhere. "And the Lord God will give to him the throne of his father David, and he will reign over the house of Jacob forever, and of his kingdom there will be no end."[2]

Now notice the words *reign* and *forever.*

Jesus is born, and then wise men appear, asking questions. Notice who they are looking for: "Where is he who has been born king of the Jews? For we saw his star when it rose and have come to worship him."[3]

Two words here: *king* and *worship.*

Herod perceives a potential threat to his power, so he gathers all the people and asks where the Christ is to be born. The chief priest and scribes open a scroll, point to the prophet Micah, and tell him Bethlehem: "And you, O Bethlehem, in the land of Judah, are by no means least among the rulers of Judah; for from you shall come a ruler who will shepherd my people Israel."[4]

Herod hears the word *ruler* and doesn't like it. Afraid of Jesus' rule and authority, he kills every firstborn boy two years and younger from in and around the region of Bethlehem.

Fast-forward. Jesus is now thirty years old. His cousin and good friend, John the Baptist, is in the wilderness of Judea preaching, "Repent, for the kingdom of heaven is at hand."[5]

Does it strike you as strange that he uses those words? I get the whole repentance thing, but what is this business about "the kingdom of heaven"?

The Tempting

While John is baptizing, Jesus is led by the Spirit into the wilderness. After a forty-day fast, the devil makes an appearance. he knows Jesus is hungry, so he tests Him with food. But that's what he says on the surface. his point lurks beneath the surface. he questions and mocks His identity: "If you are the Son of God, command these stones to become loaves of bread."[6] Jesus quotes the very words Moses spoke to the nation of Israel some fifteen hundred years prior—Deuteronomy 8:3. It is written, "Man shall not live by bread alone, but by every word that comes from the mouth of God."[7]

These are no simple words Jesus is speaking. The Scripture He quotes is embedded in the words Moses spoke to the nation of Israel on the day they were leaving the desert, after forty years, and crossing over the Jordan into the promised land. This is the day they became a nation, a nation feared by the world, and this comes on the heels of the greatest clash of kingdoms in the history of history—the God of the Hebrew slaves versus all the gods of Egypt. God the Father, the God of Abraham, Isaac, and Jacob, has made good on His promise that He spoke to Moses and the people in the exodus when they camped in the desert before the mountain of God: "If you will indeed obey my voice and keep my covenant, you shall be my treasured possession among all peoples, for all the earth is mine; and you shall be to me a kingdom of priests and a holy nation."[8]

God has taken a people who've known slavery for four hundred years—the children of the children of the children of slaves—and remade them into a nation of priests. That promise was coming true on that day when Moses reminded them that they can't live on bread alone.

Jesus' words to satan aren't simply a historical reminder, and they aren't simply a shot across his bow, nor is it scriptural wrangling in which satan has the upper hand. Jesus' words are a reminder of satan's complete and total defeat then and of the defeat he's about to suffer. In the same way Moses led God's people into the promised land, Jesus is about to walk out of this desert and lead God's children back into the kingdom of their Father. A reckoning is coming, and this simple phrase about bread is Jesus lighting the first of the bunker-busting nuclear bombs that are about to detonate inside satan's kingdom.

The dynamic between the two is interesting because Jesus and satan have known each other a long time. satan was once an angel. I tend to think he was an archangel tasked with tending to Jesus but I can't very well prove it. Then satan rebelled. Unlike Jesus, he thought equality with God was something he could grasp—even though he, like you and me, is a created being.[9] For his rebellion, God the Father cast satan out of heaven, but not before he deceived a third of the angels and took them with him.

satan's singular motivation is the same thing he wants now: worship. It's why he does what he does. It's the reason he set himself up in a rival kingdom. At least he thinks he's a rival. In truth, Jesus has no rival. But make no mistake: for a time, God has given and allowed satan to have a measure of authority and dominion. satan is the prince of the power of the air, and with his power he wages war against the saints (Eph. 2:2; Rev. 13:7).

Back to the tempting.

satan takes Jesus to Jerusalem and sets Him on the pinnacle of the temple, telling Him if He really is who He says He is to throw Himself down—the remaining angels will catch Him. satan supports this idea by quoting Psalm 91. Jesus again responds with the Word: "You shall not put the Lord your God to the test."[10] Notice that these words occur two chapters earlier than the last and in the same chapter as the greatest commandment—where God warns His people not to go after or bow down to other gods.

Things aren't panning out like satan hopes, so the devil takes Jesus to a very high mountain and shows Him all the kingdoms of the world in all their glory. The greatest civilizations ever on display in the height of their power. Babylon. Persia. Egypt. Greece. Rome. Britain. Maybe ours. Must have been quite a sight. satan waves his hand across the timeline, "All these I will give you, if you fall down and worship me."[11] In my mind Jesus scratches His head. Chuckles even. Maybe He files His nails with an emery board. Remember, satan the created is speaking to his Creator. And while satan has a measure of authority and power as we saw in the life of Job, we need to remember that he's speaking to the One who gave it to him. Jesus "spoke, and it came to be; he commanded, and it stood firm."[12] "He is the radiance of the glory of God and the exact imprint of his nature, and he upholds the universe by the word of his power."[13] In short, Jesus created everything at which the two of them are currently looking.

Jesus knows it's time to get to work. He turns slightly, raises an eyebrow, and says, "Be gone, Satan! For it is written, 'You shall worship the Lord your God and him only shall you serve.'"[14]

During that exchange, Jesus quotes Deuteronomy 6:13 and 6:16—which causes me to wonder what verses 14 and 15 say. Why does He quote either end but not the middle? Why does Jesus bookend 14 and 15 but not verbalize it? Is He sending a message? I don't know but I do wonder. Let's look at it: "You shall not go after other gods, the gods of the peoples who are around you—for the Lord your God in your midst is a jealous God—lest the anger of the Lord your God be kindled against you, and he destroy you from off the face of the earth."[15]

On the surface Jesus says don't test God, and worship Him only.

But between those two Scriptures is a promise of what happens to those who do. Is that promise a reminder to satan of what he's got coming? I'm guessing here but I tend to think so. I think Jesus' response to satan in the tempting is both defensive and offensive. Defensive in that He rebuffs every one of satan's temptations. Offensive in that He reminds satan that what satan believes is a temptation is actually the beginning of the end for him. A subtle reminder that God the Father is currently in the process of finishing what He started in Genesis 3. I think Jesus is reminding satan of the total and complete defeat he once suffered, and the irrevocable and absolute defeat he's got coming. Jesus, the serpent crusher, is reminding satan that the crushing is coming.

And these words are a dagger to what remains of satan's heart.

Notice the tension. The tug-of-war. A kingdom lies in the balance. This is a struggle for power. For rulership. Jesus has it by right. satan wants it by whatever means necessary. This is nothing new. From before the beginning of time, the struggle has been for power and for governance and what comes with it—worship and dominion.

Jesus descends the mountain and hears that John the Baptist has been imprisoned, so He returns to Galilee and begins His public ministry. What does He say? "Repent, for the kingdom of heaven is at hand."[16]

Sound familiar? And notice the words "at hand." The wait is over. The kingdom is here now. The time has begun. The clock is ticking.

The Kingdom Is Here. Right Now

Jesus dives headlong into His public ministry. Preaching. Teaching. Healing. Cleansing. Casting out. And wherever He goes, He proclaims the gospel of the kingdom of heaven. Or the gospel of the kingdom of God.

Luke recorded Jesus as saying: "I must preach the good news of the kingdom of God."[17] Shortly thereafter, Jesus sends out His disciples with the same assignment: "to proclaim the kingdom of God and to heal."[18] Before they leave, He tells them: "Proclaim as you go, saying, 'the kingdom of heaven is at hand.' Heal the sick, raise the dead, cleanse lepers, cast out demons. You received without paying, give without pay."[19]

So they do. They proclaim "the gospel of the kingdom." Heal the sick and cast out demons. In the process, the kingdom of darkness is routed. Completely. The disciples discover there are three things that cannot stand in the kingdom of heaven: sin, demons, and sickness. They are incompatible with the kingdom of God. Such is the power of the kingdom.

In the Sermon on the Mount, Jesus' very first statement has to do with the kingdom: "Blessed are the poor in spirit, for theirs is the kingdom of heaven."[20] At first glance it seems strange to start with this, unless you were the king ushering in a kingdom.

Later, at their request, Jesus is teaching His disciples to pray: "Our Father in heaven, hallowed be your name. Your kingdom come, your will be done, on earth as it is in heaven."[21]

The first thing out of Jesus' mouth as He taught them to pray has nothing to do with salvation or the forgiveness of sins or salvation. He will get there. But the priority is addressing the Father as Father, revering Him—or worshipping Him—and then inviting and desiring what He desires: His kingdom here on earth. Embedded in the words themselves is submission and yielding. Totally and without reservation. Complete and absolute.

"Your kingdom." "Your will." Jesus is teaching His followers that those who pray this are rightly related to His God. Which is Jesus' intention.

He is teaching them that entrance into the kingdom of God is conditional upon doing the will of the Father: "Not everyone who says to me, 'Lord, Lord,' will enter the kingdom of heaven, but the one who does the will of my Father who is in heaven."[22] He tells them to "seek first the kingdom of God and his righteousness, and all these things will be added to you."[23]

Throughout His earthly ministry, Jesus' message began as and continued to be the gospel of the kingdom. "Jesus went throughout all the cities and villages, teaching in their synagogues and proclaiming the gospel of the kingdom and healing every disease and every affliction" (Matt. 9:35).

Not only was it His message, but He expected that same message to be the message of those who followed Him: "And proclaim as you go, saying, 'The kingdom of heaven is at hand'" (Matt. 10:7).

Jesus "went about all Galilee, . . . preaching the gospel of the kingdom, and healing all kinds of sickness" (Matt. 4:23 NKJV). When He preached the kingdom of God, the opposing kingdom was forced out of hiding. The healing ministry of Jesus occurred within the kingdom of God. I have bumped into people who want healing without being in the kingdom, without submission, but I'm not sure it works that way. Yes, Jesus healed the Syrophoenician (Canaanite) woman, but only Jesus knew her heart. If we want forgiveness, deliverance, and healing, we would do well to come running inside the gates of the kingdom.

Jesus spoke of the kingdom of heaven or the kingdom of God nearly 150 times. By my count, the only idea upon which Jesus spent more time is the revelation of God as Father. Hence the previous chapter. If we gather all the words of Jesus and separate them into piles, the two largest would be *Father* and *kingdom*. Everywhere He went, He spoke of these two. And it's not as if Jesus stopped talking about the kingdom after His resurrection: "He presented himself alive to them after his suffering by many proofs, appearing to them during forty days and speaking about the kingdom of God" (Acts 1:3).

My question for you is simple: Is this the gospel you proclaim? Even more, is this the gospel you believe? Are you preaching a check-the-box gospel that ends in salvation? Or a gospel that ends in a kingdom surrendered to a King—of which salvation is the door? The difference matters.

A Clash of Kingdoms

If you doubt that you and I exist in the midst of a clash of kingdoms, hear Jesus: "And if Satan casts out Satan, he is divided against himself. How then will his kingdom stand?" (Matt. 12:26). The implication is that satan has a kingdom. Jesus continues with, "If it is by the Spirit of God that I cast out demons, then the kingdom of God has come upon you" (Matt. 12:28). The litmus test is black and white: How do we know the kingdom of God has come upon us? Demons are cast out. Sickness and disease are healed. And sin is forgiven. When we exercise this authority, Jesus promises to give us the keys to this kingdom: "I will give you the keys of the kingdom of heaven, and whatever you bind on earth shall be bound in heaven, and whatever you loose on earth shall be loosed in heaven" (Matt. 16:19).

We already have the keys. He gave them to us. How many of us use them to loose and bind?

You and I were born into this present age, and this present age is at war. From the moment we opened our eyes at birth, we found ourselves living in the midst of a conflict of rulers of kingdoms. The eternal tug-of-war between darkness and light. When we understand the gospel of the kingdom, our prayers change and we desire His kingdom come and His will be done. In sincerity. And not just because we learned it by rote memorization in Sunday school or on the ball field. When we adopt the gospel of the kingdom, our focus changes from seeking happiness or what satisfies us to what satisfies Him.

On the day He was crucified, Jesus was arrested, mocked, spit on, punched, his beard plucked out, beaten with rods that drove the crown of thorns down into His skull, and then He stood before Pilate. Pilate entered his headquarters, sat, crossed his legs, studied Jesus, and then called Him forward: "Are you the King of the Jews?" This is *the* question. "Jesus answered, 'Do you say this of your own accord, or did others say it to you about me?'"[24] I think Jesus asked because Pilate's denial broke Jesus' heart. He was giving him a chance to remember. Jesus fashioned Pilate from dust. Breathed into him the breath of life. Made him a living soul. And yet here he stood, rejecting his King. Pilate brushed Him off. Deflected: "Am I a Jew? Your own nation and the chief priests have delivered You over to me. What have you done?" Jesus gave him another chance: "'My kingdom is not of this world. If my kingdom were of this world, my servants would have been fighting, that I might not be delivered over to the Jews. But my kingdom is not from the world.' Then Pilate said to Him, 'So you are a king?' Jesus answered, 'You say that I am a king. For this purpose I was born and for this purpose I have come into the world—to bear witness to the truth. Everyone who is of the truth listens to my voice.'" Again Pilate deflected, "What is truth?"[25]

Pilate is Exhibit A in how *not* to approach Jesus. Mental head games masking the utter depravity of your heart. Pilate sat on the throne of Pilate's heart. Not Jesus.

Compare Pilate's posture to the words of Jesus: "Unless you turn and become like children, you will never enter the kingdom of heaven" (Matt. 18:3). And, "whoever does not receive the kingdom of God like a child shall not enter it" (Mark 10:15).

To enter the kingdom of heaven, something about our nature must become childlike. So, what characterizes a child? He trusts and obeys his Father. He jumps headlong into His arms. He doesn't fear the water.

Jesus had little patience for the scribes and Pharisees and the message they preached: "You shut the kingdom of heaven in people's faces. For you neither enter yourselves nor allow those who would enter to go in" (Matt. 23:13). Can we look at our own message with such honesty? Further, he gives His kingdom "to a people producing its fruits" (Matt. 21:43).

When I read the words of Jesus and I compare them to the message I most often hear in Christendom, I find myself squinting one eye and scratching my head. Are we proclaiming the whole gospel? I mean, really. The one Jesus proclaimed. A watered-down gospel is not the gospel of the kingdom. How many of us are honest enough about the message we either proclaim or believe? Is there something about the gospel we preach that prevents others from entering it? And what is the fruit of our gospel? Are we producing fair-weather acquaintances who want to be saved from the pain and fire of hell but tuck tail and run at the first suggestion that they bend the knee and lay down their crowns, or are we producing bond servants on their faces before their King, pursuing holiness over their happiness, whispering, "Lord, Your will be done"?

Let me be blunter. In the kingdom Jesus proclaimed and ushered in, the kingdom was preached, sickness healed, dead raised, demons cast out, lepers cleansed. Does your gospel produce that fruit?

If the end of the age won't come until "this gospel of the kingdom [is] proclaimed throughout the whole world as a testimony to all nations," will our message help usher the end, or delay it (Matt. 24:14)? Let me ask it this way: If you were traveling in a foreign country and someone offered you a glass of water saying with a smile, "It's 95 percent pure," would you drink it? Of course not. Because what's in the other 5 percent can kill you. I'm trying to ask if you and I have 95 percent of the good news and yet we're selling it as 100 percent? Are we giving people water that will result in their death?

In my experience, we have communicated to the drowning and the dying that Jesus is our Savior, but we have neglected to tell those flailing in the water that the reason He alone is able to save is because He is Lord—of all.

Everyone wants a Savior. Not everyone wants a Lord.

Big difference.

Preaching Which Gospel?

For much of my life, I've heard "the gospel" preached. And I praise God for those who herald the Word of God and His promises and rescue the wounded and the broken. Please hear me when I say that. But there is a difference between "the gospel" in today's vernacular and "the gospel of the kingdom" in the words of Jesus, and the difference is not just semantics.

In "the gospel" we hear about being saved, born again, how our sins are forgiven, and how the blood of Jesus does this. And yes, this is all absolutely true. Again, praise God. But, "the gospel of the kingdom" tells us why.

In some ways, "the gospel" preached today is a watered-down version of "the gospel of the kingdom." Words matter. Some more than others. And "of the kingdom" matters a lot. In "the gospel," Jesus is my Savior. A selfless and willing sacrifice to pay what I cannot. Again, yes, He absolutely does that. I am not dismissing that nor am I reducing its value. But why?

"The gospel of the kingdom" tells us the larger story. Prior to arriving here, Jesus was the King of a kingdom. And He still is. Yet, because He loves us, He disrobed, took off His crown, and took a swan dive out of the throne room to arrive here on a rescue mission *so that* He can restore mankind to a right relationship with the Father and join Him in His kingdom. In real simplistic terms, Jesus' arrival here and what He alone offers us is to fix what was broken in the garden. The reason for unmerited salvation is not just escaping hell. That's a nice byproduct. But it's because we were designed—from before the beginning of time—to live with the Father and the Son in His kingdom. Under His governance. The reason for the salvation, the reason for the sacrifice, the reason for the payment in blood, is to give us one more chance to stand before the Father, point to the Son, and declare through the stratosphere, *"Jesus is King of Kings and* LORD *of all!"*

Saying so is not just lip service. According to 1 Peter 4:17, judgment will begin with us, and the Father checks all hearts at the door. The Father sees through us and He knows whether we have in fact submitted without reservation or we've just taken out fire insurance. The good news of the gospel of the kingdom is that Jesus is returning to resume the governance of the human race.

In other words, the Father knows the difference between those who just want a Savior and those who cry out, "LORD!"

Whether we take up residence in "the gospel" or "the gospel of the kingdom" depends on our posture. The condition of our heart. The angle of our neck. The bend in our knee. The position of our hands. For Jesus to be Lord, we submit and yield—without reservation—to His lordship. His reign. His dominion. His governance. The good news of the gospel of the kingdom centers around Him and who He is. In making Him Lord, we take us off the throne of our hearts and put Him on it. It means we are no longer the boss of us. It means we do what He wants, not what we want. It means we lay down our lives for the King without question, every day. It means we are way more concerned with holiness than happiness.

So, which is the gospel you believe? Is Jesus both Savior and Lord or do you just want fire insurance? Have you bought into this Christianity thing simply to check the "I'm going to heaven" box? Or are you a sold-out and radical member of the kingdom of heaven with your face flat on the floor before your King?

Don't answer too quickly. Dig around. Make sure.

Not Far or Near?

During Jesus' ministry, He had an interesting exchange with a scribe. A learned man who had spent much of his life studying the law. In religious terms, he was a churchgoer. He was there every time the doors opened. He could quote Scripture backward and forward. Those on the outside looking in thought that if anyone was a member of the I'm-going-to-heaven club, it was this guy.

The scribe comes to Jesus and asks Him which is the most important commandment. Jesus responds with the *shema*: "'Hear, O Israel: The Lord our God, the Lord is one. And you shall love the Lord your God with all your heart and with all your soul and with all your mind and with all your strength.' The second is this: 'You shall love your neighbor as yourself.' There is no other commandment greater than these.'"

The scribe nods and responds: "You are right, Teacher. You have truly said that he is one, and there is no other besides him. And to love him with all the heart and with all the understanding and with all the strength, and to love one's neighbor as oneself, is much more than all whole burnt offerings and sacrifices."

Jesus responds with, "You are not far from the kingdom of God."[26]

I've been told that Jesus is encouraging the scribe that he's closer than the other Pharisees. That there's hope for him. Maybe, but I'm not so sure. I tend to think he's not submitted. Not yielded. I think he's giving Jesus lip service. Whatever the case, I know one thing for certain:

Not far from is not in. It's 95 percent.

Contrast Jesus words of "not far" with Paul's words to the Ephesians: "But now in Christ Jesus you who once were far off have been brought near by the blood of Christ" (Eph. 2:13). "Not far" is standing outside the kingdom. "Brought near" is sitting in the throne room.

Big difference.

I don't know the scribe's heart, but I wonder if he knew the law but had yet to submit and yield his will to the Lawgiver. If he was still on the throne of his own heart. If so, then—in the words of one of my spiritual heroes—"He was a self-made man worshipping his own creator." What we say with our mouth reveals what we believe in our heart. Paul tells this to the Romans, and in doing so reminds them of what the prophet Joel had said nearly six hundred years prior: "If you confess with your mouth that Jesus is Lord and believe in your heart that God raised him from the dead, you will be saved. For with the heart one believes and is justified, and with the mouth one confesses and is saved . . . For 'everyone who calls on the name of the Lord will be saved'" (Rom. 10:9–13).

Are you "not far" from the kingdom of God? Am I?

Here's the thing—only you and Jesus know your heart. You and He alone know who sits enthroned in you. And there are only two options: Him or you. You and I can talk about it until we're blue in the face, but at the end of the day, convincing each other matters none at all. We as Christians are good at pretending, at wearing two faces, so what we project on the outside may not be true on the inside. When Peter says that judgment must begin at the house of God, I think He's talking about you and me: "It is time for judgment to begin at the household of God; and if it begins with us, what will be the outcome for those who do not obey the gospel of God?" (1 Peter 4:17).

Are we 95 percent or all His? Jesus is returning to a priesthood that is sold out. All in. Nothing held back. Him or nothing. Anything less than that is "not far."

Which is a hundred trillion miles away.

I'm trying to counter the argument or the teaching that you can receive from Jesus what cost Him everything without giving Him all of you. Unreservedly. In the kingdom of God there are no partial converts. No 95 percent converts. The 95 percent are on the outside staring in, wailing and gnashing their teeth. When Jesus said, "If anyone would come after me, let him deny himself and take up his cross daily and follow me," He was not kidding (Luke 9:23). And doing so means there's going to be a daily execution. Paul knew this. It's why he said, "I die every day" (1 Cor. 15:31).

What's being put to death? The thing in you that says "I wanna do what I wanna do when I wanna do it how I wanna do it, and I'm not asking anybody's permission." It's called your "self" and it's the part of you focused on you and not Him. Picking up your cross and stepping one foot across the threshold of the kingdom of God means you enthrone Jesus in you, and the proof is in your praises. Jesus addressed it with the Twelve this way: "Who is the greater, one who reclines at table or one who serves? Is it not the one who reclines at table? But I am among you as the one who serves. You are those who have stayed with me in my trials, and I assign to you, as my Father assigned to me, a kingdom, that you may eat and drink at my table in my kingdom and sit on thrones judging the twelve tribes of Israel" (Luke 22:27–30).

Somehow the thief on the cross knew Jesus was the King of a kingdom, and yet he'd only known Him a few hours—and I seriously doubt it had anything to do with the sign above Jesus' head. This is why he told Him: "Jesus, remember me when you come into your kingdom" (Luke 23:42).

We cannot receive the unmerited and priceless gift of salvation without absolute submission to the King who offers it. The Father will not allow it. Why? To do so makes a mockery of His Son's sacrifice. This is the writer of Hebrews:

> It is impossible, in the case of those who have once been enlightened, who have tasted the heavenly gift, and have shared in the Holy Spirit, and have tasted the goodness of the word of God and the powers of the age to come, and then have fallen away, to restore them again to

repentance, since they are crucifying once again the Son of God to their own harm and holding him up to contempt. For land that has drunk the rain that often falls on it, and produces a crop useful to those for whose sake it is cultivated, receives a blessing from God. But if it bears thorns and thistles, it is worthless and near to being cursed, and its end is to be burned. (Heb. 6:4–8)

See those words "fallen away"? The Greek word is *parapipto* and it occurs only once in the New Testament. It means to defect. If you defect, or scornfully turn your back upon another, you reject submission to the ruling authority and seek asylum in a rival kingdom.

In the garden of Eden, man lived under the righteous reign of the Father. God and Adam walked together in the cool of the mornings. This was the Father's plan. His delight. Interestingly, in the garden of Eden, Adam was given dominion and governance as long as he obeyed. But when he chose the rival kingdom led by a rebel, God kicked him out. God gave man what he wanted. But you can't have one foot in one kingdom and one foot in the other any more than you can be a little bit dead. If you're dead, you're dead. There's no sorta-alive. You are either 100 percent alive or 100 percent dead. Alive and dead can't coexist. Period.

The gospel of the kingdom, or good news of the kingdom, is *not* simply that our sins are forgiven. Of course that's good news. But *why* are our sins forgiven? What's the point? The reason salvation matters, the reason the blood of Jesus cleanses us, redeems us, sanctifies us, and makes us holy as He is holy, is because the Son of God is returning to rule and govern His kingdom, here, and we're invited in.

That's the good news.

But, there's only one way into the kingdom of God, and the road is narrow and the cost is more than any of us can pay in a thousand lifetimes. We can never pay the fine for our rebellion. God knows this and He loves us despite our total and complete depravity, so the Father—in His infinite love—sent His Son to do what we could not. This is the wonder and majesty and I-just-can't-believe-it-ness of the gospel of the kingdom. The

Father sent the Son on a rescue mission to return with His children to His kingdom. Maybe this resonates with me because I write stories. I'm not sure. All I know is that the Father loves His creation and He invites us—created rebels, housed in the kingdom of darkness—to become His very own children. To transfer us out of the kingdom of death and darkness into the kingdom of the Son of His love. His offer is illogical, unimaginable, and his love unfathomable.

Paul told the church in Thessalonica: "You know how, like a father with his children, we exhorted each one of you and encouraged you and charged you to walk in a manner worthy of God, who calls you into his own kingdom and glory" (1 Thess. 2:11–12). In the kingdom of God, you and I are no longer slaves; we're children and coheirs.

What other king, anywhere at any time, shares his reign, equally, with his subjects?

I am trying, however feebly, to bring you beyond what can possibly be limited to a rational decision of your mind where you make a "decision for Christ," "receive salvation," raise your hand, or maybe walk down front and add your name to a roster, into a gut-check decision of your heart of which only you and Jesus know the truth—where you walk into the throne room, before the King, and then, like the twenty-four elders around His throne, cast your crown at His feet and cry out, *You alone are worthy!* Knees bent. Head bowed. Face to the floor. Hands raised. Heart submitted.

A Savior is thanked. A King is worshipped.

I have met people who seem genuinely surprised to find out that to receive the salvation Jesus offers requires that we submit to His reign. They scratch their heads and ask, "You mean to tell me that I have to give up my will, what I want, for His will and what He wants?"

That's exactly what I'm telling you.

They stammer, "But I thought all I had to do was repent of my sins. Make a decision for Christ and ask Him into my heart?" Yes, all of this is true and repentance is foundational, but repentance alone will not grant you access into the kingdom. Entrance into the kingdom of heaven, eternity with Jesus, occurs when we submit and come under His dominion and His governance. No submission, no new address.

One of the more beautiful transformations I have witnessed in my life in ministry is seeing those who were once a long way from Jesus encounter Him. When prodigals return, they don't have to be convinced of their own depravity and wretchedness. They know the extent of their mess— it's usually smeared across their faces—and when they meet Him they are shattered by the fact that the Father doesn't point and say, "I told you so." Doesn't poke them in the chest and exact payment. Doesn't shame them. He lifts their chin and covers their face in kisses. This is the inexplicable love of the Father, and when we encounter Him, we can't wait to fall at His feet. Whenever I've watched this unfold, I am reminded that deliverance is for the desperate.

That said, when we come to Jesus, we can't simply knock on the door and ask Him to be our Savior while standing with indifference at the threshold of the kingdom. To do so is to thumb our nose at the offering. There is no salvation outside the kingdom of heaven. It's all or nothing. He either is King of the universe who spoke us into existence and upholds all things by the word of His power or He's not. There's no middle.

Only within the kingdom are sins forgiven, all sickness healed, and demons driven out. "But if it is by the finger of God that I cast out demons, then the kingdom of God has come upon you" (Luke 11:20). If you're standing outside the kingdom, you've rejected His offer and His dominion. You've defected.

There is the possibility that someone who dearly loves Jesus, who worships Him as Lord, and who's also prayed for healing for themselves or a loved one, maybe for a long time, and not received it, might ask, "Are you telling me that I'm not healed because I haven't really yielded to Him in my life?" No. I'm not. Please don't hear that. I don't know why sometimes Jesus-loving-and-worshipping people aren't healed. I wish I did. But that's not what I'm saying. I'm simply listening to the message I often hear preached, and I think it's a counterfeit. It's watered down. It's 95 percent.

And its fruit is dead people who think they are alive.

As a result, I'm trying to cause you to question the true nature and condition of your heart. To turn the mirror on yourself. Because, in truth, only you and Jesus know the answer. Are you seeking first the kingdom, or do you just want escape from your present circumstances? Are you hoping to go from bad to good or dead to life? 'Cause there's a difference. Jesus didn't die to make bad people better. He stretched out His arms to bring dead people to life.

Who Is This Jesus?

We live in a culture in which we sing songs stating that I have a friend in Jesus or He's closer than a friend or something along these lines. And if you know me, you know I love those songs. But in calling Jesus "friend," have we somehow reduced Him? Lessened His deity? Jesus delights in being closer to us than a friend and He desires intimacy with us unlike any other, but as He scoots up next to us and wraps His arm around our neck and covers our face in kisses, let's remember who He is. Let's don't forget whose breath is actually breathing down our neck.

When Peter affirmed Jesus as the Christ in Caesarea Philippi, Jesus responded with: "Blessed are you, Simon Bar-Jonah! For flesh and blood has not revealed this to you, but my Father who is in heaven" (Matt. 16:17). See that word, *revealed*? That's exactly revelation and what is needed. John, in his book of Revelation, told us that when he beheld Jesus in His resurrected, glorified body, there were twenty-four elders flat on their faces worshipping Him. They'd cast their crowns at His feet. Stacked up like hubcaps in a junkyard. They were singing, "Worthy are you to take the scroll and to open its seals, for you were slain, and by your blood you ransomed people for God from every tribe and language and people and nation, and you have made them a kingdom and priests to our God, and they shall reign on the earth" (Rev. 5:9–10).

In his ears, John heard more than one hundred million angels singing in unison, "Worthy is the lamb who was slain" (Rev. 5:12). Everyone John could see was worshipping Jesus. Flat out on their faces. They were seeing the same revelation—Jesus as He is.

To the Philippians, Paul described Him this way: "God has highly exalted him and bestowed on him the name that is above every name, so that at the name of Jesus every knee should bow, in heaven and on earth and under the earth, and every tongue confess that Jesus Christ is Lord, to the glory of God the Father" (Phil. 2:9–11).

The writer of Hebrews put it this way—quoting Psalm 45: "But of the Son He says, 'Your throne, O God, is forever and ever, the scepter of uprightness is the scepter of your kingdom'" (Heb. 1:8).

Forever and ever.

Every knee. Every tongue. Everywhere. Jesus is Messiah. *Yeshua HaMashiach.* The Anointed One. *The* Lord of all lords. *The* King of all kings. The One who avenges us. To Him has been given all dominion. Of every kingdom everywhere. He's been given all authority—over all authority. And His kingdom cannot be shaken (Heb. 12:28). And for the record, satan can't stand any of this. he hates the fact that you and I are talking about all this.

Where the Rubber Meets the Road

My question for you is, while you are willing to be saved, are you prepared to be governed? Because you cannot separate salvation from government. Are you willing to let Him put a bit in your mouth and lead you where you do not want to go? A warhorse is useless in the battle unless he willingly gives the reins to someone else.

Has everything that pertains to you been brought under Jesus' control? Let's just start with a tough one: finances. Do you tithe? *Well, I don't have to; I'm under the new covenant, and not under the law.* Absolutely. And I thank God for it. The new covenant is a better covenant with better promises and we are free from obligation, "for the law of the Spirit of life has set you [and me] free in Christ Jesus from the law of sin and death" (Rom. 8:2).

But before we use the new covenant as a license to sin, Abraham raises the bar. Before the Law was given, when he stood in the valley of the five kings, he gave a tenth of all. Doing so was worship. Evidence that he had willfully come under the dominion of the ruling King. It flowed from the outpouring of His heart.

One of the best indicators of whether someone has truly yielded to God Most High is shown in what they do with their money. If they tithe before they pay taxes, before they spend a single penny on themselves, if they willingly and gladly give over and above their tithe, then I have a pretty good idea that they've knelt not just their body but their whole heart before the King.

The response I normally receive from people who don't tithe is, *Well, I can't afford to.* Stop. None of us can afford to. We don't give out of surplus or abundance when the whim suits us. We give out of obedience. Out of love. We give before we figure out if we can afford to. Tithing is not a budget line item. Why? It's a faith thing, and without faith it's impossible to please Him. If you are not tithing faithfully, or if you are tithing begrudgingly or not gladly, then chances are really good that you have set yourself up as king of your own kingdom. Which, in essence, means you trust you to take care of your needs more than you trust Him. And notice what's happening here: I'm telling you this but I'm not asking you for a penny of your money. I don't want anything from you. I have not included a giving envelope with this book. I don't want your money. But I am poking at you and trying to get you to ask yourself if you hold fast to your money tighter than you hold fast to the King who shed His blood for you.

This is God speaking through the prophet Malachi just before the prophets fell silent for four hundred years:

> For I the LORD do not change; therefore you, O children of Jacob, are not consumed. From the days of your fathers you have turned aside from my statutes and have not kept them. Return to me, and I will return to you, says the LORD of hosts. But you say, "How shall we return?" Will man

rob God? Yet you are robbing me. But you say, "How have we robbed you?" In your tithes and contributions. You are cursed with a curse, for you are robbing me, the whole nation of you. Bring the full tithe into the storehouse, that there may be food in my house. And thereby put me to the test, says the LORD of hosts, if I will not open the windows of heaven for you and pour down for you a blessing until there is no more need. I will rebuke the devourer for you, so that it will not destroy the fruits of your soil, and your vine in the field shall not fail to bear, says the LORD of hosts. Then all nations will call you blessed, for you will be a land of delight, says the LORD of hosts. (Mal. 3:6–12)

Jesus said, "It is more blessed to give than to receive. . . . Give, and it will be given to you. Good measure, pressed down, shaken together, running over, will be put into your lap. For with the measure you use it will be measured back to you" (Acts 20:35; Luke 6:38). Blessing comes with giving. And don't miss the "with the measure you use" part. He's not kidding. How about this one? "For God so loved the world, that he gave . . ." (John 3:16). God gave to us. Period. If we withhold giving to Him, do we really love Him?

Honest question: Are you robbing God? Who do you trust more with "your" money? You or God?

The Exchange

Sometimes it's difficult for me to comprehend the totality of the kingdom of God. But it's not so tough to comprehend what the blood of Jesus does in the kingdom. This is what I mean, and it returns us to the cross, which is good. Inside the kingdom, sin is forgiven, demons are cast out, and all sickness is healed. These three prove the existence of the kingdom. But what brought this about? What ushered this in?

Let's go back to the cross. *Tetelestai. It is finished. It is perfectly perfect. It is completely complete.* Maybe this is why the writer of Hebrews said, "By a single offering he has perfected for all time those who are being sancti-fied" (Heb. 10:14).

So, what exactly was and is finished? What was made perfectly per-fect or completely complete? Well, a lot. In a grossly simplistic form, Jesus took on Himself all of the bad stuff in us and due to us—our unholiness—and exchanged it for all the good stuff in Himself and due to Himself. Paul described the exchange this way, "He made Him who knew no sin to be sin on our behalf, so that we might become the right-eousness of God in Him" (2 Cor. 5:21 NASB). It's totally illogical—He took what was due to us and gave us what was due to Him. Our sin for His righteousness.

Isaiah described it this way seven hundred years before the cross: "All of us like sheep have gone astray, each of us has turned to his own way; but the LORD has caused the iniquity of us all to fall on Him" (Isa. 53:6 NASB). See that word *iniquity*? The Hebrew word is *avon*. It's an all-encompassing word. It means not only guilt, sin, rebellion, and iniquity but also all the consequences due us as a result of our guilt and sin. *Avon* = sin + conse-quence. He took our guilty verdict and served out the sentence. Which was death.

Implied in the words "It is finished," is the assumption that something else has begun. And that something is the kingdom of heaven.

This exchange is the mystery of the cross, and it is required to place man back in the presence of God. Until you understand what was taken from us and what was given to us, you can't understand the kingdom. To me, the aspects of this exchange are best articulated by one of my spiritual heroes, Derek Prince. I can't improve on his explanation, so I've copied it here with permission.

Don't gloss over. Don't skim. Slow down. Let it sink in. Every provi-sion needed for your total and complete return to and before a holy and righteous God—to make you holy—is here. When you read them, notice that what is listed first is what occurs in the kingdom of darkness and what follows is God's unmerited remedy to remove us from that kingdom and return us to His:

- Jesus took our *punishment* and gave us His *forgiveness* (Isa. 53:4–5).
- He was *wounded*, that we might be *healed* (Isa. 53:4–5).
- He was made *sin* with our sinfulness that we might be made *righteous* with His righteousness (2 Cor. 5:21).
- He died our *death* that we might receive His *life* (Heb. 2:9).
- He endured our *poverty* that we might share in His *abundance* (2 Cor. 8:9).
- He bore our *shame* that we might share His *glory* (Heb. 12:2).
- He endured our *rejection* that we might have His *acceptance* with the Father (Eph. 1:5–6).
- He was made a *curse* that we might enter into the *blessing* (Gal. 3:13–14).
- He was *cut off by death* that we might be *joined to God eternally* (Isa. 53:8).
- Our *old man was put to death in Him*, that *the new man might come to life* in us (Col. 3:9–10).

Let me point out the obvious: left side is the kingdom of darkness; right side is the kingdom of heaven. And while every bit of this provision is available to everyone who would receive Him, the exchange *occurs only in the kingdom of heaven*.

Which do you want? And what are you prepared to do to get it?

There is no salvation outside the kingdom walls. And outside the city walls there is no righteousness, only rebellion.

By reasons of unmerited grace, Jesus took our punishment, our wounds, our sin, our death, our poverty, our shame, our rejection, our curse, and piled it on His own shoulders. Then He let His accusers kill Him. In so doing, He crucified our old man. Put him (us) to death along with all the consequences due us. Then He resurrected a new man in his place. This is why Paul told the Galatians, "I have been crucified with Christ. It is no longer I who live, but Christ who lives in me. And the life I now live in the flesh I live by faith in the Son of God, who loved me and gave himself for me" (Gal. 2:20).

If you study this list in the exchange, nothing is left out. No exceptions. When Jesus shouted *tetelestai* out across the stratosphere, He gave us His forgiveness, His healing, His righteousness, His life, His abundance, His glory, His acceptance, His blessing—and He did all this through the new man, which He breathes to life in us. Paul told the Colossians that God the Father has literally "delivered us from the domain of darkness and transferred us to the kingdom of his beloved Son" (Col. 1:13).

Elsewhere, he told the Ephesians:

But now in Christ Jesus you who once were far off have been brought near by the blood of Christ. For he himself is our peace, who has made us both one and has broken down in his flesh the dividing wall of hostility by abolishing the law of commandments expressed in ordinances, that he might create in himself one new man in place of the two, so making peace, and might reconcile us both to God in one body through the cross, thereby killing the hostility. (Eph. 2:13–16)

Both Jew and Gentile alike have been transferred and brought near. I think if we really understood the depth and truth of that reality, we'd never get off our face. Here's my summation of the exchange that occurred to transfer us from the kingdom of darkness to the kingdom of the Son of His love: *there is more mercy in Him than sin in us.*

The cross proved and continues to prove this.

Every day.

The Only Solution

The only solution to the sum total of all human misery and pain is the establishment of God's kingdom here. His kingdom is His solution. Not current governments, not current rulers, not political parties or new legislation. I love my country, and I thank God for it. I think our system of government may well be the best ever created by man, but that's just it.

Man created it. So, from the beginning, it too is broken. It contains a fatal flaw, and the flaw is us.

Left to ourselves and our own devices, we will rot like fruit in a bowl. Decay is resident in us. It's called sin. As a result, we're all rotten and we stink. Literally. Rotting from the inside out. And there's nothing we can do about it. The Lord reminds us by giving us a physical body that mirrors our nature. From toothpaste to deodorant to perfume to body spray to baby powder to scented toilet paper, fabric softener, air fresheners, and baby wipes, we try to mask it and cover it up but, given time, we will stink again. We don't like to admit it, but every time we eat, something stinky will come out the other end. Not a single one of us exits the bathroom without a foul odor. That is the undeniable and indisputable truth of you and me. All the money in the world won't change that. The same is true for our physical bodies. We might nip, tuck, inject, and sculpt, but sooner or later things will fall, wrinkle, and flap.

That may gross you out, and you may not like me for saying it, but this is the ugly, irreversible truth of us. And it is a mirror reflection of our spiritual nature. Rotting from the inside out.

When this life comes to an end, you and I are dust returning to dust: little more than worm food. Given this, what do we really have to be arrogant about?

Absolutely nothing.

And if you think you're a self-made man or woman and you've worked hard, or maybe you've built a hundred-million-dollar company or a billion-dollar empire, let me quote Paul: "What do you have that you did not receive? If then you received it, why do you boast as if you did not receive it?" (1 Cor. 4:7). I am not suggesting that you and I haven't worked hard. You may have. But a lot of people have worked hard. You and I would do well to humble ourselves now at a time of our choosing, while there's still time. Because there will come a day and time of His choosing when your judgment will occur; and according to Scripture, if you haven't humbled yourself by then, it's too late: "For we must all appear before the judgment seat of Christ, so that each one may receive what is due for what he has done in the body, whether good or evil" (2 Cor. 5:10).

The clock is ticking.

Missing the Kingdom

It seems popular today to write away hell or erase it. To suggest it's not real. Or lessen the circumstances of our rebellion or try to make our condition seem not so bad. To suggest that we'll all get to heaven by different roads. That a "good" God would never send people there.

That's a lie from the pit of hell. There are some who will not enter into the kingdom of heaven.

This is Paul:

Do you not know that the unrighteous will not inherit the kingdom of God? Do not be deceived: neither the sexually immoral, nor idolaters, nor adulterers, nor men who practice homosexuality, nor thieves, nor the greedy, nor drunkards, nor revilers, nor swindlers will inherit the kingdom of God. And such were some of you. But you were washed, you were sanctified, you were justified in the name of the Lord Jesus Christ and by the Spirit of our God. (1 Cor. 6:9–11)

You think God is serious about this? Here is Paul describing those in the kingdom and those out:

But if you are led by the Spirit, you are not under the law. Now the works of the flesh are evident: sexual immorality, impurity, sensuality, idolatry, sorcery, enmity, strife, jealousy, fits of anger, rivalries, dissensions, divisions, envy, drunkenness, orgies, and things like these. I warn you, as I warned you before, that those who do such things will not inherit the kingdom of God. But the fruit of the Spirit is love, joy, peace, patience, kindness, goodness, faithfulness, gentleness, self-control;

against such things there is no law. And those who belong to Christ Jesus have crucified the flesh with its passions and desires. (Gal. 5:18–24)

Look back across these three paragraphs. Paul has just described every one of us.* Including me. So, what's the difference between those outside the kingdom of God and those in it if we're all a bunch of black-hearted sinners?

Those in the kingdom crucified their flesh. Repented. Submitted. Cast their crowns at His feet. And they confessed Him as Lord.**

All of us get eternity. It's guaranteed. The free gift of God allows us to choose which kingdom we spend it in. Our first problem is that we have

---

* He does much the same thing in his letter to the Ephesians: *But sexual immorality and all impurity or covetousness must not even be named among you, as is proper among saints. Let there be no filthiness nor foolish talk nor crude joking, which are out of place, but instead let there be thanksgiving. For you may be sure of this, that everyone who is sexually immoral or impure, or who is covetous (that is, an idolater), has no inheritance in the kingdom of Christ and God. Let no one deceive you with empty words, for because of these things the wrath of God comes upon the sons of disobedience. Therefore do not become partners with them; for at one time you were darkness, but now you are light in the Lord. Walk as children of light* (Eph. 5:3–8).

**To whom has the Father promised the kingdom? To those who love Him (James 2:5). Is it difficult to obtain? No. Jesus said, *Fear not, little flock, for it is your Father's good pleasure to give you the kingdom* (Luke 12:32). The implication is that they (i.e. we) love Him more than we love us. We see this kind of love in the description of the faithful in Revelation: *And I heard a loud voice in heaven saying, "Now the salvation and the power and the kingdom of our God and the authority of his Christ have come, for the accuser of our brothers has been thrown down, who accuses them day and night before our God. And they have conquered him by the blood of the Lamb and by the word of their testimony, for they loved not their lives even unto death* (Rev. 12:10–11).

The kingdom of God is not geographical, nor is it bound by time. Nor does it consist in talk, but in power (1 Cor. 4:20). Paul said, *For the kingdom of God is not a matter of eating and drinking but of righteousness and peace and joy in the Holy Spirit* (Rom. 14:17). Notice that the kingdom is *in* the Holy Spirit.

No Holy Spirit? No kingdom of heaven.

When Jesus said, "repent" what exactly did He mean? He told us in Luke 15. The story of the prodigal son. I wrote about this to a great extent in *What If It's True?* but I want to add one thing here. Notice what the prodigal said to himself: *But when he came to himself, he said, "How many of my father's hired servants have more than enough bread, but I perish here with hunger! I will arise and go to my father, and I will say to him, 'Father, I have sinned against heaven and before you. I am no longer worthy to be called your son. Treat me as one of your hired servants.'" And he arose and came to his father. But while he was still a long way off, his father saw him and felt compassion, and ran and embraced him and kissed him. And the son said to him, "Father, I have sinned against heaven and before you. I am no longer worthy to be called your son"* (Luke 15:17–21).

The son has humbled himself and in his mind and heart, he is now on the level of a servant. Aware of his own unworthiness and no longer calling himself a son, he walks home prepared to serve the Father.

The Father, on the other hand, has other ideas.

a bastardized version of repentance. To Jesus, repentance meant repent and submit. In contemporary culture, it means to be sorry that you got caught, clean up your act, and enroll in fire insurance. Two thousand years ago, repentance included submission. Face on the floor. Hands lifted high. Today it's been deleted. Eyes roaming indifferently. Hands shoved in pockets. We're afraid to speak the truth because we don't want to hurt someone's feelings.

But the requirement stands.

Repent.

When you come to Jesus, you give up your rights. All of them. You keep nothing. That means everything you want. Everything which we fight for on earth becomes stubble at His feet. Every affection, every desire, every emotion. Everything. Walking through the gates is a complete, total, and unequivocal surrender. We demand nothing. We enter His presence with our hands (and heart) held high, palms out, fingers loose. Clutching nothing. Whatever we're carrying is His for the taking. This means people, practices, purposes. Absolutely everything. If He chooses to give them back, great, but the giving and the taking is up to Him.

So with what right are you standing before Him? What demand do you bring?

Entering the Courtroom

Here's my take, as a fiction writer, on this whole deal. And maybe this four-page story gets the point across better than the pages that precede it. Remember, this is fiction, and I've written it in first person for a reason.

I enter the courtroom. Bound. Chains rattling. All eyes on me. Leading up to the trial, the headlines declared me "The Worst of the Worst." The bailiff seats me behind bulletproof glass as the King enters. All rise, save me. Why would I rise? He's about to kill me. The King takes His seat, and with His permission, the proceedings begin. The judge asks me how I plead. I mutter with smug indifference, "Not guilty." While I'm at it, I give the King the finger.

The prosecution brings out a book. Actually, several books. The record of my wrongs. Starting at the beginning, He details my life's work. The list is long but, in short, I am a rebel who committed treason, led a mutiny, and willingly aided and abetted the enemy. All in an attempt to overthrow the King. The beloved King seated above me. Moans and murmurs bubble up out of the public seats. Midway through the reading, the prosecution lowers an IMAX screen, clicks a button, and begins playing the video of my life's work. The first few images are met with silence, but are soon followed by screams, tears, and finally cries for justice. Off to my left, someone vomits. The courtroom is in an uproar. The judge slams his gavel and demands silence. The King wipes away either tears or sweat. The prosecution continues.

For days.

By week's end, the galley is enraged and foaming at the mouth. Several members of the public have been arrested trying to bring weapons into the courtroom. The King sits cross-legged, tapping His fingers, eyes trained on me. Someone leaks a copy of the video to the media. In minutes, the demonstration outside the courthouse turns violent. Armed troops are called in to prevent protesters from storming the courthouse. Fires and looting spread for blocks. Their chants echo through the windows.

They are calling for my head on a platter.

Back inside, we continue to watch the video of me. Murder. Mayhem. Chaos. Adultery. Every drug known to man. Catastrophic theft. Insurrection. School bombings. Playgrounds littered with parts. Assassination attempt after assassination attempt on the life of the King. The video paints a timeline strewn with bodies and people and hopes and dreams, and framing it all is my smiling, grinning, smug little face.

I did what I wanted, when I wanted, how I wanted, whenever I wanted, and I asked no one's permission. I lived for me. Period. Finally, the video displayed one of my mountain homes where the view stretched for miles. Epic parties. Filth untold. In the great room, I'd installed a replica of the

King's throne. Surrounded with half-dressed and undressed women. Sex slaves at my beck and call. Minions. The video continued showing me, sitting on the throne, stabbing a life-sized doll of the King. Mutilating Him. In the last frame, I cut off His head and pose for the camera.

Back in the courtroom, there's little deliberation.

The jury files in and the bailiff makes me stand as the judge takes his seat. The verdict is read. Guilty on all counts. The King again wipes either tears or sweat. The judge asks me if I have anything to say. For the second time, I give him the finger. The time for talking is over. The time for dying has arrived. The judge slams the gavel, "Death by firing squad." The bailiff wastes no time. He walks me to a holding cell and strips me to my underwear. My tattered clothes lie in a pile. The smell curls his nose. I'm not much to look at. He then leads me to the yard. Dead man walking. Straps me to a pole. Beyond the bars of the prison, the city is shouting. Screaming for blood. They press against the gates. Testing the locks. The troops wrestle to hold them back. It's not long now. I stare at the rifles all staring at me. I wonder how it will feel when the bullets tear at my flesh and rip my face off. Will I feel anything? Even now, I can feel the heat of my destination rising up around my feet.

I look around for the last time, and one thing strikes me. I am alone. Utterly and completely. Not one single friend can be found. The bailiff speaks to the riflemen, "Ready!" They level them at me. Each is aimed at my face. I could stick my finger in the end of the barrels. "Aim!" The rifles steady. At least it will be quick.

One second. Two. Their knuckles turn white as they place pressure on the triggers.

A voice speaks quietly to my left. He's calm. Collected. "Stop." The barrels lift and we turn. The King has appeared. Walking toward me. He's young. Beloved. Beaming. The crowd cheers. Women faint. Children dance. He stands before me. Studies me. I read his face, and despite my every attempt to end his life, I see no anger there. Only sadness. Tears streak His cheeks. With little notice, He takes off His robe and hands it to an attendant. Followed by the ring on His hand. As He does this, I am struck by the knowledge that He is wearing my clothes. My soiled rags.

These are no clothes for a King.

He steps closer. His face inches from mine. His breath on my face. I can smell Him. I am waiting for the condemnation. The words I deserve. Then He does the strangest thing. He kisses me and then whispers through a smile, "You are . . . the joy set before me." The bailiff unties my ropes, and the King places a thick envelope in my hands. When He turns to face the rifles, the bailiff lashes Him with my ropes to the pole, steps back, and shouts, "Fire!"

Bullets tear at His flesh and almost rip his head off His shoulders. The shockwave slams Him against the pole then drops Him, limp and bullet-riddled, to the ground. Eyes still open. The life that was there seconds ago is gone. His blood collects into a pool and seeps into the grass. Warm and red. And as it does, I can hear it crying out from the ground.

The crowd disperses and I am left alone with the body of the dead King.

That night, I stand at the window of a high-rise building. I'm dressed in a brilliant, white linen shirt. Unstained. It smells like the King, and I'm pretty sure I shouldn't be wearing it. The carpet is soft beneath my bare feet, and I am not repulsed at the smell of me.

I look over my shoulder because I know me and I don't belong here. Any minute, armed men will walk through that door and escort me back to the pole where they will finish their count. I study the streets below but there are no crowds.

Minutes pass, but there are no footsteps. The silence is deafening.

I press my face to the glass, stare out across the world laid out below me and I can see for more than a hundred miles in every direction. Nothing about my present situation makes sense. The unopened envelope sits on the table next to me. My hand shakes as I open the envelope revealing a handwritten letter followed by several legal documents.

The letter begins, "Dear Son—" and the handwriting belongs to the King, but I can't wrap my head around it. It can't possibly be true. So I read it again. There must be some mistake. Then a third time. I can't figure out who He's talking to. I stare out the window. According to the letter, I now own the building I am standing in, and every building for miles in every direction. Further, I own the land, every house, and every beast for more than a hundred miles in every direction. I keep reading, but it is the next revelation that brings me to my knees. A birth certificate. Mine. Yellowed from age.

The date of the letter catches my eye. Someone has made a colossal mistake. I turn to page one of my arrest record—the books they read in court—and the letter predates my first conviction. I empty the remaining contents of the envelope to find a thick stack of accounting spreadsheets. A debt ledger. Mine. I flip through it. Debits and very few credits. The ones I accrued over my wasted life. The last time I looked at my balance due, it was a number I couldn't pay in a hundred lifetimes. When I flip to the last page, afraid of what I know I owe, I am awestruck.

A zero balance.

The knowledge swims around my head, and the enormity of it settles somewhere in my heart—the King filed the adoption papers while I was busy writing my book. Accruing insurmountable debt. While I was trying to kill Him and grab His power. My strength fails, I hit my knees, and somewhere in that fog my heart is pierced with the knowingness that He didn't disown me when He had every right. When He could have. What's more, He didn't shame me. When He should have. What I am holding in my hand, if it is true, tells me that the King paid all my debts, served my sentence, and gave me all He had.

He made me His own.

A noise behind me. An older man. Beard. He resembles the King. His scent is somehow familiar. The picture on the desk suggests they are related. Father and Son. I peer around Him but there are no armed guards. His face is not threatening. He steps closer. His breath on my face. I hold up the documents. "Is this true?"

A tear breaks loose. A smile. And He nods. "Every word."

I point to the books, stacked in the corner. The ones used by the prosecution. "But—" I stammer. "I'm guilty. Don't you realize? I did all this.

Every last thing." I point to the picture of the Son. "And He didn't do a thing." I shake my head. "You killed the wrong man."

He says nothing.

I scream, "But why?!"

The Father wraps His arms around me, and that's when it hits me. He sent His Son. To rescue me. To do for me what I could not do for myself. When I wasn't worth rescuing.

I am undone.

If you've just read this story only to wipe your brow and think, *Gee, I'm glad I'm not that bad*, you're wrong. You are. It's your story. I wrote it in first person so you could read about you. And so I could read about me. Every one of us is that evil. We may not have acted on it, but it is our nature. We are treasonous, mutinous rebels hell-bent on assassinating the King. That's the truth of us. We are evil, rotting from the inside out, and you don't improve us or make us better or coach us out of it or cover us with deodorant or body spray. You crucify that old man. Cover him with the blood of Jesus. Bury him with Jesus. And then let Jesus—who alone is King—raise him to life. This is why the gospel of the kingdom is good news.

Maybe you disagree. Maybe you compare yourself to others and think, *I'm not that bad*. Maybe you point to that person over there: *They're worse than me!* Maybe you look at our prisons and you think, *I've not done that!*

Listen to what Scripture says. And remember, when we say "Scripture" these are the words proceeding from the mouth of God Himself.

- "The LORD saw that the wickedness of man was great in the earth, and that every intention of the thoughts of his heart was only evil continually" (Gen. 6:5).
- "The heart is deceitful above all things, and desperately sick; who can understand it?" (Jer. 17:9).
- "The fool says in his heart, 'There is no God.' They are corrupt,

doing abominable iniquity; there is none who does good. God looks down from heaven on the children of man to see if there are any who understand, who seek after God. They have all fallen away; together they have become corrupt; there is none who does good, not even one" (Ps. 53:1–3).

- "What comes out of the mouth proceeds from the heart, and this defiles a person. For out of the heart come evil thoughts, murder, adultery, sexual immorality, theft, false witness, slander" (Matt. 15:18–19).

- "What comes out of a person is what defiles him. For from within, out of the heart of man, come evil thoughts, sexual immorality, theft, murder, adultery, coveting, wickedness, deceit, sensuality, envy, slander, pride, foolishness. All these evil things come from within" (Mark 7:20–23).

Don't kid yourself. According to the Father, we really are that bad. In fact, we're a lot worse than we think. But here we are. Faced with the truth of us.

This is why Jesus proclaimed the gospel of the kingdom.

It may also be that some part of this is layered revelation. Maybe some of us can understand the nature of our King only after we've received the free gift of salvation. Maybe our hearts know first the freedom of forgiveness, and only then are we convicted with the depth of our problem and our dire need for a King. Maybe some of us cannot understand lordship until we have salvation. Okay. Maybe it's walk then run. I think He's okay with that. I have a feeling that His ways are higher than mine and He's not surprised by what we need or the depth of our depravity. He's known it all along.

I do know this: it is His kindness that leads us to repentance, His grace that instructs us to deny ungodliness and worldly desires, and the encouragement of the Scriptures that gives us hope (Rom. 2:4; Titus 2:11–12; Rom. 15:4).

The choice is yours.

All of us fall into a couple of categories. Maybe you call yourself a Christian but you did so primarily to check the I'm-going-to-heaven box and to renew your fire insurance, and you care little for Jesus the Christ. Or maybe you've been duped and deceived and have spent most of your life worshipping another god. Or, maybe you've given your finger to the world and everyone in it and you've never really repented at all.

Whatever your condition, here's your chance.

Jesus commanded us to "seek first the kingdom of God and his righteousness, and all these things will be added to you" (Matt. 6:33). Notice those words *seek first*. Later He said, "If you abide in me, and my words abide in you, ask whatever you wish, and it will be done for you" (John 15:7). Now notice those words, *it will be done*.

I ended the last chapter by stating that we all choose a father. Either the father of lies or our Father in heaven. Why write that again? Because choosing a kingdom is, in reality, choosing a Father.

What if we fell flat on our face before His throne, pressed our palms toward the heavens, and shouted at the top of our lungs, *"King Jesus! Be lifted high! Be lifted high! Worthy is the Lamb!"*? And while we're screaming, what if we step out of the kingdom of darkness and into the kingdom of God the Father?

What if we just did that?

Let's Pray

Father, I'm a rebel, born into the enemy camp, housed in the kingdom of darkness. I'm not worthy of You and there's nothing in me that deserves any part of You. I accrued a debt balance I couldn't pay in ten thousand lifetimes and yet when You saw it, You paid it. In full. But You didn't stop there. While I was busy accruing insurmountable debt, hell-bent on aiding and abetting the enemy, trying to grab Your power, You filed adoption papers and gave me the right to become Your son.

Because there is more mercy in You than sin in me, and because You loved me before the foundation of the world, You took my punishment and gave me Your forgiveness, You took my wounds and healed me, You took my sin and made me righteous with Your righteousness, You died my death so I may receive Your life. You endured my poverty to share with me Your abundance. You bore my shame, to share with me Your glory. You endured my rejection so that I might have and know the acceptance of my Abba Father. You were made a curse so that I might enter into blessing. You were cut off in death that I might be joined to God eternally. And You put to death my old man, so that You might come to life in me.

What kind of King does this? Why didn't You shame and disown me, and serve me the death sentence I deserve, when You had every right? Abba, this knowledge is too much for me. I'm undone. The fact that You served my sentence, gave me all You had and made me Your own means You did for me what I could never do.

All I can do is surrender, so I do. I give You all of me and worship You with all I am and all I have. Father in heaven, I hallow Your name and I choose You, Your kingdom, Your righteous reign, and Your sovereign dominion. I wholeheartedly yield and surrender all my rights, my will, my desires, everything I consider "mine," and I choose Your will be done. Here on earth as it is in heaven. Nothing matters more.

When I see me in light of You, my strength fails and I hit my knees. Today, now, forever, I'm Yours. I can say with all my heart, Your kingdom come. Your will be done. In Jesus' name.

Let's do one more thing: let's agree with and speak over ourselves what Paul proclaimed to the Ephesians. Let's make this our confession and shout it out across the stratosphere. And I've changed the pronouns to make it personal:

My Father, My King, I was dead in my trespasses and sins in which I once walked, following the course of this world, following the prince of the power of the air, the spirit that is now at work in the sons of disobedience—among whom I once lived in the passions of our flesh, carrying out the desires of the body and the mind, and was by nature a child of wrath, like the rest of mankind. But God, being rich in mercy, because of the great love with which you loved me, even when I was dead in my trespasses, made me alive together with Christ—by grace I have been saved—and raised me up with him and seated me with him in the heavenly places in Christ Jesus, so that in the coming ages he might show the immeasurable riches of his grace in kindness toward me in Christ Jesus.

For by grace I have been saved through faith. And this is not my own doing; it is the gift of God, not a result of works, so that I may not boast. For I am his workmanship, created in Christ Jesus for good works, which God prepared beforehand, that I should walk in them.

I remember that I was at that time separated from Christ, alienated from the commonwealth of Israel and a stranger to the covenants of promise, having no hope and without God in the world. But now in Christ Jesus I who was once far off have been brought near by the blood of Christ. For this reason I bow my knees before the Father, from whom every family in heaven and on earth is named.[27]

CHAPTER 12

I Raise My Hand

Jesus is reclining at the table. John rests on one side. Peter on the other. The rest of the Twelve lie in a circle around Him. It is Passover. Although, this one will be a little different.

Jesus speaks:

"I have earnestly desired to eat this Passover with you before I suffer. For I tell you I will not eat it until it is fulfilled in the kingdom of God." And he took a cup, and when he had given thanks he said, "Take this, and divide it among yourselves. For I tell you that from now on I will not drink of the fruit of the vine until the kingdom of God comes." And he took bread, and when he had given thanks, he broke it and gave it to them, saying, "This is my body, which is given for you. Do this in remembrance of me." And likewise the cup after they had eaten, saying, "This cup that is poured out for you is the new covenant in my blood. But behold the hand of him who betrays me is with me on the table. For the Son of Man goes as it has been determined."[1]

Jesus' words puzzle His friends. There's a lot here. Suffering? New covenant? Betrayer? Their heads are spinning. No one wants to be the betrayer. They're worried. Peter asks John to ask Jesus who it is. Jesus dips the bread in the oil and gives it to Judas. "What you are going to do, do quickly."[2] satan enters Judas, and Judas walks out. No explanation. No goodbyes. It's the last time the Twelve will ever eat together. Notice what Jesus says: He establishes the new covenant with Judas still seated at the table. It's one of the most beautiful pictures in Scripture of the unmerited love of God—He is extending forgiveness before the sin. He is cutting the covenant with the one who will cut Him.

Judas closes the door, and Jesus sits alone with the remaining Eleven. They're confused and have no idea what's about to happen. If they did, they might have acted differently. Interestingly, the next sentence in John's gospel records an amazing observation: "So, after receiving the morsel of bread, he [Judas] immediately went out. And it was night."[3]

"Night" is an apt description.

Covenant

Libraries are dedicated to this thing called "covenant." And for good reason.

A covenant is an agreement. A promise between two parties. It's a type of if-then statement, such as: "If I do this for you, then you will do that for me. And if you do that for me, then I will do this for you." One such covenant might be: "If I protect you, then you will serve me and work for me. And if you work for me and serve me, I will protect you. But if I fail to protect you, you are free from serving me; and if you fail to serve me, I am free to no longer protect you. And this covenant, or contract, is valid as long as we are both living. The moment one of us dies, the living member is free from the agreement."

Simplistic, yes, but you get the idea.

Covenants are "cut," which means in a true covenant there is a shedding of blood. Think circumcision or the wedding night. The first covenant was between God and Adam as evidenced by the shedding of blood when God killed animals in the garden to provide skins to "cover" Adam and Eve's flesh and, more importantly, their sins, as they walked out of the garden. There are many covenants in Scripture, and they are always with or through a person: the covenant with Noah, Abraham, Moses, David, and the new covenant.

Each of these is the means by which God relates to and enters into relationship with humanity. With us. I don't know why He chooses this way of relating to us; He just does. That's what makes Him God and not us. He does what He wants, when He wants, however He wants, and He asks no one's permission—and I'm totally okay with that. I trust Him completely.

When God enters into relationship with us through covenant, He makes a way for us to approach Him. Sin separates us from Him, and He doesn't like that, but He refuses to brush it under the rug; so He created a manner, or method, or avenue by which we can return to His presence despite the sin that separates us. Covenants are simply God's way of dealing with our sin and allowing us access to Him despite that sin.

A lot has been made about the "harshness" of the old covenant. The Mosaic law. All the don't-dos and thou-shalt-nots. The problem was not the covenant or the Law, but our utter inability and compete unwillingness to live up to it. The Law was perfect. Nothing wrong with it at all. A perfect tutor designed to lead us to Jesus. Would I have wanted to have grown up under it? Of course not. I know me, and I wouldn't have lasted five minutes. But let's remember, the problem was neither the covenant nor the Law. The problem was and is us. God in His mercy allowed us that covenant so when we get to Jesus at the table and He lifts the cup and utters the words "new covenant," we understand how truly significant and miraculous the love of God really is. We also realize how utterly and completely unworthy we are of a new one.

Let's Back Up

In Genesis 14, Abram, along with 318 members of his household, rescued his nephew Lot in the Valley of the Five Kings. To do so, he chased the kings essentially the length of what will become the land of Israel—from the Salt Sea to Dan, which is one of the headwaters of the Jordan River. An interesting picture, from death (salt) to life (fresh water bursting out of the ground).

After that rescue, Abram was standing in the valley where he was unexpectedly met by Melchizedek, who is one of my favorite people in Scripture. We don't know much about Melchizedek, but what we do know, we learn primarily from the writer of Hebrews:

> This Melchizedek, king of Salem, priest of the Most High God, who met Abraham returning from the slaughter of the kings and blessed him, to whom also Abraham gave a tenth part of all, first being translated "king of righteousness," and then also king of Salem, meaning "king of peace," without father, without mother, without genealogy, having neither beginning of days nor end of life, but made like the Son of God, remains a priest continually. (Heb. 7:1–3 NKJV)

I tend to think that Melchizedek was a preincarnate version of Jesus, but I can't prove it. What I can prove is what He did with Abram.

He brought out bread and wine.

Notice, too, what He is doing. He brought out bread and wine in the city of Salem. Today we call that city Jeru-Salem. Or the New Salem.

Notice Abram's response. Abram received the bread and wine, and then gave Melchizedek "a tenth of everything" (Gen. 14:20). When the five kings started to negotiate for the return of their goods, Abram shook his head. He wouldn't negotiate.

Why?

Because, Abram said, "I have lifted my hand to the LORD, God Most High, Possessor of heaven and earth" (Gen. 14:22).

Strange, don't you think? Abram met a stranger, the priest of Salem, who brought out bread and wine. As a result, Abram gave Him a tenth and raised his hand—to God Most High.

This is significant. But why?

The first time we see bread and wine in Scripture, it is followed with the

raising of a hand and a voluntary tithe. These are the willful expressions of cove-
nant. Of an oath. An agreement between two parties.

Here is how and why this becomes significant. From there, this hand-raising thing begins to permeate Hebrew culture. Lesser and greater kings used this gesture to establish and renew covenant with one another. A raised hand signified the reestablishment of the covenant. The one doing the raising was saying, "I am submitting to you." The two are renewing an oath. A commitment.

How do we know this is important to God?

In 590 BC, prior to the final fall of Jerusalem, God was speaking to the elders of Israel through the prophet Ezekiel. Notice the number of times God said He raised His hand in Ezekiel 20 (NKJV):

- verse 5: "I chose Israel and raised My hand in an oath. . . . I raised My hand in an oath to them, saying 'I am the LORD your God.'"
- verse 6: "I raised My hand in an oath."
- verses 15–16: "I also raised My hand in an oath . . . , but [they] profaned My Sabbaths; for their heart went after idols."
- verse 23: "I raised My hand in an oath."
- verse 28: "I had raised My hand in an oath."
- verse 42: "I raised My hand in an oath."

This is God speaking to us about His promise to be in covenant with us. And if God is using this language to describe His expression toward us, should it be important to us?

This is King David (NKJV):

- "Hear the voice of my supplications when I cry to You, when I lift up my hands toward Your holy sanctuary" (Ps. 28:2).
- "Thus I will bless You while I live; I will lift up my hands in Your name" (Ps. 63:4).
- "Let my prayer be set before You as incense, the lifting up of my hands as the evening sacrifice" (Ps. 141:2).

The point is this: hand lifting has its roots in the renewal of covenant. Prior to the Last Supper and "the new covenant," it was *the* expression of covenant, and it's no mistake that Hitler chose this action to express loyalty and commitment to himself. Hitler's adoption of a hand raised is a bastardization of what Abram did in the valley and what Jesus did on the cross.

Why Covenant?

Jesus' use of the words "new covenant" should make our fuzzy little heads spin off our shoulders. When broken, every covenant requires an acknowledgment that it was broken, and then payment is made to keep the covenant in force. If the breaking is acknowledged and sufficient payment is made, the covenant remains intact and relationship continues. If not, then the covenant is broken. No covenant and no relationship.

Problems arise, however, when we're talking about sin, because payment for sin is expensive. And the greater the sin, the greater the payment. God's not playing. He takes this seriously even if and when we don't. In brass tacks, that means if you've lived for more than about five minutes, you're so far in debt that you couldn't pay your balance in a hundred lifetimes. Again, I don't understand why; I just know it is. When we all stand before God maybe we'll have a better understanding. I think we will, and I don't think He'll have to say a word. I think we'll just know. Until then, I'm suggesting we take His word that it means what it means.

In every case, these covenants are God's self-initiated approach to reaching down out of heaven and snatching us back from the *avon*—the iniquity, the rebellion, and the consequences due us from that sin (Isa. 53:6). Covenants are evidence of His *chesed*—His unmerited mercy, lovingkindness, patience, forgiveness, and love. And none more so than the new covenant Jesus "cut" with us at the cross. Covenants are God's reaching back across the stratosphere to return us to Himself when we've denied Him or disobeyed Him for the ten thousandth time.

My point is that covenant matters to God. In truth, I can't think of anything that matters more. Covenants between God and man are life-and-death agreements.

But you and I have a bit of a problem. We don't value covenant today the way God values it or the way Jesus valued it at that dinner or the way He does right now seated at the right hand of God the Father.

Case in point: look at marriage. Marriage today doesn't mean what He intended it to mean. We break marriages all the time. Treat them with as much interest as the wrapper on a candy bar. Covenant with God is the genesis of, "In sickness and in health, till death do us part."

But God hasn't changed. Hasn't wavered. Hasn't rethought His decision-making paradigm. He means what He means, and He never changes (Mal. 3:6). If the idea of covenant today has lost its meaning, or we value it less than we should, or we look at covenant with cavalier indifference and thumb our nose at the notion that we owe God something, the loss of that meaning or the growth of that indifference has nothing to do with Jesus. If anything, the strength of that covenant has grown because it now stands on two thousand years of agreement and Him living up to His end of the bargain.

Covenant describes God's relentless and never-ending pursuit of us. Even when we were running the other direction. Covenant is how He makes a way for us to get to Him, and into His kingdom, despite all the stuff that threatens to separate us and prevent us access.

Don't miss this—God created mankind for His pleasure, placed him in a garden, and gave him the right to rule and reign so long as he obeyed Him. And from the moment Adam and Eve disobeyed, God has been doing everything possible to return His creation to that place of intimacy.

If you spend time here, your understanding of the love of the Father might swell a bit.

Why This Way?

Jesus on the cross finished His priestly duty. Atonement. Redemption. Justification. Sanctification. Blessing. For all who would follow Him, He bridged the gap between the kingdom of darkness and the kingdom of heaven.

But who set this up? Why this model?

God is a God of covenant. Period. And within His covenant, the only way to atone for sin is through the shedding of blood. Why? I don't know. But let's back up.

What was God doing when Adam and Eve ate the forbidden fruit? He was walking in the garden in the cool of the day, looking for them. His intention was, is, and always will be to *be with* His children. It's why He made us. He really wants to spend time with us. There's just one problem: He's holy and we're not. Sin in the garden upended this. Notice, Adam rebelled, and God kicked him out of the garden. This means every child of Adam—that's you and me—is a rebel born into the kingdom of darkness. This is our beginning condition. It's who we are before we open our eyes.

So God, in His love for us, created a way for us to get to Him. A way that allows unholy people access to Holy God. That way was and is covenant. It's a deal between two parties defined by, "I'll do such and such . . . if you do such and such." Our problem as people is that we have never kept up our end of the deal. So God, desperately wanting to bring us back to Himself just because He loves us with a crazy kind of love that we can't fathom, created a covenant with us in which He keeps up both ends of the bargain. Hence, Jesus on the cross. Think about the ridiculousness of this. The God of the universe, who spoke us into existence, is promising to keep up both His and our ends of the deal.

Only in covenant does God establish permanent relations with us.

Outside of covenant there is no relationship with God.

I won't pretend to improve on the thousands of books written on covenant, but I do want to take a little different approach. Maybe look at it through a different light, allowing Scripture to comment on itself. I want to leave Jesus and His brothers at dinner and back up about a thousand years. There is a picture embedded in the life of David that shows us, in beautiful array, the love of the King for His people and the extent to which

He will go to bring us back into His presence and restore to us everything that was lost in the fall.

David and Jonathan

King Saul stares down on the battle and watches in awestruck amazement as a diminutive, ruddy shepherd boy raises a sword nearly as long as he is tall and cuts off the head of the dead giant at his feet. All Israel shouts and descends the hill—swords drawn, battle axes swinging. The enemy's champion is dead. The Philistines flee in terror. A complete and total rout.

Saul, a wrinkle between his eyes, turns to his second-in-command and whispers around the side of his hand. "Whose kid is this?"

Abner shrugs. "It's the harp boy."

"Are you kidding me?" Saul says, "Bring him to me."

Abner walks out of the tent, whistles, and ushers David inside. Scripture says Abner "brought him before Saul with the head of the Philistine in his hand."[4]

Freckle-faced David, sling draped over his shoulder, sweat on his cheeks, four stones in a bag at his belt, elbow deep in Goliath's blood, walks into Saul's tent still carrying a dripping head. As he stands there, he is holding—better, he has decapitated—the very thing that scared Saul to death. And notice who else is present in the tent: Jonathan, Saul's son and the rightful heir to his throne.

David is not new to Jonathan. In the months prior, he's heard David play for his father when Saul was tormented by an evil spirit. He'd also been at the battle watching Goliath call out all of Israel when not one of Israel's finest warriors dared take on the champion. Jonathan had watched this play out across the weeks, he was privy to his father's private conversations, and he is standing there in his father's tent when this sweaty shepherd, still huffing from chasing Philistines, walks in dripping blood on the king's floor.

The enormity of this moment is not lost on Jonathan. Scripture goes on to say, "As soon as he [David] had finished speaking to Saul, the soul of Jonathan was knit to the soul of David, and Jonathan loved him as his own soul."[5]

Brothers from different mothers.

Two verses later, Jonathan "made a covenant with David, because he loved him as his own soul." In expression of the covenant, Jonathan gives David his robe, armor, sword, bow, and his belt. In so doing, he is visibly giving David the authority of his succession to his father's throne. We don't know exactly why Jonathan did this except that Jonathan must have seen in David something he did not possess. Whatever it was, it was enough to convince the would-be king to hand over his crown. I think it was the mantle of authority that had come to rest on David when Samuel had anointed him, but it's just my guess. Saul must have seen it, too, because David's fortunes quickly change.

Saul becomes jealous and tries to kill David. Several times. Commands his servants to kill him. Even tries to pin him to the wall with a spear. Twice.

In the worst of times, when Saul is chasing David from one end of the land of Israel to the other, Jonathan and David meet, and Jonathan says, "'If I am still alive, show me the steadfast love of the LORD, that I may not die; and do not cut off your steadfast love from my house forever, when the LORD cuts off every one of the enemies of David from the face of the earth.' And Jonathan made a covenant with the house of David, saying, 'May the LORD take vengeance on David's enemies.' And Jonathan made David swear again by his love for him, for he loved him as he loved his own soul."[6] Later, when Saul's pursuit of David has spun David into a frenzy, the two friends meet in a meadow. Scripture says they wept together. But David more so. Then Jonathan says to David, "Go in peace, because we have sworn both of us in the name of the LORD, saying 'the LORD shall be between me and you, and between my offspring and your offspring, forever.' And he rose and departed, and Jonathan went into the city."[7]

Despite Jonathan's love of David, Saul is relentless in his pursuit.

He can't stand the thought of someone else assuming his power. David continues to outrun Saul, skirting the edges of Israel and staying in the strongholds in the wilderness. The rock crevices in En Gedi. I described this in great detail in *What If It's True?* so I won't rehash here, but Saul and three thousand men swarm the Dead Sea in search of David. Needing to relieve himself, Saul retreats into the caves where he takes off his clothes. While he is in that vulnerable place, David spares Saul—and when Saul learns of this, he makes David promise that he will not cut off his descendants after him. So David swears to Saul.

That's twice David has sworn with the house of Saul—even though the house of Saul is trying to kill him.

Later in the wilderness of Ziph, with Saul still in hot pursuit, Jonathan says to David, "'Do not fear, for the hand of Saul my father shall not find you. You shall be king over Israel, and I shall be next to you. Saul my father also knows this.' And the two of them made a covenant before the LORD."[8]

That's three times David has given his word to the king and/or his son.

Realizing Saul will not stop, David flees, the story twists, years pass, and eventually Saul brings about his own demise—trying to match David's greatness in a battle against the Philistines. David hears the news from a servant fleeing the battle: "The people have fled from the battle, and also many of the people have fallen and are dead, and Saul and his son Jonathan are also dead."[9]

Jonathan dies with his father. Probably within arm's reach. And I'm pretty sure when David heard the news, his heart broke. In sorrow, he writes a song and tells the children of Judah to teach it to their children. It's called the "Song of the Bow." In it, he says, "How the mighty have fallen in the midst of the battle! Jonathan lies slain in your high places. I am distressed for you, my brother Jonathan."[10] The word for "distressed" there means to cramp or to be in anguish. It paints a picture of a man doubled over in pain.

Scripture also records something else at this time. Almost an aside. If you're reading quickly, you'll miss it: "Jonathan, the son of Saul, had a son who was crippled [lame] in his feet. He was five years old when the news about Saul and Jonathan came from Jezreel, and his nurse took him up and fled, and as she fled in her haste, he fell and became lame. And his name was Mephibosheth."[11]

The boy's name is pronounced *Me-fib-oh-sheth*. Once you get used to it, it kind of rolls off your tongue. Try it. "Mephibosheth." Now, to make it easier on us, we're going to call him "Bo."

We don't know much about him. Only that his grandfather was the mighty King Saul—anointed by Samuel himself. And his father, Jonathan, was next in line. That makes Bo of a royal bloodline, and—as the only named son of Jonathan—heir to the heir of the king. In short, Bo would have been king.

At an early age, Bo knew a life of comfort. Security. Warmth. A full stomach. Servants at his beck and call. He knew the honor due royalty and the benefits of it. Scripture doesn't say this, but I see him dancing around his house without reason. Why? Because kids dance without reason.

But while he's playing as a five-year-old, his grandfather and dad are killed in battle. News of their death reaches home, and in haste, Bo's nurse picks him up to flee the house. Panic. Fear. Chaos. The beginnings of mourning. Heartfelt cries. The king and his son are dead. It's the crumbling of Bo's Edenic world.

We don't know exactly what happened next. We know they're running and she's carrying him, but something happens. Either she trips, falls, and drops him or she falls on top of him, but whatever the case Bo does not seem responsible for the injury that would forever define him. In the blink of an eye, his entire world—his family, his health, his birthright—is ripped from him.

The life he once knew, he knows no longer.

David returns to Jerusalem, assumes the throne that is rightly his, dances before the ark as he brings it into Jerusalem, writes the incomparable Psalm 24 about "this King of glory!" and then tells his unimpressed wife Michal, "I will become even more undignified than this."[12]

David, the man after God's own heart, becomes the great king.

Then at the pinnacle of his life, with the crown on his head, and for reasons we don't know, in a time of rest, maybe even of reflection, David remembers his promise.

His covenant to Jonathan.

And don't miss the subtlety—no one would have blamed him had he not. Despite the fact that Saul tried for years to kill him, Scripture says something amazing. David turns and asks a question of those around him, "Is there still anyone left of the house of Saul, that I may show him kindness for Jonathan's sake?"[13]

Ziba, a servant who had worked in the house of Saul, says, "There is still a son of Jonathan; he is crippled in his feet."[14]

David asks, "Where is he?"

"He is in the house of Machir the son of Ammiel, in Lo-debar."[15]

Chances are good that David had never met Bo. He didn't call for him by name or feature, so I'm thinking he'd never heard of him. Look at how Ziba refers to him: "crippled in both his feet." Being crippled was Bo's identifying mark. The connotation was "outcast." "Disqualified." "Less than the rest." Further, because he's lame, he's not allowed in the temple and has no access to the priest. He is a man alone, without God and without the hope of God.

Think about this dynamic. Bo has lived with two lame feet. Interestingly, we know he is married and has a son, but he has ambulated this world by crawling on his belly or scooching along on his butt, because he can't walk. He crawls to the bathroom, crawls to bed, crawls to the dinner table, and crawls down the row of his garden. He sees life from two feet off the ground, forever looking up. Some have suggested he walked with crutches. Maybe, but I don't think so.

Bo has grown up living with the daily, physical reminder that his grandfather's sin caused his deformity. And make no mistake about it: he's deformed. He's known throughout the kingdom as the lame son of the slain king.

Do you think he was haughty? Full of himself? I don't think so. Whatever the case, Bo lived with the wound both in his feet and in his soul.

Imagine his surprise when he is summoned. For some unexplained reason, he's been brought before the king. In his mind, he's about to die.

Bo crawls into the King's court, dragging his legs behind him like two lengths of hemp rope. I'm tempted to say he pulled himself up to David's throne, but I don't think David let him get that far. I think David took one look at his face, and the great king hopped down off his throne and squatted before Bo.

Imagine the interaction: David sits next to Bo, and Bo—fearing death—buries his face on the ground.

David whispers, "Mephibosheth?"

Nose in the carpet, Bo says, "Here is your servant!"

Think back to David and Jonathan's friendship. The friend he wept with is dead, killed with the sword, and here, crawling on the ground, lies the only living reminder. What if Bo had Jonathan's eyes? Facial features? David would know it. Do you think he was reserved at the sight of them? This is the same king that danced in a loin cloth before the ark. Wrote Psalms. Sang at the top of his voice. I don't find him unfazed or indifferent.

I find him undone.

In my mind, the Charles Martin translation, David either lies on the ground next to Bo, or better yet, he lifts his chin to see his eyes and then picks up Mephibosheth and sets him in the chair next to his, because read what he says next: "Do not fear, for I will show you kindness for the sake of your father Jonathan, and I will restore to you all the land of Saul your father, and you shall eat at my table always."[16]

I love that part.

Bo is incredulous. Can't believe it. This is the sword who chopped off the giant's head. Bo responds, "But King, 'what is your servant, that you should show regard for a dead dog such as I?'"[17]

Bo's own words give a revealing glimpse into his heart. *Dead dog*. But Scripture holds a tender place for dogs. Remember the Canaanite woman at the feet of Jesus?[18]

David summons Ziba, Saul's servant, and says, "All that belonged to Saul and to all his house I have given to your master's grandson. And you and your sons and your servants shall till the land for him and shall bring in the produce. . . . Your master's grandson shall always eat at my table."[19]

Bo's Story Is Our Story

I used to wonder why Bo's story was included in the Bible. At first, he struck me as an also-played. A footnote. An unlucky casualty of war who got dropped. Then I started thinking about it. David's care of Mephibosheth had nothing to do with Mephibosheth. David exhibited covenant faithfulness to Mephibosheth based on his covenant with Jonathan. Mephibosheth was adopted into the king's court and lived out his days in the king's throne room and at his table because the king loved his father. This is complete and total unmerited grace and mercy.

And Bo's story is my story. Yours.

The king of this world fears you, and he understands your birthright probably better than you do. As a result, he wants your head on a platter. Wants to pin you to the wall. Through no fault of your own, you were born into this war. Somewhere back in your past, he attacked—waged war—you were rushed from the table, dropped, maimed, and crippled. Been crawling around on your belly most of your life. Nothing but a dead dog. Nibbling scraps from the dumpster.

And while that may describe your or my circumstances, it is not the truth of our identity. Listen to what the Word says about you:

- "The Spirit himself bears witness with our spirit that we are children of God, and if children, then heirs—heirs of God and fellow heirs with Christ, provided we suffer with him" (Rom. 8:16–17).
- "If you are Christ's, then you are Abraham's offspring, heirs according to promise" (Gal. 3:29).
- "So you are no longer a slave, but a son, and if a son, then an heir through God" (Gal. 4:7).
- "The mystery is that the Gentiles are fellow heirs, members of the same body, and partakers of the promise in Christ Jesus through the gospel" (Eph. 3:6).
- "Listen, my beloved brothers, has not God chosen those who are

poor in the world to be rich in faith and heirs of the kingdom, which he has promised to those who love Him?" (James 2:5).

The truth is this: you're heir to the King.

I know how this strikes some of you. You look in the mirror or at the world that surrounds you, or maybe you just look at your feet. At all the places where you're broken. Then you poke yourself in the chest. Your voice raises. "I don't feel like an heir!"

I don't blame you, but your qualification is not based on what you feel. The truth often does not agree with your and my emotions. If you disagree, read the Psalms. David often commands his soul when it was at odds or not in agreement with God's Word. Your qualification to eat at the table is not based on your perception of yourself. It's got nothing to do with you. It's based on His promises: "See what kind of love the Father has given to us, that we should be called children of God; and so we are. . . . Beloved, we are God's children now" (1 John 3:1–2). And, "The Spirit himself bears witness with our spirit that we are children of God, and if children, then heirs—heirs of God and fellow heirs with Christ" (Rom. 8:16–17).

Then there's this one—God is speaking through the prophet Isaiah and says this: "But to this one I will look, to him who is humble and contrite of spirit, and who trembles at My word" (66:2 NASB). You see that word, *contrite*? It means "maimed." "Lame." Strong's dictionary actually says, "Like Mephibosheth."

If you could see me, I'm fist-pumping right now.

Remember how we started this chapter talking about how Judas sold out Jesus for thirty pieces of silver? Do you know what thirty pieces of silver represents in Scripture? It is the God-mandated value and price for a slave (Ex. 21:32). In the Mosaic law, it's the amount needed to buy a slave out of slavery. Given that, here's Paul: "You are no longer a slave but a son, and if a son, then an heir of God through Christ" (Gal. 4:7 NKJV).

The lame held a special place in the heart of Jesus. Remember the paralytic lowered through the roof (Mark 2:4)? The man beside the pool at

Bethesda (John 5:5)? Remember what Jesus told the messengers from John the Baptist, "The blind receive their sight and the lame walk" (Matt. 11:5)? His care for the crippled was and is proof of His divinity. The mark of a King. If feet didn't matter to Him, then why was His last act of service on this planet to wash his best friends' feet?

What Covenants Have You Made?

Let me bring this closer to home. If you are not in covenant with Jesus, then *you are* in covenant with the enemy. Period. You disagree? When speaking of the inhabitants of the promised land, God told Moses, "You shall make no covenant with them and their gods. They shall not dwell in your land, lest they make you sin against me; for if you serve their gods, it will surely be a snare to you" (Ex. 23:32–33). The reason for this is because doing so violated the first three commandments—which are requirements for covenant with God. Most of us are not living in His promised land, but all of us are living in a land of His promises—His Word. If you are serving any other God, then you are, by definition, *not* in covenant with Jesus.

If you're not buying my argument or don't see it as seriously as I do, the good news is you don't have to defend yourself to me. Or anyone else for that matter. But one day you will stand before One who will judge you, and He will know whether your heart is wholly His or not. You won't even have to tell Him. It'll be written all over your face. I'm just trying to cause both you and me to investigate the depths of us and ask honestly where we have entered into covenant.

So look. Who is enthroned in your heart? Money? Sex? Power? Things? Manipulation? Control? Where have you raised your hand to serve another that is not Jesus? No one really knows the answer but you and Jesus. Will you give Him permission to turn on the light, rummage through your contents, and show you your heart?

Any involvement with witchcraft and/or the occult has placed you in covenant whether you intended it or not. Why? Because you sought power outside of the Holy Spirit. Fortune-telling, tarot cards, palm reading, Ouija boards, horoscopes, and any secret society or cult. You might protest, saying that you were just experimenting and you didn't really mean it. Doesn't matter. God meant it when He said, "You shall have no other gods . . . You shall not bow down . . ." (Ex. 20:3, 5).

How about your job? I'm not knocking work; we all work by the sweat of our brow, but are you more obedient to your work than Jesus? Does work, does sex, does your money get more of your heart than Jesus? Do you put more faith in your portfolio than His Word?

Let me bring it closer to home. God "cuts" a covenant with us. Through the shedding of blood, a covenant is sealed. In God's economy, without the shedding of blood, there is no covenant. Conversely, with the shedding of blood, there is covenant, whether you intend it or not. That means if you've had sex with someone not your husband or wife—be it man, woman, or animal—a covenant was cut. Sex is the consummation of covenant. God intends this to be "cut" between a husband and wife. Period. Our culture disagrees, but God has not changed His mind.

Jesus is coming back for a bride, us, and He will not wed a bride that is tethered to or in covenant with anyone other than Himself. Period.

Do the work. Ask yourself, where have you, in your heart, sought power, sought relief, sought deliverance, sought healing, sought comfort outside of God Most High? Outside of the Father? Chances are good you'll find a covenant there. And where you find false covenants you will also find curses. This is why I wrote a chapter in *What If It's True?* on blessing and curse. Because both the covenants and the curse need to be broken.

If you're feeling anxious, don't worry. The cross of Jesus is the remedy, and one drop of His blood is more powerful than any enemy. This is why He offered the new covenant and why it is such good news.

So, what do we do? Where we find unholy covenants, we break them. Unsay them. And make the right covenant. One of the reasons I love the book of Hebrews is because of how clearly and often it states that Jesus is the High Priest of our confession who welcomes us to unsay the wrong confession and make the right confession.[20] When we do so, we enter into right covenant and right relationship with Him, and that covenant forever defeats and preempts any other covenant—so long as we remain in it. The exchange at the cross is the manifest description of what happens to us and for us when we enter into the new covenant. It is, literally, the stake driven in the ground.

So what covenants do you need to break? Further, where do you need to break unholy covenants that your ancestors entered into? We are not guilty of their sin, but we can be susceptible to or suffering the consequences of their sin and their covenants. Truth is, we may not entirely know. Who of us knows exactly what all of our ancestors did? Who of us can guarantee that none of our ancestors entered into unholy covenants? Certainly not me. Because the possibility exists that they did, you and I may be living under a false covenant. And thereby a curse. If that's the case, I want to break those. Forever.*

If you reject my approach of repenting for sin we didn't commit or breaking covenants our ancestors made, let me pose this: Do you actually think that when you stand before the Father, He is going to hold this against you? That you took the repentance thing too far and repented too much? If you devour His Word, you'll find that the Father loves it when His children take Him at His Word and believe that every single word is true.

God Most High, Abba, relates to us, His children, through covenant. It's the river in which we move to and from one another. I think this is why Revelation says there is a river that flows from His throne (Rev. 22:1). No river, no movement toward. No covenant, no relationship with. Let me say this one last time: there is no relationship with God outside of covenant. This is why Jesus sat at dinner with His friends and gave us a "new covenant" in His blood. When Jesus says, "I am the way . . . no one comes to the Father except through me," this is what He's talking about (John 14:6).

Covenant is intentional—both on God's part and ours. It is not

---

* To learn more about how to break false covenants and curses, including generational curses, see chapter 8 of *What If It's True?*

haphazard or accidental. We don't "find" ourselves in a covenant. We enter into. We raise our hand. We walk the aisle.

The Banquet of the Ages

I write fiction, so let me paint you into this scene and write you into your own story.

The banquet hall is packed. Sounds of a party. Laughter. Forks on plates. A band. Dancing. Glow of a fire. Smell of fresh-baked bread. You're pressing your nose to the bottom window. Two feet off the ground. Outside looking in. Fogging up the glass. The night is cold, getting colder, and the rain has turned to sleet.

Inside there's standing room only. Oddly, everyone is barefoot and, unlike yours, their feet are beautiful. Somewhere in the back of your mind, you remember hearing stories of a gracious and kind King who fed His children at a table like that. A table of laughter and dancing and joy.

But that was before the fall.

You pull your toothpick legs and withered feet beneath you. A constant reminder. You glance at the doorkeeper. He'll never let you in. And by law, you're not allowed. What were you thinking? That glass is the closest you'll ever get. You drag yourself into the darkness. Down the street that leads away.

In the darkness, you can hear the wolves tearing the flesh of those like you. The pack is devouring those not at the table. By now, they can smell you. You can hear them growling as you approach. It's not long now. A few more feet and they'll sink their teeth into your neck, choke your jugular, and drag you into the lair where they'll eat you while you watch. Maggots squirm around your fingers and the smell of rotting flesh curls your nose. This is not what you had imagined or even hoped, but this is where they'll devour you and cast your bones upon the pile of the forgotten.

You turn, glance one last time at the banquet hall and shake your head. Longing. That's when you feel the hot air on you neck. Hear the growl. You turn and gag at the stench of his breath. His face is caked with the blood of his last victim, and his smile confirms you are next. Behind him crouch two dozen more. They circle you, eyeing the tender flesh of your legs.

This is the end.

As the alpha wolf closes his massive mouth around your head, a bolt of light flashes from above you and sends the wolf rolling like a ball. When you open your eyes, a cloaked man stands between you and the pack. Amid the flashes of light, wolves are flying everywhere. In seconds, they are gone. Only the whimpers remain.

In the silence, the man towers over you.

You hide your face. You know better. Your kind is not allowed in the kingdom. Shame shadows your face. What were you thinking?

The man stands over you, blocking your egress, proving you've been found out. Discovered. Your fate now will be worse than the wolves. The cold wind blows the sleet into your face and you shiver in the mud. You raise a hand to apologize, beg mercy, but it's no use. You've heard the stories. He's just; you're guilty. What could you possibly say? You're trespassing within the kingdom and on palace grounds. Men have been hanged for less. Even now you hear footsteps. Elite palace guards en route. Given your condition, they won't waste the death penalty on you. Following a speedy trial, they'll simply toss your body over the city wall where the wolves travel in packs and devour the rejected and the weak. The guards will stand atop the wall, warm themselves with drink and fire, and wager to see how long you'll last amid the carnage. How far you'll crawl before they consume you.

You are powerless.

As the clank of swords and shields grows closer, the man kneels in the muck and mire, studying you. His face is veiled, but His countenance registers not anger but kindness. Relief, even.

You bury your face in the mud, hoping to elicit mercy. When you do, He lifts your chin. For a moment, He just stares, and you await the blow that never comes. Finally, with massive arms and without a word, He lifts you out of the mud, cradles your useless, noodle legs in His calloused hands, and strides toward the palace. The guards file in alongside. A perfect formation. An escort for the dying.

Approaching the massive door, the light shines on His hooded face. Silver-white hair. Emerald eyes. He's unlike any man you've ever seen. He commands, "Swing wide the gates!" and massive gears clank under their weight. While the gates are opened, He speaks. His voice sounds like a mountain stream or a gentle rain on the roof. "I've been waiting for you. I'm so glad you made it." He, too, is soaked to the bone, suggesting He's been standing in the night quite a while. Then He says the strangest thing. "I've missed you."

The words echo inside your mind. *Missed you.* And yet for an executioner you've never met, His hands are tender.

He pushes the hair out of your face and points inside. To the head table. "I've set a place for you." He shouts above to a figure standing at a window, surrounded by twenty-four guards dressed in resplendent armor. "Dad," the man says, "we found him. And he has Your eyes."

The words *Your eyes* swim around inside you but find no place to rest.

The man's gaze returns to you. A single shake of His head. "An amazing likeness." The dangling of your legs embarrasses you and you wish He'd set you down before the raucous laughter begins. You've grown accustomed to it. They always laugh when the sight of the grotesque is so comical.

When He steps inside, you are met by lights, warmth, and hushed voices. All eyes stare singularly at you and your soiled and torn rags and your impotent legs. The pungent smell of you embarrasses you, but then again, how does a lame man relieve himself?

To the right is the hall of justice. Where the verdicts are handed down. Doors in the back lead the condemned to the gallows. To the left lies the banquet hall—and the smell of fresh bread and a wood fire.

Without pause, He turns left and parades you through long rows of smiling, clapping people. Certainly, they are rejoicing at your capture and the coming verdict. He carries you to the head table where rather than drop you in pile, where they can mock and spit, He places you in a seat next to His. Gently. The seat has your name on it. A band is playing music.

Until now the man has been shrouded in cloak and hood and shadow. But inside the great hall, He removes it and shakes off the rain.

You are stunned. He is brilliant. Shining like the sun. Dressed in white. It's the Prince. The Coming One. Heir to the throne. He turns and through His linen shirt, you can see the scars on His back. You've heard the stories. The legend of His capture, how they tortured Him, and the battle that ensued. How He, alone, defeated His captors and how before He returned to the palace, He emptied the prisons. Freeing those long held in chains and leading a host captive. Lastly, you know how He's spent His reign pursuing the wicked and returning for those still missing.

Knowing that you are wicked, you throw yourself to the floor and press your face to His feet. Begging mercy. Leniency. A quick death. Please.

He kneels again, lifts you quietly, and places you not in your seat, but His. It's bigger. More room. He whispers, "Wait here."

The Prince is laughing. Exuberant. Spontaneously, He begins to dance, twirling the children who gather en masse around Him. Crowds throng the banquet hall and join in. The room is spinning with light and laughter and joy and the sound of melody. On the ceiling is a spinning disco ball made entirely of diamonds.

You sit in dumbstruck amazement as the Prince dances. He is not reserved. He is not collected. He is not proper.

You are undone.

The woman seated next to you whispers, "He's dancing for you."

This strikes you as absurd. "Why?"

She smiles. "Because He found you."

This too makes no sense. "Why was He looking?"

She laughs and waves her hand across the sea of people, "He always leaves the ninety-nine to find the one."

Aware of your singular unworthiness, you drop your head in shame, only to realize that your rags have somehow been replaced with corduroy—the cloth of the King. Your skin smells of mint, rosemary, lavender, and tea tree oil and all your putrid sores are gone. Amid the commotion, He returns to you, clinks His glass with His fork, and quiets the crowd. Silence falls.

"If I could have your attention please . . ." He puts His hand on your shoulder and points to a large blank wall where your picture appears on a screen equal to a hundred IMAX projectors. It's an old picture. Everyone can see it. They look from the wall to you and back to the wall. Your discomfort grows. The I'm-a-counterfeit-and-I-don't-belong-here uncertainty spreads across your face. You slump, hoping to slide beneath the table. He continues, "Everyone, please welcome my guest of honor to dinner." Then He turns to you. Just you. You have the undivided attention of the Heir to the throne. Everything as far the eye can see or mind can imagine belongs to Him. He is undefeated in battle and He alone has done what none other could. He has no equal. He kneels. Eye level. He's whispering now. Just to you. "I'm so glad you made it. I watched you climb those steps out there and I was praying that you'd make it. That your faith would not fail." A tear rests in the corner of His eye. You've never seen joy this pure. This unadulterated. He stands, raises His glass. The applause is raucous.

More dancing erupts. The tables empty. Your eyes dart. You're not really comfortable. The sight of your feet draws you away. Ashamed, you pull the tablecloth over your lap. There must be some mistake. Mistaken identity. As soon as they uncover the truth, the party will stop and they'll leave you to the wolves. You await the laughter.

But He's not finished. He's clued into this—into you. Breaking ranks, He appears at your feet. He's kneeling. A bowl. Warm water. A towel. He pulls His hair into a ponytail and peels back the tablecloth, holding your twisted feet in His hands. For a moment, He studies your scars where the bones once poked through the skin when you fell. Tracing them with his thumb, he shakes his head. "I know you've lived with this a long time. I'm so sorry this happened."

Tears spill off His face and land in the bowl. Slowly, He dips your mangled feet in the water. You recoil but the water is warm, and His hands, so tender. Afraid but spurred by His smile, you take a chance, dip your feet in the bowl, and for reasons you can't explain the Son of the King washes the maggots and manure off your feet. The kid sitting to your left, fist-deep in a ginormous bowl of chocolate ice cream, giggles with the most beautiful laughter, "He does that for everybody." He lifts his own spotless feet. "See mine?"

When the Son is finished, He says, "Wiggle for me."

You haven't been able to wiggle your toes for years. You shake your head, "But Sire . . . I—"

He holds your feet in His hands. "Wiggle."

For the first time in memory, you wiggle your toes.

He chuckles. "Now your ankles."

You do, staring in dumbstruck amazement at ten beautiful toes, straight ankles, and muscled calves.

Your feet are beautiful on this mountain.

The look on your face brings joyous laughter from the Prince. But He pauses. Scratching His chin. He is staring at your chest. While He has fixed your feet, a deeper wound remains.

Without warning, He stands and the dance stops. All eyes on Him. He is of great renown and has many names. Faithful and True. Firstborn from Among the Dead. The One whose name is Holy. He who holds the keys to death and hades. His eyes are fire, His hair white, and His voice sounds like rushing waters or Niagara. His feet are burnished bronze— like one who walked through fire—and His sword is girded on His thigh. He is called the Lion and the Lamb, the Alpha and Omega, the First and the Last. He is radiant beyond understanding and He is the one who hand-crafted your very feet from the dust. His soul is knit to yours.

This moment—this revelation, this healing, this banquet—this is why He brought you here. He is making good on the promise you thought was too good to be true.

He lifts you to your feet. Which is strange because you can't ever remember standing. Ever. You wobble, He catches you and sets you aright.

Holding your hands, eye to eye, He speaks. "I want to correct a lie that was spoken to you long ago." He places His hand on your heart. "Erase its residue from your DNA." He lifts your chin. "You—" He inches closer, His breath blanketing you. Your eyes dart away. He smiles slightly. "Yes, you. I remember the day I made you. Fashioned you. You were then and are now perfect in every way. You are Mine. My chosen. And I will call you by name. You're heir to my throne. Co-ruler with me. Everything that was stolen from you, I am returning. All that I have is yours. And I will feed you here. Forever."

The doubt rises and you shake your head. He's lost His mind. When He figures out He's got the wrong man . . . "But, I'm not who you think."

Then He does the one thing only He could do. He calls you by your name. The name He gave you when He made you. The one written inside you.

You stammer. "But, what . . . how?"

He whispers one word: "*Tetelestai*."

Maybe you don't like my fairy tale. Maybe it's too childish. Maybe you want to poke holes in my theology. Okay. But sometimes a story says best what needs saying. What this story does explain is the inexplicable gift of the exchange. You were created for covenant, and this is how He, Jesus, upholds His end of that covenant. The new one. And this is why Jesus proclaimed the gospel of the kingdom.

One more thing: at the sound of that one word, *tetelestai*, every person in the banquet hall falls to their knees, bows, and presses their palms to the ceiling. A sea of worship.

His Father appears. A pile of crowns at His feet. The Son walks you to His Father, presents you, and without hesitation, the Father launches Himself off His throne, wraps His arms around you, covers your face in kisses, and dresses you in a robe of matchless beauty.

You raise a finger. "How can this be?"

The Father points to the Son. He's waiting. He will not dance without you.

His foot is tapping. The music rises. He beckons. "Dance with me."

Welcome to the Banquet of the Ages.

Communion

The last thing Jesus did on this earth before He walked to the cross was share a banquet with His friends. He's also promised He will share it again with us when He returns. Until then, He's commanded us to remember Him in that way. Paul told us that when we do, we proclaim the resurrection.

Here's how I want to end. I want us to take communion. Together. Some of you may have done this ten thousand times. Some of you never. Whatever the case, I want us to sit with Jesus and take communion, or to receive communion from Jesus and enter in covenant with Him and Him alone—and in so doing, break every other covenant we've ever made. In these next few moments, there will be a breaking and a making.

When Jesus did this, He used bread and wine. If you're sitting in prison, that could be difficult to duplicate. Don't worry. He'll take whatever you can offer. Including imaginative air. Some of you will argue that you need a priest to administer. Obviously, if you've read this far, I believe in the priesthood of the believer. I'm not knocking priests; I thank God for them—and if you've read my fiction you already know this—but a good priest will tell you that you don't need him to get to Jesus. And yes, you can use grape juice. I'm simply a fan of wine and, according to Scripture, Jesus is too. But I don't really think it matters. If you are alone, I'd encourage you to get with friends. To share this with them. Why? Because Jesus did. Can you take communion alone? Sure. If you're married, do this with your husband or wife. Whether you are alone or sitting with friends, whether you have access to bread and wine or not, whether you're drinking wine or grape juice doesn't matter nearly as much as the condition of your heart. Remember what the Lord said to Samuel: "The LORD sees not as man sees:

man looks on the outward appearance, but the LORD looks on the heart" (1 Sam. 16:7).

Maybe you have your own method. That's great. If not, you can read my words out loud. Maybe use them as a guide as you lead others. The important part is not what I say or how I say it, although I think it's pretty cool, but again, the condition and posture of our heart as we take and eat.

Let's return to where we started. The Passover. And remember Jesus told them this was coming, although I doubt they understood. Early in His ministry, He said:

Truly, truly, I say to you, unless you eat the flesh of the Son of Man and drink his blood, you have no life in you. Whoever feeds on my flesh and drinks my blood has eternal life, and I will raise him up on the last day. For my flesh is true food, and my blood is true drink. Whoever feeds on my flesh and drinks my blood abides in me, and I in him. As the living Father sent me, and I live because of the Father, so whoever feeds on me, he also will live because of me. This is the bread that came down from heaven, not like the bread the fathers ate, and died. Whoever feeds on this bread will live forever. (John 6:53–58)

Reclining at that last dinner, Jesus made good on that statement:

"I have earnestly desired to eat this Passover with you before I suffer. For I tell you I will not eat it until it is fulfilled in the kingdom of God." And he took a cup, and when he had given thanks he said, "Take this, and divide it among yourselves. For I tell you that from now on I will not drink of the fruit of the vine until the kingdom of God comes." And He took bread, and when he had given thanks, he broke it and gave it to them, saying, "This is my body, which is given for you. Do this in remembrance of me." (Luke 22:15–19)

Hold it right there—"Take. Eat." Notice what Jesus was doing.

He was returning us to Adam and Eve in the garden: "So when the woman saw that the tree was good for food, that it was pleasant to the eyes, and a tree desirable to make one wise, she took of its fruit and ate. She also gave to her husband with her, and he ate. Then the eyes of both of them were opened, and they knew that they were naked; and they sewed fig leaves together and made themselves coverings" (Gen. 3:6–7 NKJV).

She took and ate. Then their eyes were opened, and they knew—they were uncovered.

In saying, "Take. Eat," Jesus was returning humanity to the garden and offering a remedy for the sin that occurred there.

Jesus—the Lamb that takes away the sin of the world—was making "covering" with his very own blood. When we eat His flesh and drink His blood, we are personally identifying with the sacrifice, as with the sacrificial lamb.

When I "take and eat," I am proclaiming that He covered me on the cross by His very own blood, that His death counts for me and that He took my place.

Back to Jesus. And as they were eating, Jesus took bread, broke it, and blessed it. When He did this, He said: *Barook atah A-donai, Elohaynu Melek Hah Olahm Hamoatzee lekem meen hah aretz.*

"Blessed are You, L-rd our G-d, King of the Universe, Who brings forth bread from the earth."

Then He gave it to the disciples and said, "Take . . . eat . . . this is My body . . . Do this in remembrance of Me."

So . . . Take. Eat. This is the body of Jesus. Broken for you.

"And likewise the cup after they had eaten, saying 'This cup that is poured out for you is the new covenant in my blood'" (Luke 22:20).

"Then He took the cup, and gave thanks, and gave it to them, saying, 'Drink from it, all of you. For this is My blood of the new covenant, which is shed for many for the remission of sins'" (Matt. 26:27–28 NKJV).

Barook atah A-donai, Elohaynu Melek Hah Olahm Bo-ray pree hahgafen.

"Blessed are You, L-rd our G-d, King of the Universe, Who brings forth the fruit of the vine." Take. Drink. This is the blood of Jesus. Shed for you.

When Paul instructed the church in Corinth, he wrote:

For as often as you eat this bread and drink the cup, you proclaim the
Lord's death until he comes.

Whoever, therefore, eats the bread or drinks the cup of the Lord
in an unworthy manner will be guilty concerning the body and blood
of the Lord. Let a person examine himself, then, and so eat of the bread
and drink of the cup. For anyone who eats and drinks without discerning the body eats and drinks judgment on himself. That is why many of
you are weak and ill, and some have died. (1 Cor. 11:26–30)

This is a great place to pause and repent. Naming other covenants.
Sin. Anything that separates. Let the Holy Spirit guide you.

This right here, this moment, this breaking and this making, this
hand held high, this taking and eating—this proclaims the resurrection.

Your enemy hates it, and there's nothing he can do about it: "Since
therefore the children share in flesh and blood, he [Jesus] himself likewise partook of the same things, that through death he might destroy
the one who has the power of death, that is, the devil, and deliver all
those who through fear of death were subject to lifelong slavery" (Heb.
2:14–15).

This cup of blessing is a participation in the blood of Christ. And this
bread we break, it is a participation in the body of Christ (1 Cor. 10:16). It
is mutually exclusive from any other covenant, for by taking this blood
and this wine, we "take" of the cup of the Lord to the exclusion of the cup
of demons. "You cannot partake of the table of the Lord and the table of
demons" (1 Cor. 10:21).

Speaking of demons, look at Genesis 3:15. Theologians call this the
protevangelium. It's the first promise of the gospel. God says to the serpent, "He shall bruise your head, and you shall bruise his heel."

In communion, Jesus is crushing the serpent's head.

Lastly, let me close by attempting to show the completeness of
Scripture. Nothing is wasted. Everything is completed.

Behold, the days are coming, declares the LORD, when I will make a new covenant with the house of Israel and the house of Judah, not like the covenant that I made with their fathers on the day when I took them by the hand to bring them out of the land of Egypt, my covenant that they broke, though I was their husband, declares the LORD. For this is the covenant that I will make with the house of Israel after those days, declares the LORD: I will put my law within them, and I will write it on their hearts. And I will be their God, and they shall be my people. And no longer shall each one teach his neighbor and each his brother, saying, "Know the LORD," for they shall all know me, from the least of them to the greatest, declares the LORD. For I will forgive their iniquity, and I will remember their sin no more. (Jer. 31:31–34)

This is *tetelestai.*

Pray with Me

Jesus, I raise my hand. Here and now, I decree and declare my covenant with You. I yield to You as the greater king and receive the covenant You alone offer. I am so sorry for refusing it for so long. You alone are God and King and Savior and Lord, and no one compares to You. I renounce and revoke any and all other covenants I've ever knowingly or unknowingly made or were passed to me in the generations. By and through Your blood, I break every unholy covenant in the name of Jesus. Please forgive me.

Jesus—on the night You were betrayed, You brought out bread and wine, "cutting" a new covenant with all who would believe in You. In doing so, You crushed the serpent's head, and restored what was lost in the garden. So just as Abraham and David raised their hands in covenant—I raise mine. I want to go on record—I receive the covenant You offer and I make my covenant with You.

[So, do it. Don't just read these words. Do them. Raise your hands.]

Jesus, words fails me but they're what I have so please receive this—I thank You. And I praise You. When I think that You would enter into covenant with me and not only keep up Your end, but mine as well, I am undone. And I know I am not worthy. What kind of King does this? Only You. King Jesus, I give You all my adoration. All my affection. And all my love. This day I raise my hand and say, "You are my God. My King. And my address is in Your kingdom." In Jesus' name.

CHAPTER 13

You're in a War

I t's evening. The sun has set. Jesus is tired but the crowds throng Him. They've brought Him all who were sick or afflicted by demons. Mark, probably writing for Peter, records that the whole city had gathered at the door.[1]

Matthew records that Jesus healed them all.[2]

Healing of disease and sickness is not new in Israel. The prophets had done this. Elijah had even raised the dead. What is new is that Jesus commands the demons and they know Him by name. Like they'd met before. What's even more amazing is that Jesus casts them out with a word. This has never been seen before. Ever. This display of power is something new entirely.

Mark goes on to say, "He was preaching in their synagogues throughout all Galilee, and casting out demons."[3] Mark says it in such a way that the preaching and the casting out are commonplace. Two chapters later, Mark records an astounding detail: Jesus appoints the Twelve to do what He's doing. "To preach, and to have power to heal sicknesses and to cast out demons."[4] His instructions are simple: "As you go, preach, saying, 'the kingdom of heaven is at hand.' Heal the sick, cleanse the lepers, raise the dead, cast out demons. Freely you have received, freely give."[5]

Then Jesus tells a story about a strong man, and that no one can enter a strong man's house and steal his stuff unless he first binds the strong man.[6] His instructions have nothing to do with a physical fight.

One evening in Galilee, Peter's mother is suffering with a fever. Jesus touches her, and the fever leaves immediately.[7] Interestingly, the people who knock on the door next aren't simply the sick. They're the oppressed. The demonized. "That evening they brought to him many who were oppressed by demons, and he cast out the spirits with a word and healed all who were sick. This was to fulfill what was spoken by the prophet Isaiah: 'He took our illnesses and bore our diseases.'"[8]

Notice Jesus' process: first cast out, then heal. And pay special attention to that word, *all.*

Later, He sends the disciples out two by two, and He specifically gives them power over unclean spirits. Over the demons.[9] So, they go out, preach that people should repent, and then they cast out demons. But not with their fists. Only with their words. And the name of Jesus. They also anoint many who are sick and heal them.[10] Later, He will send out even more. Some seventy in number.

When they return, the disciples are elated. Dancing even. They can't believe what they saw and experienced. They say, "Lord, even the demons are subject to us in your name!" And he said to them, "I saw Satan fall like lightning from heaven. Behold, I have given you the authority to tread on serpents and scorpions, and over all the power of the enemy, and nothing shall hurt you."[11]

Moments later, their hearts leap when Jesus tells them, "All things have been delivered to Me by My Father."[12]

They're starting to understand: Abba Father, kingdom, power. Their eyes are being opened.

Before He is crucified, Jesus tips His hat as to what's coming. Regarding Herod, He says, "Go, tell that fox, 'Behold, I cast out demons and perform cures today and tomorrow, and the third day I shall be perfected.'"[13]

Just before He ascends, Jesus tells His disciples one last time, "Go into all the world and preach the gospel to every creature. He who believes and is baptized will be saved; but he who does not believe will be condemned.

And these signs will follow those who believe: In My name they will cast out demons; they will speak with new tongues; they will take up serpents; and if they drink anything deadly, it will by no means hurt them; they will lay hands on the sick, and they will recover."[14]

It's an amazing and all-encompassing assignment.

Jesus ascends, the disciples retreat to an upper room and begin to look back on the last three years. As they do, they realize that in over 60 percent of His miracles, Jesus first cast out, then healed. Casting out was commonplace. It occurred more often than not. And, I can find no place in Scripture where he sent someone out to minister and did not give them authority to do as He did—to cast out.

Then, early in the book of Acts, proving that they got the message, the Lord heals a lame man through Peter. He'd been lame since birth, and his healing caused quite a stir among the religious elite. They couldn't deny that something indeed miraculous had occurred because the guy was over forty and everybody knew him. While the lame man is hopping around, screaming at the top of his lungs, and unable to contain himself for joy, the skeptics are standing there with folded arms. Looking down their noses. Why? Because their power is being threatened—and they know that this new power is stronger than their power. They ask, "'What shall we do to these men? For, indeed, that a notable miracle has been done through them is evident to all who dwell in Jerusalem, and we cannot deny it. But so that it spreads no further among the people, let us severely threaten them, that from now on they speak to no man in that name.' So they called them and commanded them not to speak nor teach in the name of Jesus."

Peter and John listen to what they're saying, point to the dancing man, and shrug. Their response is a terse diss: "We cannot but speak the things which we have seen and heard."[15] And somewhere in the back of their mind, I think these words of Jesus echoed: "Truly, truly, I say to you, whoever believes in me will also do the works that I do; and greater works than these will he do, because I am going to the Father. Whatever you ask in my name, this I will do, that the Father may be glorified in the Son. If you ask me anything in my name, I will do it."[16]

In short, they believed Jesus. They took Him at His word. And because of that, they did what He did.

Some Context

Fifteen hundred years prior to these events, Moses delivers a nation of slaves from four hundred years of slavery in Egypt. Before he goes in to see Pharaoh, he argues with God and gives Him all the reasons why He should choose someone else. God says, "What's that in your hand?"

Moses eyes his shepherd's staff.

God says, "Throw it down."

He does, whereupon it immediately turns into a serpent, scaring Moses.[17] Armed with this, he and Aaron go before Pharaoh and tell him to "Let my people go." Unimpressed, Pharaoh brings forth his magicians, Jannes and Jambres.[18] When Moses tells Aaron to throw down his staff and it turns into a serpent, they do likewise.

Imagine Moses' surprise when Aaron's snake is joined by two more. Do you think, in that moment, he had a few questions for God?

Evil has power too. Given it by God Most High. No, I don't entirely understand that. I just know it to be true. Put a bookmark there; I'm coming back to this near the end of the chapter.

But watch what happens next. Aaron's snake eats their snakes. So when they leave the palace that afternoon, Jannes and Jambres have no staffs, and Aaron's is twice as thick.[19] The point is this: the deliverance from Egypt was a clash of powers, and Moses represented the power that was more powerful. But notice the requirement: Moses had to exercise the power given him in order to bring about the deliverance.

Meaning, he did not just stand there and watch God idly from the sideline.

What follows is the greatest display of power against power the world has ever seen. In the first plague, Moses tells Aaron to hold out his now-thicker staff over the waters of the Nile, and the water turns to blood, all the fish die, and Egypt stinks. Jannes and Jambres stand unfazed: "But the magicians of Egypt did the same by their secret arts."[20]

Moses and Aaron return to Pharaoh. Aaron stretches out his hand over all the rivers, canals, and pools, and immediately frogs come up and cover the land of Egypt. "But the magicians did the same by their secret arts and made frogs come up on the land of Egypt."[21]

Notice: until now, the magicians of Egypt are matching Moses and Aaron, power for power.

Moses and Aaron have got to be wondering what the Lord has brought them into. Nevertheless, they respond obediently. Aaron stretches out his staff a third time and strikes the dust so that the particles became gnats. Undeterred, "the magicians tried by their secret arts to produce gnats, but they could not."[22] Only then, when they could not match the power of Moses and Aaron, did they turn to Pharaoh and say, "This is the finger of God."[23]

Notice that phrase "finger of God." We will hear this again through the mouth of Jesus.

Jannes and Jambres succeeded with the serpent, blood, and frogs but failed with gnats. My point is this: evil had real power. It was not impotent. And defeating that power required belief, obedience, and doing.

Back to our context: Moses extracts Israel from the hand of Pharaoh by the exercise of power the likes of which the world had never seen. Not the least of which is parting the Red Sea and walking across on dry ground, only to turn around and watch a ten-story wall of water wipe out the strongest army any of the Israelites had ever imagined.

After systematically dismantling the gods of Egypt, three million Hebrews walk out of Egypt and into the desert. Once free, Moses sends spies into the promised land. Twelve men. All leaders of their tribes. Two of whom are Joshua and Caleb. The spies spy out the land and return with good and bad news. The good news is that the land is better and more fruitful than they could have imagined. Flowing with milk, honey, grapes. It's paradise. They've never seen its equal. The bad news is that the land is populated with giants. And because the people choose to listen to the ten doubtful spies rather than Joshua and Caleb, they spend the next forty years in the wilderness.[24]

With a new generation ready to do what the last would not, Joshua takes over command from Moses, enters the promised land, and God tasks Joshua with transforming a nation of slaves into a nation of priests. And the first thing required of them is to fight for what God promised them. Fighting giants.

Listen to what God tells Joshua:

Moses my servant is dead. Now therefore arise, go over this Jordan, you and all this people, into the land that I am giving to them, to the people of Israel. Every place that the sole of your foot will tread upon I have given to you, just as I promised to Moses. From the wilderness and this Lebanon as far as the great river, the river Euphrates, all the land of the Hittites to the Great Sea toward the going down of the sun shall be your territory. No man shall be able to stand before you all the days of your life. Just as I was with Moses, so I will be with you. I will not leave you or forsake you. Be strong and courageous, for you shall cause this people to inherit the land that I swore to their fathers to give them. Only be strong and very courageous, being careful to do according to all the law that Moses my servant commanded you. Do not turn from it to the right hand or to the left, that you may have good success wherever you go. This Book of the Law shall not depart from your mouth, but you shall meditate on it day and night, so that you may be careful to do according to all that is written in it. For then you will make your way prosperous, and then you will have good success. Have I not commanded you? Be strong and courageous. Do not be frightened, and do not be dismayed, for the LORD your God is with you wherever you go. (Josh. 1:2–9)

Notice what God tells the people: "arise," "go," "every place your foot treads I have given you." Also notice what He does *not* say: He does not say He will wipe their enemies out before they get there. For reasons I don't understand, God leads them into battle, which will require former slaves to pick up swords.

Pragmatically, this meant that God is requiring these people, who had never seen a battle, much less been in one, to walk into the midst of the giants who practice battle as a way of life, believing that God would do what He said. Notice God doesn't just mow down the inhabitants with lightning bolts from heaven so that the Israelites arrive and just step over the bodies. He requires that His people exercise the authority He has given them. He promises He won't ever leave them or forsake them and tells them more than once to be strong and courageous. Lastly, He tells them to do something amazing—and it's not sharpen swords, practice tactics, or march in formation. He tells them to do exactly what Moses commanded them in the Law. To meditate on that law day and night and never let it leave their mouth. Doing everything written in it.

Does it strike you as strange that God's battle plan for His people is His Word?

In the days that follow, Joshua commands the sun to stand still, which it does, and the Israelites defeat the five Amorite kings—not the least of whom is the King of Jerusalem, Adoni-zedek. After the battle, Joshua opens the cave where he's holding the kings and parades them in front of the people. When he has done so, he calls all the men of Israel and chiefs of the men of war and says, "Come near; put your feet on the necks of these kings." After they have done so, Joshua says, "Do not be afraid or dismayed; be strong and courageous. For thus the LORD will do to all your enemies against whom you fight."[25]

Joshua then kills each king and hangs their bodies in the sun, where the people can see them.

Also notice that nothing about their situation has changed. The land is still populated by giants. And the giants are bigger, stronger, and there's more of them than there are fighting Israelites.

Lastly, notice the singular condition for victory: the people must fight. War is required. God demands it of His people. For some reason, He requires His people to stand in and exercise the authority He has given them, and that battle plan includes walking into a land populated by giants and meditating on His Word—never letting it leave their mouth.

My Assumptions

I believe God requires the same from you and me today. The struggle was real then. It's real today. You and I are not walking into a land covered up in giants, but we are walking into a land of promises. His Word. And the requirement He made of them, He makes of us: believe, obey, and do.

This context helps explain, or helps me better understand, Peter's prayer after the lame man was healed. And remember, he was speaking to the religious rulers who had the authority to kill him. They'd already cut off John the Baptist's head and crucified Jesus. Add to this a terrorist named Saul who was dragging people out in the street and sticking a sword through their chests, and Peter had real reason for fear. His life was at stake. Hence, this is no idle prayer: "'Now, Lord, look on their threats, and grant to Your servants that with all boldness they may speak Your word, by stretching out Your hand to heal, and that signs and wonders may be done through the name of Your holy Servant Jesus.' And when they had prayed, the place where they were assembled together was shaken; and they were all filled with the Holy Spirit, and they spoke the word of God with boldness" (Acts 4:29–31 NKJV).

The connection I am trying to make is this: in the same way the nation of Israel walked into war that they had not started, you were born into a world at war. While I believe the story is absolutely true, I also believe it is a type and model for us. That means whether you like it or not, when you opened your eyes on planet earth, you did so on the battlefield caught between two powers. The King of the kingdom of heaven is extending His reign into and through and over the kingdom of darkness. You and I are caught in the crossfire, charged with advancing the kingdom, and the ruler we worship will determine which kingdom we advance.

Why do we wake to a world at war? Why do we open our eyes to bullets whizzing overhead? Again, I don't know. God's ways are higher than mine. I believe there will be a day when we do understand. Until then, you and I have a choice. And it's a simple one: join in or bury our heads in the sand.

In my experience, most of us bury our heads. And in my experience, not fighting does not take you out of the fight. It makes you an easy target.

I have come to believe that life is warfare. Every day, you and I wake up in a world with an enemy who's as real as the page you hold in your hand, who hates us with an evil hatred, and whose singular desire is to murder us and separate us from our Abba. This is why Peter says, "Be sober-minded; be watchful. Your adversary the devil prowls around like a roaring lion, seeking someone to devour" (1 Peter 5:8).

Notice three words: *your enemy* and *devour*.

When I've taught this, it's about here that the objections surface: "Charles, you started out teaching about healing, and I really just want to pray for the sick. So what does all this warfare stuff have to do with praying for healing like Jesus?"

In my experience, everything.

Jesus spoke about two things more than anything else: your and my Father and the kingdom of heaven. Remember when Jannes and Jambres spoke of the finger of God? When the Pharisees witnessed Jesus casting out demons, they accused Him of having a demon that allowed Him to do so. In response, Jesus said, "But if it is by the finger of God that I cast out demons, then the kingdom of God has come upon you" (Luke 11:20). Jesus was linking Himself with the power that delivered Israel from bondage. He is that power. He is also opening their eyes to the reality of the struggle they are facing.

We like to make much of David cutting off Goliath's head. And we should. But what happened on that field that day wasn't simply about a boy with a sling and a giant with a sword. It was a contest of powers. This is why Goliath said, "'Am I a dog, that you come to me with sticks?' And the Philistine cursed David by his gods" (1 Sam. 17:43).

Notice David's response:

> You come to me with a sword and with a spear and with a javelin, but I
> come to you in the name of the LORD of hosts, the God of the armies of
> Israel, whom you have defied. This day the LORD will deliver you into
> my hand, and I will strike you down and cut off your head. And I will
> give the dead bodies of the host of the Philistines this day to the birds of
> the air and to the wild beasts of the earth, that all the earth may know
> that there is a God in Israel, and that all this assembly may know that the
> LORD saves not with a sword and spear. For the battle is the LORD's, and
> he will give you into our hand. (1 Sam. 17:45–47)

Goliath cursed David by his gods. This was commonplace in battle.
But watch how David responded: "I come to you in the name of the LORD
of hosts, the God of the armies of Israel." This was a battle of heavenly
powers played out on earth. David knew this. Goliath knew this. Goliath
simply chose the wrong and weaker power. Also, notice what happened
next, and it's this part that we need to pay close attention to: "When the
Philistine arose and drew near to meet David, David ran quickly toward
the battle line to meet the Philistine" (v. 48).

Keep that in mind as this chapter plays out: David ran quickly toward
the battle line.

Admittedly, I can be intense sometimes about this whole spiritual
warfare thing. Throughout our twenty-six years of marriage, Christy
has often said to me, "Honey, sometimes you see a demon behind
every bush."

On more than one occasion, I've said, "No, sometimes I see two."

In order to pray for the sick, a warfare mentality is essential. Why? Is
every sickness the result of enemy attack? No, I don't think so. Sometimes I
think it's just the result of living in a fallen world. Some colds are just colds.
But *some* sicknesses are the result of enemy attack, and often I approach
them with this attitude. I am of the camp that if we really want to see the
lame walk, blind see, and dead raised to life, we'd do well to write or speak

this entire teaching on healing inside the warfare argument. Healing is warfare. We're kidding ourselves if we don't think it's related.

The Arguments

When I meet people who are having trouble with this idea of warfare and of casting stuff out of people that we most often can't see with our physical eyes, or that someone's affliction or sickness is due to a demonic entity inside their body—especially when that person is a Christian—they offer one of several arguments.

First, they argue that the enemy is not real. They believe in heaven but not hell. The devil is a creation of our imagination. And because he's not real, he has no real power like we see in Scripture. Somehow that has mysteriously passed out of history, and evil is just some mysterious, nebulous force. This is the ostrich-head-in-the-sand argument and it never works out well for the ostrich. The problem with this argument is, "Heaven and earth will pass away, but my words will not pass away" (Matt. 24:35).

One of the greatest tricks the enemy has ever played is convincing you and me that he's not real or that he fights fair, neither of which is true. He is real. He's been fighting guerilla warfare against the likes of us a long time. "Fair" has never crossed his mind—but he'd like you to think it has.

The second lie he's perpetrated to perfection is that not only is he real, but he's stronger than God Most High. Somehow, darkness is stronger than light. Hollywood gets some of the credit for this. Given what we've seen with our eyes, the enemy, the devil, has convinced us that he's a 747 and we're just kids on trikes. The problem with this argument is that it's based on the fundamental and illogical assumption that the created is more powerful than the Creator. This is like saying that this book I'm writing, the one you're currently reading, is more powerful, more imaginative, more creative than I am. I call this one the twisted-imagination lie.

Thirdly, they argue that a good God would never "send" you to hell. Because if He did, then He's not good. What's good about a God who would do that? This is the age-old argument from evil. It is an assault against the very nature of God and it, too, is a lie from the pit of hell. I spent an entire chapter in *What If It's True?* talking about the love of God, starting with His *chesed* or His covenantal name in Exodus 34 ending with the sacrificial death of His Son. God is love. Period. If we end up in hell, our choices sent us there. Not our Father. This is the condition of the enemy and he can't stand it. This is called the good-God lie.

Lastly, they argue that a Christian can't be possessed by a demon. I agree completely. If we are "in Christ Jesus," meaning we have repented and confessed Him Lord of all, then we are, by definition, possessed by the Holy Spirit. On the other hand, unbelievers can be possessed by the demonic, and church history agrees with this. I call this the Mary-Magdalene lie.

For us Christians, the problem we have today is the word "possession." We get it primarily from the old King James. One example is Matthew 12:22: "Then was brought unto him one possessed with a devil" (KJV). "Possessed with a devil" comes from the Greek *daimonizomai*. I find this a bad translation on two accounts. First, a better translation of "possession" would be "demonized." It means "to be afflicted by" or "exercised by," whereas the word "possession" denotes ownership. If you're "in Christ Jesus," you are owned by Him alone. He bought you with a price. His life. You can't be owned by any other. You're in the kingdom.

That said, let me pose this—if you're a Christian . . . can you still get a cold? How about a virus? Of course you can. Does getting that cold or virus make you any less a Christian? Of course not. It means you're alive on fallen planet earth. Does it mean you might have to fight some sort of sickness? Certainly. Let's say you live in the United States. Protected by a military. Governed and ruled by a government who has authority over you. Can you still be attacked by an enemy? Or, say, another country? Of course. Does that attack make you any less a citizen of your country? Of course not. Christians are owned by Christ and yet, until He returns, we can be attacked and influenced by evil spirits.

Now look at the word *devil*. Translators took the word *daimonizomai* or *daimonion* or *daimonao* and translated it "devil." This is unfortunate. There is only one devil, lucifer, whereas the word *daimonizomai* actually means "demon," of which there are many. In the same way that we can be citizens of this country and yet be attacked by foreign enemies, it's entirely possible for us as children of God—with residence in the kingdom of heaven, possessed by the Holy Spirit—to be demonized or afflicted and/or influenced by demons.

What Does God Say About Our Lives?

Now that I've posed some of the most common lies, what does God say about us? Let me list a few Scripture passages that help us.

First, "The weapons of our warfare are not carnal but mighty in God for pulling down strongholds, casting down arguments and every high thing that exalts itself against the knowledge of God, bringing every thought into captivity to the obedience of Christ" (2 Cor. 10:4–5 NKJV). Notice the location of the battlefield: the mind.

Next, "We do not wrestle against flesh and blood, but against principalities, against powers, against the rulers of the darkness of this age, against spiritual hosts of wickedness in the heavenly places" (Eph. 6:12 NKJV). We are in a wrestling match, and the enemy has a face—principalities, powers, rulers, and hosts. It's close quarters. Hand-to-hand stuff. And while we cannot see the enemy with our physical eyes, the enemy has been granted a measure of power and authority.

And then, "Little children, you are from God and have overcome them, for he who is in you is greater than he who is in the world" (1 John 4:4). If I'm not at war, then why and how would I waste my time overcoming someone, and why would a "greater" God have been deposited inside me?

What about this? "Look! The wicked bend their bow, they make ready their arrow on the string, that they may shoot secretly at the upright in heart" (Ps. 11:2 NKJV). Notice the enemy is offensive in nature. Did you or I do anything to bring about this offense, other than being born? No. Does that matter to the enemy? Not one bit.

We talked about this one earlier, but it's critical: "Be sober, be vigilant, because your adversary the devil walks about like a roaring lion, seeking whom he may devour" (1 Peter 5:8 NKJV). What is the enemy's intention toward you? John the Baptist is a good example: the enemy wants your head on a platter.

Finally, "The dragon was enraged with the woman, and he went to make war with the rest of her offspring, who keep the commandments of God and have the testimony of Jesus Christ" (Rev. 12:17 NKJV). Don't miss those words "went to make war." Did you do anything to bring that about? Did you raise a finger against the serpent of old? The Charles Martin translation says this: If you love Jesus and love His Word, there is a bullseye on your forehead whether you like it or not. I usually follow that with, "welcome to earth."

Much of *What If It's True?* and this follow-up book have focused on our need to crucify the flesh—everything from unforgiveness, pride, sexual sin, and so on. But it is here that we need to differentiate between crucifying the flesh and casting out the demonic. There's a difference. You can't crucify the demonic (only Jesus does that) and you can't cast out your flesh this side of heaven, so it helps to differentiate between what's our stuff, our carnal nature, and what isn't. The danger, in my experience, is to claim as the work of our flesh what is, in my opinion, the work of the demonic.

Let me pose one more argument, and it's possibly the most dangerous. I call this the Jesus-has-given-us-the-victory-so-just-rest-in-Jesus lie. Now hear me, yes, Jesus rendered an unequivocal, irrevocable defeat to the enemy. He alone is our defender and our avenger. Because of this we don't fight for victory, but rather from it. And yes, we do find our rest in Him. There is a rest for the people of God, and the book of Hebrews explains it (Heb. 4:9). But having said that, herein lies the rub—we are in a fight. Jesus' victory has enabled and empowered us to join Him in that. Not removed us from it.

When I've encountered folks who posit this argument, I find most do so not from a deep conviction of what they've just said but rather from the fear of what will happen to them if they don't say it, because at their root they've bought into one of the previous lies. All of which are rooted in fear. They're simply afraid to go to war and they're standing behind the rest-in-Jesus argument because they're afraid.

Also, most often this lie has come from people who've been in church a long time. When I've encountered it, I've often thought: *But why was I given armor? Why does He call me a good soldier in Jesus Christ? Why then is my struggle not against flesh and blood? Why then are the weapons of my warfare not carnal but spiritual and sufficient for tearing down strongholds? Why does He train my hands for war and my fingers for battle? Why then does my enemy the devil prowl around like a roaring lion looking for someone to devour? Why then do I overcome him [satan] by the blood of the lamb and the word of my testimony? Why then have I been given "all authority"? Why has He put a sword in my mouth? Why does He tell me to clothe myself in armor and take up a sword and cast out?*

Look, I get it. A lot of us come from traditions where we were taught all this warfare stuff has somehow faded and no longer pertains to us. That two thousand years has somehow changed the nature of spiritual warfare and the enemy's desire to wage it. Those same traditions suggest that people who talk like me do so on the fringes of Christianity. Most of us end up on TV or in prison. We're the freaks and the outliers. The crazies outside the norm. But if you put me on the outskirts because I'm preaching spiritual warfare and casting out demons, then you have to put Jesus there too. In His ministry, casting out the demonic was more common than not, and no sooner had He cast out the first demon than He told us He's given us all authority and that we will do the same and greater than He has done.

So, back to my assumption: *you are at war whether you like it or not, and you are at war with spiritual principalities and powers that you cannot see with your physical eyes.* Not fighting doesn't make you any less a target. Many of us Christians are tormented and harassed by the demonic influence and in need of deliverance. This may surprise some of you, but claiming to be a Christian and sitting in church doesn't remove the demonic from your life any more than God giving the land to the nation of Israel drove out the Anakim. Yes, they owned the land by right and deed—i.e. the land was possessed by them in the same way you are possessed by Him—but God expected His people to walk in the authority and mandate He had given them and drive them out. To conquer. Which incidentally required "belief in" and faith.

For some reason, while God was and is entirely capable of dealing with Pharaoh and his army, He sent Moses and Joshua. In the same way, He could have dealt with Goliath by a lightning bolt from on high but instead He sent David. These are not simply stories out of history. Yes, these were real people who lived and walked and obeyed and disobeyed, and they had faults and warts and great successes, but their stories were not written down simply for our entertainment to tell us who God was then. They're types for us, and in them God is telling us who He is now. He is sending us a message, and in that message is both His expectation and His hope. If you are a lover and follower of Jesus, don't let your or my need for deliverance freak you out, because it does not freak out Jesus. He's not pacing the halls of heaven popping antacids worried sick over the demons attacking us. Remember, He created them.

Jesus is totally and singularly capable of dealing decisively with whatever you present. And one more thing—your or my need for deliverance does not lessen or negate our salvation. Your enemy will whisper it does, but nothing could be further from the truth. If we've believed and confessed, we're in Jesus. It's settled. Let me ask this: If you bought a "condemned" piece of property off the courthouse steps, would you expect a little cleanup? Maybe drive out a few rodents and squatters? Of course you would. My point is this: we were all condemned until Jesus offered to buy us out of the hangman's noose. Once in the kingdom, a little cleanup might be expected.

I'm simply trying to encourage you that you might need deliverance. And if you do, the remedy is available and it's free—and what's more, it works. I'm sick and tired of a gospel of Jesus that emasculates the believer.

That takes the weapons of our warfare and either tells us we don't need them or they're impotent. We as the people of God need to take back deliverance from the mental stronghold of abnormal and, by both belief and practice, make it normal.

Jesus is the model, and our commandment is to cast out. If He didn't expect us to do it, then why give the commandment? We are His temple and the deed to our building—our body—is owned by Jesus, but when He hangs the "Under new ownership" sign out front, He may need to clear the building. And to do that, He enables us to go room to room in hand-to-hand combat and throw them out the windows.

That's deliverance.

The Root Argument

At the root of all of these arguments is the first argument in recorded history. It's what I like to call the "did-God-say?" lie. Also known as the "you-will-not-surely-die" whisper. It started with the serpent in the garden who was deceiving Eve:

> Now the serpent was more crafty than any other beast of the field that the Lord God had made. He said to the woman, "Did God actually say, 'You shall not eat of any tree in the garden?'" And the woman said to the serpent, "We may eat of the fruit of the trees in the garden, but God said, 'You shall not eat of the fruit of the tree that is in the midst of the garden, neither shall you touch it, lest you die.'" But the serpent said to the woman, "You will not surely die. For God knows that when you eat of it your eyes will be opened, and you will be like God, knowing good and evil." (Gen. 3:1–5)

Notice where the serpent attacked. he questioned the truth of what God said and what would happen. his intention was to undermine both God's Word and His motive. His heart for us. To drive an ever-so-slight wedge. To insert the possibility of doubt. It's a slick move. Crafty indeed. And the devil doesn't have to prove it or answer his own question. All he has to do is raise the question, and we take the bait by entertaining the possibility.

Two thousand years ago, Jesus "called to him his twelve disciples and gave them authority over unclean spirits, to cast them out, and to heal every disease and every affliction" (Matt. 10:1). My questions for you are these: Does that apply to you and me? Do we have that same authority? And before you answer, let me ask you this: Do we have the same Spirit?

You and I face a choice, and it's the same choice Moses, Joshua, David, and countless others faced. In a sense, we've come full circle back to *What If It's True?* Is His Word true, and will you believe Him and walk in the authority He's given you?

Or not?

When Jesus returned to Nazareth, His hometown, in Matthew 13, the local townspeople refused to believe that the boy they once knew, the carpenter's Son, was actually the promised Messiah. They were incredulous. Matthew recorded that they actually "took offense at him" (Matt. 13:57). Then Matthew recorded something unheard-of in the ministry of Jesus: "He did not do many mighty works there."

Why?

"Because of their unbelief" (v. 58).

I don't believe their unbelief had any power to refuse Jesus to perform miracles any more than the devil does. It's not as if their combined unbelief was more powerful than Jesus. Matthew says, "He did not do." I simply think Jesus chose not to perform miracles because He knew their hearts, and He was looking for a people who *pisteuo*—who "believe in"—Him.

Our authority is in the name of Jesus. Our victory is in and because of the blood of Jesus. And we maintain that victory the moment we place the name of Jesus on our lips. Has everyone I've ever prayed for been delivered or healed? Of course not. I wish they had been. Have I prayed for people who have died soon thereafter? Yes. Does this hurt my heart? More than you know. Given these "unsuccessful" experiences, should

I draw conclusions about the truth of Scripture or the nature of God's heart toward me? Should I stop praying? Should I conclude that this "stuff" doesn't work?

My response is to return to Scripture. Bury my face in it. Soak my soul in it. What does my Abba tell me in His Word? What does His Son tell me? He tells me if I've seen Jesus, I've seen the Father. When my circumstances don't line up with His Word, where does the problem lie? In His Word or my fallen world? I am staking my life on the promise that the problem lies with me and that His Word is perfect and will accomplish the purposes for which He sent it.

I can't make you believe what you won't, and I realize that for some of you I'm swimming upstream here, but we have whitewashed the ministry of Jesus to make it respectable and dignified. Spiritual warfare is not just for some of us, the superspiritual. According to the life, teaching, ministry, and example of Jesus the Christ—it's normal.

My Friend Rick

Again, there are libraries devoted to stories and testimonies of those who have been delivered from demonic influence and attack. I won't rehash them all here. But I will tell you one of mine. There are others. This one just continues to stand out.

I met him on a riverbank, which I've always found kind of cool. He was walking up and down the bank looking for his wedding ring, which had slipped off his finger. And to make matters worse, his marriage was not in a good place. He extended his hand, "I'm Rick Crowley." (And yes, everything I'm about to tell you, he's said publicly and given me permission to say here.)

Over the next few weeks I learned several things. When he was sixteen, he had a stroke and grand mal seizure. Every day since he had taken six to twelve medications a day to counter the epileptic seizures and migraines that resulted. He was a history teacher at a local high school, and the seizures had increased with such frequency that he was having trouble just making it to work. Not to mention the headaches. Add to that some personal sin, as well as his wife's diagnosis that she couldn't have children, and you can understand how he was having trouble.

I invited him to my Bible study, and he started attending. I don't remember what I had been teaching, but a couple of weeks in, I finished a lesson, was standing at the door talking to somebody, and I turned around to find Rick convulsing, pounding his head against the wall. His body was drawn up, withered, foam was coming out his mouth, and his eyes were rolled back in his head. My reaction to him was twofold: "This is not good" and "He looks afraid." The guys I'd been teaching gathered around him and laid hands on him. The seizure subsided, but my heart began to really hurt for the depth of his suffering. To this day, I've never seen one human being suffer more than Rick.

Over the weeks, we saw more of this. And we saw the frequency increase. He saw more doctors and more changes in medication than I can count. From Shands in Gainesville to Mayo and Baptist in Jacksonville, Rick made the rounds. But nothing improved. In fact, things got worse. Much worse. Slowly, I began to see a correlation between my teaching in Bible study and his seizures. Like, when I taught, he seized. Without fail. I began to wonder if there wasn't a spiritual root to his physical problem.

One night we met to anoint him with oil and pray for his healing. He was lying on the floor, we were all praying, and one of my friends, a Peter-like guy, walked over and said to Rick, "Hey, I'm going to speak something to you. I just want you to lie there and let me say it." Rick nodded. My friend placed his hand on his chest and said with no small amount of conviction, "In the name of Jesus, I rebuke you, satan."

From the second he finished speaking, you would have thought someone plugged Rick up to a powerline. His body bounced a foot or two off the ground, he screamed and growled and spit and shook and flailed—and that's about the moment I clued into the fact that while Rick was obviously very physically sick, there was a spiritual component to his suffering.

That night I poured into the ministry of Jesus and, by my own count, discovered that in 60 percent of His healings, He first cast out demons, then healed. Casting out was commonplace. I scratched my head. *I wonder if we're still supposed to do this?* Followed by: *Where does the Word tell me not to?*

So I dove in and started rebuking, binding, and casting out anything I could think of that presented itself to me. I cannot tell you I knew what I was doing. I didn't. But I was looking at Scripture, looking at the ministry of Jesus and those who followed Him, and there seemed to be a lot of parallels.

This was about when all hell broke loose.

Rick's seizures multiplied greatly, he suffered more, and on the surface, things looked really bad. I remember going to visit him one night in Mayo. They'd shaved part of his head and hooked him up to forty or fifty electrical sensors along his skull. He looked a lot like the dreadlocked alien in the movie *Predator*. The doctors were subjecting him to a series of flashing lights to bring about or cause seizures so they could read the seizure in his brain. I remember telling him through tears, "Pal, if we have to go to the other side of the globe to find healing, then we'll do it."

Interestingly, while they could visibly observe the seizures, they couldn't register or read them on the seizure reading machine. What they did find was a tumor in his brain.

A year passed. And while his physical body was in shambles, Rick's heart toward the Lord was growing. He latched ahold of repentance and began vocally repenting of every sin he could remember. Both to me and his wife. He would call at all hours of the day or night. If a memory returned, and it was sin, he confessed it. Didn't matter what it was. I heard stuff I didn't want to hear. Thankfully, I've forgotten much of it. His marriage was improving radically. Like nothing I'd ever seen. God was healing broken places. Somewhere in here I got to see a magnificent warrior of a wife emerge in Julia. To this day, one of the most beautiful things I've seen in this life is how she loved him through all of this. Even now, as I write about it, tears are cascading down my face as I think about how this woman loved this broken, and for all intents and purposes, dying man.

One doctor told her to get her affairs in order. She told the doctor, "I don't think so," and then told Rick, "Honey, pack your stuff, we're not going to be seeing him anymore."

Feeling helpless on the outside staring in, I saw how the Lord was doing a work in Rick's heart that was deeper than physical healing. Don't get me wrong—I wanted physical healing. We all did. And we were all tired of praying for it and seeing little change. But there were glimmers of hope that kept us going. One day, after he'd just suffered a seizure in which I jumped down on the floor to stop his head from slamming against the wall, Rick was out of breath, sweat pouring off his face while Julia cradled him. He looked at me and shook his head through a flow of tears, "If I have to go through a thousand grand mal seizures for the Lord to heal my marriage, I'll take them."

To this day, he's the most courageous person I've ever met. Followed closely by his wife.

During this time, I saw how calling the spirits by name and telling them to leave in the name of Jesus did have a short-term effect on Rick. After one lengthy prayer session one night, Rick went almost three weeks with no seizure. This hadn't happened since he was sixteen. We knew we were on to something.

Also, though I'm the one writing about it, in truth I played a small part in this whole thing. Rick received prayer from a lot of people, many far more experienced than I, and he and they saw powerful deliverance which, in turn, bolstered us when we prayed.

One morning, about eighteen months in, Julia called me. The seizures had returned with a vengeance and Rick was in a bad way. I was tired of the whole blasted thing. I couldn't help my friend. I felt like we were getting our spiritual tail handed to us and, honestly, I didn't have much faith in driving over there. What could I do? But I went. I drove over and the house was a mess. He'd been having seizures, and stuff was everywhere. Julia had some work stuff to do so I took over while she ran out for a couple of hours.

That left Rick and me alone, and that's when all hell broke loose again. He had what was possibly the largest seizure I'd seen. I remember speaking to some spirit and telling it to come out, and while several had responded in voices prior to this, none sounded like this one. This one was Haitian. Mind you, Rick is from Boston. He sounds like those guys in *Good Will Hunting*. But the voice coming out his mouth was clear Haitian and it hated me. He started swinging at me, and I've never heard such filth and cursing come out of a mouth. I spoke to the spirit, told it to get out in the name of Jesus. I didn't care who he was or how he got in there, he was going. Greater is He who's in me than he who's in the world. This is about where I learned that our victory is in the blood of Jesus and we maintain that victory with the name of Jesus on our lips. Also, I learned to be able to see when I was talking to Rick and when I wasn't. His eyes would take on a look that simply was not my friend Rick. Then when I told the thing to leave, Rick's eyes would come back.

After this tense exchange, where the thing was trying to choke me and curse me, Rick lay on the floor with the whole left side of his body withered up and useless. He couldn't use his arm, leg, or hand. The left side of his face was hanging down and he couldn't speak without seriously slurring his words. To make matters worse, it was at this moment he decided he needed to pee. Julia had been trying to keep him hydrated, so water in meant water had to get out. I knew he couldn't physically do that. My friend would either just pee in his pants or he'd need my help to make it to the bathroom, stand there, and he would need help with his zipper and with aim. I told him I was willing, but I also knew my Father and that He loved Rick more than I. So standing right there, I just prayed that the Lord would restore his left side. Rick stood on one leg, his right arm raised in worship, his left arm withered. And as I prayed and he worshipped, he was able to lift his left arm into the air and match his right. Within minutes, Rick stood on two feet, two hands in the air, his speech normal. I knew this because I could hear him worshipping and praising God of heaven and earth—despite his circumstances. I then watched him walk into the bathroom and get rid of the water on his own.

That was the turn. The day things changed. There's a lot more to this story and what we learned, but here's where we are: Rick has not had a seizure in eight years as of February 2020. Rick has not taken any seizure medication, or any medication of any kind, in eight years. His doctors have undiagnosed him as an epileptic. He and Julia have two boys—my godsons. His scans show no brain tumor, which stand in stark contrast to the scans that did. And he now teaches Bible at my son's high school where last year, Rick won teacher of the year.

If Rick were sitting next to you, he'd tell you two things: that Jesus heals—present tense—all diseases and that we will see the goodness of the Lord in the land of the living. If I were seated next to you, I'd say, "How can I but speak of what I've seen and heard? Signs and wonders will follow those who believe."

Now before you think I'm taking credit for any of this, I'm not. Jesus did the delivering and the healing. I know. I saw it with my own two eyes. The only thing I did was believe. And then, maybe like a shepherd boy with a sling, we all ran toward the giant who was cursing my God.

I also don't want you to think that I've always had this boldness or depth of love with everyone. I have not. At least, not yet. I'm a work in progress. Maybe you are too. Also, I haven't seen this depth of the miraculous with every person for whom I've prayed. Yes, we've continued to see healing and deliverance. Powerful, too. As recently as yesterday. But from start to finish, over more than two years of praying, Rick's story still stands out. To me, he was then and is now a man who, even with one half of his body crippled, raised his hand to God Most High, Possessor of heaven and earth, and worshipped when nothing about his present circumstances gave him anything to worship about. Rick, possibly more than anyone I know, dove into the Word, grabbed ahold of it for all he was worth, and believed it at a level I've seldom seen. He still does. When Proverbs says God's words "are life to those who find them, and health to all their flesh," Rick believed that (4:22 NKJV). Now he's teaching that to a bunch of high school kids—one of whom is my youngest son, Rives. Rather often, Rives will walk in the door from school, I'll ask, "How was school?" and he'll say, "Pretty good. Uncle Rick prayed for me in the hall."

It's one of the great joys of my life.

We Are Well Able

During this time, which seemed to stretch on for decades, I latched on to one story in Numbers 13–14 and would read it periodically. To remind me that I'm not alone. I'm retelling it here to bolster your wall. To add steel to your spine. Because if you walk here, you'll need it.

Moses sends out particular men to spy because they are "the heads" of their families. Their tribes. All twelve men are trusted, admired, respected, and their words carry weight. When they speak, people get quiet and listen.

That's why Moses chooses them.

All twelve had been slaves. Had the scars on their backs to prove it. Their dads had been slaves. Their grandfathers had been slaves. Everyone they'd ever known had been a slave. And yet, they'd been delivered out of Egypt. These men witnessed the ten plagues: water becoming blood, frogs, lice, flies, the dead livestock, boils, hail, locusts, and darkness at noon. These are the very men who had painted their door frames with lamb's blood so that the angel of God would pass over them. Sparing their first-born. And He had. These same men woke that morning to the cries and wails of the Egyptians who woke to dead children in their houses. Then there was the whole business at the Red Sea where the most powerful army in the world was breathing down their necks, about to pillage, rape, and kill, and God parted the waters, rose them up in a heap, and the Israelites walked across on dry ground. Once they reached the other side, these same men had watched the waters come crashing down and then walked the shoreline stepping over the armored bodies littering the beach. They saw the bitter waters healed at Marah by a tree. They saw manna and quail rain from the sky. Literally. And if that wasn't enough, every morning they walked out of their tents and stared at a cloud hovering over the tent of meeting, and every night they saw it replaced by a raging column of fire.

These twelve men were eyewitnesses to the greatest, most miraculous events in the history of mankind.

Given that as their resume, Moses taps them on the shoulder and they set off. Single file. Charting a course through a land that has been promised to them by the same God who did all the stuff I just listed above.

They're gone a little over a month. In that time, they walk the breadth of what would later become Israel. Upon their return, they bring back pomegranates, figs, and a cluster of grapes so large two men were required to carry it on a stick between them. When they walk back into camp, people are giddy with excitement. "Tell us! What'd you see?" Moses gathers them around the campfire, sets them up in front of the people, and they relay the story for all of Israel. One by one they stand, "Yep, it's everything we hoped. Beautiful. Lush. Green. Flows with milk and honey. Never seen its equal."

Think about that a second. That moment in time. Can you see the people's faces? Firelight dancing on their warm, red cheeks. Lighting the excitement in their eyes. How they're hugging their children just a little tighter. Smiling just a little wider. Laughing just a little louder. "Jubilant" comes to mind. For the first time maybe in their whole lives they are allowing themselves to hope and to dream and to entertain the idea that, for once, it might come true. Maybe for the first time ever, they are letting their minds wander out across a lush land. Crops in their fields. Oil in the press. Wine at their table. Children playing. Homes of their own. All promised to them by this God who brought them out of slavery—out of Egypt and out from under the hand of Pharaoh.

Then something amazing happens. One of the twelve, and Scripture doesn't say who, raises his hand. Watch as the entire crowd turns their heads in unison. Waiting for the next good word. The next promise kept. "Ummm, but you can forget all that because the cities are built like Fort Knox and the land is populated by giants."

Did you hear that? That sucking sound? That was the total deflation of the spirit of an entire people. Look at their faces now. Still smiling? Or do you see something else in their eyes as the word *giants* pinballs around the inside of their craniums?

"Yeah . . ." He continues. "The Anakim have been here quite some time. Pretty well entrenched. They run everything. Own everything. Do what they want. They devour people. We are grasshoppers in comparison."

The descendants of Anak, or the Anakim, were a race of giants that had been around a long time. They were the hands-down baddest dudes on the planet. And had been since before Abraham. Before the flood. The stories were legendary. Remember Goliath? He was one of their later descendants.

We don't know how tall they were, but we do know that the sweet little Kumbaya session at the bonfire came to an abrupt halt as "all the people wept" and then complained against Moses. The depth of their despair is registered in a single comment: "If only we had died in Egypt." As if Egypt and slavery were somehow better.

Return to the fire. To the spies as they offer proof. They point to the grapes. "The giants eat those." We know that it required two Israelites to carry back a single cluster of grapes that, by extension, one Anakim could eat out of the palm of his hand. The unspoken assumption is, if they can eat that for an afternoon snack, they'll devour you. At this point, the people begin to mutiny. "Moses is out of his mind! Run him through! Let's pick a new leader. Return to Egypt. Maybe they'll take us back!"

Do you hear that? Hear how quickly they made a 180? Funny how they've so quickly forgotten that big body of water back there.

Even God Himself is incredulous: "How long will this people despise me? And how long will they not believe in me, in spite of all the signs that I have done among them?"[26]

Take another look at that campfire. Look with spiritual eyes. Now look at all the evil strongholds and principalities perched atop the Israelites' shoulders and whispering in their ears. Those arguments that are exalting themselves against the knowledge of God. *God brought you out here to drop you off at the foot of a giant who's going to kill you. Rape your sister and mother. Enslave your children.*

What they are hearing is the same argument that came out of the mouth of Goliath.

And the fruit of that argument in them was fear. Fear is insidious. It breeds doubt. Spawns terror. Spreads like wildfire. And it is a liar.

But wait. There in the midst of wailing, of moaning, of complaining, of a full-fledged mutiny, a man named Caleb hops up on a table and quiets the crowd. He raises his hands, raises his voice, and speaks above the crowd because they refuse to be quiet. Then he says something that to them sounds utterly crazy, but to God sounds like obedience: "Let us go up at once and occupy it, for we are well able to overcome it."[27]

The word *occupy* also means to "take possession of."

Don't you love that? Every time I hear it I want to climb up on top of my house and scream at the top of my lungs, "We are well able!"

Study that picture a second. Caleb is incredulous at the people's doubt. At the thing he sees spreading throughout them. The rippling fear. In my mind, he screams this three or four times—each time louder. "We are well able. We are well able!"

The ten quickly respond before they lose face. "We are not able to go up against the people, for they are stronger than we are. . . . The land, through which we have gone to spy it out, is a land that devours its inhabitants, and all the people that we saw in it are of great height. And there we saw the Nephilim (the sons of Anak, who come from the Nephilim), and we seemed to ourselves like grasshoppers, and so we seemed to them."[28]

The fruit of this report is recorded in the next sentence: "Then all the congregation raised a loud cry, and the people wept that night. And all the people of Israel grumbled against Moses and Aaron. The whole congregation said to them, 'Would that we had died in the land of Egypt. Or would that we had died in this wilderness. Why is the LORD bringing us into this land, to fall by the sword? Our wives and our little one will become prey. Would it not be better for us to go back to Egypt?' And they said to one another, 'Let us choose a leader and go back to Egypt.'"[29]

In the ensuing clamor, Caleb the son of Jephunneh is joined by Joshua the son of Nun. Two against ten. Shoulder to shoulder with Caleb, Joshua takes up the banner. He says: "'The land, which we passed through to spy it out, is an exceedingly good land. If the LORD delights in us, he will bring us into this land and give it to us, a land that flows with milk and honey. Only do not rebel against the LORD. And do not fear the people of the land, for they are bread for us. Their protection is removed from them, and the LORD is with us; do not fear them.' Then all the congregation said to stone them with stones. But the glory of the LORD appeared at the tent of meeting to all the people of Israel."[30]

Notice the difference between "we seemed like grasshoppers" and "they are our bread."

Many times when praying for Rick, and others, I've wanted to feel like a grasshopper. It would be easier. It takes no faith to be a grasshopper. But to cross the river, to step foot in the promised land, to walk into a land populated with giants, takes a God kind of faith.

In contrast to Caleb and Joshua, the whole congregation of Israel picked up stones to strike the two men down, proving their faithlessness. God Most High, Possessor of heaven and earth, had just delivered them from Egypt with the greatest signs and wonders any of them had ever imagined, and yet, when presented with giants, they cower. And because of that, that entire generation of faithless people died in the wilderness. They never set foot in the promised land.

Forty years later, Joshua destroys the Anakim with their cities. Scripture records he "devoted them to destruction. . . . There was none of the Anakim left in the land of the people of Israel."[31]

Desert or Promised Land?

When I first stumbled on this story, several things struck me. First, I want to be like Caleb: "We are well able." Two, I want to be like Joshua: "They are our bread." And three, I want to destroy giants.

You and I face two kind of giants, and yet truth is, there is nothing gigantic about them. The first is the arguments we hear. Those I listed above. We let them live rent free in our minds. They are the arguments that exalt themselves against the knowledge of God. They are the same lies the ten spies listened to, and they need to be brought into captivity to Christ and crucified on the altar of His truth. Second are the spiritual strongholds and principalities we face. Yes, they are real. Yes, they have power. But the truth is, there has not been a demonic entity yet in the history of this universe or any other who has or can compete with one drop of Jesus' blood. When He said, "It is finished," He wasn't kidding.

The tension for you and me is simple: What do you believe? What will you believe?

What I saw in Rick, and what I often see in other people, is someone staring down a giant. And trust me, there were days, weeks, and even months when we made no headway. When nothing we prayed or tried worked. I can't explain that. All I know is that it's a wrestling match, and wrestling is hand-to-hand combat. People suffering the demonic are afraid and need someone with faith to come alongside them and say, "We are well able," and "They are our bread." Then they need to have endurance to see it through. One and done is not my experience.

If I've heard him say it once, I've heard him quote it a hundred times. When it comes to choosing whether to fight or flee, Boston-born Rick speaks in his best Scottish brogue and quotes Mel Gibson from Braveheart: "Aye, fight and you may die. Run, and you'll live—at least a while. And dying in your beds, many years from now, would you be willin' to trade *all* the days, from this day to that, for one chance, just one chance, to come back here and tell our enemies that they may take our lives, but they'll never take . . . *our freedom?*"

God led His people into a promised land. We are no different. I said it in *What If It's True?* and I'm saying it here: God Most High, Abba, is leading you and me into a land of promises. His Word. Will you believe what He's written there? Will you take Matthew 10 and do it? Preach. Cleanse. Cast out. Raise.

More often than not we forsake His written promises, choosing instead to listen to fear or our traditions. We shake our heads. Backpedal. Make excuses. "I'm not really sure."

We need a swift kick in the pants.

The enemy sits on your shoulder, constantly whispering lies. Telling you everything contrary to what God has promised. But God has not changed. His arm is not shortened so that He cannot save. He calls those things which aren't as though they are. He said it then, and He is saying it now: "Lazarus! Wake up. The time for sleeping is over. Come out." He heals all our diseases. Has given us all authority in heaven and on earth. He saw satan cast down like lightning. Defeated death and the grave. Carries the keys to prove it. His hair is white, eyes afire, feet like burnished bronze, sword girded on His thigh, and when He opens His mouth it sounds like rushing waters or the break in the pipeline, and the entire host of heaven, dressed in white linen, is lined up in battle formation behind Him. Swords clanking. Shields glistening. Horses champing at the bit.

What more do you want?!

Let me ask you a gut-check question: Whose spirit is in you? Are you more like Caleb and Joshua or the faithless ten who died in the desert? God will give you the desert if you prefer. But whether you live out your days in the desert or the land of promises is your choice. You get to choose. Grasshopper or bread.

We're all facing Anakim. Every day, we wake up in a world where they walk the streets. Welcome to earth. But the truth is this: you are well able, and they're defeated. Driven out. Cast down. Given into your hand. What you see is posturing. What you hear are lies from the pit of hell.

My experience praying for people has led me to this simple truth that I try to remember when I pray. I draw this from my experience, which does not make it absolutely true all the time (although I have found it true most of the time), but does make it practical and helpful. It might be worth writing on a 3x5 card and taping to your bathroom mirror or the dash of your car or slipping inside your Bible. I've also found it helpful in identifying the strongholds in my own life:

- Behind every stronghold is a lie
- Every lie a fear
- And every fear an idol

- Which we carved by hand (or was passed to us generationally)
- When we (or our ancestors) rebelled and surrendered to some power (for comfort, protection, provision, etc.)
- Other than the boundless love of the Father and the undefeated blood of Jesus

If you're praying for someone and bumping into strongholds (which we will talk about in more detail in the next chapter), ask the Holy Spirit to show you the idols they cling to, fears they believe, or lies they have accepted. You may not have realized it but much of *What If It's True?* walks through this very process. In the next chapter we will talk about how to break the strongholds, but in simple terms it requires renouncing, repenting, and receiving deliverance from the Holy Spirit.

The Glory of God

When Jesus met Martha outside Lazarus's grave, He said something that is easy to miss. He said, "Did I not tell you that if you believed you would see the glory of God?" (John 11:40). And don't miss the fact that He's talking about raising a dead man to life—which is what He does with every one of us. We as people want to see and experience the glory before we believe. We stand there with our arms crossed, measuring whether He is worth our belief, saying, "Prove it." The Father doesn't work that way. When did Peter see Jesus transfigured, before or after his proclamation at Caesarea Philippi? And when did God say, "This is my Son in whom I am well pleased," before or after John the Baptist said, "Behold, the Lamb of God, who takes away the sin of the world" (John 1:29)?

I've already devoted an entire chapter to belief, so I won't rehash it here, but the reason I included it before this chapter is because when you arrive here, and you're willing and wanting to pray for the sick, you need to have wrestled the belief thing.

Having just read this, some of you will say, "Charles, are you telling me that the reason I've not seen healing in some way in my life is because I don't believe enough? Don't have enough faith?"

No. I'm not. Jesus said, "Go, your faith has healed you." But little or much, we don't know how much faith they had. Scripture does not measure that. Jesus never met a sick person, held up a tape measure, shook His head, and said, "You're not quite there. Go and come back later when you have more faith."

Jesus took what they brought. And in every case it was enough. I am hoping you will hear me encouraging you to come believing that you will see. Because a man who doubts "is like a wave of the sea that is driven and tossed by the wind. For that person must not suppose that he will receive anything from the Lord; he is a double-minded man, unstable in all his ways" (James 1:6–8).

For many of you, I know that I'm pressing you to believe differently than you've been taught or believed in the past. I realize I'm questioning your foundations. Let's return to what I said in the beginning: the tangible result of the belief and faith of the disciples was easily measured. They turned the world upside down.

Unbelief turned over nothing.

Unbelief healed no one.

Unbelief delivered no one.

My prayer is rather simple: *Jesus, I believe. Please . . . help my unbelief.*

CHAPTER 14

What or Who Are You
at War Against?

Maybe you've prayed and prayed for the Lord to help you and/or heal you, and you've seen little to no change—so you're still praying. I praise God for your faith. Chances are, you might be dealing with a spiritual stronghold or fortress. Years ago in our marriage, Christy and I were praying for something that we'd been praying about for a while, and when we finished, she revealed an honest response to our prayer. She said, "I know He can, but will He?"

I can't answer you any more than I can answer her, but I do know that His very name means "My deliverer."[1] And "I am the one who avenges you."[2] He's a good Father who gives good gifts to His children. He's lavished us with His love. He loves righteousness and hates wickedness.[3] And He both commands and promises us in His Word:

- "Call upon me in the day of trouble; I will deliver you, and you shall glorify me" (Ps. 50:15).
- "Everyone who calls on the name of the Lord will be saved" (Rom 10:13 [Joel 2:32]).

- "Submit yourselves therefore to God. Resist the devil, and he will flee from you" (James 4:7).
- "Greater is He who is in [me] than he who is in the world" (1 John 4:4 NASB).
- "Having disarmed principalities and powers, He made a public spectacle of them, triumphing over them in it" (Col. 2:15 NKJV).
- "The Son of God was manifested, that He might destroy the works of the devil" (1 John 3:8 NKJV).
- "Whatever you bind on earth will be bound in heaven, and whatever you loose on earth will be loosed in heaven. Again I say to you that if two of you agree on earth concerning anything that they ask, it will be done for them by My Father in heaven. For where two or three are gathered together in My name, I am there in the midst of them" (Matt. 18:18–20 NKJV).
- "And they overcame him by the blood of the Lamb and by the word of their testimony" (Rev. 12:11 NKJV).

As I understand it, that word *testimony* means "to make the right confession," or "to say the same thing as." To say the same thing as who? The right answer is Jesus. When we say back to Him what He's said to us, we are guaranteed to make the right confession.

Does This Really Pertain to Me in this Day and Age?

Who needs deliverance prayer? Honestly? In my experience, we all do. Starting with me. There's not a single one of us walking the planet who doesn't need prayer for both deliverance from the enemy and healing of all sickness and disease.

Don't think so?

Sometimes, when I've taught this, somebody has raised their hand and asked, "But I don't really see spirits in the Bible. Where are they? What are their names?"

Let me list a few:

- a perverse spirit (Isa. 19:14 NKJV)
- familiar spirit, necromancer (Isa. 29:4 KJV; Deut. 18:11 RSV)
- spirit of deep sleep, slumber (Isa. 29:10)
- spirit of heaviness, depression (Isa. 61:3 NKJV)
- unclean spirit (Matt. 12:43; Mark 7:25)
- dumb spirit, those that affect the tongue and/or the ear (Mark 9:17, 25 NKJV)
- unclean spirit, named as "Legion" (Luke 8:29–30)
- spirit of infirmity that attacked a woman for eighteen years, bent over in her back (Luke 13:11 NKJV)
- spirit of divination (fortune-telling girl), a python spirit (Acts 16:16)
- seven sons of Sceva, the spirit leaped, overpowered, prevailed (Acts 19:14–16 NKJV)
- spirit of bondage again to fear (Rom. 8:15 NKJV)
- spirit of slumber (Rom. 11:8 KJV)
- deceiving spirits (1 Tim. 4:1 NKJV)
- spirit of fear (2 Tim. 1:7)
- Finally, John says, "Test the spirits . . . every spirit that confesses that Jesus Christ is come in the flesh is of God." Meaning, some don't confess Christ. (1 John 4:1–2 NKJV)

Let me bring this closer to home and maybe help you answer your own question: Have you ever felt enticed or harassed by something you couldn't put a finger on? Have you ever felt unable to stop doing something you are doing—even when you don't want to do it? Have you ever felt tormented? Either from physical torment (like arthritis, insomnia, something chronic and difficult to diagnose) or from mental torment (such as fear of going insane or thoughts of suicide) or spiritual torment (fear of having committed "the unforgivable sin" or asking "Am I sure I'm really saved?")? Do you have thoughts that you're pretty sure don't come from you? Have you ever felt compelled and/or enslaved to act a certain way? Have you suffered from addiction? Porn? Alcohol abuse? Have you felt compelled to steal? Lie? Commit adultery? Have you ever had a strange desire to defile your body when Jesus tells us our bodies are His temple? Have you ever been deceived? (Pride opens the door to deception and pride is both an attitude and a demonic entity.) Have you ever been sick or tired or in pain? Have you ever felt restless over a long period of time and you can't pinpoint the source?

The demonic attacks and resides in negative emotions, attitudes, our minds, our tongues, our sexual lives, and our lusts. They gain entrance to us through every type of sin including the occult, false religions, philosophies and cults, and all heresies. Personally, I believe that behind every addiction is a demon. Why? Jesus has given us His Spirit, which is a spirit of self-control (2 Tim. 1:7), so if we're not acting in control of our self then we're getting some help from an outside source and we need to cast it out.

Because of this, I've seen or known of people who have been delivered from fear, torment, anxiety, rage/anger, unforgiveness, lust, adultery, porn, addictions, rejection, gluttony, alcoholism, garrulity (which is excessive talking), gossip, lying, falsehood, shame, sickness, disease, and countless others.

The point is this: I've seen people and I know people who have come to freedom and healing when they've recognized that the problem might be an Ephesians 6:12 problem. A principality, power, and/or stronghold. And that the weapons of our warfare are as described in 2 Corinthians 10:5. Not carnal but spiritual. Freedom came when they, like Martha outside Lazarus's tomb, believed they would see the glory of God.

I'm trying to make the case that freedom and healing do in large part boil down to "What do you believe?" If you don't believe, chances are good you won't see the glory of God. And if you're not sure and you're waffling or scratching your head, let me ask you this: Are you willing to believe it? Willingness is a great starting point. Jesus can work with willingness. Whatever the case, a change has to occur in our thinking, and I think that change starts in our gut. Our will.

That change can be seen in the difference between these two

statements: "I'm sick or I'm addicted or I'm fearful simply because I live in a fallen world, and it's just a function of being human." Or, "I'm sick or addicted or fearful and the cause might be a demon, and I'm willing to give this casting-out thing a go."

For the record, not every sickness is demonic. The flu might just be the flu or a virus might just be because you got slimed at the doctor's office from a snotty-nosed kid. But I'm trying to bring about a change in your and my thinking where we believe the cause might or could be a demon, and not only do we believe that but move past that to engaging it on the field of battle.

Because again, there's a difference. The former "believes that." The latter "believes in."

How to Be Delivered: Do You Meet the Conditions?

In my experience with people who have been delivered, healed, and come to freedom, I see some consistent patterns. First, they humble themselves. They get on their faces before the throne, raise their hand in covenant with Jesus, choose His kingdom alone, and reject every other. They're honest—both about their faith and their sin. They're truth tellers even when the truth is ugly and hurts. They confess their faith in Christ. Vocally and with some gumption. They confess any known sin committed by themselves or their ancestors—with equal gumption. In fact, they pour themselves out in repentance of all sins (Prov. 28:13). No sin is too small, and they have received the gift of repentance (Acts 11:18; 2 Tim. 2:25). They recognize that the first three of the Ten Commandments are still commanded, so they break with the occult, any curses, and/or secret societies. They forgive others—especially those who don't deserve it. And finally, they actively expel (Mark 16:17)—thrust and drive out—the demonic.

Every action I've just described in the paragraph above involves our mouths. Our proclamation. Remember, Jesus is the high priest of our confession (Heb. 3:1). Study that progression and you'll find that He does not act on our behalf as our high priest until we make the right confession. Our confession actually releases the high priestly ministry of Jesus on our behalf. And what does the last line of that chapter say? They—the nation of Israel—were not able to enter His rest because of an evil, unbelieving heart. Hence they made the wrong confession and died in their sin.

I've also found some consistent hindrances. First among them is lack of repentance and/or failure to repent for a specific sin. How do you know which sin? Ask the Holy Spirit to bring it to mind. Remember the 3x5 card I mentioned above? See those words "rebelled and surrendered"? They're key because they pinpoint where we (or our ancestors) turned and did our own thing or gave up our will and chose to partner with something that is not Jesus. So look for those moments—and then repent. Lack of repentance is followed closely by lack of desperation. In my opinion, deliverance is for the desperate, and I cannot remember ever seeing a non-desperate person delivered. You've got to want it to get it. If you're still not sure, ask yourself what you don't want others to know about you. What sin do you want hidden in your closet? The one you're taking to the grave? The one you're afraid to name or speak out loud?

Also, wrong motives can also be a hindrance. Look at Simon the sorcerer. He was not desperate but wanted power rather than a relationship with the One who held the power (Acts 8:18–19). Self-centeredness is also a hurdle; it causes us to be more focused on ourselves and not on Jesus. We're focused on what we're getting out of this rather than what we bring to Him. Failure to break with the occult means that we still desire power from some source other than Jesus, and He will not allow this. This means we throw out horoscopes, Ouija boards, all fortune-telling, any form of sorcery, and all trinkets or rings or necklaces or anything attached to the occult. It means we even get rid of those expensive pieces of artwork on the wall that praise the dark world or power of the enemy. And I'm not talking about selling them and profiting off them. I'm talking about tearing them up and burning them. If you've slept with more people than your husband or wife, chances are good there's a soul tie there that needs breaking. Soulish or binding relationships are a definite hindrance, and we need to break those. Lastly, all generational curses need to be broken.

And let me interject two things before some of you become overwhelmed: First, don't dismay. The blood is the remedy. Jesus wins. Every time. Freedom and healing are on the way. Second, deliverance is an action in the battle plan, a weapon in our arsenal, but deliverance is not the end any more than a highway is the destination. We are going somewhere. That somewhere is to the Father, and deliverance is His gift to His children.

There's more—a lot more—to this whole discussion on healing and deliverance. Books, in fact. What I've written here is simply a primer. I, too, still have much to learn. Over the years, to help and arm myself, I've kept a list of Scriptures that we pray out loud over people—both when praying for healing and deliverance. And to be honest, I can't always tell the difference. This really started with praying for Rick. I've included those Scriptures in Appendix B. Feel free to add to them. The list is not exhaustive. I'd encourage you to read through them, highlight them in your Bible, write them on index cards, and use them when you pray. They work. The enemy can't stand them.

Truth is, no soldier goes into war without training. So train yourself. You can't go wrong with Derek Prince, Francis MacNutt, Francis Frangipane, and John Eldredge. There are a host of other greater teachers out there with far more experience and knowledge than I.

Also, in the last ten years, both for myself and for others, I've traveled to ministries or churches where deliverance is commonplace. And some of these places have a real mantle for this ministry. One of those places is Christian Healing Ministries here in Jacksonville. I trust them with me, my kids, and my wife. At CHM, you will not find people screaming at you, but you will find amazing prayer ministers who listen to and walk with the Holy Spirit and who will love you and help walk you out of chains and sickness. (Visit them at christianhealingmin.org.)

Let me encourage one more thing: all of us who pray for others, in any kind of deliverance and healing prayer, we're all in process. None of us is perfect. We will get it wrong sometimes. I certainly have. Please forgive us when we do. Give us a do-over. And please don't blame the Lord for the inexperience of those praying for you. Sometimes these things can take more than one prayer. My prayer with Rick took over two years, so hang in there. Also, use your discernment. Ask the Holy Spirit to guide you. Guard your heart. I'd encourage you to be shrewd as a serpent and innocent as a dove before you let someone lay hands on you (Matt. 10:16).

I can find no place in Scripture where Jesus commanded someone to preach and didn't also command them to cast out, heal, cleanse, and raise the dead. It was all part of the same package. When He sent out the Twelve, He gave them this authority, and they were amazed at the demons' response. We don't know what He told the seventy-two as He sent them out but we do know that upon their return, they, too, commented how even the demons responded (Luke 10:17). And the only person in the New Testament labeled an evangelist is Philip. Look at the fruit of his proclamation of the gospel in Samaria: "Philip went down to the city of Samaria and proclaimed to them the Christ. And the crowds with one accord paid attention to what was being said by Philip, when they heard him and saw the signs that he did. For unclean spirits, crying out with a loud voice, came out of many who had them, and many who were paralyzed or lame were healed" (Acts 8:5–7). Does your evangelism include this? For the Twelve, the seventy-two, Philip, Paul, and a host of others, it was all the same commandment. The Word was preached. The sick were healed. Demons cast out. Lepers cleansed. And dead raised to life.

Is that your ministry?

My final questions to you are these: Through faith, will you choose to believe that this is true and that it pertains to you? Will you take this scriptural basis and turn it into a way of thinking? Of doing? Of believing? Will you exercise the authority given you against the enemy trying to kill you?

When God approached Moses, Moses tried telling Him how he (Moses) wasn't the man for the job. God responded, "What is that in your hand?" (Ex. 4:2). The question before you and me right this moment is the same. What's in your hand? And will you choose to believe it? For Moses, "that" was a wooden staff. For us, "that" is the Word of God.

And while Moses got the message, the stubborn people following him weren't so receptive. God is speaking to us today what Joshua spoke before he walked the people of God into the land of God. "Choose this day whom you will serve" (Josh. 24:15). The age of passive, wimpy Christianity needs to close. The Father is raising a priesthood, a kingdom of priests who walk in belief and faith, and who do what He says. Who choose to be strong and courageous even when the giants are threatening to kill them. God is raising up priests who hop up on the table, stand shoulder to shoulder with two giants named Caleb and Joshua, raise their hands, and scream above the crowd: "We are well able! And they are our bread!"

Let's Pray

No boxer ever won a title from outside the ring. No wrestler won a match off the mat. No team won a championship from the parking lot. And no army ever won a battle except in combat—and eventually, all combat ends in hand-to-hand fighting where one side subdues the other. Where the victor stands on and holds conquered ground. Meaning? If you want to win a fight you've got to be in it.

I believe that when we really believe this, we will see the glory of God. The God of the universe is here now. And He's intently focused on you and your freedom. It's for freedom that He came to set us free. So, with expectation, let's do this on our knees, or on our face, with our hands lifted high.

The following prayer is rather simple. I've stripped it down on purpose. If you want to go further and deeper, I'd encourage you to visit one or more of several places: Christian Healing Ministries, Derek Prince Ministries, Ransomed Heart (John Eldredge), and Francis Frangipane Ministries. Yes, there are others. These are just the ones I use most often. I would also encourage you to turn to Appendix B in the back of this book where I've listed some of the Scriptures we often pray through as we pray for people. Pray them out loud. The enemy hates that.

Pray with me.

- Lord Jesus Christ, I believe You are the Son of God and the only way to God—that You died on the cross for my sins and rose again so that I might be forgiven and receive eternal life. Here and now I receive that forgiveness and that life.

- Father, I renounce all my pride and religious self-righteousness and any false dignity that does not come from You. I have no claim on Your mercy except that You died in my place, and I know there is more mercy in You than sin in me. Please forgive me of my pride. Of my rebellion. Lord, I'm so sorry. I don't want it to keep me from You any longer. Today, I choose to crucify my pride, laying it down at the foot of Your cross.

- Lord, I confess all my sins before You and hold nothing back. Especially I confess . . . [Let the Holy Spirit bring to mind any unconfessed sin. And don't hurry through this. There's no pressure here. He'll wait on you.]

- Father, I repent of all my sins. Known and unknown. Things said and left unsaid. And all my actions and thoughts not inspired by You. In this moment, I turn from every decision or action or thought based in me, my selfishness, and my wicked, black heart. I turn away from them and I turn toward You, Lord, for mercy and forgiveness.

- By a decision of my will, I freely forgive all who have ever wronged or harmed me. I lay down all bitterness, all resentment, and all hatred. Specifically, I forgive . . . [speak their name(s) out loud].

- I sever all contact I have ever had with the occult or with any and all false religions, particularly . . . (horoscopes, mind readers, mediums, fortune tellers, Ouija boards, and any and all forms of witchcraft and/or secret societies). Lord, I repent for any place where I've sought power or solace or comfort in any power other than You. Forgive me, please. In this moment, I make a full break from that false power, and I raise my hand in covenant with You and You alone. I know that it is Your blood which cleanses me from all unrighteousness, and so I plead the blood of Jesus now over my mind, soul, spirit, and body.

- Lord, I commit myself to get rid of all objects associated with the occult or false religion(s). I will purge my house now or when I get home and, regardless of earthly value, I will throw all of it in the trash.
- Lord Jesus, I thank You that on the cross You were made a curse, that I might be redeemed from every curse and inherit God's blessing. On that basis, I ask You to release me and set me free to receive the deliverance I need, which You promise me in Joel 2:32 and Acts 2:21.
- Lord, I take my stand with You against all satan's demons. I submit to You, Lord—You and You alone—and I resist the devil. Greater are You who are in me than he who is in the world. And I overcome him, satan, by the blood of the Lamb and the word of my testimony; and my testimony is this: the blood of Jesus has set me free, once and forever, from any and all attacks, schemes, plans, or activity of the enemy, and I willingly come under the full and complete *tetelestai* authority of the precious blood of Jesus.
- Having done all this, in faith and belief, I now speak to any demons that have control over me. I am a blood-bought, blood-washed, and blood-redeemed child of the Most High God, Possessor of heaven and earth, the God of angel armies, and I [Speak directly to them] command you—go from me now in the name of Jesus! Leave! Get out! I expel you! The blood of Jesus cleanses me. The name of Jesus frees me!

If you just prayed this—now, just breathe, and let me (Charles), pray over you. And you don't need to do anything. Just let the Holy Spirit have His way. He's working, even now in this moment. So relax. Just breathe in and out, let me pray, and let Him do what only He can do:

Father, I bless and praise You and You alone. I thank You for this child who is here now, resting at Your feet. Abba, I ask that You rain down, that You baptize here and now, Your child with Your presence, and Your Spirit. Invade every recess of their person, their thinking, their memories, both conscious and unconscious, and their wounds.

I speak to any stronghold, principality, power, or argument that exalts itself above the name of Jesus and, in the name of Jesus, I say, be broken. By and through and because of the blood of Jesus, I break your assignment, your attack, and command you to come out and leave. Now. No longer will you torment this child of God. In the undefeated name of Jesus, get out.

Holy Spirit, we praise You. We lift our hands in worship of You, for You alone are worthy of praise. I thank You for what You are doing in this moment and will do in the moments to come. I pray Psalm 91 over this child. I pray Isaiah 61 over this child. I ask that You come with a mighty rushing wind and fill them up to overflowing. Deliver them completely. Come, Lord Jesus. Tetelestai.

Now just praise Him.

CHAPTER 15

They Turned the World
Upside Down

Paul, Silas, and Timothy have traveled a thousand miles north-west of Jerusalem, across the Mediterranean Sea, passing through Amphipolis and Apollonia, arriving at the intersection of two major trade routes in a seaside town called Thessalonica, a thriving walled city on the Egnatian Way with a population of some 200,000. Leaders of the city are nervous because rumors about Paul and the power of his message have preceded him.

Prior to arriving in Thessalonica, Paul received the Macedonian vision, so they set sail for Troas, Samothrace, Neapolis, and Philippi—a leading city in the district of Macedonia and a Roman colony.[1]

While there, Lydia, a leading woman in the city, listens to Paul and her heart is "opened . . . to pay attention to what was said."[2] Soon there-after, she is converted and baptized and prevails upon Paul and the others to stay in her house.

As they are going to a place of prayer, the three men are met by a slave girl who has a spirit of divination. Another text reads, "a python spirit." Her owners use her for fortune-telling and make a sizable profit off her. Paul casts out the demon, saying, "'I command you in the name of Jesus

Christ to come out of her.' And it [the spirit] came out that very hour."
Seeing their chance for profit evaporate into thin air, the girl's owners
drag Paul and Silas into the city square before the magistrates and declare,
"These men are Jews, and they are disturbing our city. They advocate cus-
toms that are not lawful for us Romans to accept or practice."[3] The crowd
joins in, tears the men's clothes, beats them with rods, and puts them in
prison, fastening their feet in the stocks.

Locked to the prison floor, Paul and Silas begin singing hymns and
praying while the other prisoners listen. Inexplicably, an earthquake
occurs, shaking the very foundation of the prison and unlocking all
the doors and everyone's bonds. When the jailer wakes and sees that
he is about to lose both his job and his life because he thinks all the
prisoners have escaped, he draws his sword to fall on it. Seconds
before his death, Paul cries out, "Do not harm yourself, for we are all
here."[4] Trembling, the jailer falls down before Paul and Silas and asks,
"'What must I do to be saved?' And they said, 'Believe in the Lord
Jesus, and you will be saved, you and your household.'"[5] Notice those
words "believe in."

From there, the jailer takes them that same hour and washes their
wounds, where Scripture records an amazing thing: Paul and Silas speak
the Word of the Lord to him and all his house, who are immediately
baptized. Following their radical conversation, the jailer feeds them and
rejoices that he and his family have believed in God.

This is the context and the wave of whispers upon which Paul and
Silas and Timothy arrive in Thessalonica, where the travelers are invited
to stay in the house of a man named Jason. For the next three Sabbaths,
Paul teaches in the synagogue. In so doing, he is speaking decrees contrary to Caesar. What is he preaching? We don't know exactly, but if we
draw from Paul's other letters, we can get some idea.

To the Corinthians, Paul said, "For us there is one God, the Father,
from whom are all things and for whom we exist, and one Lord, Jesus
Christ, through whom are all things and through whom we exist."[6]

To the Galatians, he preached, "For in Christ Jesus you are all sons of

God, through faith. For as many of you as were baptized into Christ have put on Christ. There is neither Jew nor Greek, there is neither slave nor free, there is no male and female, for you are all one in Christ Jesus."[7]

To the Colossians, Paul said, "See to it that no one takes you captive by philosophy and empty deceit, according to human tradition, according to the elemental spirits of the world, and not according to Christ. For in him, the whole fullness of deity dwells bodily, and you have been filled in him, who is the head of all rule and authority."[8]

And finally, to Timothy, Paul declared, "There is one God, and there is one mediator between God and men, the man Christ Jesus, who gave himself as a ransom for all."[9]

We also know that Paul had confounded the leading Jewish authorities in both Damascus, by proclaiming that Jesus was the Christ, and in Antioch, by stating that after Pilate executed Him on a tree, God raised Jesus—His own Son—from the dead.[10] Paul ended his message by saying, "Let it be known to you therefore, brothers, that through this man forgiveness of sins is proclaimed to you, and by him everyone who believes is freed from everything from which you could not be freed by the law of Moses."[11] When the leading Jews heard this, they were jealous and incited the city—a pattern wherever Paul preached.

By including these Scriptures, I am assuming that Paul was consistent in his message, often preaching the same word from place to place. If this is true, and if he spoke similar words to the Thessalonians, and if these words came on the heels of the events in Philippi, I can imagine how the local authorities aren't too happy about his arrival. The message of the gospel of the kingdom and those who believe and practice it are a threat to their power, their influence, and their income. This hostility is the same type Jesus faced before the religious rulers after His arrest as He stood before Pilate. The Jewish leaders told Pilate, "If you release this man, you are not Caesar's friend. Everyone who makes himself a king opposes Caesar."[12]

As a result of Paul's teaching, many Thessalonians—including "devout Greeks and not a few of the leading women"—believe Jesus is the Christ, the promised Messiah and a King greater than Caesar.[13]

To Rome, this is treason. To the Jews, blasphemy.

The fact that women are included in Luke's description is significant. Leading women of the upper class, and possibly wives of leading men in the city, are swayed by Paul's message. Converted. It also says, "not a few." That means no small number. The ruling patriarchs have a problem on their hands.

Jealous and bitter city authorities are aware, and they resent their loss of power. They're also fearful that what has happened elsewhere might happen here. To counter the movement or curb it before things get any more out of hand, they form a mob, or as the KJV says, "took unto them certain lewd fellows of the baser sort," and set the city in an uproar to create havoc, accusing the trio of inciting civil rebellion.[14] (The enemy's first tactic of defense is always deception and falsehood. Same tactic, different day.) When they cannot find Paul and Silas, they drag Jason and some of the brothers out of his house and take him before the authorities, charging them with harboring those who preach this message.

Notice they're shouting, which suggests they're angry. They say, *"These men who have turned the world upside down* have come here also." Another translation reads, "These who have upset the inhabited earth." "These men" is a reference to Paul and Silas and Timothy. And all who believe like they do. They continue, "'And Jason has received them, and they are all acting against the decrees of Caesar, saying that there is another king, Jesus.' And the people and the city authorities were disturbed when they heard these things."[15]

Writing from Corinth around AD 51, in what would be his first letter to a church and possibly the first complete book of the New Testament,* Paul later described the effect of the gospel of the kingdom on the Thessalonians this way:

Our gospel came to you not only in word, but also in power and in the Holy Spirit and with full conviction. You know what kind of men

---

* While the four Gospels describe earlier events, they would not be completed in their final forms until later.

we proved to be among you for your sake. And you became imitators of us and of the Lord, for you received the word in much affliction, with the joy of the Holy Spirit, so that you became an example to all the believers in Macedonia and in Achaia. For not only has the word of the Lord sounded forth from you in Macedonia and Achaia, but your faith in God has gone forth everywhere, so that we need not say anything. For they themselves report concerning us the kind of reception we had among you, and how you turned to God from idols to serve the living and true God, and to wait for his Son from heaven, whom he raised from the dead, Jesus who delivers us from the wrath to come.[16]

How did this happen? What was the secret? Paul answers in the next chapter: "You received the word of God . . . not as the word of men but as what it really is, the word of God, which is at work in you believers."[17]

What was the effect of the message that turned the world upside down? According to Paul, they received (or heard and obeyed) the Word of God, turned from idols, served the living and true God, became imitators of Christ, sounded forth the Word of the Lord, and waited in eager expectation for the return of the Son who was raised from the dead. What did their "sounding forth" look like? Dig into that word and you'll find it means to echo, roar, or blow like a trumpet. So strong was their faith that Paul need not say anything in surrounding cities—evidence of the Word of God at work in those who believe.

What exactly does Paul do in those three Sabbaths? He opens what we call the Old Testament and demonstrates how resurrected Jesus fulfills the revelation we find there. In short, he explains how it was necessary for Jesus to suffer and to rise from the dead, saying, "This Jesus, whom I proclaim to you, is the Christ."[18]

This teaching blows their minds, and the text says, "some of them were persuaded." Said another way, some *believed in*.

Which can be very dangerous to the status quo.

From Old to New

This phrase "turned the world upside down" includes a Greek word used only by Luke in Acts and later by Paul in his letter to the Galatians (Acts 17:6 [Gal. 5:12]). The NIV translates the phrase, "caused trouble all over the world." Luke uses it to refer to a revolt, and Paul describes one who is unsettled. In both cases, the word, *anastatoo*, literally means to drive out of home, to trouble, to excite a rebellion or sedition, or to unsettle minds. Interestingly, the word comes from a root, *anastemi*, which means to stand up, be raised from the dead, or be born again. In Acts 17, the Jews are describing a state of mind or condition of their town caused by Paul and Silas and Timothy's words. Which teaching is that? That Jesus is the only begotten Son of God who was dead, buried, and rose again in accordance with the Scriptures, and that He is both Lord and Christ and currently seated at the right hand of God.

To the Jewish religious elite, this is complete and total heresy.

As the Jewish leaders have shown in the past, they don't like competition, so they are accusing Paul and Silas of instigating a revolt against their civil and spiritual rulers and disobedience to Roman law. And for claiming that there is a king greater than Caesar—a claim punishable by death, which is why they wrote *King of the Jews* above Jesus' head in three different languages when they hung Him on the cross. The word they use to describe *upside down* is no compliment. It comes from common Greek usage and is more graphic and negative in its connotation. Slang even. Notice, too, the broader context. This is not an isolated event in the lives of the Thessalonians. They've heard the rumors. And they are afraid of what might happen if people believe this gospel.

Paul's words have persuaded listeners to turn from old ways to new. From sin to righteousness. From self to other. From unforgiveness and hatred to love and mercy. To surrender to the One true King, Jesus, and yield to His kingdom. The kingdom of God. Their words have taken ignorant unbelievers and persuaded them, heart, mind, and soul, to believe in this Man named Jesus. And judging by their actions, they do. They're thronging to Him. Professing allegiance. Bowing down before Him. In fact, they're willing to die for Him. In "turning the world upside down," "upending the inhabited earth," and "causing trouble all over the world," these believers are violently advancing the kingdom of heaven, and the kingdom of satan—and all those who belong to him—doesn't like this.

Why? Because the most fearful thing to the enemy is the thought that normal folks like us actually believe this message.

And yet, there it is in the streets of Thessalonica. From the angels' promise after Jesus' ascension, to the Upper Room, to Pentecost on the southern steps, to Paul and Silas in Thessalonica, to us here on this page, the gospel has been preached—and when it is preached and believed, stuff happens. Signs and wonders kind of stuff. And worlds are turned upside down.

Slaves and sinners are transferred out of the kingdom of darkness and into the kingdom of heaven, and orphans become children who know the scent of their Father.

Let's return full circle—to the hill on which we started. That storied mountain. The disciples are staring into the sky, but Jesus is gone. They scratch their heads and descend. A mixture of sorrow, sadness, and joy. Each is bubbling with one singular question: *What now? Just what on earth do we do now?*

I've just spent three hundred pages trying to answer that, but let me paint one more picture. I want us to project down the road. To maybe what the end of our lives should look like. And in order to do this I am going to use some fictional license, because the conversation you are about to read is not in Scripture. At least not in this detail. I'm imagining what it might have sounded like and, admittedly, I could be wrong. What I do know is that a conversation did occur because God told Moses to walk his brother, Aaron, up the mountain where he would die. And so he did. This is my fictional transcript of the last walk of these two giants of the faith. This is what I think it sounded like.

One Last Walk Up the Mountain

The men are both old. Steps shorter. One of them shuffles more than the other, but it's tough to tell which one. Spittle collects in the corner of their mouths, their voices don't hold the strength they once did, and their leathery skin is tanned from decades of exposure in the desert sun. Each carries a staff, but they are leaning more on each other as Mount Hor climbs upward. They are walking slowly. Resting often. Catching their breath.

It is the last time they will ever walk together this side of death.

The sun has set. The night air has turned cool. Below them, stretched out across the plain, several million Hebrews, "all the congregation," stand quietly, watching them ascend.[19] Cries rise up out of the crowd. Women wail. Children hold parents' hands and watch with curiosity. Somewhere, somebody sounds a shofar. It is bittersweet.

God is taking one of the great ones home.

Aaron is the older. He's 123. A good speaker, he is and has been high priest of Israel for over fifty years. He, alone, has walked faithfully—once a year—into the Holy of Holies, into the cloud and very presence of God, the bells of his garment jingling, a rope tied to his foot, and painted the mercy seat with the blood of the sacrifice. Making atonement. "For the life of the flesh is in the blood, and I have given it to you upon the altar to make atonement for your souls; for it is the blood that makes atonement for the soul."[20] Aaron knows this as well as anyone.

His younger brother, Moses, is 120. Through practice—of which he has had plenty—he became a better speaker. In the millennia to follow, he will be known as the humblest man that ever lived, the greatest leader the world has ever known, and his authority is without question. He alone speaks face-to-face with God. He's on a different playing field, which is why God alone will one day bury him, and satan and Michael will contend for his body.

Neither man's eyesight is too good, but the images they want to see exist in their rear view. Right now, they're crystal clear. 4K Ultra HD. In the history of the world, it is doubtful that two brothers have ever seen more than these two. Their great-great-grandfather was Levi. The son of Jacob and Leah. And they have been preceded in death by their sister Miriam, whom they buried at Kadesh.

These two stood before Pharaoh. The most powerful, most evil tyrant the world had ever known. And they spoke the words of God. "Let my people go." Then they backed up their demand with power from on high. Blood. Lice. Frogs. Death of the firstborn. Pharaoh couldn't match it. The Hebrews walked out. Pharaoh changed his mind and released his army. A chase ensued. Moses raised his staff and stretched out his hand and the sea stood up in a heap, several hundred feet tall on either side, and the Jews walked across on dry ground. The baptism of a nation.

Pharaoh's army reached the water's edge. Swords drawn. God sent the waters down and littered the banks with bodies and armor and horses and chariots. Not a single Hebrew was lost.

So they walked into the desert where after three days and no water, they came to a bitter spring. Three million people complained; one man prayed. Moses threw a tree into the water, turning it sweet. "I am your healer."

In the forty years that follow, Moses and Aaron disciple a nation of slaves. When they walk out the other side, they will have been transformed into a nation of priests. God has made good on his Exodus 19:6 promise: "You shall be to me a kingdom of priests and a holy nation."

Their roles were different. Determined by God. Years prior, God had said to Aaron, "I give your priesthood to you as a gift for service."[21] Solidifying his role before all the people. He has served faithfully, including a fair share of mistakes. There was the golden calf—a rather large blunder early in his career—then later he and his sister, Miriam, had complained against their brother when Moses had married a Cushite (Ethiopian) woman. But to his credit, Aaron also singlehandedly saved the people. His uncle, Korah, had offered profane fire—mocking God and assuming authority not given him. In punishment, God opened up the earth and swallowed him and 250 like him. On the next day, the people "gathered against Moses and Aaron" and complained against them, blaming them for killing the people of the Lord.[22] God didn't like this either. He poured out his wrath and the Israelites began dropping like flies. Thousands dead in an instant. At Moses' order, Aaron had taken a censer and put fire in it from the altar. Then ran into the middle of the people. Into the plague. Standing between the living and the dead. Smoke wafting heavenward. Worship rising up before the throne. Around him, fourteen thousand bodies lay like pickup sticks.

In mercy, God accepted his sacrifice. And the plague stopped.[23]

But here on this mountain, God is changing the guard. Transferring that gift of priesthood and giving it to another. Aaron's son, Eleazar. Atop the mountain, the torch will pass.

Aaron is walking to his death. Moses is walking his brother home.

Eleazar, not a young man himself, walks at a short distance behind. Lest either should stumble. Tears are streaming down his face. He is listening to his father and uncle talk about the good old days. They are laughing. Remembering. Looking fifty years into the past.

Aaron nudges his brother. "You remember the look on Pharaoh's face the first time you told him to 'let my people go'?"

Moses laughs. "Thought he was going to kill me on the spot but . . ." Moses raises a finger. "To be faithful to the record, you told him. Not me."

Aaron nods.

Moses continues. "But that look was nothing compared to what happened when you threw down your rod and that snake coiled up at his feet."

Aaron is chuckling from his stomach. "Yep." Aaron wipes his brow. "I'll never forget stretching out my arms and watching all that water turn to blood."

Moses sits on a rock and leans on his staff to rest his legs. He curls his nose. "You remember the stench of all those dead fish?"

"It was nothing compared to the stench of all those frogs. And the livestock." He held his palm flat at eye level. "We piled them in heaps."

Moses swats a gnat and shakes his head. "I've never seen so many flies." He pointed to his arms. "You remember all those boils? Big as eggs. Those were some tough, stubborn people. If some other God I didn't know gave me boils, I'd have opened wide the city gates and played music while those people marched out of town."

Aaron laughs but his eyes are glassy. "Hail. Locusts." A single shake of his head. "The thing I'll never forget is the echo of all those crying mommas when they woke up and their babies were dead."

Moses is quiet. "A hard day."

A smile breaks his lips. "God Most High, Possessor of heaven and earth, obliterated their gods. One by one." He shrugs. "And then generations of slaves walked out. Arms full of Egyptian gold."

Aaron scratches his head, the admission painful. "I'd still like to take back that whole thing with the golden calf. That's my bad." He looks intently at Moses. "I'm still sorry about that." Both are quiet a moment.

Moses nods. "I'm still sorry I broke the tablets."

"Yep, but then He hid you in the rock and walked by. You saw His glory. Heard Him speak His name. His forever name."

Moses smiles. "Yes, He did that."

"None of us will ever forget when you walked down. Shining like the sun. We knew you'd been with Him."

Another smile.

They stand and begin walking. Aaron hangs his arm inside Moses'. "Any regrets?"

Moses answers quickly. "Yeah, if I had it to do over again . . ." He tilts his head to one side. "I'd speak to that rock rather than strike it."

They laugh and stare longingly over their shoulder into the distance. The promised land. Neither will step foot in it. Aaron whispers, "Would have saved us a lot of bother."

Moses again. "Next time the Lord tells me to hallow Him as holy before the people, I intend to do exactly that."

Aaron puts a hand on Moses' shoulder. "I'd say you did a pretty good job when all the rest of us did not."

Another pause. Moses is staring a long way into the past. "When we stepped up to the water's edge with all of Egypt hot on our tail. Chariots.

Horses. Bronzed armor. I said to myself, 'This is it. We're dead.' Then that water parted and—."

Aaron interrupts him. "I will never forget looking down at my feet and realizing I was standing on dry ground with waves towering on either side."

They climb higher on the mountainside. Their feet kick up dust. The sun drops further. Moses speaks solemnly, staring deeper into the past. A Technicolor slideshow of memories. "Throwing that tree into the bitter waters at Marah. Bread from heaven. Quail falling dead out of the sky."

Aaron continues the memory. "A cloud by day and a fire by night."

"If I hadn't lived it, I'm not sure I could believe it."

"You think anyone will ever believe it?"

Moses stares down at the people. "That's up to them. I just know we lived it."

They're higher now. A cool breeze filters across them. Eleazar wraps a blanket around Aaron's shoulders. Aaron speaks. "I will never forget the night the twelve returned, with all those huge clusters of grapes and pomegranates and figs, and only Joshua and Caleb had the courage to say, 'We are well able and walk us in.'"

Moses hummed in agreement. "Cost us another forty years out here."

Aaron waves his hand across the landscape. "It's right there. Just walk in and take it. We could have been eating like kings!"

They reach the top of the mountain. They are tired, so Eleazar helps them up the last few steps. They turn and stare down at some three million Hebrews staring silently back up at them. Their road together has come to an end. They have taken their last step together. Aaron whispers, remembering the words God spoke in the third month after they'd come out of Egypt when they'd come to the wilderness of Sinai. His eternal intention for His people. "The Lord took us—a nation of slaves, a people born into generations of slavery—and transformed us before our very eyes into a kingdom of priests."

Moses agrees. "A holy nation." He looks into his brother's eyes and taps him gently in the chest. "You did that."

Aaron shakes his head. "He did that."

Moses nods. "Yes, but . . . He used you."

It is time. Aaron turns, faces his brother, and lifts his arms. Moses slowly strips Aaron of his priestly garments, one piece at a time. The ephod. The breastplate. Outer garment. Inner garment. Arms full, Moses turns and dresses Eleazar. Reversing the process. Aaron watches, one hand resting on Eleazar's shoulder—passing both the mantle and the anointing. Aaron hugs his son, kisses his tear-stained cheeks, and straightens the clothes that hang on his broad shoulders. Aaron struggles to find the words. In all these years, Eleazar has served alongside him. What hasn't been said? One final encouragement. He thumbs away a tear on Eleazar's face. "The life is in the blood . . ." He tries to speak again but can't. Finally a whisper. "The life is in the blood."

Moses and Aaron turn, and Moses leads Aaron to the bed they've prepared. Aaron lies down as Moses chokes back a sob and props his brother's head on a pillow. He tries to speak but cannot. The moment is too much. Aaron was always better with words.

Aaron's eyelids are growing heavy. "Not long now."

Moses can barely speak. "You always did like to be first." Aaron nods in agreement. Moses voice cracks. He is speaking of God. "Hug Him for me."

"I will." A smile cracks Aaron's lips. "Provided I can get beyond judgment."

Moses holds Aaron's hands in his. After so many years of handling the sacrifice, the blood stains have become permanent. Moses holds Aaron's palm flat across his own. "Take the blood with you." Aaron closes his eyes and folds his crimson-tinted hands. His strength is fading quickly. His voice a whisper. "Brother?"

Moses leans in. His ear to Aaron's lips. Aaron pulls him to his chest and kisses his brother one final time. "I love you. And I have loved doing this life with you." A pause. "Don't take too long."

Aaron breathes his last, his spirit departs, and Moses and Eleazar stand on the mountain. The people of God are below. When they descend, all of Israel will mourn for thirty days.

Walking Down the Mountain

I started this book with Jesus and His disciples walking up the mountain to His ascension. At the summit, God's chariot lifts Jesus into the heavens while his friends ask themselves and each other one simple and fundamental question that will mark the rest of their lives: *What now? Just what on earth do we do now?*

You and I have spent three hundred some-odd pages walking up this mountain. We have shared you-remember-whens, how-did-He-do-thats, and that's-the-most-amazing-thing-I've-ever-heards. We have laughed, cried, and wondered at the life of our Savior and those who followed Him—all the way to death. Now, two thousand years later, we stand on this mountain staring at each other only to realize that Jesus has made good on His promise. He has clothed us with His authority and His power. It's available to us. All we need to do is ask.

As best I am able, I have tried to encourage you to not just read about the disciples and say to yourself, "Look at them," but *be* the disciples. Do the disciples. Take them off the page and walk where and how they walked. James, the brother of Jesus, said this: "Elijah was a man with a nature like ours, and he prayed earnestly that it would not rain; and it did not rain on the earth for three years and six months" (James 5:17 NKJV). I hold Elijah in pretty high esteem—so did all of his readers—but what's James saying? "A man with a nature like ours"?

He's saying, be Elijah.

Moses walked slaves out of slavery. Joshua walked priests into His promise. So, be Moses. Be Joshua.

Below us is the valley. And many of the people who live there don't know the Father. Many don't know what and who you know. You are about to close the last page and walk down. And, if I know my enemy, lies and persecution await. he hates you, he hates me for writing this book, he hates anyone who believes.

I know some of you are looking down the road. I'm not naïve. You're imagining hurdles. Roadblocks. You may not immediately see signs and wonders. Might not for some time. This may well test your resolve. Your faith. So what will you do? Will you believe your circumstances or His Word?

Herein lies the question you will answer with your life.

Jesus, God's only Son, died that we might live. He gave us His authority and clothed us with the garments of His priesthood, and as we look down the mountain, there is a body of people waiting at the bottom. It's time to walk down.

My question for you is simple: What will you do now? What on earth will you do now? Will your life be any different? Look any different? Will you believe and act any differently? Will you believe that the Word of God is, in fact, the Word of God, and will you believe that He is speaking that Word directly to you? And that He intends you to take it to heart?

My Life

Ten-plus years ago, I gathered a group of my friends. Some I knew well and some not so well. Some believed, some doubted, a few didn't know what they believed, and one or two were pretty sure they didn't. If you were looking for the apostles of this age, you would not have picked us. I don't even remember why I told them we were getting together or how I convinced them to circle up, but to their great credit, they did. From there we started walking. Together.

In truth, we were all limping. Leaning on each other. Stopping often to catch our breath.

That journey has taken us through both their and my ups and downs. Failures and successes. I'm no Aaron or Moses, and like both of them, I've made my fair share of mistakes in service, leadership, and teaching. More than I care to remember. But as I look across this last decade or more and I look at the brotherhood between Aaron and Moses, I am convinced that what the two of them encountered is exactly what God the Father—Abba—desires for you and me.

He wants to transform slaves into priests. God used Moses to walk them out, and He used Joshua to walk them in. Both are types and models for us.

God said it in Exodus. He reaffirmed it later in Peter. And He closed the Book in Revelation by saying it again. It is and always has been God's intention for you and me to live, act, and function as His priests. And in that role, God wants to exhibit His power in and through us. He wants us to hallow Him, to worship Him, to speak His Word in faith and belief, and He absolutely wants us to appropriate His blood.

He wants us to get bloody.

As I look in the rear view at where God has led this unlikely group of men, He has stripped us, washed us, clothed us, anointed us, bathed us in His blood, put His Word on our lips, tasked us with His ministry, and then set us about the work of ministering in His power and for His kingdom. He has transformed slaves into priests. As a result, we've fallen in love with Him. Deeper than I'd ever imagined. We've seen stuff we can't explain. Signs and wonders. Legit miracles for which we have no explanation. We've seen Him reveal Himself to us as Lord. As the name above all names. As God of wonders. As our Deliverer. And, yes, we've seen deliverance too. The crazy, messy kind we don't talk about in our polite churches.

If I'm honest, at times we've fallen backward. Some have walked away. We've made a pile of both personal and corporate mistakes. And I am as guilty as anyone. Yet weekly, this circle of magnificent, barbaric, repentant men has crawled back to the throne of grace. Usually with our snot-stained faces to the carpet. Our appeals have sounded something like, "Lord, it's me. I'm back."

What I have seen both in them and me can be articulated in one word. *Freedom.* I've seen men walk in freedom. And I'm still seeing it. Speaking for myself, watching that transformation has been one of the most awesome and humbling things I've ever witnessed.

To get there, we've cried a lot of tears. Felt much anger. Sensed heartbreaking pain. Admitted shame-filled stuff that we once swore we were taking to the grave. We've offered countless prayers and seen many both answered and unanswered. And I've laughed so hard I thought I'd peed myself. There is no amount of money, no riches, no worlds that you could offer me in exchange for this brotherhood, this transformation, this journey.

I've never put an end date on walking with these men who have become my brothers. We quit when we die or the Lord says otherwise. But when my eyelids grow heavy and my strength fades, I'd like to stand shoulder to shoulder with these priests as we stand at the top of the mountain and see a kingdom of priests staring back at us. A holy people. A people belonging to God. Brought out of darkness and into light. Declaring His praises. I think if that were to happen, and the Lord were to call me home as He did Aaron, I could walk into the throne room of heaven with His Word in one hand, His blood in the other, and the image of a nation of priests in my rear view.

If you walk down this road, chances are good you'll experience the gamut of emotions. Joy. Anger. Wonder. Awe. Sadness. And gut-busting belly laughter. My hope and prayer for you is that you may well come to sense and know the overwhelming presence of the Lord. And hear His voice.

I can also promise that as soon as you sign up, you need to roll up your sleeves because you've got a fight on your hands. Your enemy hates that you've read this far. The thought of you believing this terrifies him. His desire it to kill you, destroy you, steal everything you have, and when he's done, he wants to rip your head off your shoulders and defecate down your neck. But remember: he's a liar, he's defeated, and every time we walk obediently in the promises of God, we remind our enemy of his absolute and irrevocable defeat.

I have not walked you somewhere that we haven't gone. What you read here is not theory with me. It's been born out of practice. Out of the heat and friction of iron sharpening iron. Out of the blood spilled by living near the tip of the spear. Also, while I have some experience, I have much to learn. I, too, am a man in process. Still walking. Many know more and have seen more than I. But if the Lord has taught us anything, it's this: freedom is worth the pain. Transformation is worth whatever the price.

There's a lot at stake. For some of you, it's life or death. For others, it is a deeper intimacy with a King you already serve. For all of us, it's needed. Make no mistake about it, Jesus wants you—yes, you—to see Him move in power and see stuff you can't explain. To walk in a power that doesn't come from you but originates in Him. He wants you to turn around at the end of your life and look at those walking beside you and leave you scratching your head and say, "If I'd not lived it, I wouldn't believe it." And He wants you, a priest in His kingdom, to pass on that mantle and anointing to those you are raising up. What God did through Moses and Aaron is the same He commanded through Jesus—go and make disciples. And disciples don't just *believe that*. *They believe in*. They strap the bungee around their ankles and take a Peter Pan off the bridge.

Here's what I hope for you and me: I want to walk with perseverance to the end of my life. To stand before the throne having walked faithfully. In belief. In power. In obedience. In the fear of the Lord. In an understanding of His holiness and His very great desire that I walk in it. And in endurance. And when my time comes and I limp to the top of the mountain, leaning on those with whom I've walked, I want the Lord to strip off the priestly clothes with which He once clothed me and pass them on to a former slave, now clothed in the armor of light, wrapped in the spotless robe of righteousness, a sword in his mouth, who is elbow deep in the blood.

And when He does, I want to whisper to that man, "The Life is in the blood."

This book is an invitation to get bloody.

That last statement may offend some of you—but priests deal daily in blood. They are never far from the sacrifice. And ours is the shed blood of Jesus. Most of us just admire it as it pools in the bowl. This book is a three-hundred-page admonition to get it out of the bowl and let it do what only it can do.

I have saved what I'm about to say to you until right here. In this book I am making much of this idea that signs and wonders should be following us, but let me qualify that. Performing supernatural signs and wonders is *not necessarily* evidence of God's anointing or favor. satan did and can do the supernatural. he has a measure of power given him by God. Jannes and Jambres exercised that power for dark purposes. satan stirred up the Sabeans and the Chaldeans against Job, destroying all his possessions. he also has a measure of power over the elements, which he used to kill all of Job's children, and he has some power over sickness with which he afflicted Job. We don't know what Simon the sorcerer did, but we do know that he deceived people by practicing magic and amazing people with his magic arts. Luke recorded, "They all paid attention to him from the least to the greatest, saying, 'This man is the power of God that is called Great.' And they paid attention to him because for a long time he had amazed them with his magic" (Acts 8:10–11). We also know from Scripture that the antichrist will perform supernatural miracles, deceiving even the elect. Paul said, "The coming of the lawless one is by the activity of Satan with all power and false signs and wonders" (2 Thess. 2:9). And Jesus said, "For false christs and false prophets will arise and perform great signs and wonders, so as to lead astray, if possible, even the elect" (Matt. 24:24).

There is a fine line here and we need discernment to walk it. I am praying that we believe in and hope for the supernatural—that we exercise the authority and power He's given us and signs and wonders follow us—but also that when we encounter the supernatural, we do so with discernment. John said, "Beloved, do not believe every spirit, but test the spirits to see whether they are from God, for many false prophets have gone out into the world" (1 John 4:1).

Let me reiterate: performing supernatural signs and wonders is *not necessarily* evidence of God's anointing or favor. It could very well be satan deceiving you—and me. he disguised himself as an angel when the angels (or sons of God) presented themselves before the Lord, and apparently he fooled all the angels (Job 1:6). The only One to pick him out of the crowd was God. We have no Scripture to suggest that has changed. satan is really good at making you think he's not what he is. So ask the Holy Spirit to help you discern and test the spirit.

How Will We Know

God has always used "signs and wonders" to declare His glory. To make Himself known to us. We get in trouble when we just chase signs and wonders. By now, you should know I am not encouraging that, but rather to chase the One through whom the power comes by which we perform signs and wonders. Who are we to deny the miraculous? To not seek signs and wonders or treat them as out of the norm? In the life and ministry of Jesus and those who followed Him, signs and wonders were the norm, not the exception.

When Peter and John were arrested for healing the man who had been lame for forty years, Peter spoke to the Jewish leaders and said, "We cannot but speak of what we have seen and heard" (Acts 4:20). Peter was speaking from practice. From experience. How could he deny that? And Peter's proclamation of signs and wonders is not singular in Scripture. It comes in a long line of like-minded men bringing attention to the hand and work of God.

Let me end with these reminders. They are true throughout the entirety of Scripture.

- This is Moses: "The LORD brought us out of Egypt with a mighty hand and with an outstretched arm, with great terror and with signs and wonders" (Deut. 26:8 NKJV).
- This is Isaiah: "Behold, I and the children whom the LORD has given me are for signs and wonders in Israel from the LORD of hosts, who dwells on Mount Zion" (Isa. 8:18 NASB).
- This is Jeremiah: "You brought Your people Israel out of the land of Egypt with signs and wonders, and with a strong hand and with an outstretched arm and with great terror" (Jer. 32:21 NASB).
- This is Daniel: "It has seemed good to me to declare the signs and wonders which the Most High God has done for me" (Dan. 4:2 NASB).
- This is Peter on the southern steps: "Men of Israel, hear these words: Jesus of Nazareth, a man attested to you by God with mighty works

and wonders and signs that God did through him in your midst, as you yourselves know" (Acts 2:22).

- This is Luke describing the lives of the apostles: "Awe came upon every soul, and many wonders and signs were being done through the apostles" (Acts 2:43).

- This is Luke again describing the apostles' life in Jerusalem: "Now many signs and wonders were regularly done among the people by the hands of the apostles. And they were all together in Solomon's Portico" (Acts 5:12).

- This is Luke describing the ministry of Stephen: "And Stephen, full of grace and power, was doing great wonders and signs among the people" (Acts 6:8).

- This is Luke describing the ministry of Paul and Barnabas: "So they remained for a long time, speaking boldly for the Lord, who bore witness to the word of his grace, granting signs and wonders to be done by their hands" (Acts 14:3).

- This is Paul speaking to the Romans: "I will not venture to speak of anything except what Christ has accomplished through me to bring the Gentiles to obedience—by word and deed, by the power of signs and wonders, by the power of the Spirit of God—so that from Jerusalem and all the way around to Illyricum I have fulfilled the ministry of the gospel of Christ" (Rom. 15:18–19).

- And this is Paul speaking to the church in Corinth: "The signs of a true apostle were performed among you with utmost patience, with signs and wonders and mighty works" (2 Cor. 12:12).

- And finally, this is the writer of Hebrews, speaking to you and me: "Therefore we must pay much closer attention to what we have heard, lest we drift away from it. For since the message declared by angels proved to be reliable, and every transgression or disobedience received a just retribution, how shall we escape if we neglect such a great salvation? It was declared at first by the Lord, and it was attested to us by those who heard, while God also bore witness by signs and wonders and various miracles and by gifts of the Holy Spirit distributed according to his will" (Heb. 2:1–4).

My prayer for you is actually Peter's prayer after his arrest and beating by the chief priests and elders: "And now, Lord, look upon their threats and grant to your servants to continue to speak your word with all boldness, while you stretch out your hand to heal, and signs and wonders are performed through the name of your holy servant Jesus" (Acts 4:29–30).

"Yet Not . . ."

The Garden of Gethsemane. Jesus is on His face. Sweating blood. It's dripping into the dirt in front of Him. His soul is sorrowful even to death.[1] Behind Him are His friends. Snoring slightly. Before Him lies the cup of wrath. And the cross. Jesus prays, "Abba, Father, all things are possible for you. Remove this cup from me. Yet not what I will, but what you will."[2]

Eternity hangs in the balance. Literally, every thing. This is *the* moment. All of life wrapped in two words: *yet not*.

Will He or will He not drink it? His will versus His Father's will. Some have read this and assumed and even taught that Jesus' decision was a foregone conclusion. The problem with this thought is that while Jesus was 100 percent God, He was also 100 percent man. And the 100 percent man part had to decide to drink.

In the garden of Eden, Adam faced this moment and failed. In the Garden of Gethsemane, the Father gives Jesus that same moment. A do-over for all humanity. Moments later, when Jesus finds His friends sleeping, He comments, "The spirit indeed is willing, but the flesh is weak."[3] I've often wondered if He's speaking of them or Him. Or us.

Matthew records the interaction between Father and Son this way: "My Father, if this cannot pass unless I drink it, your will be done."[4] Then, as the sound of soldiers descends out of the city, across the brook Kidron, and into the garden, sword clanking against armor, Jesus tells those closest to Him: "Sleep and take your rest later on. . . . The hour is at hand."[5]

What if this is your moment? What if your hour is at hand?

Some may accuse me of dramatizing the words of this book. But am I? All of us face this moment. Where we choose His cup or ours. No, we're not Jesus, and only He could drink the Father's cup of wrath, but each of us faces a "yet not" moment where we choose forever between His will or ours.

Some of us face this moment with indifference and it passes silently. We stand muted and numb. Our heads turned slightly. Staring out of the corner of our eyes. And the Father is not interested in shaming us, so the interaction is private. He and we are the only ones who ever know.

But what if this right here is your moment? What if right now the Father is asking you to forever lay down your will and pick up His? And what if "following Him" and "taking up your cross" means taking His word to heart, hearing it, and doing it?

What if He is asking you to be Moses and lead His people out of slavery? What if He is asking you to be Joshua and lead His people into His promises?

Will I, will you, stare into our Father's face in this moment and tell Him, "If this cannot pass . . . your will be done." Or will we choose our will?

For some of you, this is that moment.

And the rest of your life hangs in the balance.

Will You?

John ends his gospel with these words: "Now Jesus did many other signs in the presence of the disciples, which are not written in this book; but these are written so that you may believe that Jesus is the Christ, the Son of God, and that by believing you may have life in his name" (John 20:30–31).

You see those words "so that you may believe" and "have life"? I share that hope and it's why I wrote what you now hold in your hands. Now it's your turn.

I've left the last few pages intentionally blank. They're for you. As best I'm able, in *What If It's True?* and here in *They Turned the World Upside Down*, I've told you what I believe. I hope you'll use the space to start or continue a lifelong conversation with Jesus. So let me ask one last time:

What if His Word is true?

What if He is speaking directly to you, and He still means these words today the way He meant them when He first spoke them?

If the answer is "yes," then:

Will you *believe in* or *believe that*?

Will you have faith? Or fear?

Will you receive the Holy Spirit and release Him to do His will?

Will you press into your Father, climb into His lap, and bury your face in His neck?

Will you raise your hand in covenant?

Will you wage war or bury your head?

Will you preach, cleanse, cast out, heal, and raise?

Some of you are afraid of your own answers. Don't be. Fear is a liar. Faith is a choice and it's never easy, convenient, or popular—especially with the fearful and the proud. Some of you are apathetic. Some of you are indifferent. Some of you are mired in resignation. A day is coming when your apathy, indifference, and throwing in the towel will get you killed. Some of you are asleep. Wake up. There's a time for sleep but this is not it. Some of you are comfortable doing what you've always done. Comfort is an idol and it's time we kill it. Some of you are unbelieving. Do you really want to stand before God with that evil heart?

Some of you are standing on the starting line, muscles taut, sweat on your brow, waiting for the gun. Your heart is pure and your eyes are fixed on Jesus. I say to you, run the race. Spend yourself for the gospel of the kingdom. Cross the finish line with nothing left in the tank. And when you stumble and fall between here and there, don't lie there. Welcome to the human race. Despise the shame and get up. Throw off everything that hinders, peel your ears back, lift your knees, throw your hands, and run with endurance. You are not alone. There's an audience in heaven, a host of a hundred million and more, and they're cheering you on. Rooting for you. Why? Because they can see the King and the crown that awaits you. Which Jesus, the Author and Finisher of our faith, will place on your head. I hope to be there when He does. What a day that will be. We will dance and sing and rejoice at the banquet of the ages as our King swallows up death and the covering.

Let me take you back to where we started. Jesus has just ascended from the Mount of Olives. Everyone standing on that mountain has one singular question resting on the tip of their tongues. They will spend, devote, and sacrifice their lives answering it. Their question is our question:

Just what on earth do we do now?

How you answer may very well turn the world upside down.

Or not.

I'm praying like crazy that you upend the inhabited earth.

I Choose

I have included this list because according to Scripture, we get to choose these, and when I do, I find myself much closer to the Father. It is by no means complete, but it's a great way to engage Scripture, and if you want to know the Father's will, you might find it here. Please feel free to add your own.

Abide
> John 15:5, 7
> 1 John 2:17

Awake
> 1 Cor. 15:34

Belief/faith
> Mark 9:24
> Heb. 3:12
> Gen. 15:6
> Rom. 10:8; 11:20
> John 3:36; 20:27–29

Bless the Lord
> Ps. 103

Boast—in the Lord, in my iniquities
> Gal. 6:14
> Ps. 34:2; 44:8
> 2 Cor. 12:5, 9

Bring every thought into captivity
> 2 Cor. 10:5

Cast down arguments
> 2 Cor. 10:5

Contentment
> Phil. 4:11–13
> 1 Tim. 6:6–10

Count it all joy when I fall into trial
> James 1:2

Decrease so that He might increase

John 3:30

Deny myself

Luke 9:23

Matt. 16:24

Endurance

Heb. 11:36; 12:2

Engage my will

Gen. 14:22; 15:6; 22:3

Job. 1:5

Faith

James 2:17–19, 22–24, 26

Heb. 11–12

Rom. 4:17

Fear of the Lord

Deut. 6:13; 10:12, 20

Josh. 24:14

Isa. 11:3

Prov. 1:7; 3:7; 10:27; 16:6

Ps. 111:10; 128:1; 147:11

Follow Him

Luke 9:23

Matt. 16:24

Josh. 24:15

Forgiveness

Matt. 6:14–15; 18:35

Mark 11:25

John 20:23

Freedom/slave to righteousness

Gal. 5:1

Rom. 6:18

Gifts of the Holy Spirit

Rom. 12:3–8

1 Cor. 12:4–11; 14:1

Give

Luke 6:38

Acts 20:35

Matt. 10:7–8

Holiness

1 Peter 1:15–16

Heb. 12:14

Honor mother/father

Ex. 20:12

Deut. 5:16

Eph. 6:2

Hope

Rom. 5:3–5

Heb. 6:19

Hospitable/generous

1 Peter 4:9

Humility/submission to authority/put on the apron of a bondservant

1 Peter 5:5–6

James 4:10

Ps. 138:6; 146:8; 147:6

Prov. 16:5, 18–19; 22:4

Hunger and thirst after righteousness

Matt. 5:6

Keep fervent in my love

1 Peter 4:8

Lay down crown

Rev. 4:4, 10

Matt. 20:16

Lay hold

Phil. 3:12

1 Tim. 6:12

Heb. 6:18

Life/blessing/good

Deut. 11:26; 30:19–20

Rom. 12:14

Matt. 5:44

Meekness

Matt. 5:5

Isa. 11:4

James 1:21; 3:13

Mercy

James 2:13

Matt. 5:7

More than a conqueror

Rom. 8:37

Not to be ashamed

Rom. 1:16

Not to bow down or serve other Gods

Ex. 20:5

Obedience

Heb. 5:8–9

2 Cor. 10:4–5

Deut. 4:29–31

Overcome by the blood

Rev. 3:21; 12:11; 21:7

Persevere

Rev. 2:3; 3:10

Pick up cross/lay down life

John 15:13

Matt. 10:38

Power of God

Rom. 1:16

1 Cor. 1:18

Praise/worship

Heb. 13:15

Ps. 22:23; 63:3; 147–150

Pray without ceasing

1 Thess. 5:17

Press on/press toward

Phil. 3:12

Priest of My house

Ex. 19:6

1 Peter 2:9

Rev. 1:6; 5:10, 20:6

Pull down strongholds

2 Cor. 10:4

Purity

Phil. 4:8

1 Tim. 5:22

James 3:17

1 Peter 2:2

1 John 3:3

Matt. 5:8

Put on the armor of god

Eph. 6:11–18

Receive the Holy Spirit

John 20:22

Acts 2:38

Rejoice

Ps. 96:11; 118:24

Phil. 4:4

1 Thess. 5:16–18

Matt. 5:11–12

Repent

Rev. 3:19

Matt. 3:2

Luke 13:3

Acts 2:38; 17:30

Resist the devil

1 Peter 5:9

Rise early

Gen. 22:3

Job 1:5

Run with endurance the race set before me

1 Cor. 9:24

Heb. 12:1

Seek Him

Ps. 34:4; 63:1

Deut. 4:29

Matt. 6:32–33; 7:7–8

2 Chron. 7:14

Isa. 55:6

See—that my righteousness is as filthy rags, chief among sinners, fallen short

1 Tim. 1:15

Isa. 64:6

Serve

Josh. 24:15

Deut. 6:13

Sober

1 Peter 5:8

Titus 2:2

Stand/hold fast the confession of my faith

Deut. 10:20

Heb. 4:14

Rom. 10:8–10

Rev. 3:3

Ex. 14:13

Eph. 6:13–14

2 Chron. 20:17

Gal. 5:1

Strength/courage

Josh. 1:9

Take up my cross daily

Luke 9:23

Throw off everything that hinders

Heb. 12:1

Truth

John 8:32; 16:13

Ps. 51:6; 63:1

Vigilant

1 Peter 5:8

Wait on the Lord

Isa. 40:31

Prov. 20:22

Wage war

2 Cor. 10:4–6

Wisdom/discretion

Prov. 2:1–5, 10–12; 3:21–23; 4:5–7

James 3:14–17

Word

    Ps. 119:9, 11

    Isa. 66:5

    Josh. 1:7–8

    Prov. 4:20–22

    Matt. 4:4

    Jer. 15:16

    Job 23:12

    Rom. 15:4

Your deliverance

    2 Sam. 22

    Ps. 18; 34:4; 40; 70; 91; 144:2

Zeal

    Num. 25:7–11

Deliverance

Deliverance Proclamations

And as Moses lifted up the serpent in the wilderness, even so must the Son of Man be lifted up, that whoever believes in Him should not perish but have eternal life. For God so loved the world that He gave His only begotten Son, that whoever believes in Him should not perish but have everlasting life. For God did not send His Son into the world to condemn the world, but that the world through Him might be saved. He who believes in Him is not condemned; but he who does not believe is condemned already, because he has not believed in the name of the only begotten Son of God.

JOHN 3:14–18 NKJV

Unless you believe that I am He, you will die in your sins.

JOHN 8:24 NASB

Through Him everyone who believes is freed from all things, from which you could not be freed through the Law of Moses.

ACTS 13:39 NASB

Our old self was crucified with Him, in order that our body of sin might be done away with, so that we would no longer be slaves to sin; for he who has died is freed from sin. . . . For sin shall not be master over you, for you are not under law but under grace.

ROMANS 6:6–7, 14 NASB

There is therefore now no condemnation to those who are in Christ Jesus, who do not walk according to the flesh, but according to the Spirit. For the law of the Spirit of life in Christ Jesus has made me free from the law of sin and death.

ROMANS 8:1–2 NKJV

Christ is the end of the law for righteousness to everyone who believes.

ROMANS 10:4

If you confess with your mouth the Lord Jesus and believe in your heart that God has raised Him from the dead, you will be saved. For with the heart one believes unto righteousness, and with the mouth confession is made unto salvation. . . . For "whoever calls on the name of the LORD shall be saved."

ROMANS 10:9–10, 13 NKJV

I have been crucified with Christ; and it is no longer I who live, but Christ lives in me; and the life which I now live in the flesh I live by faith in the Son of God.

GALATIANS 2:20 NASB

Christ redeemed us from the curse of the Law, having become a curse for us—for it is written, "Cursed is everyone who hangs on a tree"— in order that in Christ Jesus the blessing of Abraham might come to the Gentiles.

GALATIANS 3:13–14 NASB

He rescued us from the domain of darkness, and transferred us to the kingdom of His beloved Son, in whom we have redemption, the forgiveness of sins. . . . And although you were formerly alienated and hostile in mind, engaged in evil deeds, yet He has now reconciled you in His fleshly body through death, in order to present you before Him holy and blameless and beyond reproach.

COLOSSIANS 1:13–14, 21–22 NASB

By one offering He has perfected for all time those who are sanctified.

HEBREWS 10:14 NASB

He Himself bore our sins in His body on the cross, so that we might die to sin and live to righteousness; for by His wounds you were healed.

1 PETER 2:24 NASB

If we confess our sins, He is faithful and righteous to forgive us our sins and to cleanse us from all unrighteousness.

1 JOHN 1:9 NASB

The Son of God was manifested, that He might destroy the works of the devil.

1 JOHN 3:8 NKJV

I saw Satan fall like lightning from heaven. Behold, I give you the authority to trample on serpents and scorpions, and over all the power of the enemy, and nothing shall by any means hurt you.

LUKE 10:18–19 NKJV

You are of God, little children, and have overcome them, because He who is in you is greater than he who is in the world.

1 JOHN 4:4 NKJV

"In the world you will have tribulation; but be of good cheer, I have overcome the world."

JOHN 16:33 NKJV

Though we walk in the flesh, we do not war according to the flesh. For the weapons of our warfare are not carnal but mighty in God for pulling down strongholds, casting down arguments and every high thing that exalts itself against the knowledge of God, bringing every thought into captivity to the obedience of Christ.

2 CORINTHIANS 10:3–5 NKJV

Whatever is born of God overcomes the world. And this is the victory that has overcome the world—our faith. Who is he who overcomes the world, but he who believes that Jesus is the Son of God? . . .

Now this is the confidence that we have in Him, that if we ask anything according to His will, He hears us. And if we know that He hears us, whatever we ask, we know that we have the petitions that we have asked of Him.

1 JOHN 5:4–5, 14–15 NKJV

Blessed is the one whose transgression is forgiven, whose sin is covered. Blessed is the man against whom the LORD counts no iniquity.

PSALM 32:1–2

From Jesus Christ, the faithful witness, the firstborn of the dead, and the ruler of the kings of the earth. To Him who loves us and released us from our sins by His blood—and He has made us to be a kingdom, priests to His God and Father.

REVELATION 1:5–6 NASB

Through one act of righteousness there resulted justification of life to all men.

ROMANS 5:18 NASB

All of you who were baptized into Christ have clothed yourselves with Christ.

GALATIANS 3:27 NASB

He made Him who knew no sin to be sin on our behalf, so that we might become the righteousness of God in Him.

2 CORINTHIANS 5:21 NASB

You have died, and your life is hidden with Christ in God.

COLOSSIANS 3:3

"Their sins and their lawless deeds I will remember no more."

HEBREWS 10:17 NKJV

The blood of Jesus Christ His Son cleanses us from all sin.

1 JOHN 1:7 NKJV

Because you have made the LORD, who is my refuge, even the Most High, your dwelling place, no evil shall befall you, nor shall any plague come near your dwelling; for He shall give His angels charge over you, to keep you in all your ways. In their hands they shall bear you up, lest you dash your foot against a stone. You shall tread upon the lion and the cobra, the young lion and the serpent you shall trample underfoot. Because he has set his love upon Me, therefore I will deliver him; I will set him on high, because he has known My name. He shall call upon Me, and I will answer him; I will be with him in trouble; I will deliver him and honor him. With long life I will satisfy him, and show him My salvation."

PSALM 91:9–16 NKJV

Blessed be the LORD *my Rock, who trains my hands for war, and my fingers for battle—my lovingkindness and my fortress, my high tower and my deliverer, my shield and the One in whom I take refuge, who subdues my people under me.*

PSALM 144:1–2 NKJV

This is the word of the LORD *to Zerubbabel: "Not by might nor by power, but by My Spirit," says the* LORD *of hosts.*

ZECHARIAH 4:6 NKJV

You, O LORD, *are a shield for me, my glory and the One who lifts up my head. I cried to the* LORD *with my voice, and He heard me from His holy hill. Selah I lay down and slept; I awoke, for the* LORD *sustained me. I will not be afraid of ten thousands of people who have set themselves against me all around. Arise, O* LORD; *save me, O my God! For You have struck all my enemies on the cheekbone; You have broken the teeth of the ungodly. Salvation belongs to the* LORD. *Your blessing is upon Your people. Selah*

PSALM 3:3–8 NKJV

I will love You, O LORD, *my strength. The* LORD *is my rock and my fortress and my deliverer; my God, my strength, in whom I will trust; my shield and the horn of my salvation, my stronghold. I will call upon the* LORD, *who is worthy to be praised; so shall I be saved from my enemies. The pangs of death surrounded me, and the floods of ungodliness made me afraid. The sorrows of Sheol surrounded me; the snares of death confronted me. In my distress I called upon the* LORD, *and cried out to my God; He heard my voice from His temple, and my cry came before Him, even to His ears. Then the earth shook and trembled; the foundations of the hills also quaked and were shaken, because He was angry. Smoke went up from His nostrils, and devouring fire from His mouth; coals were kindled by it. He bowed the heavens also, and came down with darkness under His feet. And He rode upon a cherub, and flew; He flew upon the wings of the wind. He made darkness His secret place; His canopy around Him was dark waters and thick clouds of the skies. From the brightness before Him, His thick clouds passed with hailstones and coals of fire. The* LORD *thundered from heaven, and the Most High uttered His voice, hailstones and coals of fire. He sent out His arrows and scattered the foe, lightnings in abundance, and He vanquished them. Then the channels of the sea were seen, the foundations of the world were uncovered at*

Your rebuke, O Lord, at the blast of the breath of Your nostrils. He sent from above, He took me; He drew me out of many waters. He delivered me from my strong enemy, from those who hated me, for they were too strong for me. They confronted me in the day of my calamity, but the Lord was my support. He also brought me out into a broad place; He delivered me because He delighted in me.

PSALM 18:1–19 NKJV

Who is God, except the Lord? And who is a rock, except our God? It is God who arms me with strength, and makes my way perfect. He makes my feet like the feet of deer, and sets me on my high places. He teaches my hands to make war, so that my arms can bend a bow of bronze. You have also given me the shield of Your salvation; Your right hand has held me up, Your gentleness has made me great. You enlarged my path under me, so my feet did not slip. I have pursued my enemies and overtaken them; neither did I turn back again till they were destroyed. I have wounded them, so that they could not rise; they have fallen under my feet. For You have armed me with strength for the battle; You have subdued under me those who rose up against me. You have also given me the necks of my enemies, so that I destroyed those who hated me. They cried out, but there was none to save; even to the Lord, but He did not answer them. Then I beat them as fine as the dust before the wind; I cast them out like dirt in the streets.

PSALM 18:31–42 NKJV

They overcame him by the blood of the Lamb and by the word of their testimony, and they did not love their lives to the death.

REVELATION 12:11 NKJV

Assuredly, I say to you, whatever you bind on earth will be bound in heaven, and whatever you loose on earth will be loosed in heaven. Again I say to you that if two of you agree on earth concerning anything that they ask, it will be done for them by My Father in heaven. For where two or three are gathered together in My name, I am there in the midst of them.

MATTHEW 18:18–20 NKJV

If I cast out demons by the Spirit of God, surely the kingdom of God has come upon you. Or how can one enter a strong man's house and plunder his goods, unless he first binds the strong man? And then he will plunder his house.

MATTHEW 12:28–29 NKJV

Put on the whole armor of God, that you may be able to stand against the wiles of the devil. For we do not wrestle against flesh and blood, but against principalities, against powers, against the rulers of the darkness of this age, against spiritual hosts of wickedness in the heavenly places. Therefore take up the whole armor of God, that you may be able to withstand in the evil day, and having done all, to stand. Stand therefore, having girded your waist with truth, having put on the breastplate of righteousness, and having shod your feet with the preparation of the gospel of peace; above all, taking the shield of faith with which you will be able to quench all the fiery darts of the wicked one. And take the helmet of salvation, and the sword of the Spirit, which is the word of God; praying always with all prayer and supplication in the Spirit, being watchful to this end with all perseverance and supplication for all the saints.

EPHESIANS 6:11–18 NKJV

At midnight Paul and Silas were praying and singing hymns to God, and the prisoners were listening to them. Suddenly there was a great earthquake, so that the foundations of the prison were shaken; and immediately all the doors were opened and everyone's chains were loosed.

ACTS 16:25–26 NKJV

The LORD said to him, "What is that in your hand?" He said, "A rod."

EXODUS 4:2 NKJV

Your sandals shall be iron and bronze; as your days, so shall your strength be. "There is no one like the God of Jeshurun, who rides the heavens to help you, and in His excellency on the clouds. The eternal God is your refuge, and underneath are the everlasting arms; He will thrust out the enemy from before you, and will say, 'Destroy!' Then Israel shall dwell in safety, the fountain of Jacob alone, in a land of grain and new wine; His heavens shall also drop dew. Happy are you, O Israel! Who is like you, a people saved by the LORD, the shield of your help and the sword of your majesty! Your enemies shall submit to you, and you shall tread down their high places."

DEUTERONOMY 33:25–29 NKJV

They surrounded me like bees; they were quenched like a fire of thorns; for in the name of the LORD I will destroy them. You pushed me violently, that I might fall, but the LORD helped me. The LORD is my strength and song, and He has become my salvation. The voice of rejoicing and salvation is in the tents of the righteous; the right hand of the Lord does valiantly. The right hand of the Lord is exalted; the right hand of the Lord does valiantly. I shall not die, but live, and declare the works of the Lord. The Lord has chastened me severely, but He has not given me over to death.

PSALM 118:12–18 NKJV

If we confess our sins, He is faithful and just to forgive us our sins and to cleanse us from all unrighteousness.

1 JOHN 1:9 NKJV

We have been sanctified through the offering of the body of Jesus Christ once for all.

HEBREWS 10:10

By one offering He has perfected forever those who are being sanctified.

HEBREWS 10:14 NKJV

Their sins and their lawless deeds I will remember no more.

HEBREWS 10:17 NKJV

Notes

PROLOGUE

1. Gen. 22:8.
2. Isa. 25:6–8.
3. Acts 1:6.
4. Acts 1:7–8.
5. Acts 1:11.

CHAPTER 1: THE DEATH OF THE ONLY INNOCENT MAN

1. Matt. 27:46.
2. Matt. 27:48 NKJV.
3. Matt. 27:50 NKJV.
4. John 19:30 NKJV.
5. Matt. 27:51–52 NKJV.
6. 2 Cor. 5:21 NKJV.
7. Rev. 4:1–11.
8. Heb. 12:2, 22–24, 26, 28–29.
9. Rev. 1:5–6, 8, 13–19.
10. Isa. 52:14 NKJV.
11. Phil. 2:6, 9.
12. Rev. 22:1–2, 12–15.
13. Heb. 8:6 NKJV.
14. Jer. 31:33–34 NKJV; Heb. 8:8–12 NKJV.
15. Ex. 25:40 NKJV.
16. Heb. 8:5.
17. Heb. 7:26–27; 9:11–12 NASB.

CHAPTER 2: IT IS PERFECTLY PERFECT

1. Heb. 10:20.
2. 1 Peter 3:18 NASB.
3. Rev. 19:11–16.
4. Rev. 21:5.
5. Rev. 21:6.
6. Rev. 21:3–27.
7. 1 Peter 3:18–20.
8. Dan. 7:9–14, paraphrased.
9. John 18:11 NKJV.
10. Matt. 27:4 NKJV.
11. Matt. 27:4–5 NKJV.
12. Acts 1:18–19 NIV.

13. Ps. 69:25; Acts 1:18–20.
14. John 19:2–5.
15. Luke 8:2–3.
16. Matt. 28:2 NASB.
17. Matt. 28:4.
18. Matt. 28:5–6 NKJV.
19. Luke 24:4–6.
20. Luke 24:6–7 NKJV.
21. Mark 16:6–7 NKJV.
22. Luke 24:8.
23. Luke 24:11.

CHAPTER 3: A DEAD MAN WALKS

1. John 20:11.
2. John 20:11–13.
3. John 20:15–16.
4. John 20:17.
5. Luke 24:16–17 NKJV.
6. Luke 24:18 NKJV.
7. Luke 24:19–26.

CHAPTER 4: SHAME—THE ENEMY'S FIRST WEAPON

1. John 21:5 NKJV.
2. 1 John 3:1–2 NASB.
3. Mark 10:50.
4. John 18:15–18 NASB.
5. John 21:10 NKJV.
6. John 21:18 NKJV.

CHAPTER 5: PROBLEM NUMBER ONE

1. Acts. 9:18.
2. Rev. 1:17.
3. Acts 1:20
4. Luke 4:4; Deut. 8:3

CHAPTER 6: THEIR PROBLEM IS OUR PROBLEM

1. Mark 5:35.
2. Mark 5:41.
3. Mark 6:1–6 NKJV.
4. Mark 7:34 NKJV.
5. Mark 8:29.
6. Matt. 17:5.
7. Matt. 17:14–16.
8. Mark 9:17–18.
9. Matt. 17:17; Luke 9:41.
10. Matt. 12:30.
11. Mark 9:19–22.
12. Luke 10:17–19.
13. Mark 9:23.
14. Mark 9:24.
15. Mark 9:25.
16. Matt. 17:18.
17. Luke 9:42.
18. Matt. 28:17.
19. Mark 16:14.
20. Luke 24:36–41.
21. John 20:27, 29.
22. Lewis, C. S., *Mere Christianity*, rev. ed., (New York: Macmillan/Collier, 1952), 55.

CHAPTER 7: MOVING FROM FAITH TO FAITHFULNESS

1. Num. 13:29–30.

2. Num. 14:9 NKJV.

CHAPTER 8: THE HOLY SPIRIT

1. Luke 24:46–50, emphasis added.

2. John 14:16–19, emphasis added.

3. John 14:22.

4. John 14:23–26, emphasis added.

5. John 15:26–27, emphasis added.

6. John 16:7–10, emphasis added.

7. Luke 24:52–53.

8. Acts 1:13–14. Given Judas's betrayal of Jesus, they're down a man—numbering now only eleven rather than twelve—so Peter suggests they replace him. They cast lots, and Matthias is chosen to take his place. The apostles are once again twelve.

9. We see it in Ex. 23, 24; Lev. 16; Num. 28; and Deut. 16.

10. Deut. 16:12.

11. Ex. 23:17; 34:23.

12. Acts 2:1–4.

13. Acts 2:5–13.

14. Acts 2:14–41.

15. 2 Sam. 6:22 NKJV.

16. John 1:32.

17. Acts 2:17.

18. Acts 2:33, 38–39.

CHAPTER 9: WILLING TO BE WILLING

1. Acts 3:4.

2. Acts 3:6–8.

3. Acts 3:8.

4. Lev. 21:18.

5. Acts 3:9–10.

6. Acts 3:15–19, paraphrased.

7. Acts 4:2.

8. Acts 4:4.

9. Acts 4:7.

10. Acts 4:11–12.

11. Acts 4:17–20.

12. Acts 4:29–30.

13. Acts 4:31.

14. Acts 6:8.

15. Acts 7:48–50.

16. Acts 7:51.

17. Acts 5:42; 6:4.

18. Rev. 1:17.

CHAPTER 10: SHOW US THE FATHER

1. Luke 2:41–42.

2. Luke 2:43–44.

3. Luke 2:45.

4. Luke 2:46–48.

5. Luke 2:48–49.

6. Luke 2:50.

7. John 19:7.

8. *For you are our Father* (Isa. 63:16). *But now, O LORD, you are our Father* (Isa. 64:8).

9. *"I said, How I would set you among my sons, and give you a pleasant land, a heritage most beautiful of all nations. And I thought you would*

call me, My Father, and would not turn from following me" (Jer. 3:19). For I am a father to Israel (Jer. 31:9).

10. "A son honors his father, and a servant his master. If then I am a father, where is my honor? And if I am a master, where is my fear? says the LORD of hosts to you, O priests, who despise my name. But you say, "How have we despised your name?" (Mal. 1:6). Have we not all one Father? Has not one God created us? (Mal. 2:10).

11. Is not he your father, who created you? (Deut. 32:6).

12. Therefore David blessed the LORD in the presence of all the assembly. And David said: "Blessed are you, O LORD, the God of Israel our father, forever and ever" (1 Chron. 29:10).

13. Mark 14:36, paraphrase.

14. John 20:17, paraphrase.

CHAPTER 11: THE KINGDOM OF HEAVEN

1. Isa. 9:6–7.
2. Luke 1:32–33.
3. Matt. 2:2.
4. Matt. 2:5–6.
5. Matt. 3:2.
6. Matt. 4:3.
7. Matt. 4:4.
8. Ex. 19:5–6.
9. Phil. 2:6.
10. Deut. 6:16.
11. Matt. 4:9.
12. Ps. 33:9.
13. Heb. 1:3.
14. Matt. 4:10; Deut. 6:13.
15. Deut. 6:14–15.
16. Matt. 4:17.
17. Luke 4:43.
18. Luke 9:2.
19. Matt. 10:7–8.
20. Matt. 5:3.
21. Matt. 6:9–10.
22. Matt. 7:21.
23. Matt. 6:33.
24. John 18:33–34.
25. John 18:35–38.
26. Mark 12:28–34.
27. Eph. 2:1–10, 12–13; 3:14.

CHAPTER 12: I RAISE MY HAND

1. Luke 22:15–22.
2. John 13:27.
3. John 13:30.
4. 1 Sam. 17:57.
5. 1 Sam. 18:1.
6. 1 Sam. 20:14–17.
7. 1 Sam. 20:42.
8. 1 Sam. 23:17–18.
9. 2 Sam. 1:4.
10. 2 Sam. 1:25–26.
11. 2 Sam. 4:4.
12. 2 Sam. 6:22 NIV.
13. 2 Sam. 9:1.
14. 2 Sam. 9:3.
15. 2 Sam. 9:4.
16. 2 Sam. 9:7–8.

17. 2 Sam. 9:8.

18. Matt. 15:21–28.

19. 2 Sam. 9:9–10.

20. Heb. 2:17; 3:1; 4:14–15; 5:1, 5, 10; 6:20; 7:1, 26–28; 8:1, 3; 9:11.

CHAPTER 13: YOU'RE IN A WAR

1. Mark 1:32–33.

2. Matt. 4:23.

3. Mark 1:39 NKJV.

4. Mark 3:14–15 NKJV.

5. Matt. 10:7–8 NKJV.

6. Mark 3:27.

7. Matt. 8:15.

8. Matt. 8:16–17.

9. Mark 6:7.

10. Mark 6:12–13.

11. Luke 10:17–19.

12. Luke 10:22 NKJV.

13. Luke 13:32 NKJV.

14. Mark 16:15–18 NKJV.

15. Acts 4:16–20 NKJV.

16. John 14:12–14.

17. Ex. 4:2–3.

18. 2 Tim. 3:8.

19. Ex. 7:8–12.

20. Ex. 7:22.

21. Ex. 8:7.

22. Ex. 8:18.

23. Ex. 8:19.

24. Num. 13:1–14:34.

25. Josh. 10:22–25.

26. Num. 14:11.

27. Num. 13:30.

28. Num. 13:31–33.

29. Num. 14:1–4.

30. Num. 14:7–10.

31. Josh. 11:21–22.

CHAPTER 14: WHAT OR WHO ARE YOU AT WAR AGAINST?

1. 2 Sam. 22:2–3; Ps. 18:2; Ps. 40:17; Ps. 70:5; Ps. 144:2.

2. Rom. 12:19.

3. Ps. 45:7.

CHAPTER 15: THEY TURNED THE WORLD UPSIDE DOWN

1. Acts 16:10–12.

2. Acts 16:14.

3. Acts 16:18–21.

4. Acts 16:28.

5. Acts 16:30–31.

6. 1 Cor. 8:6.

7. Gal. 3:26–28.

8. Col. 2:8–10.

9. 1 Tim. 2:5–6.

10. Acts 13:30.

11. Acts 13:38–39.

12. John 19:12.

13. Acts 17:4.

14. Acts 17:5 KJV.

15. Acts 17:6–9.

16. 1 Thess. 1:5–10.

17. 1 Thess. 2:13.

18. Acts 17:1–5.

19. Num. 20:27.

20. Lev. 17:11 NKJV.

21. Num. 18:7 NKJV.

22. Num. 16:41–42 NKJV.

23. Num. 16:46–49.

EPILOGUE

1. Mark 14:34.

2. Mark 14:36.

3. Mark 14:38.

4. Matt. 26:42.

5. Matt. 26:45.

About the Author

Charles Martin is a *New York Times* and *USA Today* bestselling author of fourteen novels, including *The Mountain Between Us* and *Send Down the Rain*. Charles and his wife, Christy, live in Jacksonville, Florida. Learn more at charlesmartinbooks.com.